Shades of Glory

Ted "Double Duty" Radcliffe tags Josh Gibson at home plate, August 1, 1943.

Shades of Glory

★★★★★

THE NEGRO LEAGUES AND THE STORY OF AFRICAN-AMERICAN BASEBALL

★★★★★

LAWRENCE D. HOGAN
WITH A FOREWORD BY JULES TYGIEL

NATIONAL GEOGRAPHIC
WASHINGTON, D.C.

Chief author and editor, Lawrence D. Hogan
Collaborative authors: Adrian Burgos, Leslie Heaphy, Neil Lanctot, Michael Lomax, James Overmyer, Robert Peterson, Rob Ruck, Lyle Wilson
Statistical Component: Dick Clark, Larry Lester

The National Baseball Hall of Fame continues to assist the efforts of scholars to conduct further research and writing on the history of black baseball. Individuals interested in making donations in support of these endeavors, or who wish to support the work of the Negro League Baseball Players Association, are encouraged to contact Greg Harris, Director of Development, National Baseball Hall of Fame and Museum, 25 Main Street, Cooperstown, NY 13326.

ISBN-10: 0-7922-5306-X • ISBN-13: 978-0-7922-5306-8

One of the world's largest nonprofit scientific and educational organizations, the National Geographic Society was founded in 1888 "for the increase and diffusion of geographic knowledge." Fulfilling this mission, the Society educates and inspires millions every day through its magazines, books, television programs, videos, maps and atlases, research grants, the National Geographic Bee, teacher workshops, and innovative classroom materials. The Society is supported through membership dues, charitable gifts, and income from the sale of its educational products. This support is vital to National Geographic's mission to increase global understanding and promote conservation of our planet through exploration, research, and education.
For more information, please call 1-800-NGS LINE (647-5463)
or write to the following address:

National Geographic Society
1145 17th Street N.W.
Washington, DC 20036-4688 U.S.A.
Visit the Society's Web site at www.nationalgeographic.com.

Interior design by Melissa Farris

Contents

★★★★★

Dick Seay of the New York Black Yankees jumps high to make a catch in practice at Yankee Stadium, July 26, 1942.

Foreword

BY **JULES TYGIEL**

An incident would crop up here and there. They would call you a name or something. But being black we got used to that and we didn't let that deter us. Sometimes through adversity I think it made us better players because we would try harder. They would make us mad. And rather than fight or anything like that we would want to play so as to beat the opposition. We developed that kind of mentality. I think it was that kind of mentality that took us through.

—MONTE IRVIN, NEWARK EAGLES, NATIONAL BASEBALL HALL OF FAME

THE HISTORY OF AFRICAN AMERICANS AND BASEBALL ABOUNDS WITH IRONY. The ironies began in 1867 when the National Association of Base Ball Players (NABBP), the first organized league, rejected the application of the Pythian Club, an all-black team from Philadelphia, for membership.The NABBP barred "the admission of any club which may be composed of one or more colored persons," explaining, with full sincerity and without any trace of sarcasm, that "if colored clubs were admitted there would in all probability be some division of feeling, whereas by excluding them no injury could result to anyone." As African-American ballplayers navigated the shoals of baseball's evolving racial mores in the late 19th century, the ironies continued. Baseball would later decree that the game had its origins in the village of Cooperstown, New York. This assertion has no validity, but John W. "Bud" Fowler, the first known black professional player learned the game while growing up in the town in the 1860s and 1870s. The first all-African-American professional team, organized in 1885, bore the name Cuban Giants, perhaps to obscure the squad's true racial identity, though none of the players were Cuban or, due to their skin color, could play for the major league Giants of New York.

Although in the 1880s and 1890s black players and teams made appearances in predominantly white leagues, by the turn of the century baseball's color barriers had hardened. Nonetheless, rumors abounded that light-skinned African Americans were passing for white to gain entry in the major leagues. In 1901 Baltimore Oriole manager John McGraw unsuccessfully tried to sign crack second-baseman Charlie Grant by introducing him as a Native American. When clubs started signing players from Cuba and other interracial baseball-playing societies of the Caribbean, they sought assurances that these players had "pure Caucasian blood in their veins." However, as the number of "white" Latino ballplayers grew in the 1920s and 1930s, some appeared in both the major leagues and the Negro leagues, prompting sportswriter Red Smith to speculate that perhaps "there was a Senegambian somewhere in the Cuban batpile" that produced these athletes. And while major league owners defended their ban on blacks with assertions that nonwhite players lacked the inherent skills or talent to qualify for the big leagues, many observers explained Babe Ruth's prodigality with suggestions that the Baltimore-born Babe had a non-Caucasian in his family tree.

Yet another incongruity involved integrated play in a Jim Crow world. While professional baseball ardently policed its color line, African Americans competed against whites in a wide variety of venues. The early 20th-century United States offered a broad universe of semiprofessional teams representing towns, neighborhoods, churches, ethnic groups, and companies. African-American teams, both those in organized leagues and those operating independently, often found their most lucrative matchups in games that pitted them against white clubs. On the streets of Chicago, Anson's Colts, a white semiprofessional squad organized by and bearing the name of 19th-century-great Adrian "Cap" Anson, who is often portrayed as the architect of baseball segregation, routinely engaged that city's African-American teams. In 1906 the International League of Colored Baseball Clubs in America and Cuba featured two black, two

Cuban, and two white teams. A decade later, a touring All-Nations club fielded white, black, Indian, Latino, and Asian players.

Surprisingly, white fans in small-town America were often more aware of black baseball than those in major or even minor league cities. For decades, black professional teams barnstormed throughout the nation taking on all comers, entertaining black and white fans alike. Black teams participated in the California Winter League. Prestigious national competitions like the Denver Post and the National Baseball Congress in Kansas featured such Negro league standouts as the Kansas City Monarchs or individual stars like Satchel Paige and Chet Brewer playing on integrated teams. African Americans also pioneered in the international realm, incorporating teams of Cubans into their leagues, and participating in the Caribbean and Mexican baseball circuits. While on the highest levels of organized baseball, African-American athletes remained, in effect, "invisible men" on the barnstorming circuit, stars like Paige achieved legendary status.

The ironies did not abate in the post-World War II years after Jackie Robinson's breakthrough brought baseball's Jim Crow era to a close. Black America's enthusiasm for integration led to the rapid demise of the Negro leagues. "The big league doors suddenly opened one day," explained sportswriter Wendell Smith, "and when Negro players walked in, Negro baseball walked out." However, organized baseball moved "with all deliberate speed" to bring blacks into its ranks. As late as September 1953, more than six years after Robinson joined the Dodgers, only six of sixteen major league clubs fielded black players. Not until 1959, when the Boston Red Sox finally promoted a nonwhite player, did all clubs integrate. As a result, while integration opened opportunities for a relative handful of elite young African-American ballplayers, it reduced the numbers of blacks playing baseball professionally. Furthermore, major league teams rarely, if ever, acknowledged the expertise of the veterans of the Negro leagues by hiring them as managers, coaches, scouts, or front office personnel. In the enlightened age of integration, fewer rather than more African Americans would earn their livelihoods in baseball jobs.

But if the Negro leagues and other all-black teams disappeared, their style of play did not. The first generation of African-American stars, many of whom had begun their careers in the Negro leagues, introduced to the game an unprecedented blend of power and speed, of home-run hitting and base stealing that, in many respects, made the major leagues more closely resemble the game of "Cool Papa" Bell and Oscar Charleston, than that of Babe Ruth and Ted Williams. In a crowning irony, in 1974 Ruth's career home-run record, one of baseball's most sacred, fell to former Indianapolis Clowns' infielder Henry Aaron, the last remaining Negro Leaguer in the majors. By the early 21st century, African-American players held so many of major league baseball's all-time batting and baserunning records that some suggested that all statistics set before 1960 should be accompanied with an asterisk, denoting that white players in the Jim Crow years had accomplished their achievements without facing all of the best players of that age.

Perhaps the greatest irony has emerged from the evolution of Negro leagues history. By the 1960s the world of African-American baseball that had flourished so dynamically only two decades earlier had dropped from the nation's historical memory; yet today, this subject has been so thoroughly researched and rediscovered that we know more in many respects about black baseball and its intersection with the African-American community than we do of its white counterpart. As late as 1969 only one book had been written about black baseball in the Jim Crow age, and that volume, Sol White's *Official Baseball Guide*, had been published in 1907 and long since passed out of print. Indeed, finding any information about the Negro leagues in books was nearly impossible. A relative handful of pages appeared in Edwin Bancroft Henderson's *The Negro in Sports* in 1939. Multi-volume academic histories of baseball written in the 1960s by Harold Seymour and David Voigt addressed the exclusion of blacks in the 1880s, but then neglected African Americans entirely. Most accounts of the Jackie Robinson saga mentioned his brief stint with the Kansas City Monarchs, but barely scratched the surface of life in the Negro leagues.

A glimpse into the bygone world of the Negro leagues could be found in books about the first players to cross the color line. In 1953 African-American journalist A.S. "Doc" Young published *Great Negro Baseball Stars and How They Made the Major Leagues*. In vignettes about the African

Americans who appeared in the majors between 1947 and 1952, Young also discussed their careers in black baseball. Jackie Robinson included a pair of interviews with Negro league stars in *Baseball Has Done It*, his 1964 assessment of the progress of integration. Perhaps the best account of life in the Negro leagues appeared in Roy Campanella's 1959 autobiography, *It's Good To Be Alive*. Campanella, who had joined the Baltimore Elite Giants at age 15 and spent ten years with that club until signing with the Dodgers organization, devoted several lively, insightful chapters to his formative baseball experiences. Satchel Paige's autobiography disappointingly proved less illuminating, and early biographies of Hank Aaron and Willie Mays addressed their roots in black baseball only briefly. These accounts captured elements of black baseball in the 1930s and 1940s, but the earlier decades of the 20th century remained obscured.

The corrective process began in 1970 when Robert Peterson delivered his watershed work, *Only the Ball Was White*. As a boy in Warren, Pennsylvania, Peterson had watched the Homestead Grays, Indianapolis Clowns, and other barnstorming teams play against the local white semiprofessional squad. In 1966, as a journalist recently displaced by the demise of the *New York World Telegram and Sun* who was looking for an idea for a book, he recalled the marvelous players he had watched as a youth and realized how little was known about them. In *Only the Ball Was White*, the first book on the subject in more than 60 years, Peterson traced the history of blacks in baseball from the days of Bud Fowler to the debut of Jackie Robinson. He introduced Americans to early 20th-century stars like John Henry Lloyd and Rube Foster and latter-day legends like Satchel Paige and Josh Gibson, also outlining the various incarnations of the Negro leagues themselves. Peterson's invaluable appendices included descriptions of the great black players of the pre-Robinson era, league standings, box scores for the East-West All-Star Games, and a listing of hundreds of African Americans who had played for professional teams in the first half of the 20th century.

Since the mainstream press had largely ignored black baseball, discovering this history, advised Peterson, "was like trying to find a single black strand through a ton of spaghetti." But a new generation of

In this 1950 match-up between the Brooklyn Dodgers and the Philadelphia Phillies, Jackie Robinson steals home. It's a move Robinson perfected as a Negro leaguer.

researchers, inspired in part by Peterson's work, proved remarkably resourceful in uncovering sources to piece together this slice of baseball's past. Since many veterans of black baseball in the 1920s, 1930s, and 1940s remained alive, the earliest works focused on oral history. John Holway, a former analyst with the United States Information Agency, led the charge. Holway had been interviewing Negro leaguers since the early 1960s. In 1971 he began publishing transcripts of his tapes, and articles based on them, in a variety of periodicals. His first book, *Voices from the Great Black Baseball Leagues*, a collection of interviews with 18 players and Effa Manley, the flamboyant former owner of the Newark Eagles, emerged in 1975. Holway and his collaborators put forth a powerful case that the quality of play among African Americans in the Jim Crow era was equal to, if not better than, major league baseball. Not content to rely on the partisan reminiscences of the players, Holway searched for accounts of games that pitted black athletes against major leaguers. He found 445 such contests between 1886 and 1948 in which the black squads had won more than 60 percent of the games. Oral histories by Holway and others also focused on the discrimination confronted by players as they plied their trade in a segregated nation.

These pioneer efforts received a powerful boost from the creation of the Society for American Baseball Research (SABR) in 1971 In its initial year, SABR established a special Negro League Committee, offering a forum for collaboration and discussion among researchers. SABR's annual journals provided a ready venue for articles and oral histories. Furthermore, the avid researchers of SABR joined Holway and others in scanning black and mainstream newspapers for articles and box scores that would allow them to more fully re-create the history of blacks in baseball. Jerry Malloy and Ray Nemec dramatically enhanced our knowledge of the 19th-century origins of segregation in baseball. James A. Riley began compiling a comprehensive biographical encyclopedia of African-American ballplayers. Other scholars collected photographs of the black baseball experience. A host of oral histories and a handful of minor biographies and autobiographies surfaced from these efforts.

In the 1970s, the Negro leagues also attracted the attention of novelists and filmmakers. In 1973 Bill Brashler described the adventures of a troupe of black ballplayers who broke from the Negro Leagues to form their own squad in *The Bingo Long Traveling All-Stars and Motor Kings*. Three years later Bingo Long became a feature film starring James Earl Jones and Billy Dee Williams. Jim Crow baseball also served as important subthemes in novels like Jay Neugeboren's *Sam's Legacy* and Jerome Charyn's *The Seventh Babe*. *Only the Ball Was White*, a documentary based on Peterson's book, was telecast in 1980. A second influential documentary, *The Sun Was Always Shining Someplace*, appeared in 1984.

Yet, in the early 1980s, the essential library on the pre-integration era might fill less than one row on a modest book shelf. In 1983, Donn Rogosin produced *Invisible Men: Life in Baseball's Negro Leagues*, the first overview of the subject since Peterson's work. Written originally as a doctoral dissertation and based primarily on oral histories, *Invisible Men* brought the veterans of black baseball to life and also addressed the central role that both the leagues and the barnstorming squads played in African-American communities. Rogosin's book marked the beginning of trends that would characterize the next generation of Negro league scholarship: growing attention from the academic community and a shift away from a strict focus on the game itself, with a greater emphasis on social and cultural issues embodied in the baseball experience.

Thus, even as most researchers continued to amass information about the ballplayers and their performances, a handful of scholars, many coming out of universities, began to publish studies that focused on black baseball teams and their relationship to the communities that bore their names. *The Kansas City Monarchs* by Janet Bruce paved the way. Bruce portrayed the Monarchs as "a major social institution for black Kansas Citians" that united African Americans "from every walk of life." Monarch home games became "great social gatherings" and the Monarchs themselves "a community focus...for Black Kansas Citians crushed hard by discrimination." Rob Ruck followed with *Sandlot Seasons*, examining the African-American sports scene in Pittsburgh with particular emphasis on the Homestead Grays and

Pittsburgh Crawfords. Ruck created a rich fabric of sandlot stars, Negro league heroes, numbers runners, ministers, business leaders, and workers to illustrate the intersection of sports and community in black Pittsburgh.

These studies became models for a remarkable body of team histories that surfaced beginning in the mid-1990s. The Detroit Stars and the Indianapolis ABCs, the Hilldale Club of Philadelphia, the Newark Eagles, and the Homestead Grays all received highly sophisticated treatments. Authors Richard Bak, Paul Debono, Neil Lanctot, James Overmyer, and Brad Snyder revealed not only the cultural ties of the black clubs to their home cities, but also the complexities of operating black-based businesses in Jim Crow America. Negro league teams struggled with issues of black versus white ownership, the challenge of finding places to play, the use of white umpires, the dominance of white booking agents, and a fickle African-American fandom that at times showed more allegiance to segregated major league teams than their own "race enterprises."

In archives and personal collections, scholars found that several team officials had left behind considerable evidence of their activities. This enabled them to piece together the business structure of black baseball on a level that has rarely been attempted for white clubs. Michael E. Lomax, in *Black Baseball Entrepreneurs, 1860–1901: Operating by Any Means Necessary* and subsequent work on the early 20th century, painstakingly pieced together the operations of African-American professional and semiprofessional clubs, illuminating not just black baseball, but the heretofore hidden world of white semiprofessional teams and leagues. In 2004 Neil Lanctot delivered *Negro League Baseball: The Rise and Ruin of a Black Institution*, providing a remarkably comprehensive history of the Negro National and Negro American Leagues of the 1930s and 1940s.

Biographies and autobiographies of Rube Foster, Josh Gibson, Monte Irvin, Buck O'Neil, and others complemented these works. Scholars also began to turn their attention to baseball in the Caribbean, producing a rich literature on the interaction of Latino, African-American, and white baseball in Cuba, Puerto Rico, the Dominican Republic, Mexico, and Venezuela, and its repercussions in the United States.

Crucial reference volumes also began to appear. In 1992 two excellent photographic collections, *When the Game Was Black and White* by Bruce Chadwick and *The Negro Leagues: A Photographic History* by Phil Dixon and Patrick J. Hannigan, came out. In 1994 James A. Riley published *The Biographical Encyclopedia of The Negro Leagues* and SABR's Negro Leagues Committee produced *The Negro Leagues Book* including rosters, league standings, and statistical information. The indefatigable John Holway offered an even more thorough statistical compilation in 2001, *The Complete Book of Baseball's Negro Leagues: The Other Half of Baseball History*. Larry Lester, a key figure on the SABR Negro League Committee and in efforts to create a Negro leagues museum, added *Black Baseball's National Showcase: The East-West All-Star Game, 1933–1953*.

Awareness of the heritage of Jim Crow baseball had long since leapt from the printed page into other media. In 1987 August Wilson's play *Fences*, with James Earl Jones starring as an embittered former Negro league player, opened on Broadway. Larry Hogan's traveling exhibit, *Before You Can Say Jackie Robinson*, began to tour the country in 1989. The experience of blacks in baseball was a major theme in Ken Burns monumental nine-part documentary, *Baseball*, that captivated a broad audience when televised on National Public Broadcast stations in 1994. Three years later the Negro Leagues Baseball Museum opened in Kansas City.

The relationship of the National Baseball Hall of Fame and Museum and baseball's Jim Crow era parallels these broader national trends. Holway relates visiting the Hall in 1969 and finding a single manila folder with a scorecard for the Indianapolis Clowns and an article on Josh Gibson as the sole Negro league holdings in the archives. None of the Museum's exhibits acknowledged this part of baseball's legacy. Among the plaques of those commemorated as baseball immortals, none had been honored for their play in the Negro leagues. This issue had become more controversial for the Hall with each passing year. One of the most influential calls for the inclusion of Negro league veterans had come three years earlier from an unlikely source. Ted Williams had played his entire career on the Boston Red Sox, the last major league team to integrate. He had never objected to the Red Sox recalcitrance or made public statements about the issue. But in his Hall of Fame induction speech on July 25, 1966, Williams unexpectedly pronounced, "I hope that someday the names of Satchel Paige and Josh Gibson can be added as a symbol of the great Negro players [who] are not here because they were not given a chance."

Others picked up on his plea. In his epilogue to *Only the Ball Was White*, Peterson called for "recognition to the great stars of Negro baseball" in the Hall of Fame. Influential New York Daily News sportswriter Dick Young adopted the cause and the Baseball Writers Association of America voiced support for the proposal. Bowie Kuhn, who became baseball commissioner in 1969, moved to make it a reality. Kuhn, however, ran into opposition from some Hall of Fame officials who argued that Negro leaguers did not qualify because they had not played the requisite ten years in the major leagues—the irony being that Negro leaguers could not possible have met those conditions due to baseball's earlier policies. Kuhn convinced the Hall of Fame, however, to mount a special exhibit recognizing the stars of the Jim Crow era and to establish a committee of experts to select players whose exploits would be acknowledged. Satchel Paige was chosen as the initial honoree.

The plan unleashed a firestorm of protest. Peterson had already warned against the creation of "some obscure corner of the museum where Rube Foster and Satchel Paige and Josh Gibson and John Henry Lloyd can be segregated in a dusty pigeonhole as they were in life." Paige objected: "I was just as good as the white boys. I ain't going in the back door of the Hall of Fame." The controversy forced the Hall to relent. On July 6, 1971, it announced that Paige would receive full induction.

Over the next five years, the Hall of Fame Negro League Committee named additional honorees, choosing a player at each position. In addition to pitcher Paige, the Hall inducted catcher Josh Gibson, first baseman Buck Leonard, shortstop John Henry Lloyd, third baseman Judy Johnson, and outfielders Cool Papa Bell, Oscar Charleston, and Monte Irvin. The versatile Martin Dihigo, the only Latin nominee, who could have been inducted at any position, served as the second baseman. Having selected in effect an all-time Negro league all-star team, the committee disbanded in 1976. The consideration of other candidates would be left to the Hall of Fame's Veteran's Committee.

Although few people challenged the qualifications of those inducted, many noted that other equally or even more worthy athletes had been left out. Holway noted that the selections were heavily weighted toward those who had played in the 1930s and 1940s and for eastern rather than midwestern teams. Rube Foster, the dominant figure of the early decades of the 20th century who could have qualified as player, manager, or administrator, had been omitted. The 18-man Veteran's Committee, which included only two Negro league players in its ranks, Irvin and Campanella, failed to significantly redress the situation. Between 1978 and 1994 the committee chose only Foster and Newark Eagles' third baseman Ray Dandridge. In 1993 the J.G. Taylor Spink Award "for meritorious contributions to baseball writing" went to *Pittsburgh Courier* correspondent and African-American journalist Wendell Smith. The museum at the Hall exhibited a similar form of tokenism. In 1972 it unveiled a small photo montage of blacks in baseball; in 1978 it offered a permanent, but nonetheless superficial, exhibit. By 1980 the library collection had grown, but still amounted to but a few manila folders full of documents.

The 1990s brought a new awareness of the Jim Crow era to the Hall of Fame. Selection of new members remained in the hands of the Veteran's Committee, but from 1995 through 2001 electors received an additional ballot listing candidates who had played before integration, thereby enhancing the opportunity for election. Pitchers Leon Day, Bill Foster, "Bullet" Joe Rogan, Hilton Smith, "Smokey Joe" Williams, shortstop Willie Wells, and outfielder Turkey Stearnes gained acceptance. *Baltimore Afro American* reporter Sam Lacy, the dean of black sportswriters, joined Wendell Smith as a Spink Award honoree. In 1997, for the fiftieth anniversary of Jackie Robinson's major league debut, the Hall of Fame Museum unveiled "Pride and Passion: The African-American Baseball Experience," a vastly expanded and improved exhibit, which examined the history of blacks in baseball from the Civil War through the integration era. The Hall of Fame Library, meanwhile, had become a major repository for materials on African Americans and baseball.

In July 2000, Major League Baseball granted $250,000 to the Hall of Fame to fund a "comprehensive study on the history of African-Americans in Baseball, from 1860–1960." The Hall requested proposals from research teams with strong academic credentials to complete the project. In February 2001 the Hall of Fame announced that a group headed by long-time Negro league researchers Larry Hogan, a professor of history at Union County College in New Jersey, and SABR Negro League Committee Co-chairs Larry Lester and Dick Clark had won the competition. Others working on the study would include a veritable all-star team of academic experts on blacks and baseball: Bob Peterson, Rob Ruck, James Overmyer, Neil Lanctot, Leslie Heaphy, Adrian Burgos, and Michael Lomax. The committee submitted its work, *Out of the Shadows*, to the Hall of Fame in 2005. The study included an 800-page manuscript, an extensive bibliography, and a massive statistical data base of player statistics. This book represents a distillation of that lengthy analysis.

The Baseball Hall of Fame's commitment to compiling the history of blacks and baseball marked a culmination of the long struggle to incorporate the African-American experience into the legacy of the national pastime. However, one thorny problem remained. The expanded opportunity for the Veteran's Committee to select one pre-integration black player per year ended in 2001. In the next four years, no additional representatives of the Jim Crow era were added. The number of players honored remained frozen at 18. Seven of the 18 segregation-era athletes earned their fame as pitchers, but only 11 position players merited inclusion. One black catcher, Josh Gibson, appears on a Hall of Fame plaque, while universally acclaimed standouts like Louis Santop and Biz Mackey remain viable candidates. Buck Leonard remains the sole first baseman, while spectacular power-hitter "Mule" Suttles should receive consideration. There are no pure second basemen, only two shortstops, and two third basemen. Martin Dihigo remains the sole Latino Negro leaguer in the Hall, but there are other great players such as Cristobal Torriente and José Mendez.

Cooperstown also has a category that honors executives and pioneers of baseball. Several figures from the world of black baseball fall into this category. Sol White was a star player for a host of teams between 1887 and 1912, and a manager, organizer of teams, and sportswriter for several more decades. But his most enduring contribution remains his 1906 *History of Colored Baseball*, without which the first half century of blacks and baseball would have remained obscured from memory and history. J.L. Wilkinson, a white businessman who owned and operated the Kansas City Monarchs for over a half century, also deserves consideration. With the Monarchs, the All-Nations, and the House of David teams, Wilkinson pioneered on the barnstorming circuit. In 1930 he introduced a portable lighting system that helped to popularize night baseball. In the 1930s and 1940s his clever marketing helped to sustain the legend of Satchel Paige. His Monarchs developed a large number of players who went on to integrate the majors, including future Hall of Famers Jackie Robinson, Satchel Paige, and Ernie Banks. Wendell Smith described him as a man who "not only invested his money, but his heart and soul" in the African-American game. Another executive who sustained black baseball was Cumberland Posey, for more than three decades the owner of the celebrated Homestead Grays. Posey consistently fielded one of the best and most popular African-American teams. Led by Josh Gibson and Buck Leonard, the Grays won nine consecutive Negro National League pennants. In the 1940s Posey established a second home base for the Grays at Griffith Stadium in Washington, D.C., bringing great attention to the economic potential of showcasing black athletes.

Two more unorthodox figures also warrant discussion. Alejandro Pompez's contributions to baseball are indisputable. As the owner of the Cuban Stars in the 1920s and the New York Cubans from 1935–1950, Pompez introduced the top stars from Cuba to the United States, including Martin Dihigo, Luis Tiant, Sr., and Minnie Minoso. When the Negro leagues collapsed, he brought his keen eye for talent and connections in the Caribbean to his work as a scout for the New York Giants. He signed players like Orlando Cepeda, son of Puerto Rican great Perucho Cepeda, and opened up the market for players from the Dominican Republic when he recruited Juan Marichal and the Alou brothers for the Giants. Buck O'Neil is in a category all his own. As a player-manager with the Kansas City Monarchs, O'Neil would be the first to admit that his skills don't place him among the all-time greats. But he mentored many of the players who went on to pioneer integration in the majors and worked for the Chicago Cubs as a scout. In 1962 he became the first black coach in major league history. But O'Neil left his greatest mark in the 1980s and 1990s as the primary spokesperson for the legacy of the Negro leagues. On Ken Burns' *Baseball* series and myriad other venues, O'Neil charmed, entertained, and educated people about the greater glories of baseball on both sides of the color line. For several decades he has reigned as a symbol of baseball's past and the game's greatest good-will ambassador.

As this book goes to press, it is pleasing to note that these individuals, along with other worthy candidates, have been nominated for possible induction into the Hall of Fame. In July 2005 the Hall approved a special election to consider these and other candidates from the Jim Crow era for admission. The Hall established a five-man screening committee drawn from the "Out of the Shadows" research team to nominate candidates, and a twelve-person voting committee of experts on black baseball to judge the nominees. All candidates receiving 75 percent of the ballots will be inducted into the Hall of Fame in July, 2006.

Today the Negro leagues, once all but forgotten, have become virtually omnipresent. Once the flower of a segregated African-American universe, the celebration of black baseball has blossomed into a national phenomenon. Hundreds of books and thousands of websites commemorate the Negro leagues. Major league teams hold Negro league Days, where teams play in uniforms bearing the logos of the bygone clubs. Black and white fans wear hats and jerseys commemorating the Chicago American Giants, New York Black Yankees, and other storied teams of a bygone age featuring current African-American baseball superstars like Barry Bonds and

Ken Griffey, Jr.

The Negro leagues, of course, will not come back. Nor should we wish them to. Therein lies the ultimate irony of baseball's—and indeed, the nation's —racial past. The realm of black baseball was a vibrant and colorful one. It offered a panorama of innovation and enterprise, entertainment and excitement, and unparalleled athletic achievement. It enriched the lives of African Americans and of other Americans fortunate enough to witness its magic. Yet this spectacle resulted from and was made necessary by the nation's worst impulses: the cancer of segregation and discrimination that plagued the United States in its Jim Crow years. In recalling the Negro Leagues and the broader domain of black baseball, we honor the resiliency and creativity of an oppressed people. Yet we also celebrate the demise of that world and its replacement by a national pastime more fully characterized by equality of opportunity and dramatically inclusive of not just African Americans, but players from Latin America and Asia as well. The persistence of those who sustained black baseball made this possible. In retrieving their past we make a down payment on a debt that can never fully be redeemed.

—Jules Tygiel

An unknown African-American baseball club from the late 1910s to early 1920s poses for a classic team shot.

Introduction

I use my single windup, my double windup, my triple windup, my hesitation windup, my no windup. I also use my step-n-pitch-it, my submariner, my sidearmer, and my bat dodger. Man's got to do what he's got to do.

—SATCHEL PAIGE

ON AUGUST 1, IN 1943, 51,723 SPECTATORS PACKED into Chicago's Comiskey Park to watch an East-West All-Star game that would feature some of the greatest stars ever to play the game. But the top players of that era—Mel Ott, Bill Dickey, Stan Musial, and Bobby Doerr— were nowhere to be found. On this day, the fans watched the exploits of Cool Papa Bell, Buck Leonard, Josh Gibson, Leon Day, Buck O'Neil, Ted "Double Duty" Radcliffe, and Satchel Paige. There were no white faces on the field this Sunday afternoon, and very few in the stands. This was the 1943 Negro East-West All-Star Game, a match-up of the best from the Negro American and National Leagues. Two weeks before this game, the all-white major leagues played their All-Star game in Philadelphia's Shibe Park, drawing only 32,000. That the Negro League outdrew the majors wasn't a singular event. Between 1938 and 1948, the Negro Leagues' East-West game outdrew the major league All-Star game seven times.

The reason, which had become painfully obvious by 1943, was simple. These black baseball stars were every bit as good as white players. Many consider Satchel Paige the greatest pitcher of all time. Josh Gibson was called the black Babe Ruth. The list goes on and on, right on down the rosters that day. The fans at Comiskey Park had come to see baseball played at its highest level. Byron Johnson, a shortstop in the 1938 East-West game, summed it up best when he said, "Some of those critics never wanted to believe that we were as good as whites. We knew better."

This book tells the story of black baseball from the first organized games of the 19th century to the glory days of the Negro leagues in the 1920s, '30s, and '40s. It puts on display the players, owners, and fans that made the game come alive for generations of African Americans. In these pages, the special brand of baseball played in the shadows of segregation emerges in all its glory.

When baseball teams became professional in the 1870s, black Americans were facing extraordinary challenges. The Civil War had been fought, but by this time the gains ushered in by the Reconstruction era were overturned. The landmark Sumner Civil Rights Act of 1875, which sought to ensure equal access to public accommodations for all citizens, was by 1883 declared unconstitutional. During the 1890s the Supreme Court chipped away at the 14th Amendment to the Constitution, which guaranteed former slaves all the rights of United States citizens. Then in the notorious *Plessy v. Ferguson* decision of 1896, the Supreme Court upheld the separate but unequal status of blacks in American society. At the dawn of the 20th century, segregation was the rule rather than the exception.

Baseball reflected the times. Into the 1880s, some black athletes had played in "organized" white ball. By the turn of the century, as segregation laws hardened, Negro players would be barred from the white professional version of America's game. Black ballplayers would not be seen in the majors again until the 1950s.

White baseball's loss was black baseball's gain. Forced to be separate, blackball emerged as one of the greatest sources of African-American entertainment and pride. The heart of the sport was always the black community. Black baseball evolved within the context of an evolving black world of many communities, and is best understood by seeing its relationship to the entire spectrum of African-American life.

The black game started to be national and indeed hemispheric as the 19th century drew to a close. It began to incorporate an entire Caribbean baseball network, while playing white baseball teams as well in the off-seasons. These years witnessed the first of the legendary figures of the black game with names like Rube Foster, "Pop" Lloyd, Smokey Joe Williams, "Cannonball" Redding, and José Mendez playing at a level that was clearly the equal of their white major league counterparts. That evolving black baseball world reached its height in its various leagues of the 1920s, '30s and '40s.

After World War II, the Negro leagues launched the careers of Jackie Robinson, Larry Doby, Roy Campanella, Don Newcombe, Monte Irvin, Ernie Banks, Henry Aaron, and Willie Mays, players who would break baseball color barriers once and for all. Yet the Negro leagues' rosters were also filled with stars like Ray Dandridge, Leon Day, and Raymond Brown, who played out their best baseball days only to be forgotten for over three decades, with only one living long enough to smell the roses of Cooperstown.

The players who appear in these pages came to the game for different reasons. But they shared an attitude and a love for the game. Clarence "Pint" Israel, third baseman for the Newark Eagles in their 1946 championship season, expressed it well: "If you were determined to play, you played baseball, and all the guys were good ballplayers. I guess the only reason I really wanted to play is because I wanted to be good like the rest of the ballplayers. It's something that gets in your craw. It sticks with you."

It is customary to emphasize the unfairness that was at the heart of the existence of black baseball. But that is not the only story. Those who starred in the Negro leagues were playing the game they loved in front of fans who thought of them as heroes. Few have described their time on the field in the Negro leagues as memorably as Buck O'Neil, first baseman for the Kansas City Monarchs, when he said: "There is nothing like getting your body to do all it has to do on a baseball field. It is as good as sex. It is as good as music. It fills you up. Waste no tears on me. I didn't come along too early. I was right on time."

Black teams of the late 1880s to early 1990s often played for white audiences. John Milton Dabney, who would later play for the Original Cuban Giants, is seated third from the right in the front row.

Early Days

Saturday afternoon a considerable crowd, mainly dusky, assembled at the Niagara grounds to see the game between a colored nine, from Washington, who are on their travels, called the Mutuals, and a Buffalo nine, also fifteenthly amended, who rejoice in the same club title. It was a gala occasion for the colored population of Buffalo, and any number of festively attired samboes took their gaily dressed chloes out to see the game.

—Buffalo Courier, August 22, 1870

The earliest black baseball was played by slaves. Between 1936 and 1938 the Federal Writers' Project set down the reminiscences of several former slaves who recalled baseball, or something like it, having been played in their youth.

Sam Scott of Russellville, Arkansas, remembered, "I never did dance, but I sure could play baseball and make home runs!"

John Cole of Athens, Georgia, recalled life on a plantation with relatively relaxed work rules where "always on Saturday afternoon you would have 'till 'first dark' for baseball, and from first dark 'till Sunday-go-to-meeting for drinking and dancing."

Ed Allen of Des Arc, Arkansas, reminisced that white and Negro boys played ball together. Such games among young children were not unusual in the slavery South, although that changed as the youths grew older. Several of the old slaves' accounts told of the use of makeshift balls and bats. But Allen recalled to Works Progress Administration (WPA) researcher Irene Robertson, "We never had to buy a ball or a bat. Always had 'em. The white boys bought them."

For the most part, African-American team baseball became organized earlier in the North than in the South. The first recorded game between two black teams took place in the New York City area on November 15, 1859, a year in which baseball experienced a dramatic increase overall. The Unknowns of Weeksville in Brooklyn played the Henson Base Ball Club of Jamaica, in what is now the borough of Queens. The Hensons won, 54–43, an extravagant score that probably reflected a lack of good fielding more than powerful hitting.

Weeksville was an African-American settlement founded in the heart of Brooklyn in 1838. Brooklyn was made up of many such small enclaves at the time, and Weeksville gradually became a self-sufficient community among its predominantly white surroundings (less than two percent of Brooklyn's population was African American at the time). Its dozens of families included ministers, teachers, and other professionals who made up the civic backbone of black communities.

The Unknowns broke through into the white press on October 16, 1862, when a sporting correspondent for the *Brooklyn Eagle*, discovering the game between two white teams that he was supposed to cover had been canceled, stumbled instead on the Weeksville Unknowns playing Brooklyn's Monitor team. The reportage was in large part condescending in tone, as white news coverage of black baseball continued to be for decades, but the good time both the teams and the crowd were having seeped through the stereotyping:

Quite a large assemblage encircled the contestants, who were every one as black as the ace of spades. Among the assemblage we noticed a number of old and well known players, who seemed to enjoy the game more heartily than if they had been the players themselves. The dusky contestants enjoyed the game hugely, and to use a common phrase, they "did the thing genteelly." Dinah, all eyes, was there to applaud, and the game passed off most satisfactorily. All appeared to have a very jolly time, and the little piccaninnies laughed with the rest.

Memoirs of an Ex-Slave

Ben Leitner was an ex-slave and 85 years of age when the Federal Writers' Project interviewed him in 1936. The game Leitner recalled playing in his youth was very different from the baseball that emerged in the 20th century.

For one, when a group of men met to get a game started, they didn't use the word, "team." Instead, they got a "Nine" together. He recalled that if you "caught a ball on the first bounce, that was an 'out.'" There was no such thing as a mask, gloves, or "mats to protect your belly." Pitchers couldn't throw curves or "swift balls." They had to "pitch a slow drop ball." The aim of the whole game, said Leitner, "was to see how far a batter could knock [the] ball, how fast a fellow could run, how many tallies a side could make." Leitner joked that it was a "mighty poor game if [it] didn't last half a day and one side or the other [didn't make] forty tallies."

Leitner remembered a game when one of the players, Bill Kitchen, left work at his brother-in-law's store to join a nine. He went to bat, and knocked the ball way "over center field. Everybody hollered at the batter: 'Run Kitchen! Run Kitchen! Run Kitchen!' But Bill Kitchen stood right there with the bat. [He] shook his head and long black whiskers and said: 'Why should I run? I got two more licks at the ball!'" The reluctant runner was called out at the base and the umpire ruled him out. Leitner laughed: "Bill threw the bat down and said, "Damn such a game!' Folks laugh 'bout that 'til this day."

Weeksville won, 41–15, in what the *Eagle* reported was to be "the first of a series" of games. But the newspaper, its reporters presumably having successfully located white games, failed to cover the following contests.

The growth of black baseball from an unorganized amusement for any group with a ball and a pasture to more organized teams paralleled the sport's history among whites. Baseball as played pretty much by modern rules emerged in the New York City area in the late 1840s. Most of the credit for its development is given to the Knickerbocker Club of Manhattan, a group of business and professional men who used the sport as a focal point for social activities. Their ranks were composed primarily of merchants, clerks, and insurance and banking professionals, and they were "primarily a social club with a distinctly exclusive flavor....To the Knickerbockers a ball game was a vehicle for genteel amateur recreation and polite social intercourse."

New York City was the center of this evolution of baseball into a sport played by teams with consistent rosters, but it soon spread into other social classes and areas. The Knickerbockers, who might have been happy keeping the game to their own middle class, soon faced challenges from teams of "lesser" social status, such as the Eckfords of Brooklyn, a group of mechanics and shipyard builders who struck a blow for the working class once a baseball was in play. In 1858, the Knickerbockers began to share their control over the game when 22 teams met in Manhattan to form the National Association of Base Ball Players (NABBP). By that time team ball had expanded geographically as well. One club, the Eagles, was playing in California by 1859.

Team names from this early period of baseball sound quaint today. They usually could be traced to a local source. In New York City, for example, the Eckfords were named after Henry Eckford, a shipbuilder who employed some of the players, and the Mutuals were named for the fire company to which its players belonged. Although the source of some team names is now obscure, fire companies seem to have inspired the names of many. Teams, both white and black, were called "Mutuals," "Alerts," "Resolutes," and the like. Some names were chosen for their braggadocio quotient—the Uniques and Excelsiors come to mind. The Unknowns moniker adopted by the Weeksville team was not unusual, either.

The formation of African-American clubs in major Northern cities continued throughout the 1860s. The most famous earned occasional coverage in the white sporting press, surfacing in Philadelphia, Boston and Albany, New York, among other places. Back in Brooklyn, on October 25, 1867, the Monitors won what was billed in the *Ballplayers Gazette*, a sports publication of the day, as the "championship of colored clubs" by defeating the Uniques 49-17 at the Satellite Grounds in the city's Williamsburg section. The "championship" billing indicates how special the game was for black teams of that time, and the *Gazette* reported that "this match has been the theme of comment for some time in colored circles."

By this time the best African-American teams were taking the same major step in the growth of black ball that the crack white clubs had taken in the 1850s—they were journeying to each other's cities for a higher level of competition instead of simply knocking off available home teams. The big Unique–Monitor game came on the heels of a visit to Brooklyn by Philadelphia's black Excelsiors, in which they defeated the Uniques and lost to the Monitors.

The first intercity games between black teams may have been in September 1866, when the Bachelors of Albany journeyed to Philadelphia and defeated the Excelsiors and the other crack team there, the Pythians. In August 1867 the Pythians went to Washington, D.C., to play the Alerts and the Mutuals, the reigning black teams in the capital, returning the visits of both Washington clubs, who had come to Philadelphia for games in July. In a reversal of the outcomes that might have been expected, the Pythians lost their home games, by narrow margins, but won the pair in Washington. The home game against the Alerts produced some celebrity news coverage. The noted black abolitionist Frederick Douglass, whose younger son Charles was playing third base for the Alerts, sat with the dignitaries and sportswriters and viewed the game until rain washed it out in the fifth inning.

The Washington clubs should have produced strong traveling teams, since they had a bigger manpower pool from which to draw. After the Civil War, blacks flocked to the national capital, where they were given the vote in 1866 and where jobs were available, including some white-collar positions with the federal government. This led to an African-American population boom in the district, roughly tripling in number from 1860 to 43,404 by 1870.

The Washington Mutuals were composed primarily of government employees. Charles Douglass, who worked first at the Freedmen's Bureau,

Pop Watkins
The Greatest Baseball Scout in the World

Harry Hairstone, a mainstay of the Baltimore Black Sox for many years, said John Pop Watkins had "the fight in him." For this competitor, Watkins was "one of a game lot." Around the year 1905, Hairstone was playing for a white ball club, the Rochester Big Horns. The Horns were locked in a contentious game with a black squad anchored by Pop Watkins at first base. In his first time at bat the young Hairstone hit a sharp line drive down the first base line headed for two base territory. The ball never reached the outfield. Pop made a one-hand catch while falling over the bag.

"Gee old man, you're lucky," yelled the disappointed Hairstone.

"Hit them right, son," Pop yelled back, "and if I get a mile of them they're in the well."

Pop's fielding skills were the stuff of legend but his career didn't end when his playing did. Instead, Watkins was able to create a new career for himself as an accomplished scout. No less a testifier than Sol White in 1919 called Watkins the "dean of the Colored baseball profession."

Born in Augusta, Georgia, in 1857 in the days of slavery, John Watkins moved while still young to Brooklyn, New York. The young Watkins played backlot baseball. His talent as a catcher would lead to his long tenure with black baseball's first great professional team, the Cuban Giants.

He also would face some of the top white talent of his day. An *Afro American* story of 1923 records his scars from a collision at first base with the great Honus Wagner of the Pittsburgh Pirates, who crashed into him while he was taking a throw from short. That incident left him with three broken ribs. Another souvenir was a scarred lip split by a pitched ball delivered by none other than the famous Christy Mathewson.

There would be another white baseball connection for this black pioneer, one that it is difficult to credit without expressing a touch of incredulity. The title bestowed on him by the *Afro American* reporter was not "World's Greatest Black Base Ball Scout" but simply "World's Greatest Base Ball Scout." Pop's ability as a player became common knowledge to the managers of big-league clubs, and in the course of time he was sought out to take the position of scout and coach for young players. Among the many players he discovered who later became the greatest stars of the game were John McGraw, the famous pilot of the world champion Giants; Hughie Jennings, who won fame with the Detroit Tigers; John Hummel; and Al Schacht.

Pop was one of a game lot indeed.

the agency created to help former slaves make their transition to free citizenry, had been playing with the Alerts, the first of the strong Washington teams, but had gone over to the Mutuals in 1869. He was a regular for the team, sometimes its pitcher, and later president of the Mutual Club, the social organization from which the team sprang.

In August 1870, he and the rest of the Mutuals went on a road trip that was remarkably long for that period. After an August 16 game in Baltimore, where the Mutuals cowed the black Enterprise team by a 51–26 score, the team departed for upstate New York. They played seven games in a little more than a week along a 300-mile stretch roughly following the Erie Canal. Starting in the western part of the state, they overwhelmed six black clubs by mostly lopsided scores.

In Rochester the visitors had a special experience. Frederick Douglass, Charles' famous father, was living there on a farm just outside the city. He and his wife Anna played host to the ballplayers at a house that had been the last stop in the United States for slaves escaping to Canada via the Underground Railroad.

The Mutuals' enjoyed a pleasant reception overall in Rochester, where they edged a "picked nine" of players from the various white teams in Rochester, 23–19. The game drew a huge crowd. "A larger gathering was, perhaps, never before assembled on the commons to witness a game of ball," a local newspaper reported. Perhaps because Frederick Douglass himself was a respected member of the community, the press and public treated the Mutuals as valued visitors. Besides testifying to the team's baseball prowess, the reporter stated, "For gentlemanly, quiet, unassuming behavior they might be set up as a pattern worthy of the imitation of any club, white or colored." This contest, one of the first games between well-organized black and white teams, was so well received on both sides that the Mutuals returned again on September 22 for a rematch, and another victory.

The Mutuals next played in Utica, edging the local black team, the Fearless, 18–10. The Fearless was apparently a pretty good team among the black clubs along New York's Northern Tier, having beaten the Invincibles of Buffalo the year before by 70 runs to claim a "colored championship of

New York." Both they and the Mutuals were severely hampered by heavy rain, which did not stop the game from being played in extremely sloppy conditions. Baseballs were seldom replaced during games, even if they became muddy, and the *Utica Morning Herald* reporter noted, "There is a novelty about batting at a nicely pitched ball, and having your club come *kerswash* against a chunk of mud."

Before leaving the area, the Washington team defeated the Heavy Hitters of Canajoharie, a team that had won a regional tournament among Negro teams just the week before, by a lopsided 63–13. Then they moved on to the last stop, the city of Troy on the Hudson River, where they demolished the Hannibal club, 60–15. The game, played on the home grounds of the well-known white Haymakers club, with Dick Flowers of the Haymakers acting as umpire, drew 900 fans, about 600 of them white. It was reported to have been "the first public base ball match between clubs made up of colored men ever played in this vicinity." The game was actually pretty close (for 1870s ball) early on, with the Mutuals leading only 22–10 after five innings. But then the Hannibals fell apart, and the Mutuals scored 38 runs in the next three innings, until the game was called.

In sweeping their eight-game trip from Baltimore to Troy by way of Lakes Erie and Ontario, the Mutuals aroused strong curiosity. Their uniforms drew comment—white with green stockings and belts, said to resemble those of the famous white New York Mutuals. The fact that Parker, the first baseman, was an assistant superintendent of the Negro school system in Washington, and Smith, the pitcher, was a law student, was also remarked upon. The squad was described as "being composed of highly respectable and enterprising young gentlemen holding good positions in Washington."

Scheduling problems prevented the playing of the last contest in Troy with that city's Unions. Troy's white team, the Haymakers, were in the top echelon. They were the only team not to lose to the Cincinnati Red Stockings, the first truly professional team, and they became a charter member in 1871 of the first professional league, the National Association of Professional Base Ball Clubs. Although not fully professional, the

Haymakers were an example of what baseball historian David Voigt refers to as "commercialized" teams in an era when white baseball was moving toward such a status. While not paying their players directly, such teams were able to provide at least the best of them with good-paying jobs at which they were not expected to spend much time so they could turn their main focus to baseball. Although the development of black baseball lagged behind its white counterparts, the Mutuals trip showed that Negro teams were evolving as well.

THE PYTHIANS OF PHILADELPHIA

The New York metropolitan area was the Northeast's hotbed of baseball in those years, but Philadelphia was not far behind. The city had at least two crack black teams, one of which, Octavius Catto's Pythians, has been well chronicled. The Pythians' evolution from a local club shows how African-American baseball established itself in black communities after the Civil War. Fortunately, the Pythians left a written account of their doings archived in the Pennsylvania Historical Society.

The Pythians were in many ways comparable to the old white Knickerbocker club of New York. Like them, the Pythians first formed a social club for middle-class males, and baseball was the central activity around which whirled a social world of banquets and camaraderie among the leaders of the city's Negro community. The Pythians took shape in the summer of 1869. The team at first was named the Institute, from the Institute for Colored Youth, a high school for blacks from which Octavius Catto was a graduate, a teacher, and then an assistant principal. Before the summer was over, the Institute team had renamed itself the Pythians, because a number of its players were members of the black Knights of Pythias lodge.

As a social organization, the Pythians rented rooms at the Institute and laid down rules prohibiting liquor, card playing, and gambling there, as well as the use of bad language and unbecoming conduct. An extensive analysis of the Pythian club members shows it included the city's African-American upper crust. Membership was nearly 70 percent mulatto, an important distinction since social stratification in black communities favored those of lighter skins. Ninety percent of the members held lower-paying white-collar jobs or were skilled craftsmen.

The Pythians comported themselves on and off the field as a group of gentlemen. The surviving records of the club show an insistence on well-mannered behavior. Game arrangements, even with other Philadelphia teams, were made in writing. There are several examples of correspondence written in precise and ornate hands that offer challenges in the most gentlemanly terms possible. The 1867 series with the Mutuals of Washington was set in motion by this note from George D. Johnson of the Mutuals to Octavius Catto: "The Mutual Base Ball Club of Washington DC of which I have the honor to be Secretary, has instructed me to address you a friendly note, congratulatory of the high position you, as an organization, have attained in our national Game, and so to request that you will enter our Club as a friendly competitor for its honors." The response from Pythians secretary Jacob C. White was in the same vein.

The visits of out-of-town clubs were occasions for lavish celebrations. Visiting teams rarely came for one game only, and the time between contests was filled with banquets, dances, and picnics. Historian Thomas Jable concludes, "Thus baseball was part of a larger social atmosphere which brought certain African-American neighborhoods together. It facilitated social intercourse and helped instill a sense of community among those involved. But at the same time it reinforced class consciousness within African-American culture."

In the late 1860s and early 1870s, the Pythians could always count on a winning record, even when playing visiting rivals such as the Mutuals and Alerts and the Unique of Chicago. Beginning in 1867, the team lured away some better members of the rival Excelsiors, strengthening itself and at the same time wounding its local competition, so that there was no question as to who was the better black team in town. Eventually the Pythians had four separate teams, organized by ability. Catto's first team played out-of-town visitors and other top clubs.

Although individual player statistics cannot be gleaned from the sporadic press reports of early black baseball, Octavius Catto became known as the team's star. He was a convert from cricket, as were many early ballplayers, both black and white. He was also known as a brainy and consummate team manager.

The opportunity to play a white team would be a significant feather in the Pythians' cap. The black team had forged strong friendships with important figures in Philadelphia's white amateur baseball establishment. The most important tie was with the Athletics, the leading white team in the city. Although the Athletics themselves could never be persuaded to play the Pythians, which would have been the black team's greatest coup, its playing grounds were made available for the Pythians' games against out-of-town opponents, such as the Mutuals in 1867. Well-known members of the Athletics often umpired those key games, further lending prestige to the local African Americans.

Perhaps the Pythians' most important ally from the Athletics was Thomas Fitzgerald. Fitzgerald, who referred to himself as "Colonel Fitzgerald," although the rank appears to have been strictly honorary, was owner and editor of an influential local daily newspaper, the *City Item*. Fitzgerald's publication, which reflected his own opinions and interests, was progressive in its editorial outlook, and the first Philadelphia paper to provide detailed coverage of the city's baseball scene.

In addition to championing a number of local reform issues, the *City Item* vowed to be "constantly aggressive in all that relates to the quality of Man before the Law and ever striving to break down barriers of Prejudice and Caste." The *Item* published Lincoln's Emancipation Proclamation on its front page when it took effect in January 1863, regarding it as "the noblest act of the century" which "redeems the United States from the moral disgrace of complicity with slavery."

Fitzgerald's keen interest in baseball led him to be one of the founding members of the Athletic Base Ball Club in 1860, and he was its president for five years. The Colonel was perfectly positioned to take the lead in arranging an interracial baseball game. The efforts of someone from the white side of the equation would be necessary, for even in a relatively enlightened Northern city such as Philadelphia, an African-American team would not have the political and social clout to bring about a game with a white opponent.

After trying several times to arrange an interracial game, "his efforts were crowned with success on Friday, the 3d inst. [September 3, 1869], for on that day he brought together the Pythians and the Olympic Club." The game is the first known baseball contest between organized black and white teams. The Olympics piled up a 24–5 lead in the first three innings, and won 44–23. But the Pythians were, of course, the real winners of the day, having had recognition from the white sporting community finally bestowed upon them.

Fitzgerald, acting as the umpire, "never felt so honored in a similar capacity before." The Colonel was not finished, though. On September 16 he arranged a game between the Pythians and the City Items, a team of lesser ability sponsored by his own newspaper. This resulted in another first, a win for a black club over a white team, when the Pythians prevailed, 27–17.

However, the Pythians' successes did not override the segregationist tendencies that dominated early baseball. In fact, the team had already been turned down in its attempt to join the Pennsylvania Base Ball Association, the governing body of the sport in that state.

The Pythians' application had some high-powered support when the association met on October 16, 1867, in Harrisburg. Several members of the Athletics were present, yet the Pythian delegate was warned the night before the vote that support for admission was thin. Their advice was to withdraw rather "than to have it on record that we were black balled." But the Pythians' intentions were to see this through, and when it came to withdrawing, "this your delegate declined to do."

Several delegates claimed that while they favored admission, "they would in justice to the opinion of the clubs they represented be compelled, to go against their personal feelings, to vote against our admission." When the Pythian delegate telegraphed home for instructions, he was told to "fight if there was a chance." But there was none. The Pythians withdrew and ended their quest to be one with their white fellows.

The Rules of the Game

How Baseball Was Played in the 19th Century

Any longtime fan of America's pastime knows that the rules governing baseball are far from static. But they underwent their greatest changes during the last decades of the 19th century. In the earliest days of the game, leagues and teams didn't even share a single standard set of rules. Teams would often have a committee meet with opponents in advance to determine the rules for a particular game or series. These gentlemanly meetings sometimes took longer than the games themselves. During the 1870s and 1880s, however, a standard set of rules began to emerge.

As you might expect, the greatest changes involved pitching. At first pitchers did not have a mound, but pitched underhanded from a box located 45 feet from the plate, lengthened to 50 feet in the 1880s. A batter could call for a high or low pitch, according to his preference. During some seasons prior to 1880 a batter could become a runner, even if he struck out. The catcher would have to throw the runner out at first before the strikeout was recorded. Also, until 1877 a ball was ruled fair if it first bounced anywhere in fair territory before going foul.

Players experimented with different bats to see which designs would produce more hits. From 1885 to 1893, for example, flat-sided bats were legal.

In the pitcher's favor, nine balls were allowed before a walk was issued. The number of balls for a walk decreased to eight in 1880, seven in 1882, six in 1884, back to seven in 1886, down to five in 1887, and to four only in 1889. By the end of the 1880s, after several incremental changes, overhand pitching was allowed. In 1887, the rule allowing a batter to call for a pitch high or low was dropped, and a strike zone was created for the first time.

Another reason for the high scores in the early days was awful fielding. That might be expected in a game where no one wore gloves. Catchers became the first to wear gloves in 1869, followed by first basemen in 1875. After shortstop Arthur Irwin donned one in 1883, fielding gloves were adopted by nearly all players. Another aid in corralling loose balls was the developing strategy of fielders backing up one another on defense.

On a lighter note, the first coaching boxes were established in 1887, in order to curb the practice of coaches running up and down the baselines shouting and gesticulating in an effort to throw off the defense. By today's standards, 19th-century baseball was a wild and woolly game.

In December, the nominating committee of the Pennsylvania Base Ball Association made clear that it was not just the Pythians who were to be excluded when they unanimously reported "against the admission of any club which may be composed of one or more colored persons.... If colored clubs were admitted there would in all probability be some division of feeling, whereas, by excluding them no injury could result to anyone." White baseball had decided, following the practice of the society around it, that there would be no integration.

If any doubt about inequality remained, it was tragically answered on October 10, 1871, the day the city's African-American residents were first entitled to vote in a general election. Black voters were attacked to keep them away from the polls, and the local police declined to either guarantee their voting rights or quell the fighting. Octavius Catto, a teacher at a segregated school who was also an officer in a segregated National Guard unit, dismissed his students so they could get home safely. Then he left for his own home to retrieve his uniform and military equipment, since there was a chance the black unit would be called to duty to help restore order. He was nearly home when he walked past a small group of whites, one of whom accosted and shot him at point-blank range. Thus Philadelphia lost not only a leading civil rights figure, but the captain of its crack black baseball club.

BLACKBALL IN THE BIG EASY

That was how the situation in the North stood not long after the Civil War. No such formal actions had been taken against black teams in the South. Race relations there would not even allow an attempt at membership in a white organization dedicated to baseball or anything else.

While baseball grew in popularity across the South after the Civil War, it was played more on local and regional levels, and there is little evidence of popular intercity touring teams. This early "baseball lag" between South and North would find a parallel in the 20th century, when professional black baseball was played much more in the urban North and Midwest than in the South.

The post-Civil War experience of New Orleans, both in baseball and

An unidentified touring professional team from Champlain, New York.

society in general, presents an exception to the norm found across the former states of the Confederacy. The Crescent City was by far the largest city in the South and the fifth largest in the entire United States. Its location on the lower Mississippi River made it a center for river trade, and its mixed cultural heritage, which included Anglo-Saxon, French, and Spanish whites, a large proportion of free blacks, and many combinations of those groups, made it a lively place in which to live.

Baseball could be expected to thrive in such an atmosphere, and it did. It had already overtaken cricket in popularity before the Civil War began, and expanded more when the city's full social life resumed after the hostilities. "As baseball became a popular pastime for people of all classes, both black and white players founded hundreds of teams in the postwar era. Many teams existed for only a single season, but the city also had a nucleus of well-established teams that entertained fans year after year." A governing group, the Louisiana State Base Ball Association, was formed in 1868.

A Competitor Remembered

John "Pop" Watkins played first base for many seasons as a key member of the Cuban Giants. He was first and foremost a tough competitor. One of his competitors, Harry Hairstone, remembers a game late in Pop's career.

My second trip to the bat I singled a long drive to left center, good for two bases any time, but Pop hooked my foot as I turned first and down I went on my face and was lucky to scramble to the bag before the ball.

I popped to left field on my third try and on the fourth attempt I drove out a sharp liner down the field for two bases. When I turned first "Pop" made a try to repeat his same trick but I was wise this time and aimed for his foot and sliced the shoe so neatly that it fell off. He came at me fighting mad, but being a swift runner I was almost to second leaving him on first hurling maledictions to the wind.

African Americans were among the many hardball enthusiasts in New Orleans. As early as 1875 a black league staged a "state" championship game. Among the first blacks to form teams were employees of a couple of exclusive men's clubs, the Boston and Pickwick, places where upper-class and/or politically powerful men could go to congregate among themselves, and be served by others who couldn't possibly achieve their status. The players named their teams after the clubs, adding a twist to the practice of Negro teams often adopting white teams' names.

Interracial games were also frequently held, without the need for the extensive diplomacy that had accompanied the arrangement of the Pythians' contests in 1867. The interracial contact on sporting fields was marked by the comparatively relaxed state of race relations in general in the city. For example, seating at the French Opera House, the first place in America to present grand opera, displayed how the races mixed in New Orleans. The leaders of white society claimed the best seats, but the social order in the tiers rising about the orchestra section gave next precedence to "a second array of beautiful women, attired like those of the first, with no apparent difference; yet these were the octoroons and quadroons, whose beauty and wealth were all the passports needed." Then, rising toward the ceiling, came the "hoi polloi of the white race," and finally "the people of color whose color was more evident. It was a veritable sandwich of races."

The relaxed civic attitude in New Orleans allowed interracial games to continue until the mid-1880s, when the stiffening resistance to civil rights for blacks poisoned the well even there. In July 1885, two white teams protested a proposed Negro-white game and threatened to boycott white players who crossed the color line. The *Picayune* warned that any white club competing with a black team "will have to brave considerable opposition on the part of other clubs." Under this threat, other teams restricted themselves to lily-white competition.

The city's professional club, the Pelicans, and the very topflight amateur teams continued to play the top Negro teams (including the best black team, the Pinchbacks, named after Reconstruction-era governor Pinckney Benton Stewart Pinchback), but by 1890, when oppression of Negroes throughout the South had reached its peak, games between blacks and whites, which had once held the promise of wiping out the baseball color line, had ceased to be played even in this cosmopolitan city.

THE ORIGINAL CUBAN GIANTS

The Cuban Giants, formed in 1885, were the first black team to gain national renown. They were also the first team to be paid regularly rather than receiving a share of fluctuating gate receipts as they barnstormed around. They were black baseball's version of the Cincinnati Red Stockings of 1869. Both clubs mark the respective points at which astute owners made the crucial decision to forgo "wink and a nod" secret payments, and pay players as professionals.

The Cuban Giants were an amalgam of the best African-American players. Their off-the-field leader was Frank P. Thompson, a member of a vanishing profession, the peripatetic "hotelman." Skilled in keeping travelers happy, men like Thompson would move among many hostelries, south to Florida in the winter, back north in the summer. They worked in the seasons and the climes where the large tourist hotels were likely to be busiest. Thompson became an accomplished and sought-after headwaiter. He eventually settled into a winter job at the posh Ponce De Leon Hotel in St. Augustine, Florida, and a summer job at the huge Hotel Champlain on the edge of New York's Adirondack Mountains.

Both inside and outside of baseball, Thompson was an advocate of the advancement of the Negro race. Known now to baseball historians as the founder of the Cuban Giants, he also spearheaded the formation of the Progressive Fraternal International Association, the task of which was to present an annual sermon to the black hotel workers "on the unpardonable sin of race prejudice as practiced in the South." A born organizer, Thompson was later president of a black waiters' union, the National Benefit Association of Head, Second and Side Waiters. At his death in 1905 he was lauded in a newspaper biography as "possibly the most prominent head-waiter in the country."

Thompson put his first baseball team together in May 1885 in Philadelphia, his hometown. He called the team the Keystone Athletics (Pennsylvania being the "Keystone State"), and they began to play around that area. In the summer, Thompson took a job at the Argyle Hotel, a sprawling 350-room Victorian structure on 15 acres in the town of Babylon, New York, on Long Island, and he brought his team with him. The players were hired to work under him as waiters when they weren't playing ball, and as was often the case at vacation hotels in those days, the Athletics' games served to provide amusement to the white customers.

By the time the Long Island summer season had ended in October, Thompson had merged his Athletics with two other black teams, the Orions of Philadelphia and the Manhattans of Washington, DC, assembling a powerhouse squad of the best "hired guns" he could procure.

The man who brought in the Manhattans' contingent was Stanislaus Kostka Govern, known as "S.K." or "Cos" to his colleagues, a native of the Caribbean island of St. Croix. Govern emigrated to America after the Civil

War at age 13 as a cabin boy on a U.S. Navy training ship. He lived first in Washington, DC, and went into the hotel business. He worked with Thompson on the same north-south migration route among the big hotels.

Govern had been involved in black baseball with the Manhattans since 1881, and he eventually became the Cuban Giants' guiding force, managing them through the 1888 season. Besides recruiting him and three Manhattan players, Thompson also gained some financial backing from a white Philadelphia businessman, John F. Lang. The Athletics, now fully formed as the Cuban Giants, was a team of top players ready to take on all comers. They launched themselves into the big time in the fall of 1885.

While based at the Argyle Hotel, the Cuban Giants/Athletics had won six of nine games, including a tie, playing around Long Island and New York City. After picking up the Orion and Manhattan players, and with Govern in charge on the field, the team branched out to other areas and continued to win. The team won a reported 21 of 26 games in its initial season before cold weather shut down play and Govern and many of the players decamped to Florida for winter jobs.

Having no equals among black teams, the club played many white opponents, including teams in the minor league Pennsylvania State League and the Bridgeport, Connecticut team that had won the Eastern League championship. Their most accomplished opponents, though they did not defeat them, were two teams from the American Association, one of the two major leagues at that time. Both the New York Metropolitans and the Philadelphia Athletics had played less than .500 ball in the Association that year, but their post-season exhibition games with the black team were a major coup for the African Americans. The team from the Argyle Hotel was deemed "the strongest independent team in the East, and the novelty of a team of colored players with that distinction made them a valuable asset."

Over the winter of 1885–1886 the Cubans became the first of what would be many Florida winter professional black teams when they played out of the Ponce De Leon Hotel in St. Augustine, and in April 1886 the Cuban Giants surfaced in Trenton. The New Jersey capital city had lost its

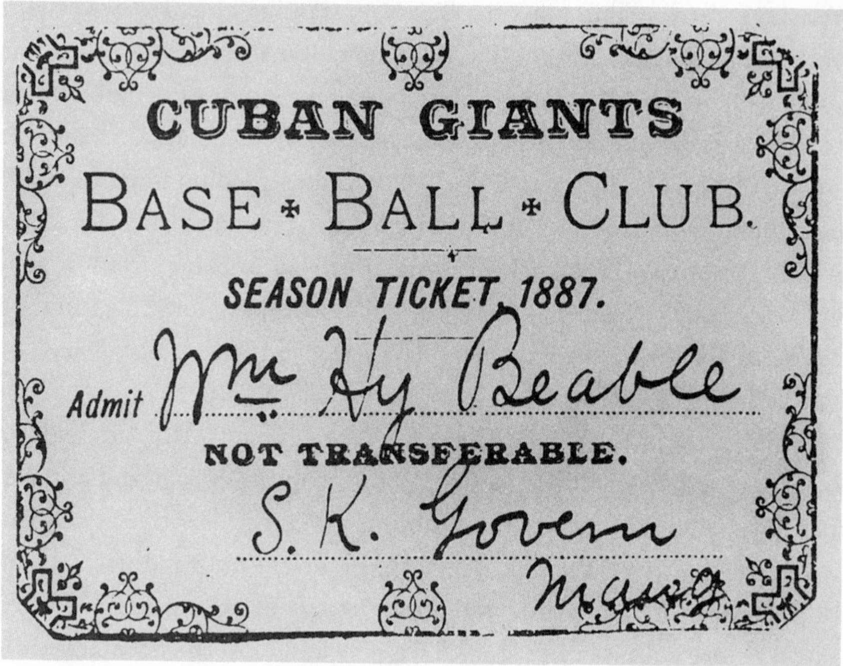

Season ticket for the Cuban Giants at Chambersburg Grounds, Trenton, New Jersey.

Eastern League franchise from previous seasons and was anxious to restore its pride as a baseball town.

Almost all the major black clubs at that time had white backing, and the Cuban Giants' second owner, John Bright, was white. Walter I. Cook, the team's first owner, also white and the youngest son of a well-off Trenton family, took over the club in the spring of 1886.

The Cubans played all that summer with a frequency that would have made other employment for the players nearly impossible. There was no waiting on tables now—the Cuban Giants did nothing but play ball. Trenton had two daily newspapers that covered the team thoroughly. Between them they reported 64 games, although the team undoubtedly played more. The Giants won 42 and lost 21, another game not being completed due to rain after three innings.

The Cuban Giants had been barnstorming their way north from their winter quarters in Florida, winning a reported 40 games along the way, when they were entreated to come to Trenton. Govern returned as manager, as did the heart of the roster that had finished 1885 so strongly.

The Giants' key players were the first black baseball personalities to be widely written about and recognized by the sports public. After the 1886 season, they were the first black team to gain fame far outside their home city. There had been outstanding players of the amateur era who were widely known locally or for their accomplishments off the baseball field. But the Cuban Giants became well known as baseball players.

The extensive coverage given the Cuban Giants in Trenton's mainstream daily papers allowed Jerry Malloy, a historian of 19th-century baseball, to examine box scores and game accounts from most of the team's 64 games. This represented a rare research opportunity since many African-American teams received coverage only sporadically in black weekly papers. In Malloy's extensive analysis of the squad, he noted the team's "potent and diversified offensive attack" and depth of talent. This was a team that "had long-ball hitters, line-drive hitters, and crafty base runners." When he looked for standout players there were several: "At the heart of the offense were the speed of Ben Boyd and George Williams and the power of Clarence Williams, Arthur Thomas and Abe Harrison."

These were the key starters:

- CLARENCE WILLIAMS, half the catching team, was a frequent outfielder the rest of the time and "the team's best all-around hitter and leading run-scorer." He wound up hitting lead-off in the second part of the season. He had three stints with the Giants, last playing for them in 1894. He played professional ball regularly until 1905, when he was 39 years old, and returned to the diamond to manage a team in 1912.
- ARTHUR THOMAS, the other catcher, also played first base and all the outfield positions. "If RBI totals had been kept, Thomas may have led the team," and he was considered a strong-armed, nimble backstop. Like Clarence Williams, he came from the Washington Manhattans.

• ABE HARRISON, one of the Philadelphia Orions, led in doubles and was second in triples, despite missing part of the season—he joined the team on June 11. Harrison had a gun of an arm at shortstop, and was also a crowd pleaser, being apt to clown for the audience when the game was not on the line. He was amazingly loyal to the Giants in a period when team rosters were often raided by the competition, sticking with the team for the rest of his career, until 1897.

• BEN BOYD was the shortstop before Harrison arrived, and the center fielder after that. He was playing high-level ball in Washington in his mid-teens (including for the Mutuals in 1875), and was one of three men from Thompson's Argyle Hotel team to show up in the Cuban Giant starting lineup.

• GEORGE PAREGO, another of the Argyle group, primarily played right field, although he was versatile, being one of two Giants to play six different positions during the season, including pitcher.

• BEN HOLMES, the third baseman, was an acknowledged off-the-field leader of the club, and was later referred to by the black newspapers as one of the organizers of the Giants. He knew both Frank Thompson and Govern in St. Augustine, where he was a member of their Progressive Association, and was with the Argyle's team when the Giants were put together.

• BILLY WHYTE, the second most used pitcher after Shep Trusty, played for top amateur and semipro teams in St. Louis and Boston before joining the Giants in 1885. He played for the Giants through 1890 and again in 1894, and became a baseball coach at Columbia College in New York City.

The Giants also had, briefly, one of the great African-American pitchers of the 19th century. In mid-June, Govern made a trip to Canada to personally obtain the services of George Stovey, a native of Williamsport, Pennsylvania, who was an itinerant star in the predominantly white minor leagues. The Giants' owner, Walter Cook, boasted that this showed Trentonians that "no expense will be spared to put a first class nine on the field."

THE SEARCH FOR TOP-FLIGHT OPPOSITION

The Trenton press and local baseball fans accepted the Cuban Giants as their own. The Trenton *Daily True American* applauded them for a May 12 victory over the Chelsea team of New York City: "The Giants are active men who play base ball for all it is worth and never lose a point that attention and hard work can secure." Walter Cook was so encouraged that he leased a playing field in the Chambersburg section of town and commenced to schedule games against some of the best talent available, most of whom the Cuban Giants defeated. Cook also had the local press refer to the team as the "Trentons," following the custom of the time to refer to teams by the names of their home cities alone, without a nickname, a move that could cement the town-team relationship even more solidly.

The Giants undoubtedly played many more than the 64 games reported in the local papers. In the gaps of several days between some published accounts they were likely barnstorming in towns away from Trenton. The opponents for the reported games fall into four categories—major league teams, minor league teams, top-notch amateur or semipro white teams, and other all-black clubs. Generally speaking, the caliber of opposition became better as the summer wore on.

They played four games against major league teams. The first, on June 9 against the Philadelphia Athletics of the American Association, was rained out after four innings, with the "Trentons" behind, 3–1. On July 21 the home team beat Cincinnati of the Association, 9–1, and on July 26 and 27 the Kansas City Cowboys of the National League came to town. The Cuban Giants won the first game, 3–2, and were trounced 13–4 the next day. No matter what the score, the presence of these teams for exhibition games while en route to their next league stand was important to the reputation of the Negro team, and to owner Cook's bank account, no doubt, since the games against the major league teams tended to attract good crowds.

Shep Trusty was Govern's pitcher of choice for almost all of the tough games. The team's leading pitcher, he was also a pretty good hitter. The *Trenton Times* called him "a phenomena [sic], being unquestionably the finest colored pitcher in the country." He pitched both 1885 games against the major league clubs, yielding only six hits to the Athletics and seven to the Metropolitans. He also faced the National League and American Association teams in 1886. He started all four contests, and pitched well in the first three, only getting knocked around seriously in the second Kansas City game, primarily because he had pitched the victory over the Cowboys the day before.

The major league teams, while not presenting their entire regular starting lineups to the Trenton fans, usually used five or more regulars among the eight position players, although the pitchers were never the teams' strongest starters. Nor were any of the three powerhouse squads in their own leagues. Cincinnati and Philadelphia finished the season fifth and sixth, respectively, in the eight-team American Association, and Kansas City was a woeful seventh in the National League, winning only 30 games and finishing a very distant 58 games out of first place. Yet the Cuban Giants' contests against these clubs represent one more piece of evidence that, if they had been given the opportunity, black players could have thrived in the majors.

The matchup that may have been the most fun, though, was one with a team from Queens, New York. The team's home grounds were not far from a resort hotel on Flushing Bay owned by the club's proprietor, Harry Hill. Hill was a flamboyant Englishman with a horseracing background who ran the most popular "concert saloon" in Manhattan. Concert saloons, forerunners of the modern nightclub, featured a stage for performers and "wait-girls" who might also double as prostitutes. Hill's place, just off Broadway, attracted a high-class crowd, including city, state, and federal officeholders, and professionals who came to mingle with racetrack and other sporting types.

Harry Hill liked baseball, and he liked a party. The Cuban Giants went to Flushing to play his team on June 13, as part of the day's entertainment. Hill had the Giants ferried across from Manhattan on a chartered steamboat and sped to his hotel by coach. The baseball contest, won by the Giants, 9–7, was intermingled with dinner, supper, and a reception attended by 300 or 400 people. The Cuban Giants were playing baseball to amuse the crowd at a big hotel again, but this time as special guests, not employees, a considerable step up in their status, not to mention that of African-American baseball.

Late in the summer, the Giants played two all-black teams. They dispatched the Alpines, from Brooklyn, "would-be colored champions of the country," by a 24–0 score on August 24. On August 14, the Giants smashed a New York team by a 25–4 score, putting to rest the challenging team's claim for a mythical "colored championship of the United States." This team, the Gorhams, would have to be reckoned with in the future, however.

The games against Eastern League teams constituted a large portion of the Giants' higher-grade schedule. Accounts exist of contests against four of the five league teams that finished their schedules that year, two opponents from New Jersey—Newark and Jersey City—and two from Connecticut—Bridgeport and Hartford. The five games with Newark produced a sharp rivalry, and the games were covered fully by the newspapers in the cities. The *Trenton Times* led off a July 6 story on a victory by the Giants, the first win over Newark after two losses, in this way: "Newark's pet team was forced to bow their heads in humility yesterday, when the hard hitting and skillful playing of the much-laughed-at Trentons left them one behind at the close of the ninth inning." The *True American* noted later that month that the Giants had overcome racial prejudice on the part of Newark's team and fans, and that "the newspapers over there now refer to them as 'Trenton's crack club.'"

Although the team's play had won over other cities' fans, the color line had not been erased. The Giants were to discover this fact of baseball life when they suffered an experience very similar to what had befallen the Pythians in Pennsylvania 19 years before. The Eastern League, as was the case with many minor leagues in baseball's formative years, found that the optimism that launched eight teams in the spring was not sustained by paid admissions. By mid-July the league was down to six members, still a balanced and sustainable number, when the Meriden, Connecticut, franchise gave up the ghost. Cook and Govern, ever alert to a chance to promote their product, applied to have the

Cuban Giants take Meriden's place. The manager of the Eastern League's Long Island club, one of the early season hardship cases, was quoted in May with an evaluation that the Giants "could beat one half of the Eastern League clubs," yet the directors of the league rejected Trenton, preferring to finish the season with an unbalanced group of five clubs, rather than let a group of blacks into their midst.

Meriden had Frank Grant, a rising young African-American star, on its roster when it folded, and the newspaper there flogged the Eastern League powers in print for blocking Trenton. "The very white men from Hartford, Waterbury, Bridgeport, Newark and Jersey City were too 'stuck up' to be in the League with black men, but probably the dread of being beaten by the Africans had something to do with the rejection of the application of the Cuban Giants. Black as these excellent Trenton ball tossers are they are whiter than some of the managers of the League. Meriden is glad that it is out of a League in which a race prejudice is so strong that a first-class club is refused admission simply because its players are black."

CUBAN GIANTS ON THE ROAD

Despite the plaudits the Cuban Giants were gathering in the local press, not enough fans were coming out to see them play, and home attendance became a problem. As early as July 29, the *True American* noted, "The Trenton Base Ball management complain of the light attendance at such good games as yesterday's—a close 4–2 loss to Newark. There wasn't enough taken in to pay the Newarks' guarantee." On August 11, attendance at another hotly contested game, a 4–3 win over Bridgeport, "did not suffice to pay the day's expenses, and the management are heartily discouraged." Cook and Govern laid down a challenge to Trenton fans: "It was officially announced last night [a Wednesday] that unless the patronage is more liberal on Friday and Monday, there will be no more games played here this season. The management have a number of good-paying dates in other cities and can secure more." The two "challenge" games were the ballyhooed "colored championship" match with the

Gorhams and a tilt against Jersey City with defector George Stovey pitching for them, so attendance went up.

But by mid-September Cook announced that he was pretty much shutting down operations in Trenton due to poor attendance. He said the team would finish on the road with games scheduled in Pennsylvania, New Jersey, up the Hudson River Valley in New York, and out to Brooklyn. Other than the travel the schedule entailed, this did not present much of a hardship. The Giants had already been spending most Sundays playing Harry Hill's and other teams on Long Island, where reportedly "more money is realized there on one game than could be obtained in Trenton on half a dozen."

The Giants were unquestionably a great draw on the road. During a period when the arrival of a crack outfit was a real event in small- and medium-sized communities, their local opponents often feted the black team royally. When the Giants arrived in Poughkeepsie, New York, to play the local club on September 14, their opponents and "the celebrated brass band of that city" met them at their hotel. Both teams then paraded in uniform to the ballpark, and despite cold, wet weather "were greeted with a large audience." Cook and a partner announced plans to take a team, apparently including several members of the Giants, to Havana, Cuba, in December and January to exploit their popularity.

The Giants reportedly had won 113 games and lost only 30 by mid-September 1887. Then again, the same publication later reported their entire season record as 107–54. As is often the case with black baseball statistics, it is hard to say which count, if either, was precise. However, the record was undoubtedly brilliant since the team kept all its best players through the season, and added some new talent, most notably versatile infielder Jack Frye and pitcher Bill Malone.

The Giants continued to play teams from all levels of baseball, including those from the high-level minor International League, which had several black players (including George Stovey) on its rosters. A swing through the Midwest in 1887 produced victories over the Cincinnati club, the second-place team in the American Association, and Indianapolis of the National League. The Giants almost upset the National League champion, Detroit, losing a lead late in the game for a 6–4 defeat.

But much worse than losing was being refused a game at all. This happened in September when the players of the St. Louis Browns of the American Association struck rather than play the Giants in New York City. The team had several injured players, and that appeared to figure into the decision, but the men's petition to Browns owner Chris Von Der Ahe explicitly stated, "we...do not agree to play against negroes tomorrow. We will cheerfully play against white people at any time, and think by refusing to play, we are only doing what is right."

Von Der Ahe, who was in breach of contract with the Cuban Giants and with the thousands of fans stood up as a result of the walkout, was furious. He read the mutinous Browns the riot act and threatened to release all the players. In the end he settled financially with the Giants' new owner, John M. Bright of New York, and the players suffered no apparent penalties for their mutiny.

JOHN BRIGHT SUCCEEDS WALTER COOK

Bright, a veteran baseball entrepreneur, had joined Walter Cook, who had been ill for several months, in running the team at the beginning of the 1887 season. When Cook died on June 24, Bright became the financially controlling force behind the Giants, and would remain so for many years.

John Bright, who was also white, was more the typical baseball entrepreneur of those days, but he was a good one. If he had sources of income other than sports promoting, reports of them have not survived the passage of years. Bright was already familiar with the Cuban Giants. He was probably the promoter of a game in Weehawken, New Jersey, in October 1886, when 3,000 fans turned out to see the Giants play the Jersey Blues. Bright arranged a pregame ceremony during which he presented floral bouquets to Govern and each of the Giants' starters. It may not sound manly today, but flowers were a perfectly proper gift for a ballplayer in the 19th century. Bright took the opportunity to praise the Giants "for their good ball playing and gentlemanly conduct upon the field during the season just passed."

In August 1888 the now Bright-owned Giants took part in a four-team tournament around New York City for the "colored championship of the world." Their opponents were the Keystones of Pittsburgh with Sol White on the roster, the Norfolk Red Stockings, and the Gorhams, a much improved squad from the team the Giants had thrashed a year before. The tournament brought together teams that represented the spectrum of topflight black ball at that time. The Giants and the Gorhams were fully professional traveling teams, and the Keystones had broken out from being merely a western Pennsylvania regional team the year before, primarily through the signing of White. The Red Stockings, one of a few black touring teams from the South, highlighted the difference in general ability between the crack Northern and Southern teams by coming in dead last in the tourney.

The Giants, still the predominant black team, with a reported 103 wins in 129 games, won the tournament, with the Keystones finishing a creditable second. In his 1906 *Baseball Guide*, Sol White wrote that the Keystones were "the surprise of the meet," losing only to the Giants and winning all their games with the other two teams. The games were well attended and included the sort of touches that accompanied important contests. Once George Williams of the Giants was about to hit "when a little girl ran out onto the field and presented him with a large bouquet. George blushed, and then hit a grounder which the Gorhams' shortstop caught and sent to first base a second ahead of the robust captain's big toe."

The Giants' trophy was a silver baseball, engraved with the names of the four teams, donated by John Bright, the Giants' owner. Bright likely cooked the tournament up in the first place, since several of the games were held on the grounds in Hoboken, New Jersey, where the Giants often played. A silver ball was a common tournament prize in those days, but this particular sphere surfaced 58 years later to become a footnote to Negro baseball history. Original Giant Ben Holmes, still the team's third baseman in 1888, wound up with possession of the ball. Settling in the Newark, New Jersey, area, he dusted off the silver sphere and allowed it to be tossed by heavyweight boxing champion Joe Louis in the first pitch ceremony for the first Newark Eagles home game in the 1946 Negro Leagues World Series.

George Stovey had returned to the club to pitch in 1888, and the redoubtable infielder Frank Grant joined them in 1889. A New York paper enthused over them toward the end of the 1888 season: "The Cuban Giants, who, by the way, are neither giants nor Cubans, but thick-set and brawny colored men, make about as stunning an exhibition of ball playing as any team in the country.... They play great ball, but, outside of that, they do more talking, yelling, howling, and bluffing than all the teams in the League put together. There is a sort of 'get' spirit among them, which carries the spectators back a good many years in ball playing, and from a spectative point of view, it is one of the best teams in the city to see."

The description of the team's "talking, yelling, howling, and bluffing" is without a doubt a reference to the common practice of the black touring teams to clown their way through pregame practices, and sometimes games themselves if the competition wasn't too keen, in order to amuse the paying customers. Players would engage in elaborate fielding pantomimes with invisible baseballs during practice, and Sol White said, "Every man on a team would do a funny stunt during a game back in the eighties and nineties." The players would also carry on loudly from the sidelines during the game—"coaching" was what it was called, but there was a low burlesque quality to it.

The *Cleveland Gazette*, an African-American weekly paper, portrayed in its July 21, 1888, issue the "comical coaching" of the Cuban Giants as the first and third base coaches, undoubtedly shouting at the top of their lungs, "instructed" a runner on first to get a move on:

> *Coacher at third bass* [sic]—Say, what're you doing over there standing on that base? Are you married to that bag? Come, honey, get a move on.
>
> *Coacher at first base*—For goodness, child, do move off that base. Get a divorce from it and travel down to second; there's a bank of molasses candy on that second bag, just waiting for you.

Coacher at third base—Yes, and here's your supper right on this third bag. What's that, Mr. Umpire? Did you call a strike on that ball? Oh for goodness sake come off that band wagon and give the child a chance.

Keeping in mind that the black teams more often than not were playing for white fans, this may have been just what the audiences expected from Negroes. In the minstrel shows, white performers in blackface, and subsequently some blacks themselves, put on broad parodies of Negro life. Minstrel music was succeeded late in the 19th century by the even more demeaning coon song, which added monetary greed and violence "to minstrel images of watermelon, chicken and possum that supposedly typified the race." Amazingly, to today's observer, African Americans soon began to write and perform coon songs, since "they had to sell what people were buying."

The clowning of the best black baseball teams fit right in with this racist societal influence on entertainment. Making a fool of oneself on the diamond was part and parcel of taking admission money from as many white folks as possible. While doing so, the "fool" as artist might of course transcend the clown role in the enthusiasm, fun, and creative expressiveness of what came to be viewed as baseball art.

The Cuban Giants played on until the mid-1890s, when an economic depression killed them off, along with much of Negro professional baseball, for a short while. Their heyday didn't survive much past 1890, as competitors naturally flocked to imitate and succeed them on the mythical African-American baseball throne. Yet the Cuban Giants of the late 1880s remain the benchmark against which all of the other black teams of that era are measured.

COMPETITORS FOR THE GIANTS—THE GORHAMS

The original Giants' success invited competition, and the Gorhams from New York City in 1886 became the first imitator to gain renown. The team was owned by an African American, Ambrose Davis, and run by a black man named Benjamin Butler, who made his primary living as a theatrical manager. The club got its unusual name from a tavern at 204 Thompson Street in lower Manhattan owned by an Alexander Gorham. Although nothing is known about Gorham's saloon, the neighborhood at the time was a place of "vile rookeries" in the "black-and-tan slums," so named for the skin colors of those who lived there.

The Gorhams appear to have had no permanent home field, being mostly a traveling club that barnstormed around the area of New York City. Davis and Butler apparently knew that to be able to book games with good local white clubs, they would have to be recognized as playing on a level with the one really good black team, the Cuban Giants. Beginning with the 1886 contest in Trenton, when they swaggered in for a "championship" game, only to receive a sound thrashing, they constantly pursued matchups with the Giants. As Sol White said, the Gorhams "hooked up with the Cuban Giants at every opportunity and by hard earnest endeavor played them to a standstill upon all occasions, until at last victory crowned their efforts." The victory occurred in 1887 when the Gorhams managed to defeat the Giants, 4–3, in Newburgh, New York, a Hudson River resort destination for New Yorkers that the Gorham club had adopted as its home that season. In 1888 the Gorhams were invited along with the Giants to play in the "silver ball" championship tournament, which the Giants eventually won.

By 1889 the Gorhams began to pick up better players, including Sol White, pitcher John Nelson, and position players Oscar and Andrew Jackson, all of whom made regular appearances on the rosters of the best black clubs in the late 1880s and early 1890s. Still, the Gorhams were not really of the Cuban Giants' caliber, at least not yet.

In 1889 these two top African-American teams entered an otherwise white minor league, the Middle States League, an outfit that lay outside the pale of organized baseball, which is to say it was not a partner to the National Agreement between major and minor leagues. Minor league teams, and major league ones, too, were anxious to play exhibitions against the best black clubs. It was only a further step along the road to profits to fit them into a regular league schedule.

The league began the season with six clubs, at one time had eight, and

Fun with the Colored Boys

In the 19th century, black touring teams were more often than not playing for white fans. In May, 1883, the Cleveland Leader offered this description of an interracial game between Cleveland and St. Louis:

The colored boys of Cleveland yesterday met with the dusky blonds of St. Louis in the ball field, and the enemy captured the Cleveland lads in a manner that was remarkably wonderful to see....There were many handsome black eyes watching the home team from the grand stand, and it is quite probable that our boys wanted to appear so fine before their fair admirers that in trying to outdo themselves they made some very grave errors, so the girls should let the boys down as light as possible in getting defeated, for they were slightly responsible for it....Milligan came up, looked at the ladies in the stands, and smiled a smile that seemed to say "Watch me bring those two fellows in on my three-base hit." He fanned the air with his timber three times in the most desperate manner and took his seat on the players' bench. Trip gave Milligan the laugh, and then stepped up to the bat and did the same thing, much to the astonishment of a maiden who was hoping to see him pound the sphere out of sight. So the Cleveland lads went out in the first, and the St. Louis chaps began to run the bases in a most discouraging manner chalking up four runs before they could be retired....The game could have been much worse, but it was not. In fact it was better than was looked for, some really good plays being made by both sides. The Clevelands were a little weak in their catcher, he passing some balls that ought to have been stopped, and the Blue's first baseman failed to hold on to some balls that he should have clenched on to. His faculty for dropping the ball and then kicking it away from him before he could pick it up was startling. The Black's shortstop was a dandy, and if he had played ball as successfully as he made a grand stand mash, he would have stopped some of the balls that he did not, and would not have pulled up so much grass. Everybody had just what they went out for, lots of fun, and the boys ought to have had a much larger attendance.

—Cleveland Leader, May 10, 1883

finished in September with five. Despite the instability, the Cuban Giants, who represented Trenton, finished with a record of 55–17. Officially, they were seven percentage points behind league leader Harrisburg, although both teams claimed to be champions based on their interpretations of several protested games. Harrisburg was eventually declared champion, based partially on a finding that Trenton had to forfeit four games in which nonregulation baseballs were used. The Giants' opponents had supplied the balls, but this did not seem to matter. Despite the apparent warm welcome extended to the black teams, this could have been last-minute recognition by the league powers of, as the *Meriden Journal* had put it, "the dread of being beaten by the Africans."

The Gorhams jumped into the league on June 29, replacing a steadily losing Philadelphia club, which had quit to play independent baseball. The black team represented Easton, Pennsylvania, where they soon were asked, upon the complaints of white customers, to leave the hotel where the players had been lodged . The Gorhams drew poorly in Easton and dropped out of the league in late August to barnstorm, leaving a 14–20 record.

Articles in the *Harrisburg Patriot* during the 1889 season complained of the on-field demeanor of both the Giants and the Gorhams, calling them "dirty foul-mouthed ball players." "Why cannot a Negro Base Ball Player be just as respectable as a White one?" the *Patriot* inquired. "There was much complaint about admitting the Cuban Giants, principally on account of their color," the newspaper reported on June 10 before getting down to the issue that always seemed to underlie discrimination against the black clubs. "And now they are proving their superior strength against all the other clubs in the league the complaints have become more general and bitter."

The Middle States League did not survive after 1889, but was reorganized for the 1890 season as the Eastern Interstate League. By then, however, the original Cuban Giants would be broken up when key members of the Giants were lured to play for rival clubs. Over the winter of 1891 John Bright recouped all of his players and entered the Cuban Giants in the Connecticut State League for the 1891 season. The Connecticut league, a small, poorly organized regional circuit, looked upon the Cuban Giants as a key drawing card. Bright, continuing the practices that had brought him criticism, apparently saw the league's schedule as merely filling out his barnstorming tours. The Giants were already being taken to task for skipping league games—including one in Meriden, where the fans turned up to honor Frank Grant, their former hero—when the entire league went belly-up in June.

The back and forth of these years continued apace. Bright's players were now snapped up by Ambrose Davis's Gorhams. Davis opened his wallet and conducted a full-scale raid on the Giants that permanently knocked them out of their elite position as the top African-American squad. Before the dust settled that summer, the Gorhams had almost all the best black players in the country, most of them ex-Cuban Giants. And S.K. Govern, renowned as the Giants' first field manager, was now running their opponents' show, to boot. Among the notables, Arthur Thomas and Clarence Williams shared the catching; Stovey, William Seldon, and Malone were the pitchers; the infield was George Williams, White, Grant, and Andrew Jackson, from first around to third; and Oscar Jackson was the centerfielder.

Davis changed the Gorhams' name to the Big Gorhams, and they certainly were. The team lost only four games all summer, winning either 39 or 41 in a row, depending upon what account is read. Although they undoubtedly feasted on local amateur and semipro teams to compile that stellar record, White, who saw nearly every outstanding black team for years, ranked the Big Gorhams as one of the two best Negro teams ever, "the best of the old bunch, i.e., those playing before the turn of the century."

What Sol White seemed to identify as Bright's major shortcoming could well have contributed to his undoing. White classed Bright "at the head of all men who dabbled in the [black] game." But, White noted, the owner "was extremely selfish in his financial dealings" and his players "were always called upon to help him in an idea," a vague assessment that seems to imply that assurance of Bright's profits, not the players' salaries, was given first consideration. Ambrose Davis's offers were too good to refuse, and as White himself said, the interests of owners and players "generally work in the opposite directions. The owner of a base ball team is in the business to make money for years to come, while the player is in

One of the last integrated clubs to play before the 20th century era was this team from Findlay, Ohio (ca 1894).

the game to make the biggest rake off in the quickest time, never knowing just when he will have hard luck and fail to keep up a hot pace."

The national economic downturn that led first to The Panic of 1893 and later to a depression beset the aspirations of both owners and players in the mid-1890s. Black baseball was insufficiently funded at best. African Americans and their businesses were the first to feel the pinch. The Gorhams, big on the field, vanished from the major black baseball scene after their 1891 season, and not even John Bright could put a Cuban Giants touring team together in 1892. Bright had the Giants traveling again in 1893, but three years later most of his good players deserted him for a rival, apparently because they could get better deals than under his seemingly penurious rule.

For the Giants' rivals, the Gorhams, the decline was much swifter. An early season exhibition contest in 1892 with the New York Giants illustrates the club's fall from prominence. On April 7 the *New York Sun* reported that the Gorhams strolled into the Polo Grounds in a cakewalk. They were adorned with new uniforms and "swallow-tail coats, an ensemble that "gave them a very attractive appearance." Two hours later "the Gorhams dragged themselves out of the grounds looking as though they had been engaged in an unsatisfactory argument with a tornado." The game was over in the third inning when the Giants scored thirteen runs. They went on to score nine in the sixth, one in the seventh, and seven in the eighth, winning 36–1. The contest was mercifully stopped after eight innings because both clubs were "exhausted." To add insult to injury, only 500 spectators witnessed the fiasco. The Gorhams staggered through the rest of the season in a daze. Although Ambrose Davis continued to operate the club throughout the 1890s, primarily as a weekend enterprise, the Gorhams would never regain their prominence of the late 1880s.

PRESENT AT THE CREATION

In his poem, "The Negro Speaks of Rivers," Langston Hughes looks back across the centuries to junctures where blacks were present in significant ways. They were there at the dawn of civilization. They helped raise the Pyramids, built huts along the Congo, and watched Abe Lincoln go down the Mississippi. I was there, the poet says, before human blood flowed in human veins.

There has been much dispute about where America's national pastime finds its origins. Baseball was played by slaves in the pre-Civil War South. It had a significant presence in black urban communities of the North in the game's infancy. Its best players were challenged by a post-Civil War racial order. In the sport's first professional decades, some of its best players forced themselves by their sheer ability onto the rosters of the best teams, and by the century's last decade they established a permanent place in the history of the game through its finest team, the Cuban Giants. It seems more than fair to say that African Americans were present in significant ways in baseball's first decades—present, indeed, at the creation.

Moses Fleetwood Walker (third row, center) broke into professional Negro baseball with the Toledo club on the North Western League in 1883.

Before Jim Crow

In 1878 John "Bud" Fowler batted a puny .153 with two hits in 13 at-bats in three games for the Lynn, Massachusetts team in the International Association. On May 1, 1884, Moses Fleetwood Walker, playing the catcher's position for Toledo in the American Association, went 0 for 3 with two passed balls and four errors. Walker finished the season with a respectable .263 batting average in 42 games. In that same year Fowler, now playing for the Stillwater, Minnesota team in the Northwest League, batted .302 in 48 games.

Quite aside from statistics, there was something much more important about their mere presence on the field of play. Fowler's 1878 appearance marks him as the first black professional player in organized baseball. Moses Walker would long be heralded as the first American Negro to play in a major league game, beating Jackie Robinson by 63 years.

If the America of the late 19th century was a time of black firsts it also produced black "lasts." George White served in the United States House of Representatives from 1896 to 1900. He was the last black congressman who were products of a Reconstruction era filled with hope for an integrated America, where men would be judged on the basis of the quality of their character and performance rather than the color of their skin. Congress would not see his kind again until the election of Chicago's Oscar DePriest in 1929—and not see his kind in fair numbers until the Voting Rights Act of 1965 finally began to secure for black Americans a franchise that had been promised in the 14th and 15th Amendments to the Constitution. Coincidentally, it was about that same time that major league baseball finally began, a decade and more after Jackie Robinson's entry, to reflect in its number a fair percentage of African Americans.

In post-Reconstruction America, integration was on the decline. The Supreme Court decision *Plessey* v. *Ferguson* in 1896, upholding a Louisiana statute segregating railroad cars, underlined how much Reconstruction had failed. The segregation that emerged after this historic court case came to be known collectively as Jim Crow laws. While Jim Crow laws started mandating segregation, poll taxes and other barriers successfully eroded the voting rights of African-American males in Southern states .

During the chaotic baseball period of the 1870s and 1880s, as the professional game was claiming a dominant place for itself on America's sporting scene, players, both black and white, were often lured away by other teams offering more money. Recruiting black players for a black team was one thing. It would seem quite another to sign them for a white club. But Jim Crow was not yet rigidly in place in society as a whole, and in the baseball that was a reflection of that society.

The most notorious instance of this luring of black to white involved George Stovey's arrival and then quick departure from the Cuban Giants in 1886. Stovey, an angular hurler with an assortment of effective breaking pitches, was said by a colorful, though anonymous, sportswriter of the time to be able to "throw a ball at the flag-staff and make it curve into the water pail." The hurler was as renowned for his temper as his curves. Pat Powers, who was to be his manager before the 1886 season was over, described him as "one of the greatest pitchers in the country, but is headstrong and obstinate, and, consequently, hard to manage."

Stovey first pitched for the Cuban Giants in that season on June 21 against the Bridgeport Eastern League team. He struck out 11 batters and gave up only four hits, but poor fielding support led to a 4–3 loss. Four days later he was signed away by Jersey City's white Eastern League team. Jersey City, which had gained Trenton's 1885 white franchise, sent manager Powers to visit Stovey in the dead of night to pull off the caper. Powers later gave an exciting account of the transaction, claiming he had spirited Stovey away from a group of Trenton fans out to stop the pitcher's flight, bundling the two of them into a carriage and hightailing it to a distant train station, where they caught a train to Jersey City in time for the next day's game.

Cook and Govern protested, of course, but Jersey City played financial hardball. The Giants' most frequent topflight games were with Eastern League teams willing to play exhibitions against them. The Jersey City representatives made it clear that the Eastern League president would ban future games against teams from his league if Stovey was not released. Jersey City paid Trenton a cash settlement, the valuable playing dates with Eastern League teams remained on the Giants' schedule, and Stovey went on to have an outstanding season in the Eastern League, winning 16 games and holding opposing batters to a meager .167 batting average. He returned to Trenton once that season, as the pitcher for Jersey City when they beat the Giants, 8–4. He gave up only six hits in a nine-inning complete game and struck out twelve, in case anyone in Trenton had forgotten what they were missing.

The contest for Stovey's talents points up an interesting aspect of black baseball in the mid-1880s. Even though the threat of the Jersey City team and the Eastern League to withhold valuable playing dates had the Giants' management over a barrel, this was a business negotiation between two sides that were somewhat equal. This indicates general acceptance of the black team by members of the white baseball power structure, reinforced by the fact that Jersey City wanted Stovey at all. The color line in professional baseball was not yet firmly drawn, and crack black players were sometimes sought after by Eastern and Midwestern teams that were otherwise composed of white men. Stovey was by no means the first black player to show up on a white team, although there were never many at any one time, and the Negro player usually stood in splendid isolation as the only African American on the field.

According to one account, George Stovey was even a candidate for the major leagues. Sol White reported that an attempt by the New York Giants to sign him after the 1886 season was quashed by the virulent opposition of Adrian "Cap" Anson, a powerful force in the league who was opposed to integrated baseball. It appears the Giants still made an offer for Stovey and his black battery mate, catcher Moses Walker, after an exhibition game against the Newark International League team in April 1887. The deal fell through because Newark wisely refused to part with its two starters just before its season began.

BLACK BASEBALL'S FIRST HISTORIAN

The limited opportunities for black baseball players in organized professional baseball had a contemporary chronicler who took pains to record early African-American baseball. This writer was King Solomon White, a standout player and manager before taking up his pen.

Sol White grew up in Bellaire, Ohio, a town across the Ohio River from Wheeling, West Virginia. One of his earliest baseball memories was of being asked to play for one of the three white teams in town due to a player shortage, bolstering the observation of Ray Stannard Baker that segregation was less of an issue in smaller communities where the Negro populations were of no great size or presumed threat. White recalled playing against a team from Marietta, Ohio, which was captained by a fellow named Bancroft Johnson, later famous as the founder of the American League.

White's best years as a player were with the great Philadelphia Giants teams of the first years of the 20th century. He founded the team with two white Philadelphia sportswriters. One of them, H. Walter Schlichter, also a sports booking agent, acted as the Giants' business agent, while White played first base and was the captain, a position analogous to being a playing manager.

Although he had a stellar career on the field, his major contribution to black baseball was a book. *Sol White's Official Baseball Guide*, published in 1907, was a slim 128 pages, including 14 pages of advertising. In the preface White claimed, "Since the advent of the colored man in base ball, this is the first book ever published wherein the pages have been given exclusively to the doings of the players and base ball teams." This was no idle boast.

White's accounts tracked the progress of the major teams and identified their owners, players, and managers. His writing provides a detailed source of early African-American baseball that would prove invaluable to later Negro baseball researchers. The teams' schedules were so peripatetic, so many games were played in places with scant sports reporting resources, and the white-run press paid so little attention to Negro ball that it would almost be necessary to canvas all the newspapers published throughout the Northeastern United States to find what Sol White set down in his little volume. In addition, the book included 57 photographs of black teams, players, and club executives. Many of these images are the only likenesses we have of the players and other personalities of the period. Jerry Malloy, the leading 19th-century black baseball scholar, called the book "the Dead Sea Scrolls of black professional baseball's pioneering community."

White candidly identified specific racial problems, from Southern white players who would refuse to play with or against blacks, to hotels "generally filled from the cellar to the garret" when traveling black players looked for a room. He also named names, identifying eventual Hall of Famer Adrian C. "Cap" Anson of the Chicago National League team, a revered figure in white ball, as someone with "repugnant feeling, shown at every opportunity, toward colored ball players." While White gives Anson more blame than he is probably due for promoting baseball segregation, it is nonetheless a necessary correction in the lore of the Chicagoan's storied career.

White concluded that "in no other profession has the color line been drawn more rigidly than in baseball." Through a series of mathematical calculations he showed that black professional players from the top Negro teams made less than the average white minor leaguer and less than 25 percent of an average major league salary. "The disparity in the salary of a major league player and a colored player is enormous," he wrote, "especially when it is taken into consideration that, were it not for color, many would be playing in the big league."

By the 1980s there were only three known copies of the book still in existence, one each at the Baseball Hall of Fame Library and the New York

Sol White
Present at the Creation

As a player and manager holding down shortstop for the 1902 Philadelphia Giants, Sol White suffered through a playoff loss for the eastern championship of black baseball to the long established Cuban X Giants. The young Rube Foster led the way for the Cubans. There was only one way to retaliate. The next season Foster was lured to Philadelphia, and the results were reversed as Foster won both Philadelphia victories to take the best of three series for their first championship. Under White's direction, the Giants would win three more titles in a row. Later, Nat Strong would say, "The 1901–05 Philadelphia Giants were the best team in the history of the game."

Sol White was 19 when he began playing professionally in 1887 for the Pittsburgh Keystones, a member of the short-lived League of Colored Baseball Clubs, the first effort at organizing African-American teams in the baseball-rich Northeast and Atlantic Seaboard regions. After the Colored League failed, he returned to Wheeling to again play with a professional white team in the Ohio State League. Thereafter White played the infield with the top independent black teams of his day, appearing between 1889 and 1907 with the New York Gorhams, the Cuban Giants, the Page Fence Giants, the Cuban X Giants, the Chicago Columbia Giants and the Philadelphia Giants. In a time when the best black players often changed teams annually, or even during seasons in response to higher salary offers, White was always sought after by the best squads.

He spent all or parts of five seasons in white organized baseball's minor leagues, one of a small group of blacks in otherwise white organized baseball before the color line descended in the 1890s. In 1889–1891, he was part of an unusual arrangement in which entire professional Negro teams were hired to represent minor league cities, another milestone in black baseball history to which White was a direct witness. He "crossed over" again in 1895, when black penetration into white organized baseball had about ended for the next 50 years, to play for the Fort Wayne, Indiana team in the Western Interstate League. Sol White had an overall batting average of .359 in middle-range minor leagues, giving a glimpse of the talent that could have enriched a major league team.

Public Library's African-American black culture center, and one in the hands of a private collector. But the resurgence of interest in black baseball resurrected White's history, and it has been reprinted twice since 1984. His work still stands as an indispensable record of the early days of black baseball, produced for us by an experienced, educated, and enthusiastic scribe. The man and the task were well joined.

If the major leagues were attracted to outstanding black players, so were the minors. When the opportunity arose in 1890, the Harrisburg Ponies of the short-lived Eastern Interstate League leapt at the chance to sign Clarence Williams to catch and, even better, Frank Grant to play infield. The latter was coming from the Cuban Giants, whom he had joined after a stint with the Buffaloes of the International League. Long before it was time for the game to begin, it was whispered around the crowd that Grant would arrive on the 3:20 train and play third base. Here is how the local *Harrisburg Patriot* reported Grant's arrival: "Everybody was anxious to see him come and there was a general stretch of necks towards the new bridge [the ballpark was on an island in the Susquehanna River near the railroad station], all being eager to get a sight at the most famous colored ball player in the business. At 3:45 o'clock an open carriage was seen coming over the bridge with two men in it. Jim Russ' famous trotter was drawing it at a 2:20 speed and as it approached nearer, the face of Grant was recognized as being one of the men. 'There he comes,' went through the crowed like magnetism and three cheers went up."

The crowd's enthusiasm was understandable. With the possible exception of George Stovey, Frank Grant was the best African-American player in the white minors.

With Grant on the Harrisburg Ponies roster, his team battled the York Colored Monarchs for first place in the early going in the Eastern Interstate League race, although the Monarchs gradually pulled away. On July 21 the Monarchs, winners of 40 of 56 games, were ahead by more than 100 percentage points in the standings when the pennant race suddenly ended. Harrisburg halted it by abruptly leaving the league to become a member of the Atlantic Association. Deprived of one of its chief draws, the Eastern Interstate League, which actually never included a team from any state but Pennsylvania, collapsed in short order.

One consequence of Harrisburg's membership in the more prestigious Atlantic League was a requirement that it jettison its two black players. The Atlantic Association was founded in 1889 in an attempt to create a high-level minor league along the Eastern Seaboard. It had teams as far north as New England, but also stretched just beyond the Mason-Dixon Line to Baltimore, Maryland; Washington, D.C.; and Wilmington, Delaware. African Americans were not welcome, a stance that was blamed on some white players from existing clubs, although it seems the management of those teams were not inclined toward any racial experiments either. But the Association was nearly on the rocks by mid-season and inclined to be less picky. A compromise on Harrisburg's blacks was reached—by agreeing to release Clarence Williams, the less skilled of the African Americans, Harrisburg was able to retain the services of Grant throughout the summer of 1890.

THE FIRST BLACK PROFESSIONAL

The finest example of the 19th-century era of integrated baseball is the itinerant ballplayer John W. "Bud" Fowler. He is believed to be the first African American to play professionally in otherwise white leagues, in 1878 for teams in Lynn and Worcester, Massachusetts. The best research on his career has established that he played in 13 different professional minor leagues in an 18-year period, with numerous other engagements with independent pro teams woven into his checkered career. He has been tracked to diamonds from Montpelier, Vermont to Santa Fe, New Mexico, and that only includes his appearances in organized leagues.

Fowler was not, in fact, his real last name. He was John Jackson when he was born in 1858. It is pretty well established that he acquired his nickname because he himself frequently referred to people he would meet as "Bud," but why he chose to take another surname is an unanswered question.

FROM POLE TO POLE

Barbering was Bud Fowler's second trade, and he traveled the country pursuing that occupation and baseball, whichever promised to pay him a salary for the month in question. Chatting with a Cincinnati *Enquirer* writer while promoting the Page Fence Giants, he claimed he had played for the crack Washington Mutuals in 1869, but as his vital statistics show, he was only 11 at the time. That data likewise shoots a hole in a long-accepted account that he began his professional career in 1872. His 1913 obituary claimed that he played in the 19th century for the Chicago White Sox, the most outlandish claim of his career, one for which he probably was the source.

His spiel for the *Enquirer* was undoubtedly exaggerated, but there are many grains of truth in the writer's characterization of his career: "Bud has played match games for trappers' furs. He has been rung in to help out a team for the championship of a mining camp and bags of gold dust. He has played with cowboys and the Indians. He has cross-roaded from one town to another all over the Far West, playing for what he could get and taking a hand to help out a team."

Many of the professional teams for which Bud played failed to finish their seasons for financial reasons, a fate not unusual during baseball's early era. Sometimes entire leagues sank under Fowler, as was the case when he played for the Terre Haute, Indiana team in the Central Interstate in 1888. When this happened he would pack up his equipment and head off to another employment prospect, often several states away. For instance, he wound up with Santa Fe in the New Mexico League after his Indiana gig folded.

Throughout his travels, he always was a very good player. Researchers have dug up box scores from 465 games he played in accepted minor leagues during 10 seasons between 1878, when he played briefly in Massachusetts, through 1895, when he put in 31 games at age 37 with Adrian and Lansing in the Michigan State League. Overall, Fowler hit .308. He didn't have long ball power, but he was fast. He stole as many as 46 bases in a season, and led the Western league with 12 triples while with Topeka in

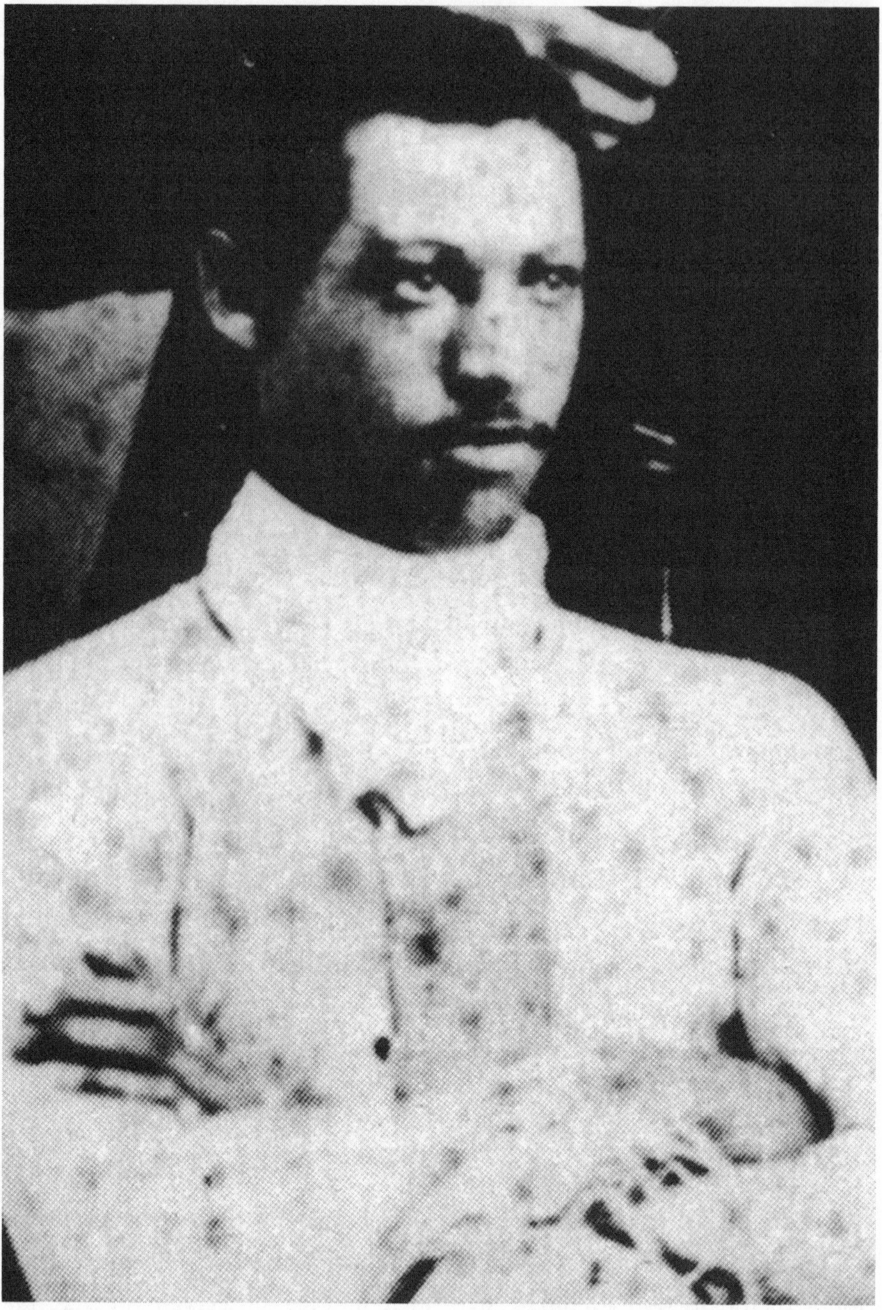

Moses Walker's 1884 season with a Toledo team in the American Association marks him as the first African-American major leaguer.

1886. He played about every position on the diamond at one time or another, although he usually could be found at second base. The research turned up 33 pitching outings. Although he won only eight games against 14 losses, he allowed only 11 hits and walks per 9 innings. This statistic must be judged in light of poor support from his teammates, a result of the general lack of good fielding in the period before gloves came into common use and the low level of leagues in which Fowler played.

Fowler seemed to have had little interest in playing for the crack all-black teams. He was probably the best African-American player of his day never to have played for the Cuban Giants, for example. The few team photos that include him show him as the only black face, or maybe one of two, on otherwise all-white teams, despite evidence that he sometimes left squads because of blatant discrimination. This happened in 1881, when he was pushed off the semi-pro Guelph, Ontario team and again in 1887, when Binghamton, New York, of the International League, although struggling in the bottom of the standings, mysteriously found it could get along without its .350-hitting colored second baseman. Fowler did not always take these slights equably, particularly when they occurred on the field. He fought one white base runner in the Nebraska State League in 1892 after a collision on a close play at second. He and Frank Grant, as International League infielders, were supposed to have fashioned wooden shin protectors to keep their legs from being bruised by oncoming runners.

THE DOOR CLOSES ON INTEGRATED BASEBALL

Bud Fowler, apparently the first African-American player in organized baseball, was also one of the last when, in 1895, he jumped the Page Fence Giants to play in the Michigan State League. Appropriately enough for this well-traveled player, he also participated in the high water mark for blacks in the International League in 1887. Research has discovered 33 black players between 1878 and 1899 on the rosters of clubs in organized white baseball, not counting the wholesale importation of black teams to represent cities in otherwise white leagues.

These pioneers, particularly in the higher-level leagues, represented some of the best African-American ballplayers of their day. While Jackie Robinson is generally credited with integrating major league baseball in 1947, it has long been accepted among baseball historians that the big-league color line was actually broken in 1884 in Toledo, Ohio by a pair of brothers, Moses and Welday Walker.

Before turning to them, it should be noted that, in 2003 and 2004, new information was discovered that points to an earlier major league appearance by an African American. A researcher looking into the biographical backgrounds of obscure major leaguers found that William Edward White, who played one game at first base for Rhode Island's Providence Greys in the National League in 1879, was black. White was a 19-year-old Brown University player who was recruited for a game on June 21 when the Greys' regular first baseman was injured. He had a good debut, even getting a hit in four at-bats. But he never played again for the Greys, or anywhere else in the majors.

Moses Fleetwood Walker was the first of the two brothers to make a major league lineup, and the manner in which he achieved it was far less dramatic than Jackie Robinson's debut. Walker, a handsome and articulate fellow whose father was a physician and an ordained Methodist minister, could have thrived at a number of professions, but gave baseball a try. He had played for college teams at Oberlin College in Ohio and at the University of Michigan when he signed up with Toledo for the 1883 season, a recruit probably more highly educated than all his white teammates.

The Toledo team at the time was a minor league club in the Northwestern League. The fierce competition for profits and turf on the major league level led in 1884 to the formation of the Union League, a rival third big league challenging the National League and the American Association. One response by the American Association was to expand from eight teams to twelve, and the Toledo franchise was one of four newcomers. The club opted to keep Walker and the rest of the better Toledos on its roster for the 1884 season. Walker, a 27-year-old catcher, played in 42 of Toledo's 110 games during a period when the absence of protective

Memories of Moses Walker

Toledo once had a colored man who was declared by many to be the greatest catcher of his time. Tony Mullane was pitching for Toledo, and he did not like to be the battery partner of a Negro.

"I had it in for him," Tony admitted years later. "He was the best catcher I ever worked with, but I disliked a Negro catcher and whenever I had to pitch to him I used to pitch anything I wanted without looking at his signals. One day he signaled me for a curve and I shot a fast ball at him. He caught it and walked down to me.

"Mr. Mullane," he said. "I'll catch you without signals, but I won't catch you if you are going to cross me when I give you a signal."

And all the rest of that season he caught me, and caught anything I pitched without knowing what was coming.

—Hugh Fullerton
New York Evening World

gear, including padded mitts, resulted in routine injuries such as swollen hands and broken fingers that limited all catchers. He hit .263 without much power. In July, Walker's brother, Welday, who was 25, joined the team briefly and played five games in the outfield, hitting .222.

Neither brother had a chance to extend his major league career. The American Association's expansion in the midst of the attendance war helped to crush the Union Association, but it also resulted in self-inflicted casualties. Three of the new members, including Toledo, were unable to support themselves financially, and dropped out. By the end of the season, the American Association was once again an eight-team organization. Moses Walker's catching skills were still in demand. He played another five years in the high minors before turning to other pursuits, primarily because events were making life for black players in white baseball more tenuous.

For African Americans to play in white organized baseball, three groups had to agree: team management, the fans, and the rest of the players. It didn't hurt if the home sporting press was supportive as well. While some racist incidents involving fans have been recorded, fans were for the most part color-blind—they applauded a good performance and booed a bad one. It should be noted, though, that most black players played in Eastern states and in the northern part of the Midwest, where there was more tolerance of blacks in general.

Team managers were, by and large, out to field the best teams they could. They usually made nondiscriminatory judgments and stuck with players who delivered results. As the number of blacks joining team rosters grew and as more black players excelled, however, white players grew increasingly dissatisfied. Baseball had created a situation nearly unknown in the American society of the time: Black men were taking white men's jobs. There were only so many spots on the roster, since expansion was driven by attendance and profits, not the number of skilled players. When enough white players on a team complained to management, the officials almost always wound up siding with the white ballplayers.

Until the mid-1880s very few black athletes played in the minors and, after Toledo's withdrawal took the Walker brothers out of the American Association, none played in the majors. In fact, until 1886 only one African American other than the Walkers and Bud Fowler played in organized baseball and that was Jack Frye, a first baseman for Reading, Pennsylvania, in the Interstate Association in 1883.

But by 1886 five blacks were listed on minor league rosters. Fowler was with Topeka in the Western League, Frye was now with Lewiston in the Pennsylvania State Association, and three men were on rosters in the Eastern League. Fleet Walker was catching for a second season for Waterbury, Connecticut; George Stovey jumped the Cuban Giants to pitch for Jersey City; and Frank Grant played second base, the outfield, and occasionally pitched for Meriden. When the Meriden franchise turned turtle and sank for lack of finances in the middle of July, Grant was snapped up by Buffalo in the International Association.

In 1887 the International League had seven black players, five of whom were regulars. Stovey and Fleet Walker played for Newark, Grant was still with Buffalo, Fowler had surfaced with Binghamton, and Robert Higgins, an accomplished pitcher who had played segregated ball in his hometown of Memphis, was with Syracuse. Randolph Jackson, an upstate New Yorker, was signed as an infielder by Oswego after a bid for George Williams, the star second baseman of the Cuban Giants, was rebuffed. William Renfroe, another pitcher from Memphis, made a few appearances with Binghamton.

There also may have been an eighth black player, although the race of catcher Dick Male, briefly with the Syracuse Stars at the beginning of the season, is in doubt. It was hinted that Male was a Negro, but he denied it in the press. Syracuse, which had a contingent of players who were tough on blacks, released him before the start of the regular season. In a mysterious twist, black catcher Richard Johnson soon appeared on the roster of the Zanesville, Ohio team in the Ohio State League. Researchers have never been able to say that Male and Johnson were the same man, but there is substantial evidence that they were.

The International League was almost a major league. Buffalo, in fact, had been a big-league city through 1885 when, in a deal that drew protests from around the National League, all the players from its floundering franchise had been sold to fellow-league member Detroit, who kept the best players and disposed of the rest. The International, formed by the merger in 1886 of the New York State and Ontario Leagues, was primarily arranged around Lake Ontario in northern New York State and Ontario, Canada. The spine of the league lay along the Erie Canal, with teams in the major industrial cities of Syracuse, Rochester, and Buffalo, and the smaller cities of Oswego and Utica, as well as in Toronto and nearby Hamilton in Ontario. The 1887 league lineup also included Binghamton, the largest city in an industrial area in south-central New York that specialized in making shoes, and Newark and Jersey City in northern New Jersey, whose franchises had become available when the Eastern League collapsed.

The location of the franchises played a role in the hiring of blacks. Not only was the area located far from the segregated South, but the league included several large cities with significant African-American populations. On paper, 1887 was a fine season for the blacks in the International League. Grant hit and walked to a .366 average—42 points above the league average— during an experimental year in which bases on balls counted in the batting average. Fowler, playing second for Binghamton, hit .350, and Fleet Walker caught regularly for Newark, where Stovey won 35 games. Higgins, recruited from Memphis, won 20 for Syracuse, and was rated a solid hitter and extremely fast base runner. But while they were excelling on the diamond, forces were at work that gave each of them misery.

Bud Fowler was gradually becoming the star of the weak eighth-place Binghamton team when he was essentially forced out of the league during the first week in July by his white teammates. There were murmurs in the local press about dissension in the club, and on June 27, when the team was in the upstate-New York city of Oneida playing an exhibition game, nine white players sent a telegram to the team's directors saying they refused to play anymore "if the colored players, who have been the cause of all our trouble, are not released at once." The management responded by levying a $50 fine on each of the protestors, but temporized significantly by suspending payment until it was seen if the team's play could improve.

Fowler appears not to have wanted to put up with either the resistance of his teammates or the pusillanimous support from management, and extricated himself gracefully on July 2 by penning a letter asking for his release to join the Cuban Giants, which Binghamton had played in an exhibition only four days previously. William Renfroe's release was not accompanied by a graceful, face-saving letter, but he was soon gone, too. Randolph Jackson's stint with Oswego had ended on May 31, when the team went out of business due to lack of cash. Grant, Walker, Stovey, and Higgins all survived the season, since their teams were financially sound and they were all exceptional players. But they were each targeted racially, usually subtly, but sometimes dramatically.

Higgins endured the first recorded insults. The Syracuse team had been substantially revamped in the off-season after falling from first place in 1885 to sixth in 1886, and management had signed several players thrown out of jobs when the Southern League folded. These Southerners, in an age when regional differences were pronounced, formed a clique that made them hard to handle. They became notorious for making their best fielding efforts when they were behind pitchers they liked, and laying down on the job for those they did not.

Not too surprisingly, the dissidents would not field for Bob Higgins. In Higgins' first regular season game with the Stars, when he pitched against Toronto, Syracuse lost 28–8, but 21 of Toronto's runs were unearned. Higgins reportedly remained calm in the midst of this chaos, although his white catcher was fined and suspended for his lousy play. The Syracuse Southerners were so obvious in their dislike of Higgins that a *Sporting News* writer called them the "Ku-Klux coterie."

Insubordination that showed itself so blatantly on the field and affected the team's fortunes could not continue, and it didn't. Higgins won 20 games that season, and a story of his shutout victory over Newark on August 4 reported that the home crowd "went wild over the perfect work of the Syracuse team. Higgins, the colored pitcher, more than distinguished himself, and the rumor that has been going the rounds that the team would not support him is knocked into a cocked hat."

Higgins' presence still caused off-the-field disruption, however, some of which became publicized. The team portrait was to be taken at a photography studio on Sunday morning, June 5. The whole squad showed up except for two men. Manager Joe Simmons confronted one of them, pitcher Dug Crothers, who freely admitted he had boycotted the photography session because he didn't want to sit for a picture with a black man. As he later explained in the press, "I am a Southerner by birth, and I tell you I would have my heart cut out before I would consent to have my picture in the group." When Simmons heard the comments, he immediately suspended Crothers. The player insulted his manager and then punched him.

Higgins wasn't the only African-American ballplayer of the day who experienced trouble during team picture-taking. Reportedly, Frank Grant had a similar experience in 1886 when several white players on the Buffalo team refused to have their pictures taken with him. Other than jibes from some followers of arch-rival Toronto yelling "Kill the nigger" every time he came to bat in that city on September 1, there is little record of overt

FRANK GRANT
THE BEST OF THE BUNCH

A hometown contemporary remembers that Frank Grant "could do more tricks with a baseball than anyone I ever saw. Kick a grounder with [his] feet to bounce up into his hands. Catch a ball behind the back before Rabbit Maranville was born."

Grant grew up in rural Williamstown, Massachusetts, in an area where blacks were a minority, but were generally well-accepted members of the community. As a youth he was always asked to play ball with groups that, except for his talented brother Clarence, were usually all white. The young Grant ran in fast company for such a small town, with his brother having played for a time with the Cuban Giants, and another of the group, Bob Pettit, having had a three-year major league career.

Grant left home for Plattsburgh, New York, in 1885, playing that summer for a team at the Hotel Champlain in the Adirondacks, organized by Frank Thompson, who was the headwaiter. Then it was on to Meriden, Connecticut in the Eastern League in 1886, where he hit .325. Though he was a few weeks shy of age 21, he was already renowned as a speedy, lithe, and talented infielder when he joined Buffalo in the International League, one step below the majors. There he improved on his Meriden showing, hitting at a .340 clip, finishing third in the league in batting and winning two of four games he was called on to pitch. His fielding was flashy and highly competent. During his time in Buffalo, which lasted through the 1888 season until he joined the Cuban Giants, a sportswriter referred to him as the "Black Dunlap," a very flattering comparison to Fred Dunlap of the National League, considered the best-fielding big-league second baseman of his day.

A contemporary account captures the esteem in which Grant was held by keen baseball observers:

There is no position on the ball field that demands greater agility, endurance of a race horse and sound judgment than that of second baseman. He must of necessity be as wiry as a cat, possess the endurance of a race horse and command unerring discrimination. In the history of the diamond probably no player more fully met these requirements than does Frank Ulysses Grant, the famed second baseman who now does such fine work for the Cuban Giants, of Trenton, New Jersey. Wherever he has played he has quickly become a favorite, alike with the audience

Frank Grant was an outstanding player in the integrated minor leagues of the 1880s.

and with the trained managers of the great teams. He is short and compactly built and weighs 160 pounds, is a fine sprinter, an almost certain catcher and has made an excellent batting record. Were it not for the fact that he is a colored man, he would without a doubt be at the top notch of the records among the finest teams in the country.

racism directed at him that season. However, he went into a deep batting slump in July and August, and began to be criticized by Buffalo sportswriters for poor fielding. His fielding problems may have stemmed from his being targeted, as reportedly was Fowler, by white runners barreling into second base.

The most public repudiation of African-American ballplayers happened to George Stovey, despite the brilliant season he was having. His 35 wins, against only 15 losses, led the league and included 4 shutouts during a period in baseball history when holding an opponent scoreless was difficult due to normally porous fielding. Stovey's considerable temper seems to have been in check during this highly successful period, and a passing racial slur of the type that routinely found its way into press coverage of the black players brought a rebuke from a fan in Rochester. "The young man simply discharged his duty to his club in whitewashing the Rochesters [9–0 on June 26]. Such comments certainly do not help the home team; neither are they creditable to a paper published in this Christian community. So far as I know, Mr. Stovey has been a gentleman in his club and should be treated with the same respect as other players."

He was not treated the same, however, 15 days later when Newark played an off-day exhibition game against the Chicago White Stockings, one of the best known major league clubs of the day. Although the Chicago team—the forerunner of the present-day Cubs, not the White Sox—was destined to finish only in third place in 1887, it had won the National League pennant in four of the previous six years and was baseball's best team of the 1880s. Led by the immensely talented and popular Cap Anson, its manager and hard-hitting first baseman, the White Stockings would create a very lucrative off-day for Newark's Little Giants at their home field.

Countering the best with the best, Newark manager Charlie Hackett announced on the 13th that Stovey would oppose Chicago. But at game time he was not on the mound, and neither he nor Walker, his catcher, made an appearance. The story in Newark was that Stovey was too ill to pitch that day, but the *Toronto World*, which generally disapproved of black players in the International League, let the cat out of the bag: "Hackett intended putting Stovey in the box against the Chicagos, but Anson objected to his playing on account of his color." Anson had displayed racist behavior before. In 1883 he had threatened to cancel an exhibition game between his White Stockings and Toledo, then still a minor league team, if Fleet Walker was allowed to play. Toledo called Anson's bluff and Walker participated that year. But the threat of a great deal of lost revenue from the game allowed Anson to win this one.

Opinion toward black players was also shifting in the top councils of the International League. The directors of the league in Buffalo met the very day Anson was drawing a color line in Newark. When the subject of Negro players came up, it was reported, "Several representatives declared that many of the best players in the league are anxious to leave on account of the colored element, and the board finally directed Secretary White to approve of no more contracts with colored men." The Newark *Daily Journal* writer covering the team clearly thought this decision was a poor one, partly because it would hurt Newark's chances of success, and partly on moral terms. "Now let the league adopt a resolution that any of its players who behave in an ungentlemanly manner upon the field shall be expelled and see how rapidly some of the clubs will be depleted," the *Journal* wisecracked. "It is safe to say that Moses F. Walker is mentally and morally the equal of any director who voted for the resolution."

This action did not, in and of itself, end the opportunities for black players in the league. Grant, Stovey, Walker, and Higgins were still under contract in the midst of the season, and since Buffalo and Syracuse were opposed to the ban and stood up for their players, three of the four returned for 1888. While there was talk of rescinding the ban on black players, that never occurred. However, Buffalo and Syracuse forged a deal that allowed Grant and Higgins to stay with their clubs, and also let Syracuse sign Fleet Walker. Stovey went off to play in the New England League with Worcester. The arrangement did not include any provision for new black blood to enter the league. As these three played out their

The 1887 Buffalo Bisons International League during a short period of integration.

strings, the International League would shun African Americans until Jackie Robinson broke in with the Montreal Royals in 1946.

To Sol White, the seven men in the International League proved that "colored players possessed major league qualifications." He believed that Fleet Walker, Stovey, Grant, and Fowler "would have been drafted by the National League or the American Association had they been of the opposite complexion." It is always a matter of conjecture to speculate which minor league players would have made the grade in the big leagues, but White is certainly correct that these men would have been given a chance to prove themselves if discrimination had not finally pervaded professional baseball.

The timing of the end of the International League's welcome to blacks was particularly notable, because in 1890 major league players, tired of salary and other disputes with major league owners, took a bold step. They lined up financial backing and formed the Players League, which for that season meant the existence of three competing major leagues. It also produced a 50 percent increase in the number of big-league teams and a concomitant increase in the number of major league roster spots. The high minors produced much of the talent to fill these new positions, but black players of the likes of Stovey, Grant, Higgins, and Walker were not even considered.

By the century's end black baseball players had been thoroughly segregated. But while the tide had turned against them, the situation was not hopeless by any means. The best black teams were, as always, highly sought after as barnstorming opponents, even if they were expected to clown for the fans as well as play well. More important, the best teams were developing local followings in their home cities. It was no longer true that the best colored baseball clubs had geographically indistinct names like the Cuban Giants, the X Giants, and the Gorhams, and could have been from anywhere. Among the strongest independent teams in the early years of the 20th century were the Philadelphia Giants, the Chicago Union Giants, and the Brooklyn Royal Giants. Teams might hit the road for long stretches, but they now had roots, too, and advertised them. This gaining of specific identities set the stage for progress toward more economically stable teams and the opportunity to form a lasting Negro league. Virtually none of the notables of 19th-century black baseball, except Sol White, were still active when these changes came about. The improvements were built upon their years of effort, which had made black baseball an accepted part of American sports.

A Negro league player takes to the field in this early 20th century photograph.

The Great Independents

The race people of Philadelphia and vicinity are proud to proclaim Hilldale the biggest thing in the baseball world owned, fostered, and controlled by race men....We are proud to be in a position to give Darby citizens the most beautiful park in Delaware County, a team that is second to none and playing the best attractions available. To affiliate ourselves with other than race men would be a mark against our name that could never be eradicated.

—Ed Bolden, Philadelphia Tribune, 1918

The major leaguer Moses Walker, who in the heady days of the 1880s came closer than any other African-American ballplayer to achieving parity with whites before being "segregated out," became in his middle age a strong advocate of voluntary separation of the races. In 1908 he wrote a pamphlet, "Our Home Colony: A Treatise on the Past, Present, and Future of the Negro Race in America," that set forth in 48 well-written pages the case for African Americans giving up on the long-denied vision of equality in America.

The opportunity for advancement did not exist for Negroes, he wrote: "We see no possible hope that the Negro will ever secure the enjoyment of this social freedom or equality. Without it, he can never expect full and complete development." Walker didn't even think God would intervene, despite the prayers of well-meaning people from both races. "The whole trouble is that the Creator had endowed His people with every power and means to attend to their own physical needs, and if they fail in the use of these faculties they may sit until the end of time waiting for outside help." Assisted by his brother, Welday, Moses Walker opened an office in Steubenville, Ohio, to promote resettlement to Africa, and lectured on the subject until his retirement in 1922, two years before his death.

To understand the despair of ex-baseball players Moses and Welday Walker, turn to historian Rayford Logan's aptly titled *The Betrayal of the Negro*. By 1901, the "nadir" year as he terms it, blacks had clearly been assigned to their "ugly" place in American society. Logan characterized that place as "a terminal that seemed indestructible. On the pediment of the separate wing reserved for Negroes were carved Exploitation, Segregation, Disfranchisement, Lynching, Contempt."

These years were filled with racist events, but there were hopeful signs as well. Hope can be found in the reminiscences of Walter White, who in the 1910s came north from Atlanta, where he was born and reared, to assume a leadership position in the NAACP. Across the next four decades, this position would make him one of the most eminent and productive black leaders in American history.

In his memoirs, *A Man Called White*, he recollected how close he came, around the time when the Walker brothers were turning away from America toward Africa, to losing his life as he and his father faced down a mob bent on killing African Americans—and how close, too, that mob came to making him into an embittered hater:

> In the quiet that followed I put my gun aside and tried to relax. But a tension different from anything I had ever known possessed me. I was gripped by the knowledge of my identity, and in the depths of my soul I was vaguely aware that I was glad of it. I was sick with loathing for the hatred which had flared before me that night and come so close to making me a killer; but I was glad I was not one of those who hated; I was glad I was not one of those made sick and murderous by pride.

In his tour de force, *The Omni Americans*, Albert Murray tells us that more needs to be made of the "possibility that the legacy left by the enslaved ancestors of Blues-oriented contemporary U.S. Negroes includes a disposition to confront the most unpromising circumstances and make the most of what little there is to go on, regardless of the odds—and not without finding delight in the process or forgetting mortality at the height of ecstasy." There must be something back there in that history, Murray asserts, to account for the "admittedly infectious exuberance, elegance and nonsense" we find wherever we turn in the history of African Americans.

Is there not, in Walter White's refusal to allow those who hated to turn him into a hater, a considerable piece of the joy, elegance, strength, and exuberance that Albert Murray alludes to as an often overlooked legacy of slavery? Should we be surprised to find similar qualities in the black men who played and ran baseball in the early years of the 20th century?

A CHANGING GAME

From the early to mid-1890s, black professional baseball experienced decline in the East and reorganization in the Midwest. The changing attitude of business toward baseball, and the efforts of local businessmen to organize the Windy City's white amateur clubs, contributed to the emergence of the Chicago Unions as the Midwest's premier African-American team. The Unions began as a local stay-at-home, playing games on Chicago's "prairie land," and passing the hat to meet expenses. By 1890, management began to try to transform the amateur club into a full-time operation by signing top-level players and barnstorming the nation for gate receipts.

This same period was grim for the top club of black baseball's founding decade, the Cuban Giants. They rarely scheduled games outside the New York area. While the Giants continued to play more than a hundred games annually, their days as the dominant black professional team were behind them.

In contrast, by 1895 two African-American entrepreneurs had laid the foundation that resulted in elevating the black game in the Midwest. Drawing from the early success of the Cuban Giants, Bud Fowler, along with Grant "Homerun" Johnson, formed the Page Fence Giants in Adrian, Michigan, using the familiar draws of showmanship, comical coaching, and top-level baseball. What made Fowler's scheme unique was that a private business provided the necessary start-up capital. At the same time, William Peters began to improve his Chicago Unions' profitability through the creation of rivalries with the top white semi-pro clubs in Chicago. In addition, to maximize profits, Peters began to book as many as three games on a single Sunday. By the end of the 1895 season, the Page Fence Giants and the Chicago Unions were ready to challenge the Cuban Giants for black baseball supremacy. While the Page Fence Giants would have only a short-lived existence, the growth of the Chicago Unions had important consequences for the future.

THE RISE OF PRAIRIE BASEBALL

The Chicago Unions' rise to prominence coincided with the emergence of semiprofessional baseball in America's second city. In 1882 the Chicago Amateur Baseball Association (CABA) was formed to serve primarily as a booking agent for local clubs. The Association secured leasing agreements on several parks throughout the city and organized playing schedules for each of them. By 1887 CABA had obtained leases on four enclosed ballparks with extensive seating capacities. The Whitings, as members of the newly formed rival City League, signed an agreement to use the White Stockings' West Side Park on any open Saturday. The rest of the City League games were played "on the open prairie," as Chicago's regular parks were often called.

The Unions emerged within the context of these white semipro clubs organizing into leagues. The club's principal organizers were William S. Peters, "Abe" Jones, Henry "Teenan" Jones, and Frank Leland. Their business strategy of pooling resources with other African Americans had its roots in black communities of the late 18th century. Early black entrepreneurs recognized that if they were to succeed, it would come only through economic cooperation. No help in obtaining capital could be expected from white America. These baseball owners understood, though, that they had to go where the money could be made. That meant scheduling games with Chicago's white semipro clubs, as well as securing leasing agreements with white park managers.

From 1887 to 1890 they operated their club as a weekend enterprise, passing the hat to meet expenses. To attract top white semi-pro teams the Chicago club offered incentives. Besides dividing gate receipts, the Unions offered a side bet—ranging from $25 to $50, and sometimes as high as $100—to the team that won the game. Side promotions could add to the day's festivities, as well as gate receipts. In one game between the Brightons and the Unions, the African-American club promoted a foot race between players from each club. The winner received $50 plus an extra $10 from CABA. In another game between the Unions and the Models, the winning team received a gold ball and a silver-mounted ebony bat.

In 1888 the Unions played the Pinchbacks of New Orleans for the "Colored Championship." A championship series was a way black baseball owners promoted the game. To compete for the colored championship, a club from the South, for example, would have to defeat all the black clubs within their respective region. They would then issue a challenge to play against the top team from another area. Once a black club defeated the top black clubs from every region, they could proclaim themselves the "World's Colored Champion." Although this informal means of determining the champion would lead to controversy, it did generate a lot of publicity for the black game.

The Pinchbacks, considered the best African-American professional team in the South, conducted a barnstorming tour of the North and Midwest during the 1888 season. A three-game series was scheduled with the Unions, and in the first game the Chicago nine surprised the Louisiana club, 4–1. In the second game, a reported crowd of 1,800 fans watched the Pinchbacks even the series, scoring two runs in the top of the ninth inning and winning 6–5. The third contest was never played. Evidently the Unions were tougher opponents than the Pinchbacks expected, and the Southern team probably left town to save face. Playing these two closely contested games established the Unions' reputation as one of the crack teams in Chicago.

The following year a series of games was played between the Pinchbacks, the Unions, and the Resolutes. Another black club from Chicago, the Resolutes had acquired William Renfroe, the pitcher who played with Bud Fowler on the International League Binghamton Bingos in 1887, but he went down in defeat, 9–5, to the hard-hitting Unions. The following day the Pinchbacks hit Renfroe hard and early en route to a 17–11 victory. Much to the dismay of Abe Jones, the Pinchbacks then defeated the Unions. The possibility of developing a Midwest-South rivalry was lost when the Pinchbacks rejected Jones's challenge to another contest, as well as his follow-up offer for a three-game series with a side bet as high as $150.

On April 2, 1890, the *Chicago Inter Ocean* reported that the Unions would open the season as a full-time operation. Frank Leland, a graduate of Fisk University and former player for the Washington Capitols, was appointed field manager and given the responsibility to sign the best available talent. He was to elevate the Unions to the same plateau as the Cuban Giants and compete for the colored championship. The Union organizers set up a barnstorming schedule to play regional teams. The club played Sunday games in Chicago and traveled throughout Illinois, Indiana, and Michigan during the week. Much like the Cuban Giants, the Unions sought to expand their market potential by creating a demand for their club in numerous locales.

The Unions' initial efforts yielded only marginal results. But in 1894 William Peters, now at the helm, formed a partnership with Al Donigan and secured a lease on playing grounds on 37th and Butler Streets, on Chicago's South Side. Frank Leland remained with the club to serve as the secretary and traveling manager on road trips. The new location was easily accessible by either the State Street or Halsted Street cable car lines.

Moving to such an ideal site, easily served by the streetcar lines, provided a home base for their ever more profitable barnstorming tours.

THE BIRTH OF AN INNOVATIVE ENTERPRISE

Midwestern black ball gained more notoriety in 1895 due to the combination of a flamboyant ball player and a white manufacturer of wire fences who liked publicity. In 1894 Bud Fowler was playing in Findlay, Ohio, for a team with no minor league affiliation. Bud had made more than one circuit through Findlay during his long career, but this time he wasn't just passing through. He had a plan to put together an African-American team to be called the "Findlay Colored Western Giants." Fowler and his only black teammate in Findlay, shortstop Grant Johnson, would form the core of the team. A native of Findlay, Johnson was a college-educated long ball hitter. At the outset of his career playing shortstop for the Findlay Sluggers in 1894, he hit 60 home runs—thus the nickname "Homerun." Sol White states that Johnson, in connection with Fowler, conceived an idea of a "colored team traveling in a private car and giving street parades prior to every game."

For all his organizational ability, Fowler was not able to find enough financial backing for a Findlay team, but a white businessman in Adrian, Michigan, a town 50 miles southwest of Detroit, bought his pitch. Adrian, while not a large community, was a good baseball town, often with teams in the low minor leagues. J. Wallace Page, president of the Page Woven Wire Fence Company, decided to tie his company's name to an unusual product, a black baseball team in a predominantly white part of the country. According to the *Adrian Daily Times and Expositor*, "Local baseball enthusiasts are much interested in the enterprise." The paper added that it was "not impossible that Fowler's scheme may succeed."

Fowler's baseball team was named the Page Fence Giants, although it also had the Monarch Bicycle Company of Massachusetts as a lesser sponsor. Bicycling was a major participant sport at the time, with "wheelmen" clubs of cyclists nearly everywhere, and the Giants worked Monarch bicycles

The famous Page Fence Giants, in the late 1890s, were among the first clubs to tour.

into their routine. They usually arrived at a town for a game by rail in a private railroad car that was hooked onto local trains to take them around the region. Their car, emblazoned with the team name, gave the club a touch of class, but also conveniently provided a place to eat and sleep along routes where a dozen black men might have trouble finding lodging or a restaurant that would serve them. Upon disembarking at the station, they would cycle through town in uniform, drawing crowds down to the diamond.

When matched against inferior local talent, as they often were, the Giants put on a show by resorting to the on-the-field stunts common to the barnstorming black teams, and undoubtedly expected by the white audiences who came down to see the colored stars. Billy Holland, a pitcher with the Giants in the early stage of a 15-year career, was described by the local newspaper as "funner than an end man in a minstrel show."

The Page Fence Giants were exclusively a traveling team, making no effort to establish a home base. A two-game series with the National League Cincinnati Reds illustrates their typical pattern. An advertisement was placed in the newspapers announcing the Page Fence Giants' arrival to

Homerun Johnson
Waiting for a Good Pitch

Grant Johnson, a stellar shortstop at the turn of century, appeared for most of the great black clubs, among them the Page Fence Giants, the great Philadelphia Giants clubs of 1905–06, the Brooklyn Royal Giants, the Leland Giants, and with the legendary Lincoln Giants. A reported 60 home runs in his rookie season for the semi-pro Findlay Sluggers earned him the sobriquet he would carry for the rest of his baseball career, even though for many seasons in the Deadball Era he averaged only ten.

Called "Dad" by other players, he was "a favorite with the crowds with his witty sayings, good playing and good conduct winning him many friends."

He was known as a student of the game, and often put his many years at the bat into words. According to Johnson, there were two requisites to being a first-class hitter: confidence and fearlessness. Though best known as a home run hitter he learned early on not to swing for the fences. From Johnson's perspective, any pitcher worth his salt would rather, when the game is on the line, "face the mighty swinger to the cool steady batter who tries to meet the ball and place it to the best advantage."

He put his advice into action. In 1910, playing for the Havana Reds, his .412 average outhit Sam Crawford and Ty Cobb of the Detroit Tigers when they toured Cuba. That same year, during the most storied run of his career, he hit a reported .397 for the Leland Giants, while they went 123-6 for the season. For the Lincoln Giants from 1911 to 1913, he batted .374, .413 and .371. Grant Johnson not only slugged home runs, he collected a few other hits besides.

their city. *The Cincinnati Enquirer* reported that the Giants would conduct "a street parade on bicycles and put up a good article of ball." On game day, souvenirs were distributed to the fans with a picture of the Giants on one side and a picture of the Page Wire Frence Company on the other. The Giants played a spirited contest against the Reds in the first game before losing, 11–7. Page center fielder Gus Brooks, the paper reported, "made three wonderful catches," and Bud Fowler, at age 49, was "as spry and as fast as any man on the field." The *Enquirer* reported that every "colored barber, wine boy, and palace car porter" who could get the day off attended the game, and, seated in a segregated pavilion, they cheered with "shouting and jubilation." The second game was a different story. The game was over in the first inning, when the Reds erupted for eleven runs and won 16–2.

In 1895 their business manager, Augustus S. "Gus" Parsons, booked 156 games in 112 towns in seven states. The Page club started poorly in the month of April, winning only two of eleven games. But by late June the Giants caught fire and went on several winning streaks for the remainder of the season. They began to dazzle fans with their showmanship, comical coaching, and competitive baseball. Grant Johnson once executed a cartwheel around the bases after hitting a home run. Even the servants occasionally got involved. Will Gaskin, the cook, rapped five hits against the Romero club. The Page club also played many close games against top-level semi-pro clubs, illustrating their ability to play at a high caliber .

The Giants barnstormed throughout Ohio, Indiana, Illinois, and Michigan in their first season and turned a profit. But Bud Fowler had greater aspirations for his team. By mid-July, rumors circulated in the press that the Giants would embark upon an international barnstorming tour. *The Detroit Free Press* reported that the Page club, along with Minneapolis of the Western League, would play 40 games in England at the end of the regular season. The *Adrian Daily Times* reported that nine men selected from various clubs of the Michigan State League would travel with the Giants to Honolulu, Hawaii, and play for an entire month. Both clubs would then barnstorm Australia and New Zealand for approximately three months. Five players from the Cuban Giants would accompany the Page club. No evidence has been uncovered to indicate that either of these tours ever occurred, but they do illustrate Fowler's uncanny ability to generate publicity.

The Page Fence Giants concluded their 1895 season with a benefit game. Their opponent, known as the Detroits, was composed of professional white players who made Detroit their home, such as major leaguer

Sam Thompson, who played on the champion Detroit club of 1887; Washington shortstop Frank Scheibach; and Boston pitcher Ed "Kid" Nichols. Unfortunately, rain marred the series and only one game was played, with the result that many of the star players refused to participate. Only 150 fans watched the Giants drub the Detroits, 16–2. During their successful first season the Giants won 118, lost 36 and tied two, playing before an average crowd of 1,500.

The team members apparently were paid regularly at the going rates for the best black players, at least $75 and perhaps as much as $100 per month. The pay attracted fine players. Homerun Johnson, shortstop and chief slugger, was a key member of the team throughout its four-year existence. Bill Malone, the former Cuban Giants and Gorham pitcher, closed out his career with the Page Fence team, and George Wilson began an illustrious ten years of pitching with them. Charlie Grant, one of the preeminent black infielders of the early 20th century, a second baseman like Frank Grant but no relation to him, also got his start in Adrian. Fowler, ever restless, left the team he had created before the 1895 season was over to play with Adrian's entry in the white Michigan State League. The ever present player and scribe, Sol White, replaced him at second base.

THE RISE OF THE CHICAGO UNIONS

During the middle years of the 1890s, while the Page Fence Giants secured their place in the ranks of black baseball, William Peters continued to build rivalries with other semi-pro teams. A seasonal rivalry, particularly on Sundays, meant a big payday for semi-pro clubs. Club owners attempted to develop such rivalries with at least two or three independent clubs.

Two of the top white semi-professional clubs in the Windy City, the Edgars and Dalys, filled that role for the Unions in 1895. That season the Dalys were the Unions' fiercest rivals. A three-game series was scheduled, with the winner receiving a purse worth $500. The Unions took the first game, 18–9, but lost the second, 12–8. The final game of the series was played on September 15 at the South Side City League grounds. The

Chiefs Need Not Apply

Baseball historian John Holway recorded a story that illuminates these segregated times. During spring training in Hot Springs, Arkansas, John McGraw, manager of the powerful Baltimore teams of the early 1900s, spotted a hot prospect: Charlie Grant, star second baseman for the Page Fence Giants and later the Columbia Giants. Because he was light-skinned, McGraw signed him as "Chief Tokahoma, a full-blooded Cherokee Indian."

Yet the chief was unmasked at a Chicago exhibition game, when hundreds of black fans came to cheer "our boy, Charlie Grant." "If McGraw keeps this Indian," said White Sox owner Charles Comiskey, "I'll put a Chinaman on third base."

Unions' center fielder, Al Hackley, who won the Douglass Cycling Club Cup for most hits in the series, led his club to a 9–8 victory. The reported crowd of 3,600 in the series finale illustrates the importance of seasonal rivalries for independent clubs.

The creation of Sunday doubleheaders was the second way Peters sought to improve the Unions' profits. On June 15, the *Inter Ocean* reported that the Unions would "meet all comers" every Sunday. Peters scheduled two games, the Schroeder Brothers in the first and the Cranes in the second. Both ended in Unions victories. On August 7, Peters booked three games at Unions' Park with the Schroeder Brothers, the Lake Views, and the Altmans. Unfortunately, the results were not reported in the press. Therein lay a fundamental flaw in Peters' plan—sporadic press coverage. Consistent reportage was needed to generate publicity and stimulate fan interest. This shortcoming would be overcome as the Unions rose to prominence.

Through these mid-years of the 1890s the Chicago Unions and the Page Fence Giants made good progress in becoming full-time operations. Both clubs elevated the black game in the Midwest to the point that they were ready to challenge the Cuban Giants for black baseball supremacy.

THE NEW CUBAN GIANTS

Despite being only a shadow of their former selves, the Cuban Giants were still one of the elite semi-pro clubs in the East. From 1892 to 1895, J. M. Bright constructed a moderate barnstorming pattern for his team, rarely playing games outside the New York area. While Bright secured a leasing agreement to play games in Norwalk, Connecticut, he coveted more the Sunday games on the Long Island grounds. One of those games attracted 1,200 fans, and another drew 1,000. Throughout this period the Giants almost exclusively played white semiprofessional clubs.

On April 20, 1893, the New York Sun reported that J. M. Bright had hired a new field manager. According to the Sun, Frank Grant would "have full control of the men." One can likely see here how race shaped the business relationship between black players and white owners. Although several of the original Cuban Giants continued to play for Bright, the players appear to have had an estranged relationship with their enigmatic owner. But if the players wanted to sustain their elite status in baseball's semi-pro circles, not to mention receive regular pay checks, they had little choice but to play for a white owner.

As player-manager, Grant served as a liaison between white owner and black players. Management and players recognized that both sides needed each other in order to function. This complex relationship between white ownership and a black labor force continued to play out among black clubs well into the 20th century.

In 1896 the Giants' owner would face his most serious challenge: another white owner from Brooklyn. Edward B. (E.B.) Lamar, Jr., a 28-year-old from a New York City family acquainted with both business and baseball, was gradually persuading most of Bright's team to switch to his outfit. Over the course of a few years he also snapped up many other topflight stars. S.K. Govern became Lamar's field manager. Sol White, one of the first defectors, assessed Lamar very favorably in his later historical writings: "His efforts were in the interest of his team, and he was held in the highest regard by the players."

Lamar's team carried on a hard-fought competition with Bright's Giants for most of the remaining years of the decade. The first battle occurred even before a ball was thrown, when Lamar christened his new squad the "Cuban X Giants." Sticking the "X" in the middle of the name of his team was a form of brand-name theft that appeared to pass legal muster. Lamar noted, "We are informed legally that the name of Cuban X Giants is not incorporated and that we have a perfect right to the use of same." The fact that fans in smaller cities and towns might confuse his team with the venerable Cuban Giants was probably no small advantage to his fledgling operation.

In order to avoid confusion, Bright renamed his club the "Original Cuban Giants," sometimes replacing "Original" with "Genuine" or "Wonderful." Other than giving his team a slightly revised new name, his initial response to the Cuban X Giants' formation was to ignore their existence. Lamar issued an immediate challenge to a series of games to be played either in Brooklyn or at the Polo Grounds; the winner would receive all of the gate receipts. Bright did not respond. But the competition was likely a factor in the decision of the Original Cubans' to replace some weaker performing players in 1895 with "younger blood."

Throughout the 1896 season the Cuban X Giants and Cuban Giants maintained their dominance over white semi-pro clubs. The excellent performances of both teams led one fan, calling himself "Admirer," to call for a season-ending series between these clubs. The unnamed admirer further suggested that part of the proceeds be donated to a hospital of the players' choosing. Such a series would have been a fitting conclusion to a fine year. In response, Lamar stated that he had made several attempts to arrange a series between the two clubs with no results. Once again, J.M. Bright snubbed the X Giants.

Even as Bright ignored Lamar's request for a series, the Cuban X Giants set out on their first extended barnstorming tour. The rise of the Page Fence Giants and the Chicago Unions, along with the emergence of the top white semi-pro teams in the Windy City, made the trip economically feasible. Moreover, the Western League, the precursor to the American League, was willing to play games with black clubs when their schedules permitted. The era of barnstorming tours was kicking into a higher gear.

E.B. Lamar named his team the Cuban X Giants.

WHO ARE THE REAL COLORED CHAMPIONS?

The Page Fence Giants began the 1896 season without their founder and innovator, Bud Fowler. He had formed a black baseball club in Muncie, Indiana, with the intent of "wrestling the laurels from the Page Fence Giants." In his absence, Gus Parsons and Grant Johnson ran the team and barnstormed the Midwest for gate receipts.

At the outset of the season, the Giants embarked on a long tour throughout Wisconsin, Minnesota, Illinois, and Indiana. According to the *Free Press*, the Page club won 35 straight games. In June the Giants began a 40-game schedule throughout Michigan, beginning in Hillsdale with a 15–5 victory. Unlike the previous season, Parsons scheduled more games in the club's home base of Adrian, Michigan.

By late July 1896, press reports were announcing a series between the Page Fence Giants and the Cuban X Giants for the "Colored Championship of the United States." The two clubs would crisscross the state of Michigan, playing seventeen games. The series was significant for several reasons. For the Cuban X Giants, it elevated their status as a touring team. Playing for the colored championship also brought national attention to the black game.

The Page Fence players began the series poorly with a close loss in the opener, 8–6, and then were manhandled 20–13. In game three the Pages demolished the X Giants, 26–6, and proceeded to win the next three games. After ten games the Page Fencers led the series six games to four. They proceeded to win five out of the next seven games and won the series eleven games to six. The Michigan club received a commemorative silver medal engraved with the inscription: "1896 Page Fence Giants Champions." More important—although the reporting was sporadic—the series received national press coverage in the *New York Sun*, *Detroit Free Press*, and *Sporting Life*.

Crowning the Page Fence Giants as colored champions, however, was premature. Neither the Midwestern nor the Eastern Giants had played the top black club within their respective regions of the country. Bright refused to play the Cuban X Giants in the Eastern Leagues, while the Page club did not play the Chicago Unions in the Midwest.

Meanwhile, the Unions continued their barnstorming pattern of a weekly tour through Midwestern states while returning to Chicago for Sunday games. Frank Leland functioned as the team's traveling manager, with William Peters remaining in Chicago. Their travels took the club through a wide swath of the Midwest, during one stretch going on a seven-game winning streak against "the best teams in Michigan."

In late September, a triangular series between the Edgars, Unions, and J. M. Bright's Original Cuban Giants was conducted for another "Colored Championship of the World." This series marked the first time since 1888 that the Cuban Giants toured outside the New York area, and the X Giants much-publicized colored championship series with the Page Fence Giants was a major cause. The three clubs and "several local followers" contributed to a purse worth $1,000.

The triangular series began with the Unions playing the Edgars at the latter's home base at Elgin Athletic Park. The Edgars took a 3–2 lead into the ninth inning, but in the bottom of the frame Unions' shortstop William Joyner hit a double and then scored on what would be Gus Hopkins's game-winning home run. The 4–3 victory typified the close games the Unions and Edgars played against each other, fueling the fire of their fierce rivalry.

The Unions, however, performed poorly against the Cuban Giants. William Peters' club took an early 5–2 lead into the seventh inning, when the Giants broke the game open, scoring four runs in the seventh and seven in the eighth, winning the game 16–5. The Unions were their own worst enemy, committing nine errors in the contest. The following day the Giants knocked the Unions' star pitcher Harry Buckner out of the box early and took a 10–3 lead into the seventh inning. The Unions mounted an unsucessful comeback in the later innings but eventually lost 11–9. The Cuban Giants had also swept the Edgars in their series and claimed the $1,000 purse.

But who were the "real" colored champions? Both the Page Fence Giants and Cuban Giants were spectacular in their respective championship series, but no evidence has been uncovered to suggest that either J. M. Bright or Gus Parsons attempted to arrange a championship series between their respective clubs. Efforts would be made to resolve this impasse in the upcoming season.

BRAGGING RIGHTS

J. M. Bright's preparations for the 1897 season included an ambitious undertaking for his Original Cubans. Bright planned a western barnstorming tour throughout Ohio, Indiana, Michigan, and Canada. The Cubans would also play the Page Fence Giants, but it would not be for the colored championship. According to Bright, a colored championship series could only occur "when all the crack colored clubs enter into a tournament." He did try to organize such a competition, inviting the Page Fence Giants, the Pinchbacks of New Orleans, the Red Stockings of Norfolk, Virginia, and the

Chicago Unions to face off against each other, but he failed to obtain agreements from the invited clubs and the tournament never took place.

That same season E. B. Lamar and his Cuban X Giants embarked on one of the most successful extended barnstorming tours of the late 19th century. The tour was scheduled so that the X Giants would play several black clubs in a colored championship series. They also played the top white semi-pro clubs of Chicago, teams in smaller cities and towns like Marion, Ohio, and eventually the National League's Cincinnati Reds.

Concurrently, William Peters booked several Sunday games with the top black clubs of the South and East and billed them as colored championship series. In May, the Chicago Unions began a "colored championship series" by playing the Page Fence Giants. A reported crowd of 5,400 fans watched the Unions nip the Giants behind Harry Buckner's hitting and pitching. Chicago trailed 4–3 when the Unions broke the game open with four runs in the seventh and won 7–6.

It should be noted that Harry Buckner was one of the leading players of the era. He not only was "head and shoulders above" other pitchers, but he could also catch and play both infield and outfield. One contemporary called him a "speed marvel." Starting with the Chicago Unions, he would jump from team to team, like so many stars of the time. By 1909 he would join the Brooklyn Royal Giants, forming part of a formidable pitching rotation that included Andrew "Rube" Foster, Dan McClellan, and Walter Bell. That team would dominate Eastern teams during his two-year tenure there.

In June, the Cuban X Giants invaded Unions' Park for a three-game series that included a Sunday doubleheader. Once again, the Unions aided in their own defeat, committing five errors in the first game and losing 14–5. The Unions won the second game behind Billy Holland's excellent pitching, but their poor defense proved their undoing in the third game. Union fielders committed eleven errors and lost the game 14–9, thus allowing the Cuban X Giants to claim victory over the colored champions of the Midwest.

Their touring next took the Eastern club through St. Louis, southern Illinois, and Indiana. By July 1, the long-touring X Giants had played 35 games on their extended western swing, winning 28 of them. Late August

Hoodoo in Texas

Of all the professional trainers who plied their art in black baseball, none garnered more respect than William "Doc" Lambert. Lambert's baseball pedigree stretched from the 1890s through the 1930s. His training career included stints with major league clubs and a host of Negro professional teams. One of the games he remembered best was played in 1898 when he was with the Staten Giants, a team consisting of a father and his nine sons. They played the local Calvert, Texas, team featuring a young Rube Foster in his hometown.

As Doc remembers the scene, old man Staten had a habit of chewing roots and spitting on the ball, claiming that this gave his boys good luck. But even as a youthful player, Foster had a trick or two of his own. After Staten had deposited his 'spell' on the ball, Rube called for the horsehide, strode from the pitchers mound to the batter, waved his hands about the ball, muttered some hocus pocus, and told Father Staten that if he busted that apple it would explode and kill him, or else hoodoo him for life. The Statens—and Doc—fell for Rube's line, and nary a hit did they get that day.

—Pittsburgh Courier, April 4, 1925

brought J. M. Bright's Cuban Giants to the Windy City. The Unions were itching for this rematch after their poor performance the previous season, and in three heavy-hitting affairs, the Unions swept their Eastern rivals.

Upon the Cuban Giants' return to the East, J. M. Bright finally relented to a championship series with the Cuban X Giants. Three games were scheduled on consecutive Sundays in Weehawken, New Jersey. After winning the opening game 11–9, the Cuban Giants lost the next two games, enabling the Cuban X Giants to proclaim themselves the "World's Colored Champions."

Clearly, these informal standards for determining the colored champion were flawed, yet this conflict generated valuable publicity for the black game. Several black clubs, particularly from the South, desirous of elevating their status, began to challenge the Cuban Giants or the Cuban X Giants for black baseball supremacy.

Through the off season E. B. Lamar and J. M. Bright continued squabbling, and a proposed ten-game series for the 1898 season fell through. Instead, the Cuban X Giants devised a barnstorming tour with the Chicago Unions. From the beginning, only the games played in Chicago were billed as a colored championship series. A series of games was scheduled throughout Wisconsin, Illinois, and Michigan. Simultaneously, both clubs scheduled games with white semi-pro teams on open dates. Harry Buckner and James Robinson dueled to a 3–3 tie in the first game of the colored championship series. After the Cuban X Giants won the second game, the final contest proved to be a slugfest. The Giants took a 6–3 lead in the first, only to fall behind 10–7 after six innings. After scoring one run in the seventh, the X Giants mustered a three-run rally in the eighth to pull of an 11–10 X Giants win. For the second straight year the X Giants defeated the Unions for the colored championship.

Upon their return to the East, J. M. Bright agreed once again to a three-game series with the Cuban X Giants, but the younger club continued their dominance by winning in two games. For the second straight year, the Cuban X Giants had a spectacular season. They played 136 games, winning 101, losing 31, and tying four.

COLUMBIA GIANTS JOIN THE FRAY

As the 1890s ended, barnstorming grew less prosperous for the Page Fence Giants, and the team went out of business after the 1898 season. Its demise cleared the way for an even more successful team. The leading players migrated to Chicago to become the Columbia Giants, owned by black Chicagoans Julius Avendorph and Alvin Garret. Columbia Club members came from the ranks of Chicago's African-American elite, and Avendorph was Negro Chicago's "undisputed social leader from 1886 to about 1910." From the outset, the Columbia Club attempted to operate the Giants as a full-time operation, leasing a playing ground on 39th and Wentworth Avenue, on Chicago's South Side.

Although the Columbias seemed to be no threat at first to William Peters'

Unions, they arrived in Chicago at a time when the Unions' business relationship with the top white semi-pros began to disintegrate. Peters' booking of touring black clubs into Unions' Park for Sunday games, particularly the Cuban X and Cuban Giants, led to bitter feelings among white operators wanting a big payday. For instance, in 1898 Peters canceled a game with the Marquettes, to schedule what turned out to be the first game of the colored championship series with the Cuban X Giants. In addition, the winner-take-all series and the substantial side bets on some series with white teams further strained the black-white baseball relationship. Plus the Unions' dominance over white semi-pro clubs could have made the latter reluctant to play them, in spite of the economic reward. A black club consistently beating a white one was a hard pill to swallow for whites in 19th-century America.

By early September, the Columbia Giants issued a challenge to the Chicago Unions for the city's colored championship. At first William Peters avoided the Columbia club, upset when that team signed pitcher Harry Buckner away from the Unions. However, according to Sol White, out of consideration for the public, the Unions agreed to a five-game series. Consideration for his own pocketbook might have been a factor as well for Peters, given the Columbia squad's attendance at Sunday games. It was a high-stakes match, as both clubs agreed to a winner-take-all format, and a $100 side bet on each game. To offset the potential losses, the Giants and Unions scheduled additional Sunday games on the same day they faced each other. The first game set the tone. A reported 9,000 fans packed Unions' Park as Giants pitcher Harry Buckner shut out his former teammates en route to a 1–0 victory. After that the Unions were never in the series, as they lost the next four games. A new champion was emerging in Chicago.

THE REAL CUBANS COME TO PLAY

The developing rivalries continued to permeate the 1899 season, and a significant new factor was added when an all-star squad from Havana, Cuba toured through New York and New Jersey and also challenged the Cuban X Giants to a championship series.

As Stetson Palmer in *Baseball Magazine* noted, "One of the principal fruits of the Spanish-American War [was] to make Cuba a nation of baseball fans." Actually, baseball had made its way south to Cuba around the same time it began to flourish in the North American Midwest. A number of Cubans who figured prominently in baseball's development on the island learned America's game while attending schools in the United States.

Credited by some chroniclers as the "father" of Cuban baseball, Nemesio Guilló attended Springhill College in Mobile, Alabama. In 1864, he returned to Cuba at the age of seventeen, having spent six years at the Alabama school. Included among the belongings the young Cuban brought back were a bat and a baseball. His baseball equipment was "the first to be seen in Cuba, and little known even in the United States, where the game was just then catching on."

Cuba's first big leaguer, Esteban Bellán, was also sent north for his education. In 1868, Bellán gained the distinction of being the first Cuban to perform on a U.S. college varsity team, playing on the Rose Hill club (present-day Fordham University). Three years later the Cuban infielder left school to join the Troy Haymakers (National Association), thereby becoming the first Latino major leaguer. Dozens of Cubans and Latinos joined Bellán in studying at Fordham during this period. Included in this group were Teodoro and Carlos Zaldo, who attended Fordham in 1875-77 and were among the original members of the Almendares Base Ball Club in 1878, one of Cuban baseball's most storied teams.

By the mid-1880s the national pastime of the United States had sunk deep roots into Cuban soil. Sporting papers like the *New York Clipper*, *The Sporting News*, and *Sporting Life* included coverage of Cuban baseball dating back to the formation of the Cuban professional league in 1879. Meanwhile Cuban publications like *El Score* and *El Baseball* carried news of Cuban participants in North American baseball at every level from high school to professional, allowing Cuban baseball fans to follow the feats of their countrymen wherever they lived.

The Sporting News announced in the summer of 1899 that a club made up of Cuban players would tour the United States from August to

September. The All Cubans team was managed by Abel Linares and field manager Agustin "Tinti" Molina, both experienced baseball men who had made trips to Florida. The All Cubans 1899 tour would open a new era of Latino-North American baseball.

The All Cubans were impressive in their head-to-head competition against white semi-pro teams. On July 28 they easily defeated a picked team, 12–4, in Weehawken, New Jersey. Three days later, a reported crowd of 1,800 fans watched the All Cubans lose a close game with the West New York Field Club, 8–5. The Mountain AC club also played tough against the All Cubans. The score was tied 3–3 going into the eighth, when the Cubans erupted for four runs in the bottom of the frame and coasted to a 9–3 win. The Cubans finally met their match in Jersey City, New Jersey, as the Jerseys trounced them, 14–4.

In mid-August, the All Cubans challenged the Cuban X Giants. According to the *New York Sun*, the All Cubans protested "against the Cuban X Giants posing as representatives of Cuba." To resolve the alleged dispute, a contest was scheduled on the St. George cricket grounds in Hoboken, New Jersey. Behind the five-hit pitching of James Robinson, the Giants defeated the All Cubans, 7–3. The game was never in question as the Giants scored five runs in the first three innings. The All Cubans licked their wounds and challenged the Cuban X Giants to a second game, the winner to receive all the gate receipts. The game was tied 3–3 going into the fourth inning, when the Giants erupted for five runs in the bottom of the frame, coasting to an 11–6 victory.

In spring of 1900 the Cuban X Giants played a series in Havana against several Cuban clubs. By March 16 the Giants had played seven games on the island, defeating the Franciscos 10–5. The Cuban clubs provided the Giants some fierce competition, however. On March 22 the San Franciscos gave the Giants a tough fight before bowing to defeat, 10–8. On March 29 the Havanas lost a 4–2 heartbreaker to New York. On March 30, 1900, a Cuban club finally defeated the Cuban X Giants. The Criollo team swept the Giants in a two-game series that culminated the New York club's barnstorming tour. Although the Cuban X Giants won 13 of 15 games, Criollo's victories reinforce historian Roberto Echevarria's assertion that Cuban baseball had come a long way. Moreover, Criollo's wins whetted the appetite of Cuban impresarios who saw an opportunity to capitalize upon the sport's potential for commercial gain. After all, a Cuban club had defeated the most dominant "colored baseball" team in the United States.

BLACK CLUBS GO TO WAR

In the meantime, animosity between the Chicago Unions and Columbia Giants increased. From the outset, Sol White states that both clubs were at "loggerheads" with each other. The Columbia club's defeat of the Unions in 1899 ranked them among the elite in Chicago's semi-pro circles. In 1900, the Columbia Giants defeated J. M. Bright's Cuban Giants, and the Unions defeated the Cuban X Giants, marking the first time the Windy City club beat the New York nine in a series. But a disputed championship for local supremacy between the Columbia club and the Unions intensified the resentment.

In spite of this dispute, the Columbia Giants further elevated their status with a season-ending match with Charles Comiskey's White Stockings. Comiskey had moved his club from St. Paul, Minnesota, to Chicago as part of Ban Johnson's effort to make his Western League, to be renamed the American League in 1900, a second major league. At the same time the "Old Roman" took for his team the familiar old nickname "White Stockings," and shortened it to White Sox two years later.

A two-game series was scheduled between the Sox and the Giants at the latter's home grounds. In the opener the Columbias scored four runs in the first three innings, and when Harry Buckner held the White Stockings' hitters in check, the Giants won 5–3. The second game lasted only four innings, as rain shortened the contest with the White Stockings in the lead 8–4.

The Columbia Giants' rise in status resulted in a war over players, however, and the eventual dismantling of both the Giants and the Chicago Unions. On April 5, 1901, the *Inter Ocean* reported that the Unions had signed Harry Buckner and star left fielder John Patterson away from the Columbia Giants, and the raiding continued a month later with the sign-

Abel Linares
Cuban Pioneer

By the end of the 19th century Abel Linares was already a veteran baseball executive in Cuba who at different times in a long career operated teams in the Cuban professional league. These teams introduced a number of Latino players to the United States sporting scene, including future major leaguers Adolfo Luque, Armando Marsans and Rafael Almeida.

Linares' Cuban teams, the All Cubans and, later, the Cuban Stars, barnstormed the U.S. black baseball circuit from 1899 through the late 1910s. The tours typically started in March and lasted until early September.

In addition to his role as team owner, the Cuban baseball impresario regularly handled arrangements for barnstorming tours of Cuba by black and major league teams, and from 1902 to 1904 penned a sports column, "Cuba's Chapter," for *The Sporting Life*.

Through the entrepreneurial efforts of Linares and fellow Cuban executives such as Alex Pompez, working relationships with their North American counterparts were forged. Baseball men like Rube Foster, Nat Strong and Ed Lamar assisted their Cuban associates in plotting out itineraries and securing accommodations among other tour details. These North American baseball entrepreneurs were in a position to aid the Cuban promoters to book the better venues and to schedule exhibition games that had strong revenue potential. This interaction resulted in both sides increasingly incorporating talent from each other, which elevated the quality of America's game in the 1910s.

ing of two other star players. The Columbia Giants were left in a crippled condition, but they managed to finish the season.

Adding to the confusion was the formation of a third club. Frank Leland apparently had grown weary of being Peters' lieutenant, and realized that the Unions' business relationship with white semi-pro teams was weakening as the leading clubs in Chicago disbanded. In August

Clarence Lytle was listed as a pitcher on the 1906 roster for Frank Leland's Giants.

1901, Leland broke with Peters to form the Chicago Union Giants. As the name illustrates, several players from the Unions and Columbia Giants made up this new club. There were now three black teams operating in the Windy City.

Leland's break with Peters resulted in the Unions losing their lease on Unions' Park. For the remainder of the season Peters' old Unions club was relegated to a traveling team. The decline of the Unions and the player raiding that decimated the Columbia Giants brought to an end the East-West connection with the Cuban X Giants. With the decline of Chicago's teams, there was no incentive for Eastern black teams to travel to the Windy City.

The 1901 season did end on a positive note. The new Chicago Union Giants and the Columbia Giants agreed to a season-ending series for that ubiquitous "Colored Championship of the World." A best-two-out-of-three series was scheduled on consecutive Sundays at Charles Comiskey's American League Park. The Columbia club was victorious in the first game. In the second game, 400 fans braved the cold and, according to the *Inter Ocean*, both clubs played on a field that "was fit for mud horses." The game was tied at two when the Columbias scored one run in the seventh inning and won, 3–2, proclaiming themselves the "Colored Champions of the World."

BROTHERLY LOVE FOR BLACK BASEBALL

In 1901, after watching a heavily attended game between the Cuban X Giants and the Philadelphia Athletics at Columbia Park, H. Walter Schlichter was struck by the idea of a strong black club representing the Quaker City. The next year Schlichter, in conjunction with Sol White and Harry Smith, a sports editor for the *Philadelphia Tribune*, organized the Philadelphia Giants. Their formation shows once again African American entrepreneurs working within the white power structure. This meant negotiating with white semiprofessional owners, park managers, and, in this case, a white business partner.

The by now familiar White was the driving force behind the Philadelphia Giants, but little is known regarding the backgrounds of Harry Smith and H. Walter Schlichter. Smith served on what eventually became the oldest continuously circulating African-American newspaper in the United States. Promoted as the "Voice of the Black Community," the *Tribune* sought to represent the interests of the majority of America's citizens of African descent. Schlichter was the sports editor of the white *Philadelphis Item*. The Giants benefited tremendously from the increased press coverage provided by his paper. More important, Schlichter's connection to the white baseball world was instrumental in the club playing in the Philadelphia Athletics' Columbia Park when the American League club was on the road.

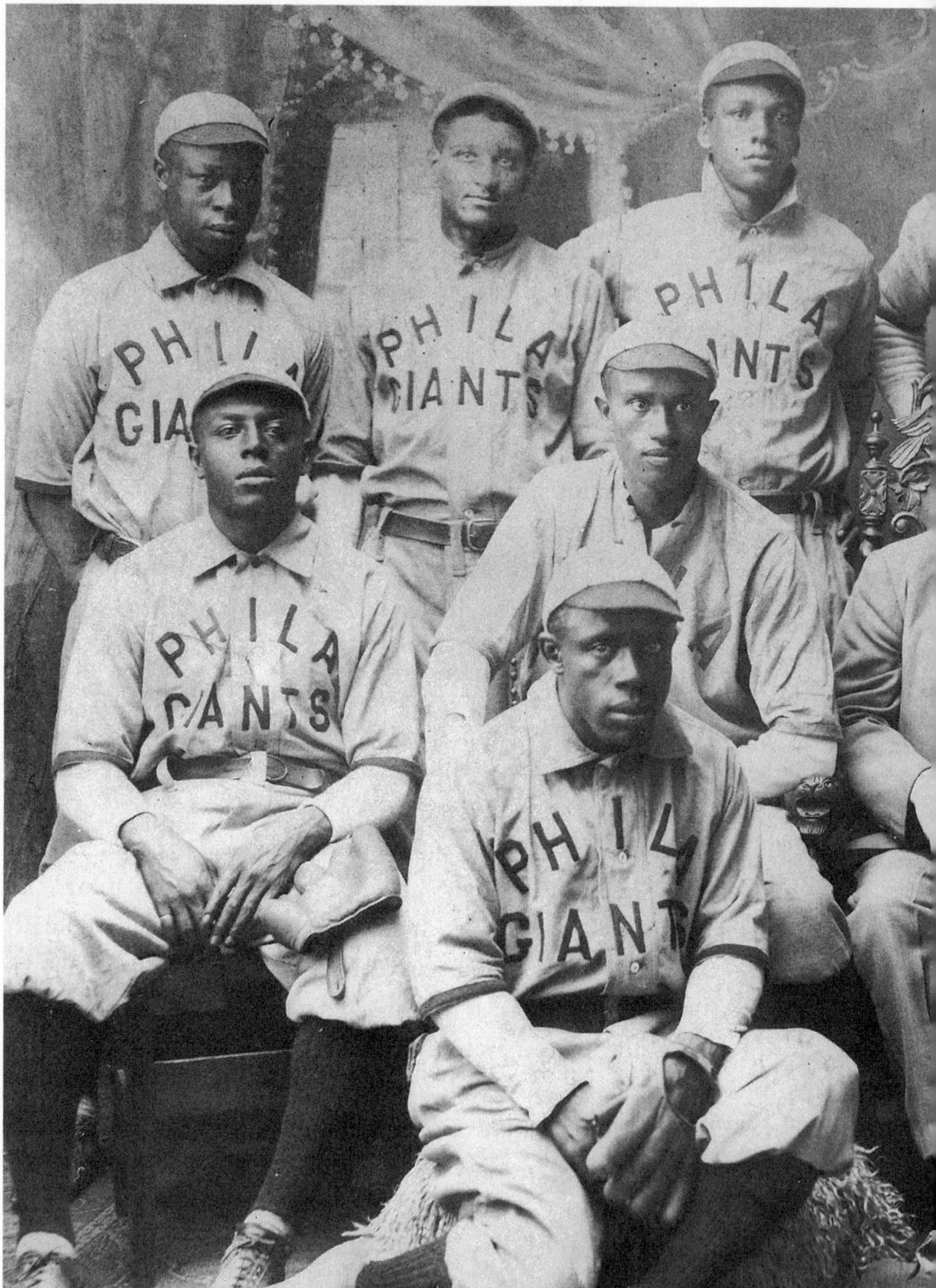
PHILA
GIANTS

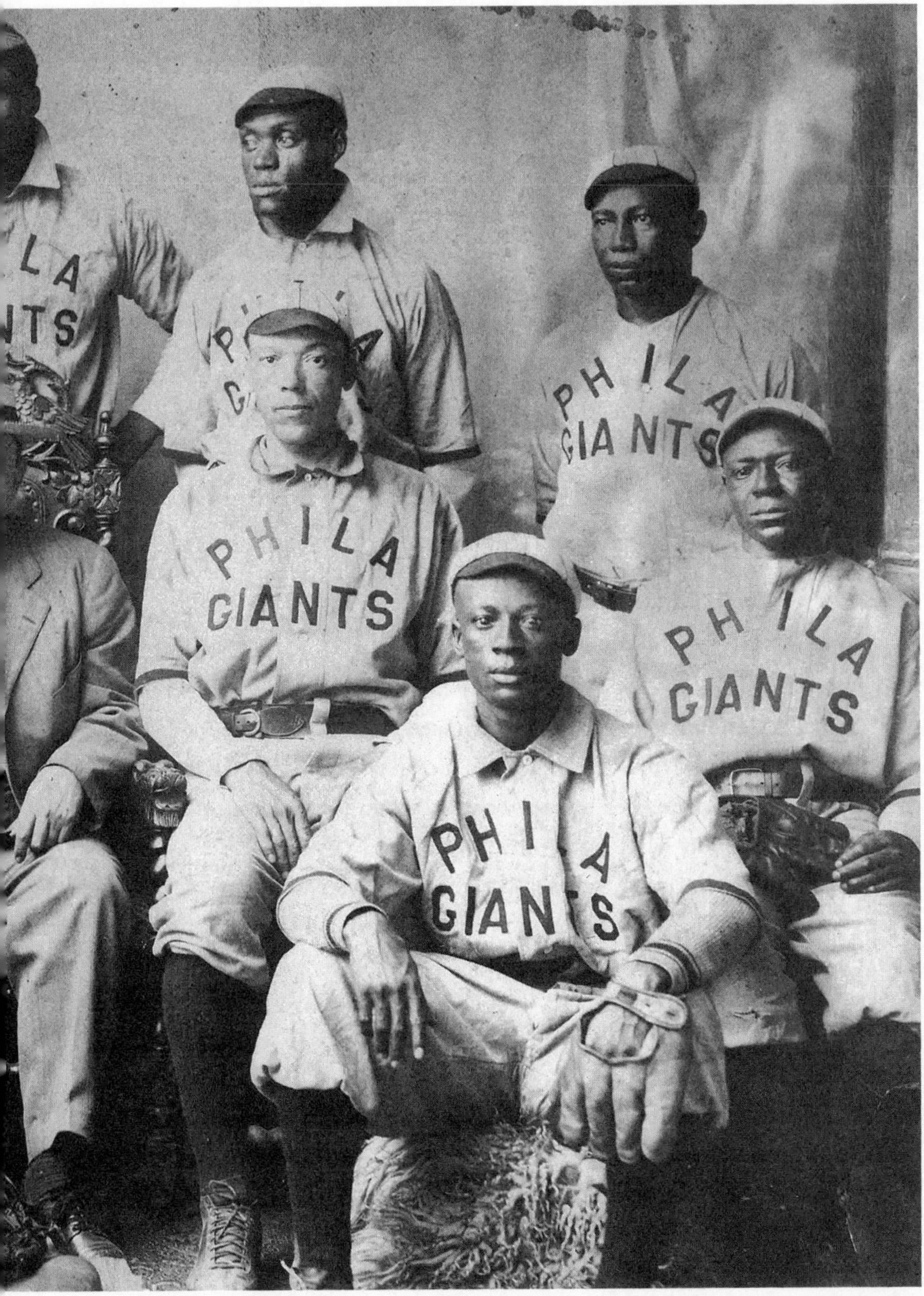

The Philadelphia Giants were the dominant Eastern black club in the early 1900s.

The Philadelphia Giants were made up of several prominent black baseball veterans and some upcoming young stars. Among the older players were catcher Clarence Williams, an original member of the Cuban Giants; his brother George, the team's shortstop; and the great Frank Grant at second. The pitching staff was bolstered by John Nelson and Charles "Kid" Carter. Nelson had played previously for the Cuban X Giants. Andrew "Jap" Payne began as a 19-year-old outfielder with the Giants, and in the next 17 years he developed a reputation as a player who could help a team in many ways.

The Giants were promoted along the same lines as the black independents of the late 19th century—a talented black club catering to a white clientele. They toured the states of Pennsylvania, New Jersey, and New York, and by the end of May had won 16 games and lost four. They also played in one of the first reported night games in baseball history. On June 3, the *Item* reported that the Giants would play John O' Rourke's Cosmopolitans under the lights at Columbia Park. The grounds were to be illuminated by "an engine mounted on a track on wheels, with detachable poles, wires, and lamps which [could] be put up and taken down in a few hours." Evidently, the fans were not amused by the spectacle. A reported 400 fans journeyed to Columbia Park and they "did not go crazy over the game." The six-inning contest was a fiasco, as both clubs committed 15 errors with the Giants winning 15–13.

Throughout their inaugural season the Giants issued several challenges to the Cuban X Giants for the "World's Colored Championship." Cubans magnate E. B. Lamar snubbed the upstarts, supposedly claiming the Philadelphia players had been "knocking" the X Giants, and if both clubs played in an actual game some of the Philadelphians would be "injured." A more plausible explanation is that since several of Lamar's former players played for the Quaker club, the Cuban X Giants' reputation would be tarnished if they lost the series.

By Ocober, the Philadelphia Giants had compiled an 81–43–2 win-loss-tie record. They culminated their opening season with a two-game series with the American League champion, the Philadelphia Athletics. Prior to the series, both teams were honored with a "big parade" to commemorate both clubs' successful seasons. Two hundred escorts and a brass band accompanied the clubs, and several of the city's leading politicians took part in the parade. The American League champions soundly beat the Giants in both games, however, 8–3 and 13–9.

In 1903, Sol White bolstered his club by acquiring Harry Buckner, William Binga, Robert Footes, and John Patterson. William Binga, who began his career with the Page Fence Giants, was regarded as one of the top third basemen in the black game. Veteran catcher Robert Footes had played previously with the Chicago Unions and the Chicago Union Giants. John Patterson, a versatile player who could play second base and the outfield, was a member of the Page Fence Giants in 1895, their founding year.

The 1903 season provides evidence of the Giants' ability to generate revenue, for the average attendance at Giants games was 2,722. Their largest reported attendance was in New York against the Murray Hill Club at Jasper Oval. Eight thousand fans witnessed a hard-hitting affair. Three runs in the bottom of the ninth resulted in a 14–13 Giants win.

In September the Philadelphians again challenged the Cuban X Giants for the "World's Colored Championship." Ten games were scheduled between the two clubs in New York, Philadelphia, and Harrisburg, although only five were played. In the first contest, the Cuban X Giants' star pitcher Rube Foster scattered six hits en route to a 4–2 victory at Columbia Park. On September 14, both clubs played a doubleheader at Ridgewood Park in New York. A reported crowd of 7,000 watched the Cubans win 8–1. In the second game, Philadelphia scored five runs in the fourth inning en route to a 5–2 victory. It was the Giants' only win, as the Cubans swept the final two games.

After their poor performance against the Cuban X Giants, White continued to strengthen his ball club. He lured pitching nemesis Rube Foster from the X Giants and added pitcher Danny McClellan, outfielder Pete Hill, and catcher George "Chappie" Johnson. At the same time, White signed a lease to play the Giants' home games at Broad Street and Jackson Avenue in the Quaker City. This move, no doubt, was predicated on the

Giants playing more games in Philadelphia to maximize revenues. They were no longer required to schedule home games around the Philadelphia Athletics' schedule.

One of the best pitchers in the early 20th century, southpaw Danny McClellan had a career that lasted nearly 30 years, spent mainly with the Philadelphia Stars. Though lacking an overpowering fastball, he relied on an assortment of off-speed curves. They served him well, because he's known best for throwing the first perfect game in black baseball history. In 1903 McClellan faced the minimum of 27 batters during a game against York, Pennsylvania of the Tri-State League.

The Philadelphia Giants scheduled tougher competition to establish their reputation as one of the best of black baseball's crack teams. In August, the All Cubans team from Cuba played the Giants in what was promoted as an "international contest." Kid Carter gave up seven hits en route to a 6–1 Giants victory. On August 17, a second game was scheduled between the two clubs. In a pitchers duel, All Cubans hurler José Munoz prevailed, 3–2.

In September 1904 the Philadelphia club again challenged the Cuban X Giants for the "World's Colored Championship," and a best-two-out-of-three series was scheduled in Atlantic City, New Jersey. In the first game, four thousand fans witnessed a spectacular performance. Rube Foster struck out 18 batters, scattered 7 hits, and defeated the Cubans, 8–4. Foster also collected three hits, including a triple, and scored one run. The Cuban X Giants turned the tables in game two behind Harry Buckner, 3–1. Rube Foster faced off against Dan McClellan in the rubber game for the Philadelphia Giants. The Cuban X Giants took a 2–0 lead into the fourth inning, but Foster struck out six batters and gave up only three hits for a 4–2 victory. According to the *Item*, the Philadelphia squad's defeat of the Cuban X Giants was a "big surprise even to their strongest admirers." An amusing moment occurred in the seventh inning. The X Giants catcher Clarence Williams deliberately ran into Sol White at first base, making him drop the ball. White chased him all the way to second, challenging him. When Williams turned around and put up his fists, Sol White promptly tagged him out.

The Quaker City club crowned their successful season with a final contest with the All Cubans team. The *Item* proudly proclaimed that the Giants "made good their claim for the colored championship" by defeating the All Cubans, 13–3. Foster out-pitched All Cubans ace José Munoz, striking out 14 batters and giving up only five hits. By the end of September, rumors circulated that the Giants had issued a challenge to play the American League New York Highlanders, who were in a close pennant race with the Boston Red Sox. The challenge went unanswered, however.

The Philadelphia Giants' defeat of the Cuban X Giants marked the start of a new era in black baseball in the East. The prestige brought on by becoming the colored champion resulted in the Giants' management team's desire to expand the club's market potential, both nationally and abroad. This aspiration occurred simultaneously with dramatic changes taking place in New York and in Cuba.

BLACK BALL IN BROOKLYN

In 1904, John W. Connors formed the Brooklyn Royal Giants, the first club in New York that was exclusively black-owned and black-operated since the early 1890s. Connors represented a new type of black entrepreneur who became involved in the management and ownership of black baseball teams. A migrant to Harlem from his native Portsmouth, Virginia, Connors personified the black middle class that began to emerge in the early 20th century. Between 1890 and 1920, segregation and discrimination were pivotal in the creation of a petit bourgeoisie of professional ,and businessmen relying primarily for their livelihood on the black masses. They were self-made men, of humble origins, and the majority of them were darker-skinned than the old upper class. They were also less likely to be descendents of antebellum house slaves or of free people of color. The new black elite formed an ambitious middle class, and the more successful among them achieved upper-class status before World War I.

It was no coincidence that black entrepreneurs within the ranks of the new black middle class would be attracted to the black baseball business. Black economist Abram L. Harris found that African-American business fell primarily within four main categories: amusement and recreation enterprises, real estate, retail trade, and personal service. Recreation and amusement enterprises such as professional baseball teams did not require a substantial financial investment and, if successfully managed, could yield a high return.

The Royal Giants began by playing the majority of their games in New York and New Jersey. For their first season Connor secured the services of Homerun Johnson from the Page Fence Giants to manage the club. By the next season the Brooklyn Royal Giants challenged the Philadelphia Giants for their colored championship. A three-game series was scheduled in Atlantic City, New Jersey. In the first game, 1,200 fans watched the Philadelphia Giants shut out the Royals, 2–0. The second game was tied at 6 in the ninth inning before the Royal Giants went down in defeat, 7–6. The Philadelphia Giants swept the series and defended their title for a second consecutive year, as Danny McClellan gave up 2 runs and 8 hits in a 7–2 victory. Yet despite losing the colored championship, Connors would become the first African-American owner from the East to transform a ball club from a stay-at-home to a touring team.

A changing business attitude toward baseball contributed to the rise of semiprofessional leagues and associations. Industrial supervisors responded to their workers' need to improve the quality of their lives not by altering the industrial system, but by adding recreation and other programs and services for their workforce. Two other factors contributed to this rise. Newly built trolley lines linking towns and neighborhoods led to more leagues in cities and suburbs. And under the influence of the Progressive Era's Playground Movement, city governments began to view organized recreation and sports as a good way to curb juvenile delinquency and "Americanize" immigrant children.

In 1906, approximately 100 clubs in New York and New Jersey formed the Intercity Association (IA). The IA's objectives were to secure better playing facilities, to induce park commissioners to lay out diamonds in various parks, and to develop better relations with police authorities regarding Sunday games, which were vital to semi-pro clubs. In order for a club to become eligible for entry into the Association, it had to be "regularly organized, officered, and uniformed."

The presence of the Intercity Association encouraged entrepreneurs to create a lucrative enterprise—booking semiprofessional games. The key to a booking agent's success was his ability to gain control of key ballparks. This control enabled the agent to schedule clubs he deemed most attractive to the public, generating the most revenue. The booking agent could also determine which clubs got the better dates—primarily Sundays and holidays—and charge a ten percent fee for his services. Ballpark control meant that a booking agent could make or break a semi-pro club by keeping a club either very busy or very idle.

NAT STRONG TWISTS ARMS

In New York, Nathaniel Colvin "Nat" Strong saw a promising opportunity booking semiprofessional games. He was a sporting-goods salesman by trade who had a previous track record in Negro league ball. One of his first successful teams was the Murray Hills club, who played the Philadelphia Giants in 1903. Strong owned the Ridgewoods baseball club, and he was also a member of the New York Athletic Club. In March 1907, Nat Strong became president of the Intercity Association.

This marked the start of Strong's 28-year reign as the booking power in New York. To be profitable, both black and white semiprofessional clubs had to deal with Strong to schedule games at the best parks and secure the best playing dates. This relatively small-time operator gained so much power because of his ties with Tammany Hall, in particular with Andrew Freedman, owner of the National League New York Giants from 1895 to 1901. As a close friend of Richard Croker, the machine's political boss, Freedman came into control of most of the suitable locations for baseball fields through leases or options.

John Henry "Pop" Lloyd

Greatest Player in the National Game

"Bacharach Manager Now Shares Honors with Speaker Lamb and Chas. Dressen" shouts the headline in a July, 24 1924 issue of the *Philadelphia Tribune*. An old John Henry "Pop" Lloyd had taken to the field and was surpassing even the feats of his youth. Lloyd exploded any preconceived notions of how old an athlete could be and still play great ball by banging out eleven straight hits. He proved in the later years of his career that a veteran player can tie a world's record. It's a record that young ballplayers are still striving to match .

John Henry Lloyd was, baseball historian Jim Riley tells us, a "complete player who could hit, run, field, throw and hit with power, especially in the clutch. He was a superlative fielder who studied batters and positioned himself wisely, got a good jump on the ball, and possessed exceptional range and sure hands with which he dug balls out of the dirt like a shovel." Honus Wagner said, "I am honored to have John Lloyd called the black Wagner. It is a privilege to be compared to him."

Pop Lloyd began his professional career in 1906 when Ed Lamar brought him to the Cuban X Giants. The next year he jumped to Sol White's champion Philadelphia Giants, and he would continually jump teams after that, staying only in Chicago for a four-year tenure with Rube Foster's American Giants, helping the Giants claim three Western championships and victories over the Eastern champions in 1914 and 1917. "Wherever the money was, that's where I was," Lloyd would say later in life.

When asked in 1949 at the dedication of the stadium named in his honor if he regretted that his playing days were long past before the color line in baseball was erased, "Pop" Lloyd replied: "I do not consider that I was born at the wrong time. I felt it was the right time, for I had the chance to prove the ability of our race in this sport, and because many of us did our very best to uphold the traditions of the game and of the world of sport, we have given the Negro a greater opportunity now to be accepted in the major leagues with other Americans."

John Henry Pop Lloyd was inducted into the National Baseball Hall of Fame in 1977.

Shortstop John Henry "Pop" Lloyd; considered by some to be one of the game's greatest.

Although his primary focus was on white semi-pro baseball, Strong was tempted by the ambitions of Sol White and H. Walter Schlichter in Philadelphia and of John Connors in Brooklyn to become involved in the scheduling of black baseball games as well. Inspired by the barnstorming tours of Cuban clubs, Strong saw an opportunity to expand his booking control even beyond American shores.

THE FIRST NEGRO LEAGUE

The 1906 season witnessed a virtual explosion of black independent clubs within a hundred-mile radius of New York, New Jersey, and Pennsylvania. Among the clubs that emerged were the Quaker Giants of New York, Wilmington Giants, New York Giants, Baltimore Giants of Newark, and Keystone Giants of Philadelphia. Adding to the expansion were Abel Linares' Cuban teams that had been touring the U.S. since 1903. According to Sol White, "of the many Cuban teams that have visited America, the strongest was the Cuban Stars of Santiago de Cuba. They were organized in 1905 and composed of all Cuban players." Several of these clubs, in conjunction with the established black teams—the Philadelphia Giants, Genuine Cuban Giants, Cuban X Giants, and Brooklyn Royal Giants—became members of the International League of Colored Baseball Clubs in America and Cuba (ILBCAC).

Formed by William Freihoffer and John O'Rourke, the culturally diverse ILBCAC—two black, two Cuban, and two white teams—began operation with six clubs: the Cuban X Giants, Philadelphia Quaker Giants, Cuban Stars, Havana Stars of Cuba, Philadelphia Professionals, and Riverton Palmyra; league offices were located in Philadelphia. Several ILBCAC games were scheduled on the playing grounds of the National League Phillies and the American League Athletics. In addition, these semi-pro clubs continued to play the bulk of their games against other independent teams outside of league play.

On July 24, 1906, the Philadelphia Giants and the Wilmington Giants replaced the Cuban Stars and the Philadelphia Quaker Giants as ILBCAC members.. The Philadelphia Giants and Wilmington Giants assumed the expelled clubs' place in the standings and their league schedule.

The Philadelphia Giants' entry into the ILBCAC coincided with the club enjoying another spectacular season. In early spring they embarked on their first extended barnstorming tour, traveling through western Pennsylvania, Ohio, and Illinois. Upon their return East, the Giants scheduled a series of games with the Brooklyn Royal Giants, building what would be a storied rivalry between the two clubs.

On May 31, the Royals played the Giants to a 0–0 tie, with "Pop" Andrews dueling Rube Foster to a standstill. On June 4, an 11-hit attack and three runs aided Foster in the top of the ninth inning en route to a 7–4 victory. A reported 10,000 fans witnessed the Giants defeat the Royals, 11–6, on August 26 at Washington Park in Brooklyn. The club finished the season with an impressive 108–31–6 win-loss-tie record.

At season's end, the Cuban X Giants played the Philadelphia club for the "World's Colored Championship." Simultaneously, both clubs played for the Freihoffer Cup to determine the winner of the ILBCAC pennant since both teams had finished the season with identical records. On September 3, the Giants defeated the Cubans and won the Freihoffer Cup, and three days later they played the Cubans for the colored championship. The Cubans scored three runs off Giants pitcher Danny McClellan in the fourth inning, before the Quaker City club tied the game in the seventh. Philadelphia scored two runs in the top of the ninth inning and defeated the Cubans 5–3, to lay claim again to the "World's Colored Championship."

H. Walter Schlichter then issued a challenge to the major league teams, calling for a best-two-out-of-three series to determine "who can play baseball the best—the white or black American." The Philadelphia Athletics evidently answered the challenge. Though Connie Mack's Athletics had a dismal season, finishing in fourth place in the American League, they boasted one of the game's finest pitching staffs in Eddie Plank, Charles "Chief" Bender, and the infamous George "Rube" Waddell. In the first game, the Athletics led 5-1 going into the ninth inning behind the excellent pitching of Plank. The Giants rallied with three runs in the bottom of the ninth before bowing in defeat, 5–4. In the second game, the Giants were no match for the eccentric Waddell. He pitched a two-hit shutout en route to a 5–0 win. Despite this disappointing series, the Philadelphia Giants had a spectacular season.

On October 22, 1906, the ILBCAC was joined by the National Association of Colored Baseball Clubs of the United States and Cuba (NACBC). Formed in Brooklyn, the organization included four of the top black baseball teams in the East: the Philadelphia Giants, Cuban X Giants, Brooklyn Royal Giants, and the Cuban Stars. A primary objective of the Association was to safeguard "the property rights of those engaged in colored baseball as a business, without sacrificing the spirit of competition in the conduct of the game." In other words, the member clubs meant to prevent players from jumping to new teams every time they were offered a new salary. This move would immediately backfire because players could still jump to teams outside of the NACBC, such as the new Giants in Chicago.

THE LELANDS BECOME GIANTS

From 1902 to 1906 black baseball in Chicago underwent a period of decline and reorganization. With the dismantling of the Columbia Giants, Frank Leland's split with William Peters left two black clubs, the Chicago Unions and the Chicago Union Giants, operating in the Windy City in very different ways.

William Peters operated his Unions as a traveling team and maintained his association with white semiprofessional organizations. On April 7, 1903, the *Inter Ocean* reported that Peters was named treasurer of the Amateur Managers' Baseball League. Two years later, Peters renamed his club the Union Giants, and they won a reported 112 out of 122 games. Yet they never regained their prominence of the mid- and late 1890s. Peters seemed content to operate a traveling team and pass the hat to meet expenses.

Frank Leland, on the other hand, moved his club to Auburn Park on

A booklet promoting the Leland Giants, Rube Foster's first Chicago team.

79th Street and Wentworth Avenue, and made efforts to develop a local fan base. In September 1904, the Leland's Union Giants played J. M. Bright's Cuban Giants for the "Colored World's Series." A best-two-out-of-three series was scheduled at Auburn Park, where the Cuban Giants swept the first two games, winning the Colored World Series. In 1905, Leland renamed his club the Leland Giants.

The rise of the Leland Giants coincided with the breakup of the Philadelphia Giants. Despite their phenomenal success on the field, several players on the Philadelphia team were unhappy with the salaries they received. Following Rube Foster's lead, they left the Quaker City club and traveled to Chicago to join the Leland Giants. As a result the Leland Giants emerged as the premier black baseball club in the Midwest.

The Leland Giants' rise to power was due primarily to the efforts of one man—Andrew "Rube" Foster. His ascendancy as both their manager and booking agent marked the start of his dominance of black baseball in the Midwest. Foster was born in Calvert, Texas, in 1879, the son of a presiding elder of Calvert's Methodist Church. Devoutly religious, Foster neither drank nor allowed anyone to consume spirits in his household, but he did tolerate

Giant of the Deadball Era

A left-handed batter, Pete Hill was the first great outfielder in black baseball history. He could hit both lefthanders and righthanders equally well, and he became the backbone of the great Chicago American Giants teams for Rube Foster. Credited with a perfect eye for the strike zone, he was later called the "most consistent hitter of his lifetime" by Cum Posey, owner of the Homestead Grays. He was a contact hitter who sprayed line drives to all fields. At six-foot-one and 215 pounds, he also hit for power, often leading the league in triples during an age when home runs were still counted in single digits. Available statistics show that he hit .423 in 1910, .400 in 1911, .357 in 1912, and .302 in 1913, for a .371 during those four years. In the Cuban Winter League he batted .343 in 1908, he led the league in hitting in 1910–11 with a mark of .365, and he hit .373 in 1916–17. As the cleanup hitter for the Detroit Stars in 1921, he batted .391. Baseball historian Jim Riley has said that if an all-star team was picked from the Deadball Era, Pete Hill would have been flanked in the outfield by Ty Cobb and Tris Speaker.

Pete Hill was also a terrific defensive player, a center fielder with exceptional range and a deadly throwing arm. His great speed made him a terror on the base paths, and he was described as a "restless type, always in motion, jumping back and forth, trying to draw a throw from the pitcher." He would learn the tricks of managing a ball club from Rube Foster, and go on to manage the Detroit Stars and later the Baltimore Black Sox.

Ben Taylor, himself an outstanding hitter, said of Pete Hill: "The time was he was numbered among the greatest in the game, and will probably never have an equal as a hitter. I think he is the most dangerous man in a pinch in baseball."

it in others. Foster exhibited his organizational skills at a young age, operating a baseball team while in grade school. He left school in the eighth grade to pursue a career in baseball. By 1897 Andrew Foster was pitching for the Waco Yellow Jackets, a traveling team that toured Texas and the bordering states. In the spring of 1902, William Peters invited him to join the Chicago

Unions, but since he sent no travel money, Foster remained in Texas. Simultaneously, Frank Leland invited Foster to join the Chicago Union Giants, initiating a stormy relationship between the two men. By mid-spring, Foster quit the Union Giants to join a white semi-pro team in Michigan. When its season ended, he headed east to play for the Cuban X Giants.

From 1904 to 1906 Foster played for the Philadelphia Giants. Prior to the start of the 1907 season, he traveled to Cuba to play for the Fe club. Upon his return to the States, Foster led the players' revolt that resulted in five players leaving the Giants. Foster and teammate Pete Hill considered themselves grossly underpaid. According to Foster, "The whole team was making only $100 out of Sunday games and a proportionate amount for other games. In spite of the fact that we were the best colored team in baseball, that was all Walter Schlichter, the owner, could or would do for us." At the same time, the organizers of the National Association of Colored Baseball Clubs of the United States and Cuba (NABC) attempted to impose salary limits upon the players. As a result, Foster and four other stars left the Giants and traveled to Chicago.

Upon becoming the manager of the Leland Giants, Foster's first move was to release the players of the previous year, despite Leland's opposition. Foster wanted his own players, and he had just brought four from one of the best black teams ever assembled. Leland's failing health and his responsibilities as the newly elected Cook County commissioner led to Foster assuming control of booking the team's games. He immediately established a business arrangement whereby either gate receipts would be divided in half or he would ensure a substantial guarantee to attract the top teams.

The 1907 season marked the beginning of a barnstorming schedule that would be Rube Foster's trademark for the next decade. On February 20, the Indianapolis *Freeman* reported that the Leland Giants would embark on a spring training tour. They played white semi-pro clubs in Milwaukee, Chicago, and Joliet, Illinois, leading the paper to state that the Lelands were "about to break that strong barrier of race prejudice."

The Leland Giants benefited from the rise of several top white semi-pro clubs in the Windy City. Rivalries began to emerge with the Logan

Squares, Adrian Anson's Colts, and Jake Stahl's South Chicagos. At the same time, several black baseball clubs from the South barnstormed the Midwest during the regular season. The Louisville Giants and Birmingham Giants, for example, made Chicago part of their travel itinerary. On July 6, 1907, the *Broad Ax* reported that the Lelands would play the Louisville Giants in a two-game series, and a $500 side bet was placed on the games. The Leland Giants swept the series.

Concurrently, Frank Leland made his only attempt to organize a black professional league. On November 9, 1907, the Indianapolis *Freeman* reported a movement to form the National Colored League of Professional Ball Clubs. The circuit was to be a 13-team league spread across the Midwest. Despite these organizers' efforts, though, the league died without a pitch being thrown. Essentially, two factors led to its downfall. First was the lack of commitment by black baseball owners. According to the *Freeman*, only Chicago and Indianapolis made firm commitments. Also, several black baseball magnates feared the league would damage their business. Operating in a league format could lead to losing lucrative games with black and white semi-pro clubs within their respective region.

In lieu of playing within a black professional league, the Leland Giants launched a spectacular touring schedule. On May 15, 1909, the Indianapolis *Freeman* reported that Frank Leland's club traveled 4,465 miles playing black and white teams. Rube Foster received a hero's welcome upon his return to his home state of Texas. His reception in Fort Worth would "have done honor to the President of the United States." In Houston, the Lelands played to the "largest crowd ever at a baseball game" in that city, as the Giants swept the Texas club in three games.

A large contingent from Foster's hometown of Calvert attended one of the games. Like the Page Fence Giants before them, the Leland Giants traveled in the luxury of a Pullman sleeper, thus avoiding the prejudice of white hotel managers in the South.

The Windy City's semi-pro baseball season was notable for the long-awaited return of a formal Chicago City League, with six teams. On September 4, the Lelands clinched the City League pennant with a 5–3 win

Joe Tinker Learns a Lesson

Once when the old Chicago Cubs were champions, they played a post-season game against a colored team and had their hands full. They could not hit the pitching, and some of them "got after" their opponents who responded with good-natured ridicule of the champs. Tinker was playing a little "goat getting," and the mascot of the team, a black little fellow, was laughing at him. Tinker thoughtlessly turned around and called him "Nigger." At that moment one of the Negro players stepped up and said very quietly: "Mister Tinker, that child that you called 'nigger' is my wife's baby."

He said it with such feeling and earnestness that Tinker, in a flash, was ashamed, and turning he grasped the man's hand and said:

"I'm sorry I said that."

Tinker tells the story on himself, and adds that his respect for colored men has been greater since that time than ever before.

—Hugh Fullerton,
New York Age, January 11, 1919

over the Logan Squares. They finished the season with 31 wins and 9 losses. The Giants' pennant-winning season led a *Chicago Tribune* sportswriter to state, "While undoubtedly it is galling to many persons to see a colored nine take honors from five white teams, the Leland Giants are entitled to a place in the league by their drawing powers." The writer went on to describe how the Lelands had such talent that "at least five of them would be in the major leagues if white."

The Leland Giants culminated their 1909 season with a three-game series with the National League Chicago Cubs. The North Side contingent was the best team in the National League, winning the pennant three years in a row and finishing second in 1909. They had won a major league record 116 games in 1906. From 1906 to 1909, the Chicago Cubs won 426 games. They possessed the legendary double play combination of Joe Tinker, Johnny Evers, and Frank Chance, and boasted an outstanding pitching staff that included Mordecai "Three Finger" Brown and Ed Reulbach.

The Leland Giants and Chicago Cubs played three tightly contested games. In game one, 2,344 fans watched the Cubs defeat the Lelands, 4–1, behind the excellent pitching of Three Finger Brown. In the second game, the Lelands took a 5–2 lead into the ninth inning before the Cubs scored four runs and won 6–5. The game ended on a controversial play when Rube Foster, trying to slow down the Cubs' momentum, left the mound to consult with pitcher Pat Dougherty to determine whether the latter should relieve. This obvious stalling tactic irritated the Cubs and the home plate umpire, and when Dougherty approached the mound, the ump refused to let him enter the game. Amid the confusion Cubs right fielder Frank "Wildfire" Schulte stole home and was called safe, to the dismay of Foster and the Lelands. The final game, a tight pitchers duel between Three Finger Brown and Pat Dougherty, was called in the seventh inning because of darkness, with the Cubs ahead, 1–0.

In spite of losing the series, the Leland Giants had made tremendous progress. Yet, as was so common in those rough-and-tumble days, an ownership dispute between Frank Leland and his business partners led to his being forced out. In response, Leland formed the Chicago Leland Giants, and proceeded to raid his old club for players. His former club then took Leland to court to prohibit him from using the name Leland Giants, and the Chicago Leland Giants became the Chicago Giants. To further complicate matters, the Chicago City League issued a ban prohibiting the scheduling of games with black and Cuban clubs. The reason given by the City League was that local patrons complained about the lack of contests being scheduled between local clubs. That meant the Giants couldn't play any of the NACBC clubs traveling to Chicago. That would lead to Leland dropping out of the Chicago City League. Two years later he died at the age of 45. Joe Green, the Giants' shortstop, reorganized the team, and from 1913 until the formation of the Negro Leagues, they were the top black stay-at-home team in the Chicago area.

Beauregard Moseley, the Leland Giants' new owner, had higher ambitions in mind. Despite Leland's raiding his old club for players, the Leland Giants remained a competitive club. Foster secured the services of top

Leftfielder Willis Jones played for the Chicago Union Giants in 1911.

players, including Pete Hill, John Henry Lloyd, Pete Booker, Bruce Petway, and Andrew "Jap" Payne. Booker and Petway were both catchers, but the husky Booker, although an outstanding receiver, moved to first base to make way for Petway's exceptional skills. His arm was so strong that he had runners "hugging the bases." For example, playing in Cuba, he threw out Ty Cobb three times in three attempts in 1910.

Rube Foster's picks for pitchers were equally strong. Frank Wickware, Pat Dougherty, and Foster made the Giants' staff awesome. In October 1910, after winning 20 straight games in the East and Midwest, the Leland Giants made their first trip to Cuba. Along with the American League Detroit Tigers, the Lelands played the top Cuban clubs, including the Havanas and the Alemendares.

Moseley advocated the need for blacks to organize their own professional league. He recognized that the raiding of player rosters was a destructive force that had to be eliminated, and that the possibility of a color ban, with white semi-pro clubs refusing to schedule games with black teams, threatened their ability to generate revenue.

The prospective members first met on December 30, 1910. Eight cities were represented: Chicago; New Orleans; Mobile; Louisville; St. Louis; Columbus, Ohio; Kansas City, Missouri; and Kansas City, Kansas. The league generated a lot of enthusiasm the following year and rumors persisted of other cities joining the loop, but it died stillborn.

In 1911, Foster would split with Moseley and form the Chicago American Giants. It was not clear what led Foster to make a break, but both the color ban and two failed attempts to form a league appear to be factors. With this important move, black baseball in Chicago was about to enter a new, more long-lasting period of reorganization.

THE CUBAN CONNECTION

In 1907 and 1908, the National Association of Colored Baseball Clubs of the United States and Cuba extended its booking network to the Midwest and internationally to Cuba. On May 20, 1907, the All-Havana baseball club, responding to the resurgence of semi-professional baseball in Chicago, invaded the Windy City to play the top white semi-pro teams. The All-Havanas typified the type of baseball club that played during the Deadball Era. Pitching, defense, base running, and timely hitting were the keys to the Cuban club's success. They were led by their shortstop Luis Bustamente, considered one of the greatest Cuban players of the first two decades of the 20th century. Nicknamed "The Eel," he was regarded by Sol White as the best shortstop of his era. John McGraw called him a "perfect shortstop." A strong defender, known for his quick feet, he also had a powerful throwing arm. Rafael Almeida, the Havana's catcher, demonstrated good speed and average power, and he would later play three seasons with the Cincinnati Reds.

The All-Havanas performed admirably against Chicago's white semi-pro clubs. On May 30, they easily defeated the Logan Squares, 6–1. On June 8, the Havanas squared off against Anson's Colts, winning a fourteen-inning contest, 7–5. Of the five games reported in the press, the All-Havanas won three of them. As the *Tribune* astutely noted, the All-Havanas demonstrated "that baseball [was] no joke in Cuba."

The Philadelphia Giants would test that judgment in October 1907 on their first and only tour of the Cuban island. Despite losing several players to the Leland Giants, Sol White managed to field a competitive team for the fifth straight year, with the addition of stellar shortstop John Henry Lloyd from the Cuban X Giants. Often referred to as the black Honus Wagner, Lloyd was the complete ballplayer who could both throw and hit with power, especially in the clutch. He was a superb defensive player with exceptional range and good hands. Lloyd's defensive skills earned him the nickname "El Cuchara" in Cuba (The Tablespoon).

The Philadelphia Giants' tour of Cuba exemplified the NACBC's efforts to centralize the scheduling of games among their elected officials. Ironically, founding father Sol White did not accompany his Giants to Cuba. According to the *Philadelphia Item*, the Giants were under the management of E. B. Lamar, and Clarence Williams managed the team.

The Giants played the majority of their games against the Almendares Blues and the Havana Reds. The Blues team was Cuba's marquee club, led by José Munoz. Referred to as "the premier pitcher of Cuba," Munoz possessed a good fastball and a screwball with pinpoint control. When he was not pitching, the Cuban hurler exhibited his athletic prowess by playing in the outfield and batting second or fifth in the batting order. Armando Marsans, the Almendares' star player, played several positions and was touted as "the Cuban answer to Ty Cobb." Marsans would also play for the Cincinnati Reds. The Havana Reds, on the other hand, was the same team that played as the All-Havanas in the United States.

The Philadelphia Giants got off to a slow start. In their opening game against the Almendares, José Munoz held the Giants to four hits and shut them out, 6–0. The Blues went on to defeat the Giants the next three times they played. On November 7, the Giants finally prevailed against the Blues, 8–2, and from that point on, the Giants won four out of the next five games. However, out of the twelve games reported in the press, the Almendares won six, lost five, and tied one.

The Havana Reds were equally as tough. After losing their first two games to the Giants, the Reds won six straight games. Each match was closely contested. For example, on December 29 the score was tied at six going into the ninth inning when the Reds scored three runs in the top of the frame. The Giants scored two runs in the bottom of the inning, and with a man on third and two outs, Andrew "Jap" Payne stepped to the plate. Payne grounded out hard to Bustamente at short and the Giants lost, 9–8. Overall, the Giants knotted their series with Havana at six games each. If any more proof was needed, the Almendares Blues' and the Havana Reds' performance against the Philadelphia Giants illustrated that Cuban baseball was on par with the black game in the U.S.

In 1908 the NACBC sent three of its teams to the Midwest—the All-Havanas, the Cuban Giants, and the Philadelphia Giants. First to go was the All-Havanas. On May 30 they embarked upon their second tour of the Midwest. The tour marked the debut of Cuba's legendary pitcher José Mendez. Also known as the "Black Diamond," Mendez began his baseball career at age 16. Five years later he was pitching for Havana, and in his first game in the U.S., he shut out the Brooklyn Royal Giants, 3–0. On June 2, the *Tribune* reported that the All-Havanas played the "first game in the series for the colored baseball championship" against the Leland Giants. The Lelands took a 5–3 lead into the eighth inning before the Cuban club erupted with three runs in the eighth and two in the ninth, winning 8–7. However, the Lelands won the next five games and took the series, five games to two.

In July, J. M. Bright's Cuban Giants made their way to the Windy City. The first game set the tone for the series. Rube Foster squared off against John Nelson, and the Lelands' manager took a 2–1 lead into the fifth inning. The Lelands went on to score three runs in the sixth, four in the seventh, and six in the eighth, winning in a rout, 15–3. From that time on, the Cuban Giants were listless as they proceeded to lose the next four games.

On July 27, the Philadelphia Giants began a controversial seven-game series with the Leland Giants for black baseball supremacy. The Lelands hit Giants pitcher Danny McClellan early and often, and won 6–4. The Philadelphia Giants evened the series at one game each with a 5–4 win that took eleven innings to complete. The third game was a pitchers duel, tied at two going into the ninth inning when Leland's catcher Pete Booker singled and came home two singles later with the winning run. The Lelands crushed the Giants in the fourth game, 11–1, and took a 3–1 lead in the series.

The Philadelphia Giants rallied to stay alive. In game five, the Giants knocked Rube Foster out of the box, taking an early 6–2 lead and winning easily, 8–2. John Henry Lloyd led the Giants to victory in game six. He rapped two hits, one of them a double, batted in two runs, and scored three runs en route to a 7–4 victory. The seventh game evidently was not played. It was unclear why both clubs chose not to complete the series. It was apparent that bad blood still existed between the two clubs following Foster's defection from the Giants in 1907. When the Quaker club tied the series, Foster and White could have let their personal animosity toward each other cloud their business judgment.

DECLINE OF THE NACBC

While the evidence is limited, it appears that the International League of Colored Baseball Clubs in America and Cuba was absorbed into the NACBC, since the same clubs that made up the ILBCAC were also NACBC members. League clubs played in the ILBCAC in the East, while they functioned under the umbrella of the NACBC during their barnstorming tours in the Midwest and Cuba.

With scheduling in the hands of NACBC treasurer Nat Strong, Sol White became disgruntled in his diminished role as co-owner and manager of the Philadelphia Giants. Phenomenal success on the field and elevation to the ranks of a touring team were apparently not enough to offset his loss of control. Nothing illustrated this fact better than the Giants' tour of Cuba. E. B. Lamar and Clarence Williams running the club on the Cuban island must have irritated White. After all, it was White who transformed the Philadelphia club into one of the top black clubs in the U.S. He had managed to keep a nucleus of star players together, and had created a demand for his club by barnstorming the Midwest prior to the NACBC's formation.

Joe Williams
The Daddy of Them All

Longtime black baseball executive Frank Leland knew talent when he saw it. At the outset of Joe Williams' rookie season in the big time he alerted Chicago fans as to what to expect from their new right hander: "If you have ever witnessed the speed of a pebble in a storm you have not even seen the speed possessed by this wonderful Texan Giant. He is the king of all pitchers hailing from the Lone Star state and you have but to see him once to exclaim, that's a-plenty."

Historian Jim Riley points to three performances against major league clubs as showcasing the exceptional talent of this pitcher. In 1912, Williams shut out the world champion New York Giants, 6–0. In a second matchup, in 1915, he struck out 10 batters while throwing a three-hit shutout against Grover Cleveland Alexander and the Philadelphia Phillies, winning by a score of 1–0. In a third showcase performance, in 1917, he recorded 20 strikeouts in a no-hitter against the New York Giants (he lost the game 1–0 on an error).

His remarkable dominance of major league opposition lasted well beyond the normal span of years. In 1926, pitching for the Homestead Grays in what should have been the waning years of a great career, the 50-year-old wonder, the great veteran, the daddy of them all, pitched successive shutout victories over a team of major league all-stars in a post-season exhibition series. The big league squad included such future Hall of Famers as Heinie Manush, Harry Heilmann and Jimmie Foxx in its lineup.

That same year, Jim Keenan, involved in amateur and professional baseball for more than 25 years, 15 as owner of the Lincoln Giants, would say that the greatest pitching duel he ever witnessed was when the "Big Train" (Walter Johnson) bested "Smokey Joe" by a score of 1–0.

Williams was to the first half of black baseball what Satchel Paige was to the second, the dominant pitcher of his age. A 1952 poll of Negro baseball insiders by the *Pittsburgh Courier* gave Williams the nod over Paige by a 20 to 19 vote as the best of all time, which makes the long wait for his induction into the National Baseball Hall of Fame puzzling. Paige entered Cooperstown in 1973 as the first Negro League inductee, while Smokey Joe had to wait until 1999 to posthumously receive his due.

Smokey Joe was in his prime when he wore a Giants uniform in the early 1910s.

On April 8, 1909, the *New York Age* reported that White had officially broken with Schlichter to become the owner and manager of the Quaker Giants. Controversy arose when the ILBCAC allegedly agreed not to schedule games with White's new team. According to the *Age*, Strong supposedly told White that booking dates were not available to him. In response, White visited the various park managers in New York City and presumably received promises that they would schedule the Quaker Giants regardless of the ILBCAC's objection.

The effort to exclude White's Quaker Giants from playing ILBCAC clubs illustrated how Nat Strong benefited from the NACBC's attempt to centralize power. According to African-American sportswriter Doc Lambert, Strong refused to play his Ridgewood or Murray Hill team in other parks unless he received 35 to 40 percent of the gate receipts, or a substantial guarantee. Conversely, black clubs received no more than $500 for any game.

Operating in the nation's largest baseball market provided Strong with considerable leverage. Tapping into the New York market was one reason why Walter Schlichter sought an alliance with Strong in the first place. However, black baseball clubs had to make concessions that white clubs never did.

White also attempted to persuade Brooklyn Royal Giants owner John Connors to withdraw from the ILBCAC. At first Connors was reluctant, but by July the *Age* reported that the Royals' owner believed his team was not being given proper consideration in regards to booking dates. White tried to convince Connor, Pop Watkins, and J. M. Bright to form a new association. Bright was also at odds with Strong, resulting in the Cubans' magnate booking his own games. As a result the NACBC was split into two warring factions.

The division within the NACBC did not hinder their barnstorming, however. The Cuban Stars embarked upon a three-month tour of Indiana, Kentucky, Illinois, and Wisconsin, with the majority of their games played against Chicago's top semiprofessional clubs. Stars manager E. B. Lamar had assembled a talented Cuban team, led by their dazzling pitching combo—José Munoz and José Mendez—that could compete against any major league club in the deadball era.

How a Cyclone Starts

Smokey Joe Williams threw such a hard fastball that even the legendary Rube Foster was astonished. After the first time Williams faced Chicago, Foster told him, "Slow down there."

"Do you really want me to throw hard?" Joe asked. "If I really throw hard, you won't see it at all."

"What's your name, boy?" Rube asked.

"Just call me Cyclone."

On August 24, the *Chicago Tribune* reported that the Cuban Stars were "ordered" to return east. Upon their return, the Stars were challenged by John Connors' Brooklyn Royal Giants for black baseball supremacy in the East. Connors, along with manager Homerun Johnson, assembled the strongest Royal Giants team in its brief history. A best-three-out-five series was scheduled on consecutive weekends throughout the various parks in New York City controlled by the NACBC. A reported crowd of 6,000 fans packed Bronx Oval to watch Frank Earle outduel Stars' pitcher Luis Padron, 5–3. In the second game, Earle defeated José Mendez, 2–1, despite the latter striking out ten Royals batters. Padron prevailed in the third game with a 4–2 victory, but the reprieve was short-lived. Earle triumphed for the third time with a 5–3 win over Padron, and the Royal Giants won the series.

TUMULTUOUS SEASONS

Internal conflict continued to plague NACBC teams during the 1910 season. Typical of the manager of black teams of that era, Royals skipper Grant Johnson's responsibilities included locating and developing player talent, creating a demand for his club in different locales, and working at maintaining a good business relationship with white semiprofessional teams. After the Royals' winter tour of Florida, where they competed against the Leland Giants, each team winning three and tying two, manager Johnson sought a partnership with Connors but was refused. As Connors explained: "For the last two years I have spent thousands of dollars trying to furnish New York with a champion team, and did not think that I should give any one interest at this time." Charging that Johnson had encouraged other players to leave the club, Connors attempted to "trade" his manager to the Philadelphia Giants for John Henry Lloyd, but was unsuccessful. As a result of all these maneuverings, Johnson left the Royals and signed with the Leland Giants. Connors, nevertheless, was able to keep a strong team together, and to replace Johnson, Connors named Sol White as the Royals' new manager.

Another wedge emerged that spring within the NACBC's ownership ranks. On May 5, 1910, the *Age* reported that the Leland Giants and the Cuban Giants had been expelled by the NACBC. In other words, the association would refuse to schedule games with these clubs, and the NACBC would use its influence to ensure that neither club would get the best playing dates with top level semipro teams. The Lelands' expulsion was undoubtedly in response to signing Grant Johnson. To add insult to injury, Rube Foster lured John Henry Lloyd from the Philadelphia Giants. According to the *Age*, Lloyd did not want to play anymore with the Quaker club, and had been contemplating going to Chicago anyway. Since one of the NACBC's broad objectives was to impose salary limits and minimize player movement, the Leland Giants' expulsion was predictable. The Cuban Giants' banishment, on the other hand, was probably due to J. M. Bright falling into disfavor the previous year when he began to book his own games.

In the midst of this turmoil, the NACBC managed to send two of its member clubs on their annual Midwestern barnstorming tour. The Cuban Stars and the Philadelphia Giants made their third consecutive tour of the Midwest. Of the 37 games reported in the press, the Stars won 23 of them. Conversely, the Philadelphia Giants performed poorly. Once the centerpiece of the NACBC, the Giants' fall from prominence was swift.

As the season moved along, tumult continued. By the end of the year, Sol White broke with John Connors, and along with Roderick "Jess" McMahon, a white sports promoter, he formed the Lincoln Giants. White lured stars such as Danny McClellan, Pete Booker, John Henry Lloyd, and

Spotswood "Spot" Poles, making the Lincolns a powerful club from the outset. Along with his brother, Ed, McMahon secured a lease on Olympic Field, and pointed out that they would not give a percentage to anyone to book their games. The latter assertion was obviously directed at Nat Strong.

Spotswood Poles was a small, swift player who began with the Philadelphia Giants in 1909 at the age of 19. He would go on to roam the Lincoln Giants' center field for the next ten years. Teammate Sam Streeter claimed that Poles could outrun "Cool Papa" Bell, regarded as the fastest player ever on the Negro leagues base paths. Poles was a line-drive hitter, racking up such remarkable averages as his reported .440 in 1911, followed by .398, .414, and an eye-popping .487. He rates as a big reason that the Lincoln Giants are regarded as one of the best teams in blackball history.

Despite losing several of his best players, Connors maintained a competitive club and concurrently elevated his Royals to the ranks of a touring team. The Royal Giants barnstormed the South and Midwest from April to mid-May, playing a total of 46 games and winning 43. On July 20, 1911, Connor secured a five-year lease on Harlem Oval, located at 142nd Street and Lenox Avenue. He began renovations by covering the grandstand and expanding the seating capacity to handle 2,600 people. In addition to booking games, Connors envisioned sponsoring athletic events "conducted under the auspices of colored athletic organizations." According to the *Age*, the deal marked the first time in the history of New York City that a Negro had complete possession of an "up-to-date ball grounds." It was, for all the turmoil he had faced, John Connors' finest house in black baseball.

The formation of the Lincoln Giants and Connors' lease on Harlem Oval ended the NACBC's booking control, and the organization began to unravel. J. M. Bright had continued to book his own games after leaving the association the previous year. On August 3, the *Age* reported that the Philadelphia Giants had disbanded. Rumors circulated that E. B. Lamar would book games for the Royal Giants. On August 10, the *Age* reported that Nat Strong would represent the Cuban Stars in arranging a five-game series with the Lincoln Giants for the colored championship.

The collapse of the NACBC resulted in a scramble the next year. Cogan's Smart Set, a black team representing Paterson, New Jersey, signed several players from the Lincoln Giants. In May, Spot Poles had become disgruntled and jumped to the Royal Giants. Players jumping their contracts also took a toll on J. M. Bright's Cuban Giants, which disbanded at the end of the season.

The tumultuous 1912 season left a bitter taste in John Connors' mouth. It must have been of some comfort when the *Age*'s Lester Walton came to his defense when rumors circulated about an attempt by white owners to control all New York black clubs by forcing Connors to accept a flat guarantee instead of sharing gate receipts "The *Age* does not believe," Walton intoned, "that colored baseball fans should loyally support teams because they are managed by colored men." However, those fans "should resent any attempt to put a colored manager out of business. To see Manager John W. Connor get the worst of a raw deal would not only be a rank injustice to him, but a gross piece of discourtesy to the colored fans." But dealing with players threatening to jump their contracts, the substantial investment to renovate Harlem Oval, and white owners compelling him to accept a flat guarantee was more than Connors could endure. On July 19, 1913, the *Age* reported a transfer in the ownership of the Brooklyn Royal Giants to a contingent headed by Nat Strong. Temporarily, John W. Connors was out of black baseball.

The next domino to fall was the Lincoln Giants. The McMahons had overextended themselves with business ventures that did not pan out, and revenue generated by the Lincolns was used to cover the McMahons' debts in their other endeavors. By the end of the 1912 season, they had lost their lease on Olympic Field. In September 1913, Nat Strong announced he would book no more games with the Lincoln Giants until he got the money owed from previous games. The McMahons' bad debts resulted in a transition of ownership of the Lincoln Giants baseball club. James J. Keenan, a white sports promoter, along with Charles Harvey, secured controlling interest of the Lincolns and Olympic Field. From then on black baseball clubs in New York City would remain under white control until the collapse of the Negro leagues in 1931.

If falling baseball dominoes seemed the rule at the outset of the decade of the 1910s, much had been attempted and much learned in the years since the turn of the century that would have important consequences for the future of the black game. What had been at the outset of the period a game played by local teams that mostly toured in their own geographic areas became, in these decades of the growth of independent clubs, a commercialized amusement with professional teams in major black population centers developing their own local fan base, traveling widely outside their own regions, securing extraordinary talent, internationalizing the game with the addition of a Cuban element, and beginning to dominate the sports pages in nationally circulating weekly newspapers. Efforts undertaken during this period to build strong teams, and organize into leagues, would blossom into new realities for blackball in the mid-1910s and 1920s.

Frank Wickware, the "Red Ant," was a righthander with a blazing fastball.

Organized League Ball

The national game was put in disfavor by the narrow ignorance of leading people all over the country who believed baseball was a game to be patronized only by the sporting element and not fit for their girls and boys to see. The caliber of the players, the training they received had much to do with encouraging this idea. I came up under these conditions. I made baseball a profession, later a business. I have wiped away much of that prejudice, so much so that I know of no men who have not felt it as much an honor to meet me as I have felt it an honor to meet them, from the most prominent men in the churches to our greatest educators and college professors. They have been my staunchest friends. Their homes are open to me, and mine is to them.

—Andrew "Rube" Foster, 1921

The rise of black professional baseball teams in the early 20th century coincided with increased migration, and the institutional racism that contributed to the development of black business districts in American cities. The most significant event was the Great Migration in which African Americans in the South moved to large industrial centers in the North. Dramatically growing populations concentrated in segregated areas led to the growth of black business districts on major streets in the urban centers where the migrants located.

As black businesses increased, an array of new enterprises developed. With the increasing urbanization of African Americans in racial ghettoes, black business activity became more a part of a separate black economy. Yet enterprises owned by native whites and immigrants were located in black business districts, and these businesses, in what is called an economic detour, procured most of the black consumer dollars that came essentially from wages paid by whites.

Black baseball teams exemplified this complex economic development in the early 20th century. Black baseball entrepreneurs still maintained their symbiotic business relationship with white semiprofessional teams. They still had to negotiate with white park managers to gain access to ballparks that had easy access to city transit. By 1915 the leading black baseball teams in New York City were white-owned and operated. To establish his foundation for his booking control in the Midwest, Rube Foster took on a white partner who provided him with a ballpark accessible to the black community. Because of these circumstances black baseball entrepreneurs operated as businessmen first and "Race men" second.

Still, migration brought about one significant change. Prior to this time, black baseball clubs played for essentially a white clientele. The rise of black enclaves in the North, however, was too important for blackball to ignore. A new generation of both black and white baseball entrepreneurs would attempt to tap into this growing market.

FOSTER BECOMES THE MAN

While black baseball in New York underwent a dramatic reshuffling, Rube Foster made a series of moves that spurred his rise to the top. These included forming a partnership with a white tavern owner, expanding his barnstorming tours during the winter, reviving the East-West Colored Championship, and developing good press and community relations to defuse charges that baseball revenues were "going over to the other race," and that the American Giants were not supporting race institutions in the black community.

A crucial first step was his entering into a partnership with John M. Schorling, who had operated a sandlot club in Chicago for several years. Schorling leased the grounds of the old White Sox Park on 39th and Shields after the American League team moved into their new stadium. The White Sox had torn down the old grandstand, and when Schorling built a new one with a seating capacity of 9,000, he approached Foster with an offer of a partnership. Foster now had a ballpark and Schorling had the best booking agent and field manager in Chicago. Over the next 15 years they became one of the best management teams in baseball.

From 1912 to 1915 Foster established a barnstorming tour on the West Coast during the winter months. The American Giants played in the California Winter League, a collection of teams made up of former and current major and minor league players, and they won the California League Championship in its first season. On July 5, 1913, the *Defender* reported that the American Giants celebrated winning the championship with a parade. At the same time, Foster's alliance with Schorling enabled him to schedule games with white semi-pro teams during the week. Foster now had in place the structure that ensured the successful operation of a black team.

Foster also revived the East-West Colored Championship series. On July 5, 1913, the *Defender* reported an upcoming championship series between the Chicago American Giants and the Lincoln Giants of New York. A series of 13 games was scheduled in both cities. After nine games the series was tied at four victories apiece and one tie. The Lincoln Giants won the final four games in New York, earning the right to be called "World's Colored Champion." While Foster's American Giants lost the series, he had won the hearts and the minds of many in Chicago's black community.

The California Winter League championship and the East-West Colored Championship brought Rube Foster accolades from a prominent member of Chicago's black middle class and on the sport pages of the *Defender*. Julius Avendorph, former owner of the Columbia Giants, extolled the American Giants for "their high class baseball playing... [and] for their gentlemanly conduct on the ball field." Avendorph added that the

Dick Redding
The Cannonball

The great first baseman and manager Ben Taylor said that Dick "Cannonball" Redding had more speed on his fastball than probably any man in the world. Weighing in at 225 pounds on a compact six-foot frame, he had the build of a great speed baller. Among the moderns, Tom Seaver comes to mind. Taylor, one of the best hitters of his era, faced the Cannon often. In 1925 he testified to the futility of that experience: "From 1911 when he broke into fast company, until a few years ago he used nothing but his smoke ball. And it was impossible to hit it. I know, because I have tried."

No one equaled Redding when it came to winning big games against major league competition. A year after coming up to the black big leagues, he recorded exhibition game victories over the New York Giants and Boston Braves. Against the Jersey City team of the International League he fanned 24 batters. Carl Mays, the great submarine ball pitcher, was defeated by Cannonball in 1921 in a 15-inning contest by a score of 2–1. In that same year, by that same score, he bested Jack Scott's All-America Stars, a squad comprised mostly of major leaguers. In 1922, Babe Ruth, coming off a 59-home run season, went down on strikes three times against Redding.

Against Negro professional competition the record is equally outstanding. In his rookie season he won 29 straight games against some of the best colored teams in the country, including four victories over Rube Foster and one over José Mendez. He once struck out 25 men in a nine-inning game, facing the minimum of 27 batters. In that same year he bested the Cuban Stars without allowing a hit or a run. During his career he is credited with 12 no-hit games.

Redding once crossed the color line and hitched up with an Eastern League All-Star aggregation, joining such stars Chief Bender and Andy Coakley. Playing the regular Boston Braves with the addition of Ty Cobb in right field, Redding tossed a 1–0 shutout in 10 innings. In a second game he and Grover Cleveland Alexander battled to a 2–2 tie in 14 innings. In 1939 Alexander was numbered among the first group to be inducted into the National Baseball Hall of Fame. We are still waiting for the Cannonball to join Pete in Cooperstown's plaque gallery.

American Giants were "an example that lots of white clubs can take pattern from." When some of Chicago's black patrons berated Foster for raising his ticket prices, the *Defender* came to his defense. Chicago's black fans would "have to pay for quality and they [the fans] have certainly got their money's worth lately," referring to the colored championship. Moreover, the *Defender* reminded its readers that many of the Windy City's black fans "never knew what it was to see a game among those of their race unless forced to go to 79th Street.... Now it's a stone's throw from their homes."

Foster and Schorling actively cultivated press and community relations. In addition to raising funds for civic institutions, Schorling donated the use of the ballpark for local community activities, like the Chicago Church League championship game. Foster also developed positive press relations. He began first by granting an interview with the *Defender* that provided readers with insights about his early career in baseball. Throughout the war years he granted many interviews, wrote several articles, and became a local patron as well.

By 1915, Andrew "Rube" Foster had emerged as the dominant black baseball promoter in the Midwest. The American Giants' success on the diamond resonated well with Chicago's new black elite, who promoted civic institutions as symbols of race pride and racial solidarity.

EASY AS ABC IN INDIANAPOLIS

While Rube Foster engineered his rise as the booking power of the Midwest, three baseball entrepreneurs founded teams in Indianapolis, St. Louis, and Kansas City that would form the nucleus for the Negro National League in 1920. The first of these baseball owners was Charles Islam Taylor. C. I., as he came to be known in black baseball circles, was born on January 20, 1875, in Anderson, South Carolina. He attended Biddell and Clark Universities, and served in the Spanish-American War. In 1904, Taylor along with his brothers—Ben, "Candy" Jim, and "Steel Arm" John—organized the Birmingham Giants. In 1910, Taylor moved the club to West Baden, Indiana, and four years after that he transferred

Oscar Charleston and Bingo DeMoss of the Indianapolis ABCs, 1916.

the club to Indianapolis, where the club was sponsored by the American Brewing Company and called the ABCs. Taylor had become part owner with Ted Bowser, who owned the lease on Washington Park, the ABCs' home facility. By 1915, Taylor ousted Bowser and gained full control of the club and the lease on the park.

The most prominent player of the Taylor brothers was Ben. A slick-fielding first baseman, especially adept at digging out low throws, he is considered the best defensive player at the position in Negro league history. He was also a hard-hitting slugger, anchoring the ABCs' lineup in the cleanup spot. Recorded statistics from his time with the team in the 1920s show averages of .323, .407, and .358 during the 1920–22 seasons. Baseball historian James Riley said of him: "Modest, easygoing, and soft-spoken, Taylor was a true gentleman who maintained a fair and professional demeanor, and he was an excellent teacher of young players."

His brother, C.I., found life off the diamond more difficult. His plight in Indianapolis epitomized the kinds of challenges black baseball owners confronted outside Chicago. Taylor's break with Bowser resulted in the ABCs' being split into two teams in 1916. While Bowser's club, renamed Jewell's ABCs, played its home games at Northwestern Park, within close proximity of the black community, Taylor had leased Washington Park, home of the minor league club in the American Association. Whereas two clubs called the ABCs was a confusing proposition for sportswriter Billy Lewis, he accurately indicated that it would be a conflict of interest if both clubs scheduled home games on the same Sunday. For the next three years, these clubs competed for the same patronage and territorial control.

By 1918, the *Freeman* reported that Taylor was contemplating moving his club to another city. Like Rube Foster in Chicago in the prewar years, Taylor had become an unpopular man in Indianapolis. However, what upset Taylor the most was that the fans began to root for the visiting team, especially the Cuban Stars. Taylor viewed this behavior as a repudiation of his club and the work he tried to do in Indianapolis's black community.

On July 20, 1918, C. I. Taylor wrote an article in the *Freeman*, stating why he was thinking of moving his club. His rhetoric and actions reflected the aspirations of the new black middle class to create institutions that were symbols of race pride and racial solidarity. He sought, he said, to create an enterprise that black people in Indianapolis could take pride in. Along with the *Indianapolis Ledger*, Taylor mounted a public relations campaign to eliminate drinking, gambling, and rowdiness from the ballpark.

"There [was] no club in the country," he stated, "that has made a more enviable reputation for clean sport and good conduct on and off the ball field." Taylor then indicted his team's local followers for their disreputable behavior, and claimed he had never played in a city where the fans rooted more for the visitors than for the home team. According to his thinking, rooting for opponents resulted in disruptive behavior both from unruly fans and from certain ball clubs. He was extremely critical of the Cuban Stars, whose rowdy behavior was a direct result of the crowd pulling for them. The Cubans had become especially astute at arousing the fans by disputing every questionable and sometimes unquestionable decision the umpires made.

Even more significant were the scheduling problems. Fans did not want to see the white semiprofessional clubs play. They asked instead when the Cuban Stars or the American Giants were coming to town. The ABCs could only play the Cuban Stars three Sundays out of the season, and the American Giants once. That left eight Sundays on which the ABCs had to play other clubs. What resulted was the haunting legacy of the Cuban Giants' early years in Trenton, New Jersey. The fans showed little interest in patronizing games in which either the Cubans or the American Giants were not the opponent. In 1919, C.I. Taylor failed to organize the ABCs for a local season. Only when Rube Foster organized the Negro National League in 1920 would Taylor regroup to field a team that would become a league mainstay.

ROLLIN' AND TUMBLIN'

As much as C.I. Taylor wanted a clean game, two of his most famous players were involved in a notorious brawl on October 24, 1915. After a disputed steal, star second baseman Bingo DeMoss charged the umpire. Oscar Charleston, a future first-five Hall of Fame selection, ran in from center field and punched the umpire in the mouth. Players from both dugouts spilled onto the field and mixed it up in a reported "near race riot." Policemen armed with billy clubs were required to break up the melee, and they hauled DeMoss and Charleston off to jail.

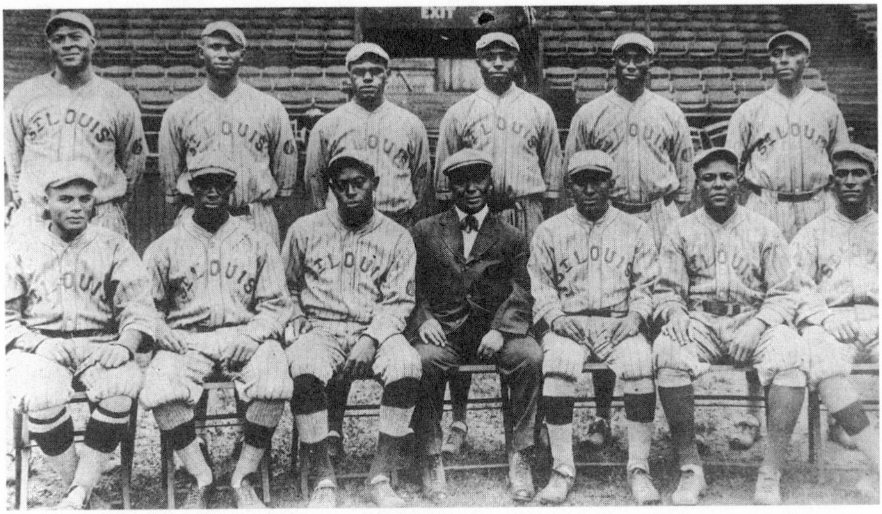

The St. Louis Giants of 1916 boasted Bill Gatewood, Bill Drake, and Frank Warfield.

TAKING THE MOUND IN ST. LOUIS

Another African-American entrepreneur emerged in St. Louis. The St. Louis Giants began as a sandlot team managed by Charles Mills, a local saloon keeper. The team was made up of mostly young player who wore cheap unmatching uniforms and earned less than sixty cents a game. In 1907, the Giants leased Koehler's Park and played primarily against white semi-pro teams on the weekends. The Giants soon became a gate attraction, outdrawing the local white trolley league. In 1910, they journeyed to Chicago to challenge the top semi-pro clubs in the Windy City. Mills then signed several talented players who made the Giants a competitive club. On September 24, 1910, the Giants played a two-game series with Frank Leland's Chicago Giants. The Chicago Giants took the first game 6–2, as John "Steel Arm" Taylor held St. Louis to five hits. In the second game, veteran pitcher Bill Gatewood trailed Chicago pitcher Walter Ball 3–1, before the club from the St. Louis scored three runs in the top of the ninth and won 4–3.

In 1911, Mills elevated his Giants to the ranks of a national touring team. He partnered with local black businessmen and formed the St. Louis Giants and Amusement Association (SLGAA). This provided Mills with the capital necessary to sign veteran black baseball players. He signed outstanding veteran players, including "Chappie" Johnson and Steel Arm Taylor. The St. Louis Giants embarked upon their first extended tour to New York. On August 10, the *Age* reported a doubleheader between St. Louis and the Lincoln Giants at Olympic Field. St. Louis won the first game, but the Lincolns hit Steel Arm Taylor early and often in the second game and won easily, 12–1.

In 1912, the St. Louis Giants made their second extended tour to New York and put on an impressive performance in defeating Nat Strong's Ridgewood club, 8–2. With their first tour of the South in 1913, the St. Louis Giants were elevated to the ranks of a touring team. In time they would become charter members of the Negro National League.

KINGS IN KANSAS CITY

Finally, a white owner emerged who would be a pivotal figure in the future league. James Leslie (J.L.) Wilkinson, known to his close friends as Wilkie, was the son of the president of Algona Normal College. While attending Highland Park College in Des Moines, Iowa, he pitched for a variety of semi-pro teams under the assumed name of Joe Green, and later signed on a team sponsored by the Hopkins Brothers Sporting Goods Store in Des Moines. When the manager of that team left, the club voted Wilkinson to assume his responsibilities.

In 1912, Wilkinson, along with J.E. Gall, organized the All Nations team. The club assembled on its roster whites, blacks, Indians, Mexicans, Cubans, and Asians. In addition, Wilkinson hired a woman, whom he advertised as "Carrie Nation," to play second base. They were a traveling team who rode in a specially built Pullman car, along with a cast of other entertainers. From 1915 to 1917, the All Nations gained notoriety by defeating the Chicago American Giants, twice, and the Indianapolis ABCs.

In 1915, Wilkinson moved the club to Kansas City, Missouri. Kansas City had the black population and access to other cities that Des Moines lacked. Kansas City also had a rich baseball tradition, dating back to the

The original Kansas City Monarchs, 1908.

1890s. Although the club fell on hard times during World War I, Wilkerson reorganized the All Nations in 1919 for a local season. They would later be renamed the Kansas City Monarchs.

The emergence of C.I. Taylor, Charles Mills, and J.L. Wilkinson was instrumental in establishing the nucleus of the Negro National League. They became important, although at times antagonistic, allies in Rube Foster's efforts to organize a league. Other clubs would also emerge during the Great Migration that would be charter members of the black Western league, but they would emerge under Foster's guidance.

A MIDWESTERN ALLIANCE

From 1915 to 1919 Rube Foster both expanded his booking control in the Midwest and built civic ties within Chicago's black community. Foster had the foresight to book as many as three games on a single Sunday when the Chicago American Giants were at home. Ever the smart business person, Foster made sure to keep Schooling Park busy when his club was on the road as well. He created still another source of revenue when he took on scheduling games for the Havanas of Cuba, and at times, Joe Green's Chicago Giants, which allowed him to collect a ten percent fee. He also booked games for two white clubs under the same agreement, the Logan Squares and the Duffy Florals.

Foster's successful barnstorming tours elevated his prestige among Chicago's African-American community but, at the same time, his efforts also benefitted the Windy City's blacks. His American Giants' phenomenal success provided black residents with a sense of race pride. News of the team's performances also bestowed some invaluable publicity upon Chicago's blacks.

The 1915-16 barnstorming tour, undoubtedly their greatest, exemplified the American Giants' heightened celebrity. They won the California Winter League for an unprecedented second time in four years. When the winter league season ended, the American Giants traveled to Cuba, playing in the Cuban Winter League, winning seven and losing eight games. They barnstormed the West and Southwest, winning 57 and losing 15. When the local season began in May, the American Giants had traveled over 20,000 miles. During this tour sportswriter Frank Young made the somewhat exaggerated claim that "the Rube" had brought Chicago more promotion than all other city enterprises combined.

The American Giants' popularity was not lost upon local politicians, who sought to create a political machine to address the black community's needs. Beginning in the 1916 local season, American Giants home openers would start off with a prominent Windy City politician or businessman throwing out the first pitch. By the 1917 season, Foster reserved a special box for Chicago's black elite.

At the same time the American Giants magnate expanded his booking control throughout the Midwest. One major step was establishing a business arrangement with major league owners in Cincinnati and Detroit to rent their ballparks. On August 18, 1917, the *Defender* announced a series of games between the Havanas and the American Giants at Redland Field in Cincinnati. Two weeks later, Foster booked games with the Indianapolis ABCs at Navin Field in Detroit.

The formation of the Detroit Stars also contributed to stabilizing Rube Foster's hold in the Midwest. The Stars played their games in the middle of a white working-class neighborhood four miles from downtown. Foster installed John "Tenny" Blount, who was involved in gambling enterprises in Detroit and was one of several vice leaders that began to emerge in the promotion of black baseball, as the Stars business manager. Selecting former American Giants outfielder Pete Hill as manager, Foster transferred several of his players to the club. To maintain controlling interest in the Stars, he held the ball players' contracts and the lease to Mack Park.

By 1919, Rube Foster had become the major booking power in the Midwest. A primary reason was the American Giants' ability to turn a profit. By July, Foster told a friend that the American Giants were "drawing double of any year here. Even adding 2300 Boxes, cannot accommodate the people." By the end of the season, Foster had reportedly amassed a profit of nearly $15,000, a far cry from his $1,000 earnings in 1907.

Despite this prosperous season, Foster recognized having the best club was not enough. He needed opponents that were evenly matched. During this time Foster started to consider creating a national enterprise. With the emergence of a black independent club in Philadelphia and the return of John Connors, that dream would come closer to being realized.

CLEANING UP IN HILLDALE

Out of a crowd of black clubs in the Quaker City that aspired to become the next Philadelphia Giants came Ed Bolden, an African-American entrepreneur whose small sandlot team would grow into a powerhouse. The story of the legendary Hilldale club begins on May 29, 1910, when Austin Devere Thompson, a 19-year-old from Darby, Pennsylvania, placed

In the 1910s and 20s, the Hilldales were mainstays of black baseball.

an advertisement in the *Philadelphia Sunday Item*. Under the column entitled "Amateur Base Ball Notes," Thompson sought to arrange games with 14- and 15-year-old traveling teams, agreeing to pay half of their expenses. Darby was an African-American "community satellite" located southwest of Philadelphia in Delaware County, just across the city line. By 1910, nearly 7,000 African Americans lived in the conveniently located borough, a 45-minute ride from downtown Philadelphia by trolley. Blacks composed ten percent of the population and were restricted to living "upon the Hill."

Little is known about Hilldale's inaugural season, but before it ended A.D. Thompson left the club and was replaced by Ed Bolden. Born on January 17, 1881, in Concordsville, Pennsylvania, 15 miles from Darby, Bolden was not a former baseball player. He was a Philadelphia postal clerk, emblematic of the black professional of that time. Asked to keep score at one of Hilldale's games, Bolden eventually assumed control of the young team. In 1911, Bolden's club amassed a 23-6 record, but even so Hilldale was indistinguishable from the dozens of clubs in the Philadelphia area. Self-promotion was essential for stimulating interest in the Hilldale Club and developing a fan base. With the exception of Rube Foster, no other black baseball entrepreneur utilized the black press better than Ed Bolden. Beginning in 1912, Bolden began bombarding the *Philadelphia Tribune* with constant press releases from March to October. He also recognized the need to develop an acceptable moral image to boost the promotion of his club. Bolden declared, "We have good grounds, and give a good guarantee for a good attraction." He advocated "clean baseball" and required his players to be "gentlemen in uniform as well as off the ball field."

Bolden soon gained control of Hilldale Park in Delaware County. Unlike the New York clubs, who were relegated to traveling status and under the control of a booking agent, Bolden was in a unique position to develop his own booking schedule with black and white clubs, for Hilldale was attractive to white semi-pro teams that lacked their own grounds. In 1914, Bolden scheduled three games against white clubs, including a game that featured a minor league pitcher owned by Connie Mack's Philadelphia Athletics. That same year Bolden's club defeated Three Links, champions of the Interborough League, for the championship of Darby.

Finally, Ed Bolden began recruiting sandlot players from other teams. Like many of the black clubs in the Quaker City, Hilldale's owner-general manager used the sports pages of the *Philadelphia Tribune* to encourage players to join his club. He acquired several players in this fashion, transforming Hilldale from a club of "small boys" to a prospective black professional club. In 1915, Bolden's Hilldale Club enjoyed another successful season, winning twenty, losing eight, and tying two. Yet the process of transformation was still in its initial stages during the prewar years. Not until the Great Migration would Bolden make his big push into black baseball's professional world.

From 1916 to 1920, Ed Bolden completed the transformation of the

Louis Santop
The Clan Darbie Siege Gun

Of the many great athletes who played Negro ball in the 1910s and early 1920s, Louis Napoleon Santop, nicknamed the "Clan Darbie Siege Gun" or "Top," stands out. Santop came to the Philadelphia Giants in 1911, where his teammates included several greats of that era, including the fine backstop, Doc Wiley, and the great Dick "Cannonball" Redding. When he left the Giants, "Top" went to Jess McMahon's Lincolns in New York, where he remained though 1916, playing with John Henry Lloyd, Pete Booker, and Spot Poles. Santop joined the Hilldale Daisies for the 1917 season, and played for Uncle Sam's Navy in 1918. In 1919 he managed the Brooklyn Royal Giants, and came back to the Daisies in 1920 to anchor clubs that would win both championships in the Eastern Colored League and a Negro World Series title in 1925.

Rollo Wilson once asserted that if Rube Foster ever wrote a history of baseball, he'd list Santop as his first-string catcher. If "Top" was good enough for Foster, shouldn't he be good enough for induction into the Hall of Fame?

Hilldale Athletic Club into a full-time business enterprise. With his motto, "clean baseball," Bolden emphasized the importance of a high moral standards. Not only were the players expected to portray this image, but so were the fans who came to Hilldale Park. On January 13, 1917, the *Philadelphia Tribune* reported that the Hilldale management had issued five warrants against five men for rowdy behavior at a game. They were successful in having four of them pay fines and costs. The episode resulted in Bolden hiring uniformed security officers to ensure the "pleasure and comfort" of his respectable patrons.

In addition to signing peace officers, Bolden also inked Hilldale's first professional players. On March 17, 1917, the *Tribune* announced the signing of Otto Briggs, a native of Kings Mountain, North Carolina. Briggs had migrated to the North with C.I. Taylor in 1914 and played for several leading Midwestern clubs. He was named the team's captain and would remain with Hilldale for most of the next 13 years. A second acquisition, Frank "Doc" Sykes, a pitcher, had played previously with the Lincoln Giants, Lincoln Stars, and the Brooklyn Royal Giants. By late July, Bolden had signed outfielders McKinley "Bunny" Downs and Spotswood Poles, and catcher-first baseman Bill Petus.

In 1918 Nat Strong turned his eye on Hilldale. He wanted to absorb the Darbyites into his monolithic booking agency, thus making inroads into the Philadelphia market. The New York magnate indicated that if Hilldale did not agree, he would put a club across the street. In addition, Strong would resurrect his former business associate, H. Walter Schlichter, to manage the club.

In response, Bolden published a letter on the pages of the *Tribune* that exemplified race rhetoric in the age of Booker T. Washington. He stated, "The race people of Philadelphia and vicinity are proud to proclaim Hilldale the biggest thing in the baseball world owned, fostered, and controlled by race men." The Hilldale leader added that his club was "proud to be in a position to give [Darby's citizens] the most beautiful park in Delaware County, a team that is second to none and playing the best attractions obtainable." Bolden concluded by stating, "To affiliate ourselves with other than race men would be a mark against our name that could never be eradicated."

Nat Strong's challenge fell flat. In the first place, Hilldale was being transformed into a top-notch black independent by signing several professional players. Second, Bolden had begun scheduling the top black clubs of the east at Hilldale Park. Fans were more willing to patronize games that included the Cuban Stars, Lincoln Giants, or the Bacharach Giants than local semi-pro teams. The club had also developed strong ties with the black community. Finally, establishing themselves as a winning club, Hilldale was a strong gate attraction for some of the top white clubs in the Quaker City.

In 1916 the club began renovating Hilldale Park. Across the next four years trees were removed from left and center field, and a new grandstand was erected. By 1920, Hilldale had extended the grandstand and built a roof to protect its patrons. That same year, Bolden secured a lease on a ballpark in Camden, New Jersey. Much like the Cuban Giants in the 1880s, Bolden could now expand his market potential in the Philadelphia area through the control of two ballparks. Bolden then made arrangements with the P.R.T Company to have all trolley lines on Walnut run straight to Hilldale Park. P.R.T. also indicated they would run extra cars from 1:15 p.m. to 6:15 p.m., making it more convenient for fans coming to and from the ballpark.

Next, Bolden began scheduling some of the leading black independent players from the East. On June 30, 1917, Nat Strong's Cuban Stars arrived at Hilldale Park. Doc Sykes pitched and lost 7–2 against Strong's hard-hitting nine. Their first win against a top black club was against Strong's Brooklyn Royal Giants. This time Sykes was in top form as he scattered five hits in nine innings, coasting to a 9–1 victory. By the end of the 1917 season, Hilldale had played six games against black independents of the East, winning two and losing four. A new baseball power was on the rise.

GOOD OLD DAYS OF LATIN BASEBALL

New York *Amsterdam News* sports editor Romeo Dougherty looked back from 1926 with considerable delight on the years before World War I, "the good old days when the Lincolns engaged in a series with the then world famous Cuban Stars when Mendez was a world-beating pitching ace and Gonzalez caught the hot ones behind the bat." The talent of the Cubans was no longer suspect. To the contrary, they were catching widespread attention. None other than New York Giants manager John McGraw stated that "if Mendez was even light enough to 'pass for white,' he would have paid forty thousand dollars for his release from the Cuban team." But it was the entire scene that made Dougherty nostalgic. "Talk about your enthusiasm: say the night before those games which were staged at the American League baseball park, none of us went to bed, and the morning of the eventful day found all roads leading to the grounds. The late Ed Warren in his silk shirt, light gray suit betopped by a seasonable straw and his winning smile; John Connors, Barron Wilkins, Casper Holstein and the entire old guard used to turn out in full force. Yes sir, those were the good old days."

The presence of Latinos in baseball in that era occurred largely as the result of Cuban-American entrepreneur Alex Pompez's foray into black baseball. A native of Key West, Pompez spent most of his adult life in New York City, where he operated Negro league teams, ran a numbers bank, and, at the end of his career, worked as a scout for the New York Giants. After learning the sports promotion craft under Nat Strong, the Cuban-American businessman decided to go out on his own. The 1916 Cuban Stars was his first professional baseball team. Pompez's Cuban Stars would from their outset play year-round in the United States and throughout the Caribbean.

During his years as a Latin baseball impresario, Pompez brought in a stream of Latinos who excelled in the U.S. black circuit. In 1917 Alejandro "Walla Walla" Oms made his debut. A left-handed batter, he was a great power hitter, with a recorded .332 career batting average. He would pace the team's offensive attack from the late 1910s into the early 1930s. The era's Cuban Stars roster included other talented Latinos such as their fabulous shortstop and leadoff hitter, Pelayo Chacón.

Pompez's first team in 1916 sent waves rippling throughout the black and white baseball circuits in the United States. The formation of a second "Cuban Stars" baseball team infuriated Abel Linares. At the height of his activity as a baseball entrepreneur, Linares took pride in having brought the first Cuban team (All Cubans, later the Cuban Stars) to barnstorm through the States in 1899. When Puerto Rican baseball promoters informed Linares about Pompez having formed a team playing under the same name, the Cuban took action. He sent an irate cable to the Puerto Rican officials who had organized the tour of Pompez's team. Linares claimed "that the authentic 'Cuban Stars' were his, that they were the same [team] that played in the Cuban championship and who traveled to the United States every year," and that history was on his side as his Cuban Stars team had toured the U.S. first. Quick to take advantage of a potential opportunity to make more money, promoters in Puerto Rico extended Linares an invitation. Let the two Cuban Stars teams battle it out on the playing field for the rightful claim to the name. It was a challenge that Linares, ever confident, could not pass up.

The March 16 matchup was advertised as a contest between the "authentic" Cuban Stars and "the imposters." The outcome would determine which team deserved the name Cuban Stars. Linares' team arrived on the island fully manned with top guns José Mendez, Cristobal Torriente, and Luis Padron, among others. But the Latino baseball impresario soon regretted accepting Pompez's invitation. Linares' team went down in defeat by a 3–2 score. Alex Pompez only added to Linares' frustration with having to coexist with a second Cuban Stars team by flatly refusing a rematch. "Not enough time," Pompez explained. His triumphant Cuban Stars were about to set sail for the United States to begin their 1916 campaign.

SOMETHING BIGGER THAN BASEBALL

During spring training in 1917, America entered the conflict that had been raging in Europe for close to three years. Black leadership struggled to formulate a strategy appropriate to their people's peculiar relationship to a nation that was deeply theirs—and yet also deeply not theirs. Yet there was little ambiguity in the response from the ranks of black baseball. Many of the best players traded in their bats and gloves for rifles and canteens to fight, they thought, for a better life for their people and their nation. Baseball ranks quickly began to be depleted, as all through that first wartime summer and into the next the soldiers' ranks swelled with black enlistees and draftees. The list was indeed impressive. Cannonball Dick Redding was dubbed "Grenade" after the war for his fighting exploits. Louis Santop traded his "Big Bertha" and his catcher's tools for the tools of war. Joe Harris, Dicta Johnson, and a host of others abandoned their baseball battles for a much more dangerous and far more consequential form of warfare.

Cristobal Torriente

The Latin Babe Ruth

We have never given Torriente the credit he deserved. He did everything well, he fielded like a natural, threw in perfect form, he covered as much field as could be covered; as for batting, he left being good to being something extraordinary.

—Martin Dihigo

The story of Cristobal Torriente, the gifted Cuban outfielder, is tragic. From modest beginnings, Torriente first played ball amid the sugar fields in Cienfuegos, Cuba. He rose to stardom playing in the black circuit in the United States only to meet a lonely death in New York City while still in his early thirties due to alcohol-induced cirrhosis. In between were stellar years on the diamond where he established a reputation at the plate as one of Cuba's best offensive imports.

When his career on the field was at its peak, Torriente's batting impressed teammates and opponents alike. But his most memorable day at the plate was probably a November 1920 exhibition game in his native Cuba. Cuban Stars owner Abel Linares had successfully scheduled a two-week visit by New York Yankees legend Babe Ruth. Tens of thousands came out to see Ruth perform, but Torriente stole the show, outslugging Babe Ruth three homers to none and earning the nickname "The Latin Babe Ruth."

The Cuban outfielder's clutch performances in the black circuit and in the Cuban winter league did not go unnoticed by major league clubs. His talents were clearly on a major league level. But performance alone would not win a player a spot in the majors. For some, Torriente occupied an ambiguous racial position. His nationality along with his skin color could have possibly gotten him into the majors. Kansas City Monarchs pitcher Chet Brewer described the Cuban outfielder as "Indian" color, which, in some instances during the 1920s, would have garnered a talented player a tryout from a major league club.

Floyd "Jelly" Gardner, a teammate of Torriente with the Chicago American Giants, witnessed firsthand the interest a New York Giants scout expressed in his Cuban counterpart in 1920. According to Gardner, the Cuban's play impressed, but something still held the scout back: Torriente's hair. In Gardner's view, Torriente would have "went up there [to the majors] but he had real bad hair— he would have been all right if his hair had been better."

In the midst of the war, black baseball continued its growth, headed toward unprecedented days to come. By 1918 the Hilldale baseball operation had become substantial enough to attract the eye of Rube Foster. On August 3, the Chicago American Giants invaded Hilldale Park for a doubleheader. The Darbyites squeaked past the "Windy City Crew," 9–8, as Louis Santop hit a two-run homer in the bottom of the tenth inning, to the delight of the hometown crowd. In the second game, Hilldale was no match for the Midwesterners, as the American Giants won easily 9–2.

Their meeting also signaled a larger development. With Foster and Bolden entrenched within their respective markets, a challenge to Nat Strong's booking control was about to occur. The next chink in his armor would appear in New York City itself.

THE RETURN OF UNCLE JOHN

From 1914 to 1919, no black clubs from the Midwest played in New York City. Black clubs in Gotham under the control of Nat Strong's monopolistic booking agency, combined with the collusive practices of white owners of semipro clubs, excluded Midwestern clubs from black baseball's most potentially lucrative market. Furthermore, Midwestern clubs were reluctant to travel east, given, as sportswriter Lester Walton described it, white owners' penchant for kidnapping players.

Instead a black club from the South would make an initial strike on Nat Strong's stranglehold. In 1916, the Duval Giants of Jacksonville, Florida, barnstormed its way to Atlantic City, New Jersey. Tom Jackson and Henry Tucker, politicians from Atlantic City, brought the Duval Giants north on behalf of the city's mayor, Harry Bacharach, and renamed the club the Bacharach Giants.

In 1919 Tucker entered into a business alliance with John Connors and New York nightclub owner and gambler Baron Wilkins, with Connors and Wilkins as the club's financial backers, and Tucker serving as the booking agent. Connors' alliance with Tucker ensured the team a home grounds in Atlantic City named Bacharach Park, and the beach resort's mayor lent his

Giving No Quarter

Baseball historian Phil Dixon has recorded a moment showing how competitive the great ones could be:

Flame-throwing Smokey Joe Williams and Cannonball Dick Redding, though once teammates, became fierce rivals. After Red-ding beat Williams at Ebbets Field, a reporter from the New York Age gathered the two for a photograph. Yet when he asked them to shake hands, both of them refused. "I'll stand beside him," Redding said grudgingly, and Williams replied, "I don't want to shake his hand."

financial backing to the club. At the same time Connor secured the lease of Dyckman Oval, located a few blocks from Olympic Field, the Lincoln Giants' home field in Harlem. Connor signed several players from the Lincoln Giants and Brooklyn Royal Giants, including Cannonball Redding.

John Connor's unexpected return to black baseball shocked Nat Strong. According to the *Defender*, secret meetings were held to exclude the Bacharachs' owner and his team from the New York market. Yet Connors had already foreseen the problem of not securing suitable playing dates. "You see," he said, "that is the reason we have leased our own grounds and, by the way, I might state that a contract had been given for the building of a new grandstand."

Strong made every attempt to block the Atlantic City deal. He began by refusing to allow the Royal Giants, Cuban Stars, or Lincoln Giants to play in Atlantic City. Strong even tried to create a rift between the Bacharach management team. On May 17, 1919, the *Defender* reported that Strong accused Connors and Wilkins of owing him money. Both Connors and Wilkins categorically denied the allegations, and Wilkins filed a defamation suit in civil court. Faced with possible litigation, Strong backed down.

Strong then availed himself of the one resource he had under his control, colluding with the white owners in not scheduling games with the Bacharachs. In response, Connors entered into a business agreement with Brooklyn Dodgers owner Charles Ebbets to rent his ballpark. This alliance came through New York Giants first baseman Hal Chase, who had a reputation as a notorious gambler. No doubt Wilkins' and Chase's paths intersected, given the nightclub owner's reputation as a gambler and bootlegger. Connor had gained access to three ballparks to schedule games, thus freeing the Bacharachs from relying on Strong's booking agency for games in Gotham. Connors had pulled off the major coup of the 1919 and 1920 season. Strong conceded defeat temporarily.

From May 22 to September 11, 1920, Connors scheduled six games between black clubs at Ebbets Field, the first black teams to play there, according to the *Age*. The Atlantic City contingent took both games of a doubleheader from Guy Empey's Treat 'Em Roughs, a local black club. On July 17, 16,000 fans watched the Bacharachs play the Lincoln Giants for the Eastern Colored Championship. The first game matched pitching legends Dick Redding against Joe Williams, and the Cannonball outdueled the Cyclone 5–0. The Lincolns won the second game 7–5. No reference can be found to a third and deciding game. In August and September, the Chicago Giants and the Indianapolis ABCs invaded Ebbets Field. In the four games with the Midwestern clubs, the Bacharachs won three.

The high-water mark of Connors' successful 1920 season occurred in October. Foster's American Giants invaded Gotham for a four-game series with the Bacharachs, three of them scheduled in Ebbets Field. Connor's Bacharachs manhandled the Windy City crew, winning three out of four. On October 15, the *Defender* reported that 15,000 fans watched Bacharachs hurlers Dick Redding and Red Ryan defeat the American Giants by scores of 5-3 and 7-3. This would be the only instance in the early 20th century when New York's black community could embrace a ball club that was both black-owned and black-operated. While his success would be short-lived, John Connor was sitting on top of the black baseball world in New York.

TIME FOR A REAL NEGRO MAJOR LEAGUE

From 1890 to 1920, black professional baseball in the United States underwent a period of tremendous growth and maturation. In 1890, only a handful of black clubs operated on a full-time basis. The limited connection of these teams to a strong home-city fan base, to financial support from black businesses, to newspapers that would follow their games, and to ballparks that they could reasonably call their home were problems still to be faced. By 1920, in contrast, several black professional clubs had a local fan base. The team were supported by black businessmen who believed in race advancement. They were the sports darlings of a nationwide press, and they had secured regular access to their own home fields with substantial penetration into major league parks. These were indeed heady times for the black professional version of America's game. Could anyone be surprised that as the 1920 season approached, a group of Midwestern black baseball owners, led by Andrew "Rube" Foster and C. I. Taylor, were ready to build a Negro National Major League in this new world of blackball?

Paul Robeson, third from right, was catcher for the 1918 Rutgers varsity team.

The New Negro

The National Association of Colored Baseball Clubs is satisfied with their lot, is resting on a solid financial foundation, and is operating in perfect harmony with other organized leagues.
—DAVE WYATT, CHICAGO WHIP, MARCH 12, 1921

IN WHAT HISTORIAN JOHN HOLWAY APTLY CHARACTERIZES AS "ONE OF the great iron-man performances of baseball history," the Atlantic City Bacharachs' Harold Treadwell faced off against the Chicago American Giants' Huck Rile in 1922 post-season play.

In the sixth inning in a scoreless game, Rile was replaced by Dave Brown, who had pitched a nine-inning victory only two days before. Treadwell and Brown continued to pitch scoreless baseball for 14 more innings. Brown gave six singles, walked two, and struck out twelve. Treadwell gave up only nine hits in twenty innings. "They couldn't see Brown," said third baseman Dave Malarcher, "and we couldn't see Treadwell." In the tenth inning Bacharach manager John Lloyd put Ramiro Ramirez in right field in place of Pete Duncan. Foster thought Ramirez had a weak arm and told Malarcher to hit one to him to test it. Sure enough, the throw was weak. In the bottom of the 20th, Treadwell walked Torriente, and Bobby Williams sacrificed. Foster told Malarcher to hit another to Ramirez, and Torriente beat the throw home by five feet.

Score: Chicago 1, Atlantic City 0. Perhaps if Duncan had stayed in the game the teams would still be playing!

This was but one golden game in what would prove to be a golden decade.

A NEW PSYCHOLOGY

The social critic Alain Locke is generally credited with giving the term "New Negro" to the era that stretches roughly from the beginning of the Great Migration in the 1910s to the opening of the Great Depression. In his 1925 essay of the same name, Locke celebrated a New Negro who was transforming the popular image of the Negro from that of ex-slave to that of culture bearer for the race. This transforming New Negro was embracing a "new psychology" and a "new spirit" that would equip him to smash all of the impediments that had long obstructed black achievement.

Equipped with a new mind-set, black artists would, in the words of Langston Hughes, "express our individual dark-skinned selves without fear or shame. If white people are pleased we are glad. If they are not, it doesn't matter. We know we are beautiful. And ugly too. The tom-tom cries and the tom-tom laughs. If colored people are pleased we are glad. If they are not, their displeasure doesn't matter either. We build our temples for tomorrow, strong as we know how, and we stand on top of the mountain, free within ourselves."

This era of the New Negro was a time when African Americans journeyed to new places to lay claim to territory that had never been acknowledged as theirs, taking possession rightfully of what had been taken from them. Among the many, many other things he would be, the superb athlete Paul Robeson was a New Negro, a journeyer to new places. The Walter Camp 1917–1918 All-American end for Rutgers University was a multisport varsity-letter winner at the New Jersey school, where he stood out for his academic as well as athletic prowess—to say nothing of the color of his skin. While best known as a gridiron star, he was an outstanding catcher in baseball. It was not uncommon to find accounts of his college athletic feats on the pages of great black national weeklies alongside stories about

Negro professional baseball. Yet for all that he did in his youth as an athlete, for all that he came to do in his maturity as a political and cultural activist, Robeson is often remembered for his voice. Most meant the singing voice. Negro leaguer Gene Benson meant the speaking voice and the words spoken as well, "Paul Robeson spoke for me. What he said, I felt and could not say as he could."

Voices like those of Hughes and Robeson, and their literary and artistic fellows in the Harlem Renaissance, had their counterparts in the masses of folk who were taking one of the most spectacular journeys in American history, leaving the rural South for the urban North in the Great Migration.

It is not possible to understand black baseball without understanding this migration. The same newspapers that reported baseball games recorded this massive movement of blacks. The most influential of these, the *Chicago Defender*, spoke to its readers in poetic terms of the feats of black baseball heroes, many of whom themselves were migrants, as it urged those suffering under Southern oppression to move North:

Why should I remain longer in the South
To be kicked and dogged around?
Cracker to shoot me in the mouth
And shoot my brother down.
I would rather the cold to snatch my breath
And die from natural cause
Than to stay down South and be beat to death
Under cracker law.

Of the ten Northern cities with more than 25,000 Negroes in 1920, all but two—Pittsburgh and Kansas City—registered gains of over 50 percent from the 1910 census. In Detroit the Negro population increased 611 percent, in Cleveland 308 percent, in Chicago 148 percent, and 59 percent in Philadelphia and Indianapolis. Chicago, the capital of black baseball, shows the magnitude of this mass movement. The 1920 census recorded 109,458, an increase of 65,355 in ten years.

Baseball organizers like Andrew Foster and Ed Bolden would create national baseball leagues from these new black cities of the North. Along with these New Negro executives and their New Negro fans, migrant players with nicknames like "Pop," "Smokey Joe," and "the Cannonball" would build careers across a wide swath of territory that would have been unimaginable before the advent of the New Negro era.

The 1920s has long been regarded as an era of literary luminaries. Perhaps that view should be widened as the historian Clement Price pictures it:

> One has to have a long memory to document Negro baseball. At least into the later 19th century. Certainly in the early 20th century when blacks are moving about this country as part of the great migration. Negro baseball surfaces as an important symbol of black accomplishment in the cities, black accomplishment on the playing field, and black business development. The New Negro Era, long known for its poets and its jazz musicians and its intellectuals, must now be reconsidered for its sports figures.

BLACK BASEBALL WAS SPECIAL

"Can a people live and develop over 300 years simply by reacting?" the novelist Ralph Ellison asks. "Are all American Negroes simply the creation of white men, or have they at least helped to create themselves out of what they have found around them?"

Like Ellison, many sportswriters of black newspapers were looking at black baseball as far more than a game. To Sports editor Charles Starkes, of the *Kansas City Call*, black baseball was a "source of interest, pride, and race glory." The sport would lead to "great strides in the development of national character." To these commentators, the baseball madness that was gripping fans as they watched the exploits of the Cubans, ABCs, and other teams was capable of generating social change. Starkes went so far as to

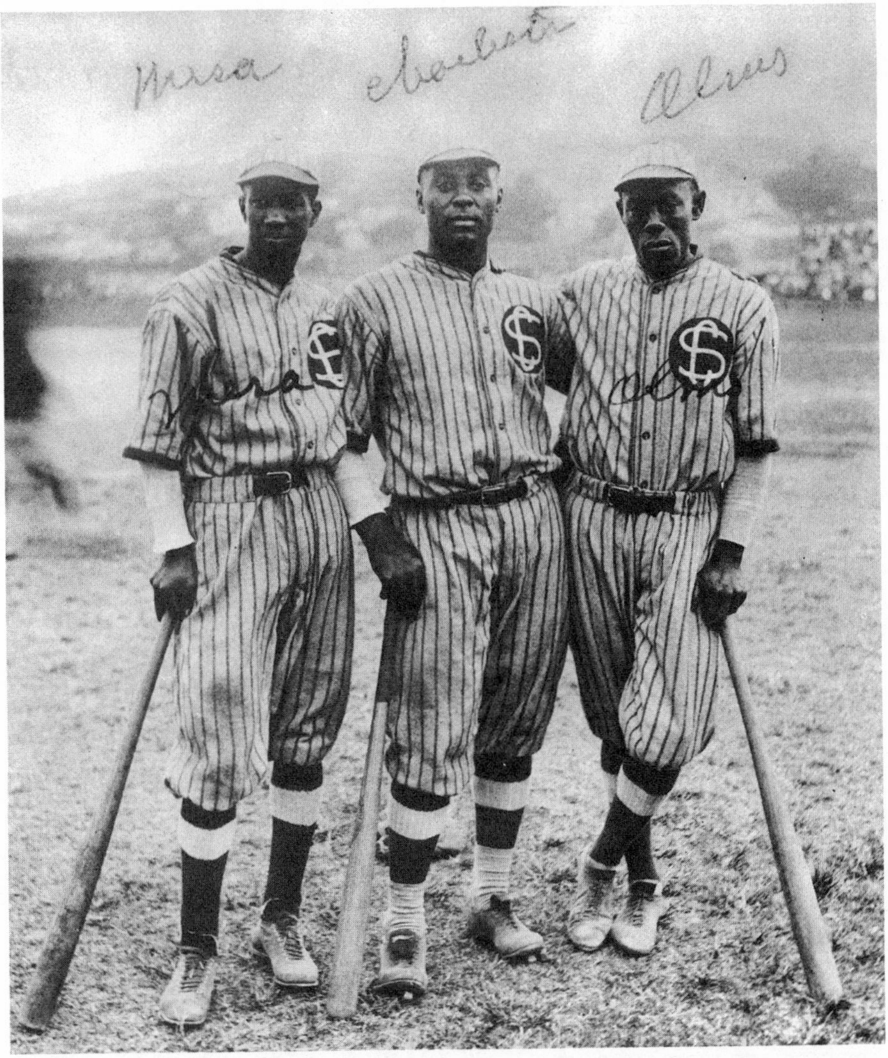

Pedro Mesa, Oscar Charleston, and Alejandro Oms in Cuba in the mid-1920s.

say: "Here in Kansas City we see baseball as a wonderful contributor to the solution of an ancient race problem."

What had black baseball done to merit such a claim? Most visible was its realization of a long-held dream, the creation of the Negro National Baseball League, founded in the winter of 1920 by Rube Foster and his cohorts in Kansas City. From its inception the National was a Midwestern

Raleigh "Biz" Mackey

The Best Backstop

None other than Ty Cobb, one of the most intense competitors the national pastime has ever known, called Biz Mackey one of the greatest catchers in the game, high praise indeed for a defensive whiz who spent the better part of three decades donning the tools of ignorance.

While the slugging Josh Gibson receives the lion's share of praise as black baseball's best catcher, a surprisingly high percentage of their contemporaries rate Mackey superior based on his all-around game. Cum Posey, a longtime black baseball executive, once said, "For combined hitting, thinking, throwing, and physical endowment, there has never been another like Biz Mackey. A tremendous hitter, a fierce competitor, although slow afoot he is the standout among catchers who have shown their wares in this nation." Infielder Jake Stephens was more succinct: "Of all the catchers, Mackey was the greatest."

Mackey's ability behind the plate is most often confirmed by those who stood on the pitchers mound. Webster McDonald, a teammate with both the Hilldale Daisies and Philadelphia Stars, said, "Biz Mackey was our catcher, the best in baseball bar none. He was an artist behind the plate." Max Manning, who threw to Mackey while with the Newark Eagles, said he "was one of the smartest catchers that I've ever pitched to."

Mackey was also known for his tutelage of young players. Said future Hall of Fame catcher Roy Campanella: "In my opinion, Biz Mackey was the master of defense of all catchers. When I was a kid in Philadelphia, I saw both Mackey and Mickey Cochrane in their primes, but for real catching skills, I didn't think Cochrane was the master of defense that Mackey was. When I went under his direction at Baltimore, I was 15 years old. I gathered quite a bit from Mackey, watching how he did things, how he blocked low pitches, how he shifted his feet for an outside pitch, how he threw with a short, quick, accurate throw without drawing back."

A player-manager until his 50s, Mackey's guidance helped a number of his players break into the big leagues after the color line was broken in 1947. According to Nap Gulley, who played under Mackey with the Newark Eagles, he was a gentle giant and one of the finest managers he had the privilege of playing for: "He could help a ballplayer to become a better ballplayer."

league, with two teams that first season based in Chicago, and clubs representing Dayton, Detroit, Indianapolis, Kansas City, and St. Louis. The Cuban Stars, operating out of Cincinnati, but with no specific home-city affiliation, rounded out the eight-team circuit. Through its first years of operation several teams joined, while others dropped out. The benefits of a league were many. Starkes wrote:

> Four years ago we had no semblance of a league, therefore as players we did not know the comparative high salaries our athletes are now receiving, and the fans had no where to lay their heads. They had to camp on the burning bleachers to watch the white sons of baseball perform their skillful play.... Baseball is a great thing for the race in a big way.... We have tasted in a national way the meaning of league baseball, and we have approved of it and declared it all right for adult and child—we the people.

The early 1920s were heady times for black baseball. But the feelings generated by league play went beyond enjoyment of good baseball and the satisfaction of seeing black athletes do well. In a much broader sense, the new level of play meant that white psychology, so far as it was "applied to Negro baseball, [was] a dead issue" wrote Starkes. It was an outlook that "implies always the superiority of the whites and the inferiority of the blacks." Social commentators like Starkes noted that years of oppression had produced among his people an "acceptance of white standards of valuation instead of creating our own after our peculiar conceptions." Under such conditions a sense of one's own identity was impaired in ways that were extremely harmful. "In our particular case psychology is the expression of a mental attitude of the white man influencing the mental concepts of the Negro and causing a certain moral depression on our part. The white man emphasized the thought of our terrible inferiority in the past, and we believed it because of our ignorance."

Black baseball showed what was wrong with the negative thinking produced by America's white psyche. "It has been recently proven too well that Negroes play the game with much more thought and snap than the average white player," the Kansas City writer confidently announced. "If you want an instance of strategy highly embodied on our part, then compare Rube Foster, our best, with John McGraw, the acknowledged white master. We dare say the Fosterian genius would tally up with the other."

Starkes even suggested that public sentiment might well crystallize to the point where "it will question the results of a world series championship between two white teams as conclusive when perhaps there are one of several colored teams in the country better than the contenders." In the meantime his prescription was "to continue to let the race hit the ball in every progressive way."

At the beginning of the 1920s, the black game had clearly become something to embrace as their own by those who played it, watched it, and wrote about it. On the professional baseball diamonds of America blacks felt they had, in Ralph Ellison's words, clearly "helped to create themselves out of what they have found around them."

FATHER OF BLACK BASEBALL

Andrew "Rube" Foster is, without argument, the central black baseball figure for the 1920s. Before founding the Negro National League, he was a player beyond compare. In September 1912 a white newspaper, the Albany *Times Union*, called him the "Black Mathewson of the national game, a great ballplayer despite his resemblance to a barrel." No greater praise could be paid to a pitcher of that day than to be compared to the great Matty. Rube's playing days made for many great stories. In one afternoon's work for the Leland Giants, he reportedly struck out Mike Dolan three times. The fine major league batsman Jake Stahl "couldn't get within speaking distance of Uncle Rube's curves." Foster claimed later to have lost only six games to opposing black teams throughout his long career in black baseball.

Early black baseball impresario Ed Lamar remembered when the young Rube joined the Cuban Giants in Zanesville, Ohio, "in 1900 or 1901" as the team came east from a western trip. Lamar compared Foster favorably in speed to major league star Amos Rusie, and took particular note of his fine curve ball. At the time the young pitcher was relying too much on his physical prowess, which got him in trouble in his first game with the Hoboken club, arguably "the best white independent club in that area." He lost in a rout, 13–0. "From then on," Lamar notes, "he made a study of the game, and every chance he had he would go out to the big league parks and watch the big clubs in action." He must have been a fast learner. Later in that Cuban X Giants season he beat the Hoboken club twice and would never lose to them again. But then, he seldom lost to anyone in his prime as the anchor for staffs on the Philadelphia Giants, Chicago's Leland Giants, and finally his own American Giants club.

Similar testimony lauds his managerial and executive abilities. When his great team came to Kansas City for an important series in the 1920s, it was his name rather than his American Giants team name that was featured in game advertisements. "It is claimed," *Pittsburgh Courier* sports reporter Ira Lewis wrote, "that the Germans learned some of their spy system from the propaganda Rube Foster used to steal away Bingo [DeMoss] from C.I. [Taylor]." In this statement Lewis captures the awe in which his contemporaries held their black baseball father.

If Rube Foster had done nothing else but play and manage the way he did, he would be remembered in baseball annals. But he did much more. He was the key figure in bringing together, on February 13 and 14, 1920, at the Negro Y.M.C.A. in Kansas City, the group of men who established the first national black baseball league at a gathering Ira Lewis characterized as "perhaps the most singular and noteworthy meeting ever held in the interest of our sport life." Foster was aptly characterized as the league's "active, militant, fighting head." Indication of how bold the move was, it was said at the time that only three of the eight founding teams were paying their players a regular salary. A contemporary claimed that Andrew

The great pitcher, Andrew Rube Foster, at bat (ca 1909).

Don't Stop Talking

Martin Dihigo would do anything to manufacture a run. Once, while leading off third base, he screamed at the pitcher, "You balked! You balked!" Dihigo continued to holler, "You balked! You balked!" as he headed toward home. Everyone stared as if Dihigo had suddenly gone mad. But when he crossed the plate and walked slyly into the dugout, the fans started laughing and erupted in cheers.

Foster acted as he did at this time "sensing the death of semi-pro baseball." After all that he and like-minded owners such as C.I. Taylor, J.L. Wilkinson, and Edward Bolden had done with their baseball teams from 1910 to 1920, a league of national scope was a natural next step.

Such a league was heralded at its outset as a great advancement for the race as a whole. According to journalist Lewis, more than sports was involved. "The workings of this league will be watched with more than passing interest by everyone. If it is successful, as we all hope, look for a further merging of colored business interests on a national scale."

Foster and his cohorts could look back in the winter of 1921 with considerable satisfaction on their league's performance. The *Chicago Whip* claimed "one million persons supported their initial effort in 1920." Cristobal Torriente and ace Dave Brown led Foster's Chicago American Giants to a first-place finish in the league's inaugural season. John Holway tells us that Brown was regarded by old-timers as the best left hander produced by the Negro leagues. To become that required a parole from a conviction of armed robbery into the custody of fellow Texan Rube Foster. Torriente's numbers would have been better if he had not played in what arguably was "the worst hitter's park in America."

For 1921 only one team, the Dayton Marcos, was missing from the original eight—but it would be eight again for the second league season with the addition of the Columbus Buckeyes. The Chicago club of founding father Foster repeated their success of 1920, this time besting the St. Louis Stars in a close seasonal race.

As a harbinger of the instability to come, in 1922 teams in Cleveland and Pittsburgh replaced the Columbus Buckeyes and the Chicago Giants of Joe Green. Foster pulled off a rare "three-peat" in professional baseball, beating out the Indianapolis ABCs for the league championship. Debuting that season for the Cubans was the great Martin Dihigo, whose remarkable versatility would make him an excellent player across a long career at every position he played—which turned out to be all nine. His Cubans team boasted what John Holway ranks as among the greatest defensive outfields of all time—Pablo "Champion" Mesa, Alejandro Oms, and Bernardo Baro. Oms could reportedly lean forward and catch a fly ball behind his back.

A BLACK LEAGUE FOR THE EAST

A meeting in the Y.M.C.A. in Philadelphia on December 16, 1922 was the second big black baseball story of the decade. In the colorful phrasing of the *Afro American* reporter covering the event, these men "knocked into a cocked hat the theory that the leading lights of colored baseball would not coincide along materially constructive lines for a permanent organization." What had proven good for Midwestern teams—putting aside their independent status and joining a league—would now be tested in the East.

Strong, independent, prosperous teams had existed for several years in major eastern cities. These clubs had regular access to their own parks. Patronage had been built up. Good transportation by train over relatively short distances made travel an affordable operation. "Men of long experience and good repute" now desired to advance the status of their baseball teams. And the fans were on board. Tired of irregular scheduling, with some crack teams hardly ever playing against natural rivals, fans in the East were ready for a regular schedule "so they could see all eastern teams mix it so they can tell who's who in the east."

Among the Eastern lights of colored baseball, several of whom were white, Edward Bolden of the Hilldale club took the leadership role. The Eastern black press proudly claimed that the formation of the Mutual Association of Eastern Colored Baseball Clubs—in popular terminology the Eastern Colored League—made baseball history. The success of the Western league venture, the existence of several major independent teams geographically convenient to each other, and the 20-year-old structure of the National and American Major Leagues made forming a second Negro major league attractive.

Ed Bolden's own club, the Hilldale Daisies, began its inaugural 1923 league season with pre-league games against tough competition. The team's aging Louis Santop was still holding down catching duties and swinging his Big Bertha with undiminished might. Biz Mackey was filling in ably for veteran great John Lloyd when not spelling him behind the plate, and with Santop, Mackey, and Lloyd on board, the Daisies had three players with Hall of Fame credentials. Fittingly, the Hilldales ended a championship season with a great battle on Hilldale Field against the Paterson Silk Sox. Not so fittingly the Daisies lost the match 1–0 despite a great performance by Hilldale pitching ace Nip Winters. Winters carried a perfect game into the ninth inning, even striking out the first five men to face him, including the heaviest sluggers on the opposing team.

Tall, left-handed Nip Winters is considered by many the best pitcher of the Eastern Colored League. His lights-out pitch was not his fastball but an outstanding curve. His dominance in the first three years of the league is shown in his reported won-loss records of 32–6, 19–5, and 21–10, including two no-hitters. With numbers like these, it is no surprise that he led his club to pennants all three years.

In between the opening win and closing loss to the Silk Sox, the Hilldale club managed to prevail against their fellow Eastern League clubs in a race that was marked by several long victory runs by the second-place Cuban Stars. In its first season, the new league also included the Brooklyn Royal Giants, the New York Lincoln Stars, the Atlantic City Bacharach Giants, and the Black Sox from Baltimore. Colonel C.W. Strothers' Giants from Harrisburg, Pennsylvania and George Robinson's ill-fated Washington Potomacs joined the league in 1924.

A Negro National League—weakened by raids from Eastern clubs in which Biz Mackey, George Scales, Clint Thomas, and Frank Warfield,

The Baltimore Black Sox were founding members of the Eastern Colored League.

among others, jumped to the new league—witnessed the deposing of the perennial champions, the Chicago American Giants, by the Kansas City team that over the years would be the strongest club in Negro baseball. The Kansas City team's stellar lineup included veteran Oscar "Heavy" Johnson at the plate and, arguably, had one of the finest pitching staffs of all time with William Bell, "Bullet" Rogan, José Mendez, and "Big Bill" Drake. Led by Johnson and their great pitching talent, the Kansas City Monarchs overtook the Detroit's Stars. The Chicago American Giants could manage no better than third place.

GROWING PAINS

By the 1923 post-season meeting of the Negro National League, black professional baseball organizations could look back at four seasons of play. Great strides had been made, but there were important issues that still needed to be addressed. Among the most pressing were the perennial scheduling problems, especially acute in 1923 after Milwaukee and Toledo dropped out of the league and the remaining teams had to play an uneven number of games. Player salary limits, excessive costs for umpires, and the quest for new teams filled out the agenda.

Pointed language in the newspaper account of the meeting alludes to the internal tension among team owners, as well as the essential problem facing the league—lack of sufficient capital. As the *Defender* reporter Fay Young put it, "Some of the present members are drawbacks who are willing to promote the success of the league from a moral standpoint, but who are lacking the necessary cash." Young, perhaps influenced by a personal relationship with the league's founding president, was more than willing to advise the baseball magnates as to how best to proceed into the future. "We believe if Foster was given a free hand to make a stock proposition of the league, sell stock to the fans, and have a governing board of directors, that things would move along in a much better shape."

In mid-December 1923, the Eastern league commissioners and team owners met in order to assess the first year's operation and plan for the second season. More corporate in its structure than its Western rival, the Eastern league had organized itself without establishing a presidency. According to the *Afro American* reporter who covered the founding meeting, "the club owners decided to roll up their sleeves and bend their efforts in unison to perfect their ideal." Such an arrangement would be severely tested when in 1924 one of the league's founding members, Nat Strong, found his Brooklyn Royal Giants expelled for failure to play out the agreed-upon schedule. As in the Midwest, scheduling posed a problem for teams that, for the most part, had to rent their ballparks and, for financial reasons, play a full non-league schedule as well as commit to league games.

League expansion occupied a large part of the agenda at the Eastern 1923 meeting, with careful consideration given to the presentations of Ben Taylor and George Robinson representing the Washington Potomacs and to Colonel Strothers of the Harrisburg Giants for admittance to the league. With such known and experienced baseball men—and noting that

José Mendez
The Black Mathewson

The Sporting Life of February, 1909 reported with much anticipation a new Cuban baseball phenom who was coming to the States. "In the party will be pitcher Mendez, who repeatedly beat the Reds and once held them down to a single hit in nine innings. This fellow is coal-black, being a native Cuban, with no Spanish blood, and several of the other players are dark as to their complexion, but as skilled on the field as any white team."

After seeing the great Mendez perform in Cuba, New York Giants manager John McGraw was convinced of the pitcher's talents. McGraw shared his interest in Mendez with a New York City sportswriter who reported that "if Mendez was a white man, he [McGraw] would pay $50,000 for his release from Almendares."

The Cuban hurler's assortment of pitches became a familiar source of misery for major leaguers. At one point in his career, Mendez compiled a scoreless streak of 25 innings pitching against the Cincinnati Reds (1908) and the Detroit Tigers (1909).

In a 1908 game, he held Cincinnati batters hitless through nine innings before settling on a one-hit shutout victory. Many major league officials, players, and U.S. sportswriters proclaimed his big league credentials. Athletics catcher Ira Thomas witnessed the Cuban's exploits firsthand during Philadelphia's 1911 tour of Cuba. "More than one big leaguer from the states has faced him and left the plate with a wholesome respect for the great Cuban star. It is not alone my opinion but the opinion of many others who have seen Mendez pitch that he ranks with the best in the game."

Philadelphia Phillies' John Hans Lobert echoed Thomas's assessment in his report to *The Sporting Life* following the team's December 1911 visit. "Mendez is some pitcher, and here on the island they call him "Mathewson in the Black," and if we could paint him white we surely could use him on the Philly team next season as well as his catcher, Gonzales."

Mendez stood tall among his peers in the American baseball circuit that linked Havana, New York City, Chicago, Tampa, and a host of other cities in between. A Latino pioneer who excelled against both major league and black baseball talent, El *Diamante* Negro (the Black Diamond) is a worthy candidate for election into the National Baseball Hall of Fame.

the "jumps" were not too far and that a compact circuit could be maintained—both applications were favorably acted upon. It was ominously noted that "the weighty matter of drafting a schedule" would be considered at next month's meeting.

CONTESTING THE WEST

Expectations were high in Kansas City as the 1924 season opener drew near. The Monarchs were the defending Western League champions, and in the off season they had lost only one top-notch player, Rube Currie, to Eastern League raiding. With a staff composed of veterans"Bullet" Rogan, Bill Drake, William Bell and manager José Mendez; a fast and unusual all-left-handed outfield in Hurley McNair, Wade Johnson and John Donaldson; and a formidable infield anchored by the steady Frank Duncan at catcher and the outstanding Dobie Moore at shortstop, they were pre-season favorites to repeat.

Carrying one 12-game winning steak into Chicago for a Memorial Day weekend clash with the American Giants, they had been emboldened by their four victories over Foster's men earlier in the month, when they had beat the Chicagoans to "a frazzle humiliating the Giants before thousands of Kansas City folks." One bright Monarchs fan, on his way from his Kansas home to attend the Decoration Day games, was also emboldened—so much so that he wrote an obituary for his club's Chicago rivals:

> Born in Chicago several years ago. Departed this life May 6. Symptoms first noticed Saturday, May 3; pulse 10 to 3. Grew weaker Sunday, May 4; pulse, 10 to 5. At death's door Monday, May 5, pulse, 3–2. In eternal rest, Tuesday, May 6, 14–10. Cause of death, worry and fractured skulls caused by heavy blows from Monarchs' bats. Contributory cause, too much Monarchs. Burial at Schorling's Park, 39th Street and Wentworth Avenue, Chicago. Pall bearers, Drake, Mendez, Rogan and Bell. Honorary pall bearers, Duncan, Moore,

> Allen, Joseph, and McNair. The deceased left to mourn their loss Treadwell and a host of friends. As it pleased the Almighty to wipe out the American Giants in four straight games, be it resolved that fitting services will be held at Schorling's Park both morning and afternoon on Decoration Day, at which time the Monarchs will be in Chicago for five straight games and to place the finishing touches on the graves already started.

As it pleased the Almighty, and the forces of Foster, any wake and burial had to wait until season's end. While the Memorial Day contests saw the Monarchs take the opener 5–1, the Fosterites won the second game 6–2. The Giants 1924 lineup was too strong to be interred so early in the fray. They would prove good enough at season's end to give the Chicagoans a .681 finishing percentage—just not quite good enough to match the incredible seasonal mark of the Monarchs.

Early in June the Kansas City club's hometown *Call* was worried that their team had lost the league lead and dropped into third place. By the end of the month the paper was celebrating series wins over Birmingham, Detroit, and the Cubans, and all but declaring the race for first to be no race at all. "It looks like they'd have to bring in a major league club to keep the Monarchs from having a walk away with this year's pennant," the reporter speculated.

By early August it did appear that a "walk away" was underway with the Giants' .605 a distant second to the Monarchs' incredible .754 league-leading percentage. September's first Sunday saw the Fosterites winning three of four from the Mendez-led Monarchs in meaningless games for an almost clinched Western championship that the *Defender* would announce the next week in a bold headline: "HILLDALE AND KANSAS CITY TO PLAY FOR CHAMPIONSHIP."

An important part of Chicago's future made an extended appearance on the Giants' staff in 1923. In late May, Bill Foster, left hander and baby brother of big Andrew Rube Foster, reportedly on his way to join his brother's team, pitched a masterful exhibition victory for the Memphis Red Sox over "Dizzy" Dismukes' ABCs. Leading citizens of Memphis offered to raise a fund for the younger version of the great Rube to defray his expenses in school and pay his scholarship during the next year if he would only remain with them and play on the Red Sox club. The fates and big brother Andrew decreed otherwise, and young Bill donned an American Giants uniform for the rest of the season. Well, almost for the rest of the season, as he, along with several teammates, left before the final games to return to college studies. Across the next decade and more, he would by some accounts outdo his brother's pitching prowess. Yet three generations would pass before William Hendrick "Willie" Foster joined Rube in the ranks of baseball immortals enshrined in the National Baseball Hall of Fame.

There was a high level of excitement as the Eastern Colored League opened its second season of play, and the spirit carried through the summer. Three weeks into July, Oscar Charleston of Harrisburg was leading the league at a hefty .421 clip. The Lincoln Giants, who led the Eastern Colored League in the beginning of July, dropped two games to the Bacharachs of Atlantic City. Jim Keenan's Lincolns went from first place at mid-season to a third-place finish at season's close, well behind the .681 championship clip posted by the Hilldale Daisies.

In the East, the 1924 season had gotten off to a bad start with excessive rain. *Courier* columnist Rollo Wilson bemoaned that, due to cancellations, teams have lost "gobs of money," and due to lack of morning practice, "pitchers are in bad shape, fielders' arms and legs refuse to function properly, and batters' eyes are befogged."

The season's lowest point, however, came off the field of play with the news that veteran Bill Pettus was in a Long Island sanatorium making an unequal fight with "the geat white plague," tuberculosis. Appeals went out across the league for donations to aid him in his difficult times. "HELP THIS MAN" pleaded Rollo Wilson in a column of July 2 announcing plans for a benefit game scheduled for September. Much admired for his steady play across a long career in Negro baseball, and for his managerial abilities with several clubs, Pettus was, said Wilson, "a staunch figure of our sporting world."

GAME DELAYED BY KLAN

The Kansas City Comets dropped a hard fought game Sunday to the Garden City, Mo., team. The score was 3–0. The feature of the game was the airtight pitching of "Hezie" Connors. The game was lost by errors in the pinches and the failure of the Comets to hit at needed times. An interesting incident too was that a Klan meeting was being held in the park when the Comets got to Garden City, which delayed the game for an hour.

—*Kansas City Call*, August 1, 1924

A near riot in Harrisburg on July 24 occured in a clash between that city's Giants and the visiting Cubans. Near the end of a tight contest, the umpire called the Cubans' Estrada out on strikes. When words ensued, Estrada's teammate Fabre threw dirt in the umpire's face, then struck him and knocked him down. Spectators and players flocked to the field, and some Cubans waded into the mob with their bats. It required great effort on the part of the police to quell the fight. In the aftermath of the fracas the umpires brought charges against Estrada and Levis; these charges included inciting a riot, assault and battery, and attempting to kill. The *Courier* reported that no arrests had been made as the Cuban players left Harrisburg immediately after the game. Ominously, the paper noted they would be placed under arrest as soon as they returned to Pennsylvania.

It turned out to be the Black Sox from Baltimore, with Jud Wilson and John Beckwith leading the way, who gave Hilldale its closest competition for league champion by finishing in second place with a .632 winning percentage. But when the season's dust had settled, it was "Clan Darbie" representing Hilldale who headed off to the Negro baseball post-season.

A TRUE COLORD CHAMPIONSHIP

What came next was arguably the biggest black baseball event in the history of blackball up to then. With two successful leagues in place after 1923, the next logical step would be the staging of a Negro World Series.

The Doctor Calls

Franklin "Doc" Sykes pitched for some fine Black Sox teams in the early 20s with players like Blaney Hall, Charlie Thomas, Joe Lewis, and Jud Wilson providing strong support in the field and at bat for their teammate on the mound. Sykes' 1922 season was one of the best recorded in the history of Negro professional baseball. In that year's campaign he took the mound for the Sox 37 times, supposedly winning 30, losing 6, with one tie, although scores for only eight games have been found.

The Kansas City Call reports on one of Sykes' memorable games with the headline, "BALTIMORE PITCHER INTO HALL OF FAME."

Baltimore, Md, Sept 21—It is the ambition of every baseball pitcher to some time during his career on the mound to pitch a no-hit no-run game. Only a few twirlers are ever able to achieve this feat, and when it is done with the least number of batters that are required to play a regular game, 27, that hurler at once strides majestically into the baseball Hall of Fame.

Last Sunday at Maryland Park, "Doc" Sykes, the ace of the Black Sox staff, felt the urge of achievement stirring within him and decided that this was as good a day as any to cross the portals of the Hall, and forthwith he went to the box against the Original Bacharach Giants of Atlantic City (who by the way are playing a far better brand of ball than the New York team of the same name), in the first game of a twin set-to, and hurled a no-hit no-run game, doing it with the additional feat of having only 27 men face him, three in each inning and without a single pass. Only two men were retired on strikes, and the game was played in exactly one hour and twenty minutes.

There had been many series billed by their promoters as contests for the "World Championship of Negro Baseball." Promoted by their participants to that status, there could be no true championship until there was a league structure. As the 1923 season progressed, fans, sportswriters, and executives expressed a growing desire for a Negro League World Series. But the one man whose opinion counted the most wasn't ready—and until Rube Foster was, there would be no World Series.

He had good reasons to hold out. Several of his league teams had lost contracted players to raiding by Eastern clubs during the preceding two baseball seasons. Ed Bolden, the key figure from the East in negotiations for a World Series, also loudly accused Foster of pocketing for the league coffers a $1,000 Negro National League entry fee, paid by the Hilldale owner when he joined the Western circuit and not returned on Bolden's withdrawal of his club from the league. Their argument grew intense. Foster labeled Bolden "a deliberate teller of lies," and claimed this showed how little the Philadelphian "meant to help advance the Negro in his profession." Bolden fired back in uncompromising terms, and even the usually reserved John Lloyd entered the fray with a public condemnation of Foster as employing "the common method of time immemorial of men of his class who have preyed on the race by posing as a 'race man.'" So, the ruler of black baseball was in no mood for a peace with the East. There would be no black World Series in 1923. "It must come in time," a *Courier* scribe intoned at the height of the clamor, "but according to Foster that time is not now."

But the idea of a World Series proved stronger than personal enmity. The World Series would wait until 1924 for fulfillment. And when it came, it came on Rube's terms.

Foster insisted that before a series could take place, there must be a clear agreement to prevent players from jumping their contracts and signing with the highest bidder. The clamor for a post-season classic reached new heights as the 1924 season unfolded, culminating in a meeting between Eastern and Western baseball magnates at the 135th Street Y.M.C.A. in New York City on September 10. An agreement was reached to stage a Negro Leagues World Series to open in Philadelphia on October 3. The contest would be between the winner of the Eastern League, Hilldale of Darby, Pennsylvania, and the Kansas City Monarchs, who had won the Negro National League flag after a season-long struggle with the Chicago American Giants.

The competitive Andrew Foster must have left that meeting disappointed that it was the Monarchs, and not his American Giants, that would set baseball history. But the league president was pleased that an arbitration commission would be appointed to handle contract disputes. "No club will have the right to interfere with players under contract with any other club in either league unless by legitimate lawful trade by club owners or by sale," the agreement stipulated. Furthermore, each club in both leagues would be given a list of players on every club within the leagues. Players whose names were on what we would call today a reserve list would not be allowed to change teams. On paper, at least, the matter of players jumping contracts—which Foster and others claimed had hurt Western franchises—had now come to an end.

Pre-series attention was extensive in the black press. The Monarchs were the clear favorite. But off-the-field results were talked about almost as much as the anticipated on-the-field outcome. The larger picture here was what this World Series meant for the future of black professional baseball. As one writer proclaimed, "The first Negro World Series marks the ending of one of the most bitterly fought baseball wars of all time." A World Series, it was said, would acquaint the fans of both circuits with all the teams, and show baseball officials the weaknesses of continued strife.

By this time baseball and the press as black institutions were joined at the hip, the growth of either in this pairing influenced significantly by the growth of the other. When the first Negro World Series came to Chicago, the Honorable Robert S. Abbott, owner of the *Chicago Defender*, threw out the first ceremonial ball. "He strode to the mound and donned Rogan's cap and glove," the account goes, "took a great wind-up and shot the ball up to the plate like a regular catcher." The premier black publisher of his time—indeed arguably in all of black history—appropriately took his place at the center of what was arguably black baseball's most important moment.

The series delivered exciting baseball. As an old fan put it about game five, "there will never be better baseball than that Hilldale half of the eighth Saturday." With the bases full and no one out, the score 2–1 in favor

Advice from the "Black Snake"

Willie Powell, star pitcher for the Chicago American Giants, told historian John Holway a valuable tip passed down to him by older veteran, Rube Currie: When he was young, Currie could throw hard as anybody. The "Black Snake, as Currie was called, once quipped "You know what their [a batters'] weakness was? A fastball between the eyes."

of the Monarchs, and the big guns of the Hilldale lineup coming to the plate, not a runner got home. The eighth game was lost by Hilldale in the ninth inning when two key errors led to three runs, a Monarch victory, and an upset Rube Currie who had brought his club to within a hairsbreadth of victory over his former Monarch mates. "The wrath of Mr. Currie was being expressed in the clubhouse in language which beggars description," wrote the *Kansas City Call* reporter. "It was cold outside, but it was plenty hot in the Hilldale quarters." Hilldale responded to Currie's wrath and took game nine 5–3.

With four victories apiece and one tie, the outcome came down to a tenth deciding game on Monday, October 20, played in Chicago. Right up to game time it was a question mark as to who would pitch for the Monarchs. Perhaps the least likely candidate was the great Mendez himself, aged veteran of many a baseball war, manager now of the Kansas City club, and under orders from his doctor after a recent operation that "he pitch no more ball this season as it might injure him permanently." But his response to his doctor was, "I don't care. I want to win today." So pitch he did, giving what has to be one of the most remarkable clutch performances in the history of America's national game.

For seven innings the game was nip and tuck with both pitchers dominating. The Monarchs broke through in the eighth when Hilldale's "Script" Lee inexplicably departed from his up-to-then very successful script, and went from an underhand submarine delivery to overhand tosses. Five runs produced a final score of Monarchs 5 and Hilldales 0. Carl Beckwith in the *Call* captures this great baseball moment:

> The temperature had dropped oodles of degrees between Sunday evening and Monday noon and fur coats predominated in the stands....Murmurs of discontent and surprise created a hum when Mendez was announced as pitcher for the Westerners. It was not hot enough for Joe so they thought. But they changed their minds. For inning after inning Joe kept the Easterners popping up or grounding out. Not a man reached second, and only four reached first. It is improbable that Mendez will ever pitch another such game. He wasn't there for a strike out record; just 'cut' any kind of way was what he wanted. He kept the Easterners popping up, hitting long flies, or grounding out all afternoon. And therein lies the answer to the win. He kept the ball, as cold as it was, under his control always.

Paid attendance for the nine-game series totaled just under 46,000. Kansas City players received $4,927.32 to split among themselves; the losing Hilldale players, $3,284.88. While there was grumbling among some players about the size of their World Series paycheck, the $3,200 divided among the Hilldale men was only a few hundred dollars shy of that club's monthly payroll. The guarantee at the outset that every player would make as much as his regular salary for the series games was met.

NEGRO MINOR LEAGUES

The many black semi-pro teams that played all through the decade helped to develop players, provided a significant source of revenue in barnstorming opponents, and spured widespread interest in the game. Numerous clubs, highly skilled and organized, traveled widely outside their home regions; they seem for the most part to have paid their players a regular salary, and they provided formidable competition in non-league contests with Negro league teams. These clubs had names that were easily recognized by the thousands of fans across the nation who came out to see them play. In one call for reform at the top, the astute Fay Young proposed that several of the best of these teams be brought into the Negro National and Eastern Colored Leagues' tent under a national agreement, thus building a relationship in scope and extent similar to that between white professional baseball's major and minor leagues.

One of the best known of these "Triple A" outfits was Gilkersons Union Giants, whose home territory covered a wide swath of the Midwest. Accounts of Gilkersons games are a constant in the *Chicago Defender* and other black papers throughout the 1920s. With the 1924 World Series naturally commanding most of the sports pages, a reader still found four game accounts in the Pittsburgh *Courier* of the Gilkersons hitting Carl Mays hard, and defeating the star Yankee right hander's Big League All Stars before large crowds in Eldora, Iowa. In Pittsburgh, Seth Hall's Keystones were constantly competing with the Homestead Grays for the baseball fans' allegiance in western Pennsylvania, while their organizer and president squabbled as constantly with Grays owner, Cum Posey.

In Philadelphia, Danny McClelland's Giants played regularly in their native area, and every summer went "nor'east" to New England, especially the Boston area, "because it is there that the money is in semi pro ball." Rollo Wilson would write in the middle of the decade, "My boy friends who are vacationing in New England as the Philadelphia Giants are having a wonderful time and winning three fourths of their battles with the natives." Joe Green's Chicago Giants popped in and out of the Negro National League in the early 1920s. And everywhere you looked, there he would be, arguably the best teacher and wiliest negotiator of them all, Chappie Johnson with his All Stars. Readers were told "by expert" in the January 3, 1925, Pittsburgh *Courier*, that "Chappie has developed more good baseball players than any man in the east, and rivals the late C. I. Taylor as a developer of young ball players."

While there was no formal affiliation between these clubs and their counterparts in the Negro major leagues, they served as a baseball training grounds to develop youngsters—and in some instances as a place to "play out the string" for oldsters. Typical items from the *Courier* in the

Sports Rialto and Baseball Headquarters, which is another way of referring to the Roadside Hotel, seethed during the day. Rumors ran like a prairie fire after a ten weeks drought. Bald-headed magnates became balder. Special traffic cops had to keep the crowds moving. And when the shouting and the tumult died Mr. Johnson revealed that he had snared a few stars to help him out during the season. According to Chappie his game bag contained George Britt of the Black Sox, Wilbur Cooper of Harrisburg, Buck Ewing whom Colonel Keenan thought he had signed, and George Washington Johnson of Clan Darbie. In addition, Carter, formerly of Hilldale and Harrisburg, was among the freight. Chappie said that lines were laid for other game and that his next haul would be even more fruitful. He whispered some names to me and when he gets those men Billy Penn will leap from his pedestal on City Hall.

The hometown of Chappie Johnson's All-Stars is Amsterdam, New York, where the team plays on Fridays and Sundays. The outfit in now on a fifteen-game trip through Albany, Hartford, Waterbury, Springfield and other Eastern League towns. Then Chappie jumps to the NY-Penn circuit and meets Binghamton, Williamsport, and Elmira. Numbered among his players are Sam Warmack, Sees Johnson, Don Perry, Dick Fels, Ridgely, Darknight Smith and Baby Hobson.

Chappie claims that Buck Ewing is the greatest catcher in baseball and that he will be the star of the men in the iron masks for the next decade. He says that he is the one catcher who can teach young pitchers how to PITCH and how to THINK. He is the biggest gate attraction on his squad.

No man in the national pastime has had a more colorful career than the 55-year-old Johnson. Even yet he can don a uniform and play a credible game at short, first, or in the outfield and the old batting eye has not forsaken him. His has been a life of ups and down, but he coined the expression which he claims the Salvation Army copped from him—"A man may be down, but he is never out."

—Rollo Wilson,
Pittsburgh Courier, April 11, 1925

mid-1920s make that point clear. Arthur "Rats" Henderson, pitching ace of the Bacharach Giants, jumped that team in 1924 to join the "hypnotic Chappie Johnson who is without peer when it comes to converting ball players to his way of thinking." In this instance the conversion wasn't permanent, as Henderson would rejoin the Bacharachs for future Negro league seasons. The same paper in the same year notes that Paul Stevens, who trained under Danny McClellan on the Philadelphia Giants, was now with the Hilldale club, as was Nick Carter, who had left Chappie Johnson to join that team. Two years later the paper reported that the young Webster McDonald and the youthful Bill Yancy, both future Negro league players, were playing with Danny McClellan's Philadelphia Giants. These clubs were also places where Negro major-league quality players could find a baseball home more personably suitable than what they found in the Negro National or Eastern Colored Leagues. The fine catcher Buck Ewing is the best case in point, with a considerable stint throughout the 1920s playing for Chappie Johnson and his All Stars when he wasn't with a Negro major league club.

Below these upper-tier teams were teams perhaps comparable to Double A minor league ball. These clubs might travel outside their immediate territory, sometimes for long distances, but played most of their games close to home. Players were likely to be unsalaried, but expenses would be covered, and they could share on a percentage basis in the attendance take. Sometimes they would use the papers to "advertise" for games. "Winston Giants Baseball Team Manager K. T. Timlic, Royal Sports Club, 1056 Trade Street, Winston-Salem North Carolina, winners of 33 straight games last season easily winning the southern championship wishes to hear from all the best teams in this country" reads the not unusual notice in the April 12, 1919, *Chicago Defender*.

Samplings of game reports from one issue of the *Defender* in the middle of the summer of 1922 give a taste of the geographic extent of the games being played on this level of Negro professional baseball. The paper has the Kentucky Reds in Atlantic City playing the Vineland nine. The Buffalo Stars are squaring off against the Tate Stars of Cleveland. It is the Illinois Giants versus Wausaukee. The Panama Red Sox are in Brooklyn while the Virginia Giants are playing in New York. The Illinois Giants are at Antigo, Wisconsin. And then there are the Cleveland Cubs, the Grand Central Red Caps, and the Kosy Korner Club, run by an Italian immigrant, Rocky Alvalony, owner of the Kosy Corner Café at 580 Lenox Avenue. Alvalony is "one of the best known sporting men in Harlem and 100% American."

A third tier of professional blackball contained the numerous semi-pro teams that stayed close to their home, with players who undoubtedly played for the enjoyment of the games and had little expectation of ever moving up the ladder to the Negro major leagues. But at times they clearly wanted to move up at least a rung or two on the black baseball ladder. This kind of team is represented well by a club the New York *Amsterdam News* headlined as "A NEW TEAM AND A GOOD ONE." Typical of the upbeat, optimistic air of the press release that a story like this was likely based on, it advertises the New York Sports as a "Colored team organized now for three years. The present team has very much pleased Manager Bonelli having met some of the fastest and hardest hitting teams in the Bronx and other places in and around NY. Their aim now is to own their own grounds. They hope to do that with outside help and are seeking the interest of all those interested in colored baseball to make that happen."

NEGRO LEAGUE BASEBALL AT MID-DECADE

While not playing in the first Negro World Series, Rube Foster's Chicago American Giants were still a powerful team, albeit challenged now for center stage in the West by J. L. Wilkerson's Kansas City Monarchs. Before the 1925 season even began, however, it appeared that the indomitable one would no longer command from the bridge of his league battleship. "NATIONAL NEGRO BASEBALL LEAGUE IS AUTOMATICALLY DISBANDED AS FOSTER RESIGNS" reads the headline in the January 3 issue of the New York Age. As with the case of Mark Twain's famous reply to reports that he had died, so too, it would be quickly noted, were the reports of Rube Foster's resignation "greatly exaggerated."

The temptation to resign may have been real. Long-held urges to get out of the league business and concentrate on his baseball team could only have been exacerbated by the nasty public quarrel he had in the 1924 off-season with J. Tenny Blount, owner of the Detroit Stars and erstwhile friend and confidant. In a series of sensational articles in the *Pittsburgh Courier* he aired much Foster dirty linen in public. Blount charged that Foster, in complete control of league affairs since its founding, had used his positions as league president, owner and manager of the key league club, and booking agent as well, to bankrupt several member teams, including Blount's Detroit Stars, in order to make money for himself.

Whatever the sources for the resignation story, the hopes of his enemies were quickly quashed. "THE NEGRO NATIONAL LEAGUE IS FAR FROM DEAD" announced the *Norfolk Journal and Guide* over a story with an Associated Negro Press byline:

> "The Negro National Baseball League is not dead and is not going to die," declared Andrew Foster… in an exclusive interview with the Associated Negro Press.… With a twist of his good pipe, and a seriousness of expression he often carries when the American Giants have made a rumble in a tight game, Foster advised, "I am merely getting rid of men who are not able to advance; I am weak from such burdens." The seriousness turned to a smile and twinkle in his eyes when he said, "That is why the kickers love their president. When he cuts off the finances he has robbed them."

Rube Foster would remain in command of league affairs in the West in 1925, and he was determined to regain control of play on the field as well. Smarting from the absence of his Giants from the first World Series, he appeared from the outset of the season to be more eager than ever to win at whatever the cost. He commanded the preseason headline in the *Courier* of March 7 with a banner that screamed "RUBE FOSTER RELEASES PRACTICALLY ENTIRE TEAM." "I need to reorganize," Rube said. "I need new men. I need youth and pep. Kansas City won the pennant last year. I am going to furnish them with real opposition this year." But it was not easy for the Rube. "It gripped at the heartstrings to let some of these players, dear and personal friends of mine, and men who have stuck with me through thick and thin, go, but I had to do it for the good of the organization."

At first his wrecking seemed to pay dividends when his revamped Giants took three games out of five from the Monarchs in an at-home series in early May. Profit dividends were realized as well when the Sunday game saw a record crowd of 18,000 at Schorling Park "go wild" as Cristobal Torriente tripled to center in the 12th inning, and then scored the winning run as the Monarchs' Johnson gathered in Dave Malarcher's sacrifice fly.

But three out of five early on was not enough to derail a Kansas City club that was touted in the preseason as boasting an infield of Lem Hawkins, Newt Allen, Dobie Moore, and Newt Joseph that "looked like a $1,000,000 combination." Rookies Nelson Dean and Chet Brewer complemented a veteran staff of Cliff Bell, Big Bill Drake, Bullet Rogan, and William Bell. The "Old Master," manager José Mendez, occasionally took the mound where he was indeed the master. The club overcame illness and injury to its $1,000,000 contingent, and as the oppressive heat of a Midwestern early July rolled into Kansas City, the Monarchs took four out of five from the Cuban Stars to clinch the first half of a split-season schedule. On their way they were the architects of humiliation for the Fostermen, constructing five straight victories in a series over the Giants in late May in Kansas City. Sore from that experience, the "rejuvenated" Chicagoans could take little consolation from early June victories against the Memphis Red Sox, and ended the first half with a mediocre 26–22 record, finishing in fourth place behind the Monarchs, St. Louis, and Detroit.

Perhaps adjusting to the newness of its lineup, and with the addition of several late-season imports such as pitcher Webster McDonald from

Wilbur Rogan
The Bullet from Kay See

"There are few pitchers in the game today, regardless of color, who look as good on the mound as Rogan. His stand is beautiful. His wind-up perfect. He is a great twirler; we venture to say another Matty or Foster."

Wilbur "Bullet" Rogan was equally talented on the mound and in the batter's box. He did not play in the Negro Leagues until the age of 30, but his fame long preceded his debut. "Bullet Rogan, star pitcher with the Kansas City Monarchs, holds the strikeout record of all times for a single game." Once while Bullet served in the U.S. Army, where he first gained his fame, his twirling left 25 batters without doing more than whiffing the breeze. Rogan's record in the service will probably stand for some time, winning 58 and losing 2. Combining a great fastball and a curve, he went on to compile a .721 winning percentage (111–43) in the Negro Leagues. Yankees manager Casey Stengel called Rogan "one of the best—if not the best—pitcher that ever pitched."

His bat produced equally prodigious numbers during his 11 seasons with Kansas City. He hit over .300 (twice over .400) in 1922-1930, and he often hit cleanup for the Monarchs. In all, he compiled a .339 batting average, 10th among all Negro Leaguers. He showed similar prowess against white teams. In 25 games against major league teams, Rogan batted .329.

With twin tools like that, Wilbur Rogan's double threat was better than just about any triple threat. He was posthumously inducted into the Baseball Hall of Fame in 1998.

the East and third baseman Leroy Stratton from Birmingham, Chicago fared better in the second half of the season. But its respectable .596 winning percentage could not match the Monarchs' .737, and the phenomenal 35–11–2 and .761 mark of the second-half winner, the St. Louis Stars.

A closely fought championship playoff series to decide whether the Kansas City squad would win the right to repeat their fall triumph of the previous year propelled the Monarchs into the second Negro League

"Unser Joe" Gets a Face-Lift

Another "hero" besides Mr. Currie emerged from the 1925 series. Joe Harris was his name—and an interesting tale attaches to him. For some reason known as "Unser" Joe, he was a World War I veteran. One of Joe's favorite pastimes in his war days, Rollo Wilson tells us, was to "make faces at every Boche machine gun he espied." One morning one of those German war tools spat a leaden stream at our hero, rearranging his face to give Joe's visage the appearance of an ex-prize fighter from the knock-down drag-out era. But this story has a happy ending. Beauty trumps disfigurement. A skin graft operation after Hilldale's 25-series triumph by a skillful surgeon was a success. Big League fans and writers are to be forewarned. "When you see a familiar squat figure slouching toward the plate, but with a strange map above those shoulders, content yourself in peace. It's the same Joe Harris."

World Series. It was fitting that the decisive seventh game 3–0 playoff clincher was pitched by Wilbur "Bullet" Rogan, whose anchoring of the Monarchs staff for many seasons to come would eventually earn him induction into the National Baseball Hall of Fame. Of his performance on that clinching day, someone was heard to say, "It was dusky, and a fast ball was needed to win. Bullet had it."

In the East, 1925 turned out to be the year of the Hilldales. They were led by their aces Nip Winters and Rube Currie. Good pitching from spitballer Winters and elongated right hander Currie characterized the entire season of the Hilldale club. On August 13 in Philadelphia, Currie yielded seven hits against a Cubans lineup anchored by the redoubtable Martin Dihigo and the veteran hard-hitting center fielder "Walla Walla" Oms. While Hilldale could garner but six hits from the Cuban Stars ace Juanelo Mirabal, Currie was still returned a winner in rather easy fashion when Bolden's crew scored a 5–2 victory. Two days later the Hilldale's third pitching gun, Phil Cockrell, the "Georgia Rose," barely missed his fifth career no-hitter when "by far the most meddlesome individual that has ever left Cuba's verdant isle for these arid states of ours, the veteran mitt artist and capable receiver, José Maria Fernandez, inserted a puny single in the fifth inning of the fracas waged at Hilldale park and deprived Cockrell of a no hit no run game." As it was, Cockrell blanked the Cubans 4–0.

At season's end Hilldale's 52–15 and .776 record outpaced the Oscar Charleston-led Harrisburg Giants' 37–19 and .660.

Still scheduled as a best five of nine games, and played this year at the home cities of the two clubs, the 5–1 rout by Hilldale over the Western champion Monarchs in the second Negro World Series is belied by the closeness of the scores. Former Monarch Rube Currie fittingly won a 2–1 Hilldale victory in game five in Philadelphia. When Phil Cockrell closed out the Monarchs with a 5–2 victory in game six, Currie was spared the need to fill the clubhouse with the foul language he had used when his teammates, through poor fielding, cost him his coveted win and world championship in 1924.

SOUTHERN PROFESSIONAL BASEBALL

By the middle of the decade, fans of blackball could look south as well as east and west. After the 1920 founding of the Negro National League, it would take three full seasons of play before the two centers of Dixie blackball, Memphis and Birmingham, turned up as league members. Neither team fared particularly well across the duration of the decade, finishing generally in the bottom half of league standings. The Nashville Elite Giants joined these two southern clubs in that "faring not so well" category for the 1929 and 1930 seasons, when the league was struggling to survive in the midst of the Depression. While competing in the league, all three Southern teams would of course play extensively outside the league schedule as well.

The decade's highlight for Southern black professional baseball would have to be the 1926 season, when Birmingham and Memphis played entirely outside the Negro National League in what was arguably, for that one season, a third Negro major league. "SOUTHERN LEAGUE FANS ON EDGE

FOR THE BIRMINGHAM MEMPHIS 'WORLD SERIES'" announced the *Chicago Defender* headline of September 11, 1926, a reference to the "Little World Series" that was to determine the championship of the South. Excitement was running high in both cities. For the series opener in Memphis there was a big parade preceding the game. People flocked to the series from all parts of the South, including a group from Birmingham with at least 2,000 people. As a sign of the intense interest in these contests, the Chicago paper shared a prediction that it would take a special company of the 24th Infantry to keep apart rival fans.

The Little World Series brought to an end a season when the league made a wonderful showing. It was an eight-team circuit with clubs stretching across a wide swath of the South. New Orleans had its Ads, joining the Memphis Red Sox, Louisville White Sox, Albany (Georgia) Giants, Birmingham Black Barons, Atlanta Black Crackers, Montgomery Gray Sox, and Chattanooga White Sox. All league teams seem to have played a more than respectable schedule of 50-plus games. Reporting of games in Northern papers like the *Defender*, which circulated widely through the South, was steady. Star players like the Negro National veteran Steel Arm Taylor had outstanding seasons. In the second half alone, the steel-armed one is said to have captured 14 games out of the 16 he started.

In 1922 a previous incarnation of a Southern Negro League had opened the season with the league champions, the Elite Giants of Nashville, as favorites to cop the title again "with the greatest galaxy of ball players ever to play under the name of Elite Giants." At season's end the headline in the *Defender* announced: "A NEW LEAGUE FOR SOUTHLAND GETS UNDER WAY, Blowing Up of Southern in Middle of Playing Season Is Cause of Action."

With promises of a new Southern League forming whose nucleus would be around New Orleans, the *Defender* reporter looked back on the "blowing up" of its predecessor that had been accomplished "partly through mismanagement and the lack of baseball experience." Among the lessons learned in the league's disappearance was the importance of giving the fans a schedule that would be played, an adequate deposit paid by each team into the league coffers, and limits on players' salaries. In spite of the optimism that resources could be found to bring a stable and profitable organized league to the South, 1926 seems to be the only year in the decade when any of these conditions came close to existing.

THE MOST EXCITING OF SEASONS

You would have to search long and hard to find a year that equals the fine, tight, well-fought professional baseball of 1926. Ironically, prospects for the year did not look particularly promising at first. National economic prospects were dismal. Writing in April, a *Courier* reporter worried over an unemployment situation that "had struck all sections. Men are idle now who will be idle when the baseball season begins. This means they will not attend many baseball games. They are playing a game of catch up and will not attend games as often as they did last season." Tough economic times, and some tough weather, did extract a price in 1926. The two Southern teams of the previous two league seasons were no longer in the circuit, and two clubs in the West, the Dayton Marcos and the Cleveland Elites, and one in the East, the widely heralded Newark Stars, were unable to complete the schedule.

As the season played out, however, it was clear that neither bad weather nor difficult economic conditions could deter Pittsburgh's wonder team. Cum Posey's Grays were still playing as an independent club outside the league structure. "Once in the lifetime of the average baseball fan," wrote *Courier* columnist William Nunn, "comes the opportunity to observe the actions of a real 'wonder team.' This club, skimming along through fair weather and foul, has succeeded in setting a mark for successive wins unequalled or unheard of before in the ranks of baseball." With superlative pitching coming from the newly acquired and ageless veteran, Smokey Joe Williams, supported by fellow top-rank starters Lefty Williams, Oscar "Four No Hitters" Owens, and Sam Streeter, they won 65 victories with only 3 defeats by early July.

In league play in the East, as the season wore down to a finish, baseball was just as exciting. "BACHARACHS, CUBANS, HILLDALE AND HARRISBURG IN GREAT 'FOUR-CORNERED' FIGHT FOR FIRST HONORS AS CLOSING WEEKS OF EASTERN LEAGUE RACE ARRIVE" announced the *Courier* headline of September 11. For reporter G. H. Lockhart, 1926 had been the hardest of seasons to pick a winner. At the opening bell the Hilldale club, "one of the greatest Negro, or better still one of the greatest teams in the country," was the favorite to be standing first at season's close. Next to them were the formidable Harrisburg Senators with the great Oscar Charleston at the helm. Looming up big later were the Lincoln Giants, led by the peer of Negro baseball, John H. Lloyd. And to be closely watched as well were Ben Taylor's Baltimore Black Sox.

Nowhere to be seen, except at league's bottom, were the Bacharachs from Atlantic City. But then the unexpected happened:

> The Bacharach Giants have astonished the world in the past six weeks. They jumped from the bottom to 'Sit On Top Of The World.' They won fourteen straight league games and have made an unquestionable bid for the flag. The strange part about the Bacharachs club is the fact that two months ago nearly every man had some ailment—knees out of joint, charley horses, pitchers with sore arms and everything that would hinder a team. But in the face of all that they rest calmly upon 'Yon Sun Kissed Hill' where fame crowns the heroes heads. They fight to prove the ability and capability of youth. They battle not to lower the standards of Negro baseball, but to raise them in order that the future may hand out more promising things to the Negro baseball world.

Their leader was Dick Lundy, also called "King Richard." Lundy, the best shortstop of the 1920s, became the Bacharachs' manager in 1926 and led them to two consecutive championships. A superb fielder, he had a gun for an arm that allowed him to play deep at short. As for his hitting, he consistently topped the .300 mark. He was joined on the left side of the infield by Oliver "Ghost" Marcelle. As a third baseman, he was known for making spectacular fielding plays, knocking down bullets, and firing to first. At the plate he was a feared clutch hitter. If he had any faults, it was his "hot Creole temper," which caused fights with umpires and other players.

With leaders like that, it was no surprise that by the end of the season the Bacharachs had a .630 winning percentage to Harrisburg's .595. They were westward-bound to the third World Series.

Who the victors would be in the West that year was anyone's guess. At season's end, a best five-out-of-nine series between first-half winner Kansas City and second-half champs Chicago was needed. When the Monarchs won three out of four on their home field, and took the first contest at the American Giants' Schorling Park grounds, the outcome seemed assured.

What no one counted on was Willie Foster—no one, that is, but the Giants themselves. Needing a sweep of a final doubleheader on September 29, manager Dave Malarcher, who assumed the team's reins that summer after Rube Foster was hospitalized, sent younger brother Willie to the mound against Kansas City's best, Bullet Rogan. Light snow was falling as one of the great pitching duels of baseball history commenced. It took nine innings for either team to score a run. That one tally came in the bottom half when pitcher Foster sacrificed Stanford Jackson to third, and with two out, Sandy Thompson hit a walk-off single to register the win for Chicago.

Historian John Holway takes us into the American Giants clubhouse after Foster's great performance. "'Who do you want to pitch the second game?' Dave Malarcher asked his players. They replied with one voice, 'Foster!' When Bullet Rogan saw who was warming up, he took the ball from the appointed starter Chet Brewer, determined to match Willie Foster and avenge the first game loss." Shortened because of approaching darkness to a five-inning contest, the score stood 5–0 when the game was called for lack of light. It is unusual for any pitcher to throw a shutout. It is rare for a hurler to pitch two in one day. Willie Foster had sparked one of the greatest comebacks in playoff history, black or white.

While the season was filled with excitement on the field, all was not smooth at its close. As late as September 6, 1926, Fay Young in his *Defender* column was expressing serious doubts that a third World Series would be played that fall. But series there was. If it weren't for what had preceded it in the regular season, it would be hard to imagine more exciting baseball than what was given to fans of the black game in the 1926 world championship.

But as the third black World Series opened, anticipation of seeing fine baseball took a back seat to different kinds of feelings. Two figures who should have been present were missing from the dugouts that each would have commanded if fate had not intervened. One would be hard pressed to find two men of the Negro leagues more deserving of being participants in this Negro League World Series than Andrew "Rube" Foster and John Henry "Pop" Lloyd. Rube had been confined since midsummer to a mental institution in Kankakee, Illinois, after a tragic breakdown that would end his great baseball career. Pop was the manager for the 1926 season of the fifth-place New York Lincoln Giants, after serving the Bacharachs for the two previous seasons as their manager.

Unlike the majors, only the second game in the series was played in Atlantic City. In an effort to boost attendance, games one, four, and five were staged in Philadelphia, with games six though eleven played in Chicago. Games one and four ended in a tie due to darkness, thus necessitating eleven games in all. Game three played in Baltimore is the most often commented upon as it featured a no-hitter by the young Claude "Red" Grier, leading his Bacharachs to a lopsided 10–0 victory. A better game baseball-wise was the deciding tenth game at Chicago. The Giants from Atlantic City outhit the Giants from the Windy City 10–4. Unfortunately for the Bacharachs, the Chicago Americans outfielded them no errors to three and, with the wily Willie Foster pitching out of several tight spots, outscored them 1–0. The storied Chicago American Giants had triumphed in their first Negro League World Series—without the great Rube Foster.

Soon the entire Negro leagues would lose their towering founder. With his demise would come the onset of the Great Depression, throwing black baseball into turmoil. The Roaring Twenties would prove to be a high point. During the next decade, the fortunes of the leagues would, for the most part, head downward.

McIntire Children's Home baseball squad, Zanesville, Ohio.

Hope for the Future

When the great little 'Cum' Posey sends the Homestead Grays against the Lincoln Giants the fur is going to fly. Posey says that New York can't beat Pittsburgh at anything and is willing to back his opinion. Line forms to the right for local mouthologists who bet, but never put up or pay when they lose."

—New York Amsterdam News, June 6, 1928

POST-SEASON 1929 WITNESSED WHAT HAD BECOME A REGULAR occurrence in recent years, black big leagues versus white big leagues. The American Giants squared off against a strong contingent of American League All-Stars led by future Hall of Famers Heinie Manush, Harry Heilmann and Charlie Gehringer. As things would have it, the black club had an answer with three of its own, Willie Wells, Bill Foster and Cool Papa Bell. Led by George "Mule" Suttles' three triples and a home run, the American Giants won the series, 3–2. Bill Foster won games 1 and 2, and dropped a close 2–0 final contest. Game three witnessed one of the great inter-racial contests of the century. John Holway describes:

> Frog Holsey and Lefty Whitehill battled to a 0–0 tie across the first six innings. In the seventh, Hudlin swung and missed a third strike, but catcher Jim Brown dropped the

> ball and Hudlin was safe on first. Batting for himself, Whitehill singled Hudlin to second, and he scored on Bill Sweeney's hit to center. The American Giants tried to rally with two out in the eighth. Steel Arm Davis and Willie Wells hit successive singles, but Mule Suttles' ground-out ended the threat.

Final score: All-Stars 1, American Giants 0.

Earlier in the decade the *Chicago Whip* had waxed eloquent about the meaning of these post-season games between the big leaguers under the headline, "COLORED STAR OUTPITCHES NATIONAL LEAGUERS FOR THE SECOND TIME." After naming the mix of major leaguers from the New York Giants, St. Louis Browns, and New York Yankees, and five other stars who played under assumed names, the writer got to the point.

> This game gives a fan a chance to get a line on our Colored stars and proves beyond a reasonable doubt that men like Joe Williams, Dick Redding, Donaldson and G. Williams as pitchers have the necessary qualifications to make good in the major leagues, and that it behooves the powers to be to get busy and stop letting their prejudice get the better of their judgment and conduct the game as a real, and only a real, red-blooded sport should be. Stop looking at a man's color, and judge his ability alone.

Long after that 1929 All-Stars series, Charlie Gehringer, who was then dean of the committee that elected veteran players to the Hall of Fame, recollected his playing against Foster and Suttles. "They say Suttles used the heaviest bat ever swung. Looking at it, I think it was true. He hit some boomers." Heinie Manush had an even more pointed observation. After a 1930 barnstorming game in which Cool Papa Bell robbed him of a sure triple, he said, "I sure am glad you colored players aren't in our league. I wouldn't ever hit .300."

CRACKS START TO SHOW

With the conclusion of the 1926 World Series, what had at times seemed impossible at the start of the decade had now happened for the third season in a row. Few would have expected at that time that there would be only one more after this one, and that the decade that had started out with such promise for the future of black baseball would face its worst season of league ball in 1927—and, by the end of the decade, no leagues at all.

Dark clouds were on the horizon even before the 1927 season started. Fay Young asked his readers whether the *Defender* had fed them too much baseball coverage. Dwindling attendance each year at baseball games made him wonder if he might not please the general public by giving more space to some other sport.

Brooklyn Royal Giants owner Nat Strong had predicted as early as August 1926 that the Eastern Colored League might be abandoned next season. Then came the news as the season was ready to open that the defending champion of the East, the Bacharach Giants of Atlantic City, with arguably the best pitching staff in the league, might not be able to play at all due to bankruptcy proceedings. With a tremendous debt facing the owners, and with salaries to pay, the club probably would be abandoned and its players allotted to other members of the Eastern League.

When the season started, several of the leagues' best players, in violation of a clearly stated rule that promised a five-year suspension, were missing in action. They were in Japan, having joined the independent Philadelphia Royal Giants on a baseball trip across the Pacific at the close of the California winter season. They would be AWOL through the first month or more of the regular league season.

Splintering was occurring at a larger level as well. The cooperation between the two leagues turned to conflict as Eastern and Western owners throughout much of the season fiercely debated the rights to Estaban Montalvo. Cuban Stars owner Alex Pompez argued that he held first rights on signing Latino "free agents" over the claims made by other Eastern League teams. In the Montalvo case Pompez contended he had a territorial basis to an exclusive market on Latino talent. The other Negro

Norman "Turkey" Stearnes

As Good As a Job

"He had a funny stance, but he could get around on you," said Satchel Paige of Turkey Stearnes. "He could hit it over the right field fence, over the left field fence, or center field fence. If you didn't pitch it in the right place for him, he would just hit the ball out of that park just about every time he came up. He was one of the greatest hitters we ever had. He was as good as Josh [Gibson]. He was as good as anybody ever played baseball."

A quiet 170-pounder, Stearnes let his bat do his talking. In 19 seasons (1923–1941), mainly with the Detroit Stars, he blasted at least 183 home runs in league games, and put up high totals in doubles and triples as well. He reportedly got his nickname because he ran with both elbows flapping, but was also known for his unusual batting stance. A left-hander, he stood with his weight forward and his toe pointed skyward, stepped in the bucket, and launched mighty blasts while choking up on a short bat.

His home run prowess was legendary. Ted Radcliffe reported that "I've seen Stearnes hit one in Comiskey Park, hit the facing of the roof in the upper deck, and it was still going when it hit." Added Buck Leonard, "I've seen Stearnes hit them out of Chicago through the wind—the wind blows steady in Chicago, especially over to the old American Giants park—but he could hit them through the wind and over the fence."

Radcliffe also admired Stearnes' defensive work in center field. "Everybody knows that Cool Papa Bell was the fastest man. But Cool Papa Bell couldn't field with Turkey Stearnes. He was faster, but Turkey Stearnes was one of the best fly ball men." Birmingham's Jim Canada testified that Stearnes "hit the ball nine miles. He was a show, people would go to see him play. He put on a lot of shows out there in the outfield, too. Hard chances, he'd make them look easy, and easy chances, he made them look hard."

Strictly a slugger in his early years, he joined the Chicago American Giants in 1932, where manager Dave Malarcher taught him to bunt as a way of utilizing his great speed. "He developed into a really diversified player after that," Malarcher said. "Turkey could bunt, and he could pull them down to first base and fly. And when his time came to hit, he could really plaster them."

Raleigh "Biz" Mackey of the Philadelphia Giants playing in Japan in 1927.

league team owners had the entire African-American market in the United States from which to scout and acquire talent.

A May 21, 1927, *New York Age* article added a racial element to what had become a highly charged situation. The paper asserted that Pompez's objection to the Lincoln Giants' claim on Montalvo was "based on racial prejudice." Perhaps believeing that Pompez's ultimate goal was to keep

Africans and Latinos on separate teams, the *Age* sportswriter elaborated, "Mr. Pompez feels that there are enough American-born ball players for the teams in the League to select from without their signing up Cubans. He feels that he should have a monopoly on all Cuban players." Caught up in the Montalvo dispute, longtime owner James Keenan at mid-season resigned from the Eastern League and for a time removed his Lincoln Giants from the league schedule.

At season's end the *New York Age* noted, "As the 1927 baseball season draws to a close and financial reports begin coming in, the Homestead Grays of Pittsburgh seem to be the only team in the East, and very likely the only one in the country, that has had a successful season from a financial viewpoint. Unfavorable weather conditions and dissension among the members of the Eastern Colored Baseball League have conspired to make this the worst season on record for the history of that organization. Unless there is a new alignment of the clubs and a reorganization of the League's management, it is being freely predicted that it will be disbanded."

Not everything about 1927 was a downer. And viewed from a different perspective, some of the downs might well be seen as ups. The 1927 spring trip to Japan by Raleigh "Biz" Mackey and friends could have been celebrated—as indeed it might well have been at the decade's beginning—as one more sign of the wonderful international reach of black professional baseball. Yet the national weeklies characterized the trip as damaging to the league structure that was already under assault from forces that would bring it down.

In the West a key question had to be faced, and the answer would have important implications for Eastern blackball as well. How were they to navigate successfully through the difficult waters of black organized baseball without Rube Foster at the helm? The "Admiral" had been felled in mid-season 1926 by a nervous breakdown, and afterward it was clear he would not be back.

At the winter league meetings in St. Louis on February 4, 1927, Judge William C. Hueston of Gary, Indiana, was approved unanimously by league directors as president. At the time Hueston was serving his second term as a municipal judge with criminal jurisdiction. Rube Foster he certainly was not—but then who could be? The story that reports Hueston's appointment notes that while his knowledge of the inside workings of baseball might be lacking, his good judgment, ability to see both sides of a debated question, and reputation for fairness would stand him in good stead as he undertook his new duties.

Unfortunately, the problems he faced made his term a troubled one. At its end he would preside over the dissolution of a league that had started out with such great promise both for organized national black baseball and for the advancement of the race.

Meanwhile in the East, the league ship was sailing into troubled waters as well, but for the first time it would have an "admiral" at its helm rather than a chairman of the board. In January attorney Isaac Nutter of Atlantic City was appointed president. By September league news took a turn for the worse as the Associated Negro Press reported the shock felt by baseball fans "at the announcement that Ed Bolden, manager of the Hilldale baseball team, has suffered a nervous breakdown." The news agency quoted Bolden's wife as saying, "The combination of baseball worries and his regular work at the Post Office has forced Mr. Bolden to leave town for treatment for ill health."

THE YEAR OF THE TURKEY

Given its down side off the field of play, it seems only appropriate that 1927 turned out to be the year of the "Turkey" on the field, although with a different turn of circumstance it could well have been dubbed the year of the "Mule." Future Hall of Famer Norman "Turkey" Stearnes had an MVP season, finishing second in home runs and stolen bases, and leading the league in doubles and triples while batting a hefty .352. He might well have been bested by Mule Suttles, who was batting .478 with seven home runs before his season ended prematurely from a beaning by Chet Brewer. After a year outside the league, Birmingham and Memphis were back in, the former with a rookie right hander who was taught control by veterans Harry Salmon and Sam Streeter, and the hesitation pitch by Bill Gatewood. No one suspected at the time that Leroy "Satchel" Paige would still be controlling and hesitating long after the Negro National League had disappeared.

Defending champion Chicago took the first half of the season, and the Black Barons from Birmingham claimed first-place honors for the second half. Having won the last four games against their Alabama opponents in regular season play, Chicago was the clear favorite going into the playoffs. That designation did not sit well with one of the Giants' most vocal fans. Fay Young, putting as he saw it the welfare of the league ahead of personal rooting interests, was hoping for a Birmingham victory. The American Giants decisively swept the Barons in the first three games of the playoffs. Rookie Paige relieved Streeter in the first inning of the fourth game with the score 4–0 in favor of Chicago and held the American Giants to two additional runs in a 6–2 loss that sent the Chicagoans into their second consecutive World Series appearance. It would not be Satchel's last appearance in post-season play.

In the East, baseball reality, as it so often does, fell considerably short of prediction. Reports in preseason from John Henry Lloyd and Alex Pompez about their Lincoln Giants and Cuban Stars considerably overstated their teams' performance. In the case of the Giants, their league season ended when owner Jim Keenan suddenly withdrew from the eastern ranks in a dispute over Estaban Montalvo. As for Pompez's squad, their third- and fourth-place finishes in the season's two halves were a disappointment to their owner, who at season's outset had modestly claimed, "We are better, faster and stronger and will cop the pennant which we lost the last half of the season last year if field generalship means anything."

The Black Sox from Baltimore, led from the dugout by great veteran Ben Taylor, seemed to be the team to beat as the early part of the season unfolded. A seven-game winning streak into early June appeared to foretell a fine season. Fine it was for the first half, when they finished a few games behind the defending champion Bacharachs. But by late August Taylor's team had dropped toward the Eastern League cellar. In reporting on a split with the Cubans, a writer for the Sox's hometown newspaper expressed puzzlement over what he was witnessing. "Ben Taylor's Black Sox failed to gain in the second half pennant race over the weekend. For some reason or another the locals have lost that old fighting spirit and just can't break into the winning column any more."

"ATLANTIC CITY WINS PENNANT" reads the headline on the *Afro*'s sports page for September 17. The paper was merely announcing what every baseball fan already knew. Baltimore was out, and the Bacharachs had repeated. At the end of the next month a headline that read "CRUEL SOX BEAT WHITE STARS" must have triggered feelings of disappointment in the *Afro*'s readers, as they watched their Baltimore black nine battle to their sixth consecutive post-season victory over a contingent of white stars who featured several major leaguers in their lineup. It would only have been natural to think, if they could do it against whites outside the league, why not to blacks inside?

A GRAND FINALE

Given all the negatives swirling around baseball in 1927, fans could not have been faulted for expecting less than memorable baseball in post-season play. But memorable it was. In fact, the 1927 Fall Classic is arguably one of the best of all the Negro League World Series. The Atlantic City Bacharachs were down four games, having lost all but the first contest by lopsided scores, against Chicago's American Giants. Just as the Bacharachs were about to lose game five on their home grounds on a dark and rainy day, they eked out a one-run victory. Assisting the win on the mound was Luther "Red" Farrellon, a sometime outfielder who had already lost two games in the series. In a seven-inning rain-shortened contest, Farrellon recorded a 3–2 victory over Willie Foster. In game six, the Bacharachs held on through ten innings of a 1–1 tie, which was eventually called on account of darkness. They then won the seventh and eighth games, which sent the series into what would be the decisive ninth game.

Frank Young wrote this colorful account of the contest on the front page of the *Defender*, October 15, 1927:

> Fighting with their backs to the wall, but fighting gamely, Dick Lundy and his Bacharachs Giants, twice Eastern League champions, fell for the second consecutive year to the American Giants of Chicago, National League victors in 1926 and 1927, and world's 1926 champions, this afternoon in a wild and wooly game 11–4.
>
> As dusk mixed with a fog settled over the field in the first of the ninth, Farrell tossed out Sweatt, Williams poked a single to right and then Umpire McDevitt ended the 1927 world series by justly calling the game.

Was there something eerily prescient about the last game, of what turned out to be the last Negro League World Series under the original league regime, being fogged and darkened out with the home team not able to come to bat in the bottom of the ninth?

Three weeks later the *Chicago Defender* carried a feature piece by insider Lloyd Thompson questioning whether there would ever be another Negro League World Series. He pointed to decreasing attendance, decreasing revenues, and scheduling difficulties as problems that would likely do in what had started with such great expectation three years earlier.

The year 1928 was a confirmation of the downward spiral of the previous season. The prediction reported in the *Age* in September 1927 was reality by April 1928, with the folding of the long-troubled Eastern Colored League and a return to independent baseball by former league teams. By early June a *Kansas City Call* sports editor explained to his readers "Why Fans Manifest Little Interest in Negro National League." He, and others, believed that the decline of the Negro leagues was not caused entirely by the national economic downturn. The leagues failed to give the fans what was promised—an operation where players would be punished for transgressions against established rules, good statistics would be available as a matter of course, and a regular schedule would be played.

In the spring of 1929, in several feature articles syndicated by the Associated Negro Press to the vast majority of black newspapers in the nation, Raymond Drake's "Negro Baseball as a Fan Sees It" recites a litany of shortcomings that contributed to the sad state of black baseball: there were weeks when some clubs would not be heard of, even though they were playing a regular game in a regular league city; when clubs won a game, immediately the result went to the press; when the same club dropped a game, it never appeared in the papers; players were dropped from a roster, and no mention of it was made in print; "dumb" owners often failed to furnish weekly newspapers with league standings; and standings would vary from paper to paper.

On a train trip from Chicago to St. Louis, Drake decided he would take advantage of his circumstances to get the real scoop. "Three, four, five newspapers are gleaned, but the mystery of the correct standing remains a mystery. I give up! In the language of that famous Amos and Andy team, 'I'so regusted.'"

Other aspects of the leagues' weak administrations elicited criticism from fans. With umpires in black baseball often chosen by the home teams and enjoying only limited authority, on-field arguments and fights regularly marred games. As one Homestead fan observed, "only in rare instances is a game ever carried through to completion without a lot of unnecessary haggling." The failure to curb endless disputes and sometimes unruly behavior undoubtedly cost the leagues support, including one fan who explained to NNL president William Hueston that he preferred "a more efficient game than your boys play. I understand inside baseball; your boys do not play it and they quarrel too much." While many critics would argue with the assertion that black players did not play "inside baseball," it was hardly debatable that the discipline present in the white game was often lacking.

The belief by some fans that they were not seeing "big-league baseball" was shaped less by the actual talent on the field and more by the general

"Eastern League Umpires Have No More Authority Than a Klu Kluxer Would Have at a Banquet of the 'Hell Fighters' in Harlem!"

During a recent game in Baltimore the batter asked to see the ball and the umps requested pitcher Strong, of the Sox, to throw it in. Strong dropped the ball to the mound at his feet and told the umpire that if he wanted to see it he might come out and get it. The arbiter told the batter, Smith of the Royals, that if he wanted to see it he might go out and pick it up. Smith accepted the invitation, inspected the sphere, and threw it over the grandstand. Strong was permitted to remain in the game but Smith and several other Royals were ejected.

During a recent game in Harrisburg, Manager Charleston is said to have hit Rats Henderson in the face for disputing a decision at the plate. Henderson and Marcelle were put out and Charleston allowed to continue. Umpire Shewall told Manager Lloyd that he, Charleston, was protecting the umpires from the bad Bacharachs. This Shewall is the same bird Beckwith beat up in Harrisburg some time since. In a letter to me John Hennerey says, "If umpires are so much for Hilldale they must think the Harrisburg Giants are the Hilldale club when they are playing the Bacharachs."

—Rollo Wilson, Pittsburgh Courier, September 12, 1925

milieu of black baseball. The baseball of the Negro leagues, with its irregular schedules, sporadic statistics, and use of home umpires, was far closer in structure to semiprofessional baseball than professional, although the level of play was much higher. Yet regardless of their talent, organizations that operated in such a manner inevitably disappointed black fans who used the white major leagues as a frame of reference. Philadelphia resident Thomas Simmons, for example, insisted that the leagues were "run on the semi-pro style and will never get the public interested in them until they adopt the big league style.... The smallest white professional league in the country is run better than any Negro league was ever run.... Very few people can get interested in a league where only two or three games are played each week."

Simmons' commentary, of course, ignored the fundamental financial problems preventing Negro league organizations from adopting a daily schedule of league games. Yet several sports observers insisted that the leagues, regardless of their income, were capable of drastically improving their administration and organization. A.D. Williams recommended a more effective use of "business methods and not petty personal grudge methods mixed with inefficiency," while Bill Gibson advocated stricter rule enforcement.

Gibson, however, doubted that the leagues would heed any suggestion, noting that "experience should have taught the different race leagues that if ten years of endeavor have not met the proper response from the fans, a change should be made. Nevertheless, experience seemingly has taught them nothing." League officials, however, were notoriously leery of any perceived interference from writers, and as Rollo Wilson lamented, "one of the most thankless jobs in the world is trying to tell club owners how they can improve on conditions. Even when they know what is wrong they will make no effort to correct it."

What must have been the widespread disappointment at the state of league affairs is found in biting commentary from Al Monroe, a respected *Chicago Whip* reporter:

"Just now however the leagues, east and west, are more or less two of a kind except for the fact that some of the western cities are drawing enough customers to warrant its continuance. They have devised an economy scheme that should save something, if not the league, by refusing to purchase stamps to supply the papers with news of their games. Frankly I am not so sure that the eastern association is still a league.... But at that we should show less interest perhaps, in as much as we have a problem right here in our own league and a problem in our American Giants. Yes, baseball will be baseball, but not as the leagues either east or west dish it up."

While the older Negro National League would struggle through the difficult depression era for several more years, that league would disappear as well after the 1931 season.

HERE COME THE HOMESTEAD GRAYS

Although Negro league baseball did not last out its first decade in the East and barely survived into its second decade in the West, there was one baseball story of the 1920s that promised a bright future.The architect of that future, Cumberland Willis Posey, Jr., would be seen as arguably the greatest success in Negro professional baseball. He was the creator of the greatest dynasty in the history of black baseball, perhaps all baseball.

Born in 1891 in Homestead, Pennsylvania to one of the leading families of the Pittsburgh area's African-American community, Posey was a sports star at his high school. The young athlete was described by sportswriter Rollo Wilson as "a fleet outfielder and a fair hitter, but always thinking." In 1911, at the age of 20, he joined a local semi-pro baseball team. The Homestead Grays were a nearly all-black outfit that seldom lost even in the teeming baseball competition around Pittsburgh. Cum Posey became captain of the squad in 1916 and was booking the Grays' playing dates by 1918. In 1920 he teamed with Charles Walker, a local businessman who had been a Grays batboy as a kid, to buy the club. Posey then quit his job to stake his future on baseball.

In a few years all vestiges of semiprofessionalism disappeared from the Grays. They played every day during the summer, leaving no time for their players to do other work. In 1922 they played 117 games, advertised by Posey as "a new independent record." The team dominated western Pennsylvania baseball and reputedly established all-time attendance records at many towns in the area. It was reported, in terms that would have pleased Posey greatly that "the popularity of the Grays is due to their behavior on the field. Their natty appearance and ability give all clubs a run for their money."

At first the Grays upgraded themselves by trying to corner the market on local talent, and they didn't always have a strictly African-American roster. Two local white stars, Ziggy Walsh and Johnny Pearson, played for them before signing professional contracts. Posey, using his team's steadily solidifying economic base to his best advantage, soon signed well-known Negro leaguers who were willing to leave league play, which was financially unstable, for the Grays' regional kingdom, which wasn't. The best of the early acquisitions was the venerable right-hander Smokey Joe Williams, who left the Lincoln Giants of the Eastern Colored League in 1925 and spent ten years in a Grays' uniform. At other times in the twenties the Grays boasted slugger John Beckwith, left-handed pitcher Sam Streeter, and shortstop Bobby Williams, among others.

These signings were in some circles construed as "raiding" the league clubs. Raiding was a practice that all club owners deplored in principle, although nearly all would do it if they believed their acts were in "self-defense" against other owners who were trying to raid their squad.

As an independent team the Grays weren't bound by the hands-off agreements among league clubs. And, to Posey's credit, he didn't protest too much when league clubs picked off individual Grays. He could afford to be tolerant, at any rate, since the balance sheet of player movements in and out of Homestead greatly favored his team. Many Negro leaguers made clear that what they appreciated most about their favorite owners were regular twice-a-month paydays. Since the Grays almost always provided these, Posey could get the best men to come to Homestead. More than half of the Negro leaguers in the Baseball Hall of Fame eventually played for Posey's Grays.

By 1927 the Grays, still operating as an independent, were playing upward of 150 games each summer, as many as teams in the white majors. Running off streaks of 43 wins in 1926 and 31 in 1927, they were winning 80 to 90 percent of their games, mostly against area semi-pro teams and clubs in the Ohio and Pennsylvania League, a minor league whose officials came to Posey to book a string of lucrative Sunday contests outside their regular schedule. Increasingly, teams from the existing Negro leagues booked the Grays on their schedule. In 1927 Homestead won six out of seven games from New York City's Lincoln Giants of the Eastern Colored League (ECL), and took two of three from Cleveland of the Negro National League (NNL) at Forbes Field in Pittsburgh. The next year the Grays won five of eight from the Giants, four of five from the Baltimore Black Sox of the ECL, and split 14 games with Hilldale.

Posey in those years also booked as many as nine games in October with a white club, the so-called "American League All Star" team. The All-Stars included big league regulars such as pitchers Rube Walberg and Jack Quinn and outfielders Heinie Manush and Harry Heilmann. Earl Mack, son of Philadelphia Athletics owner and manager Connie Mack, and a coach for his dad's team, managed the squad. Homestead never did worse than a split in these series, which were clearly big moneymakers both for Posey and Walker and the Macks. The 1927 series, for which Posey beefed up the Grays with the special addition of future Hall of Famer Martin Dihigo, was spread entirely throughout the Grays' baseball kingdom with games in Ohio, Pennsylvania, West Virginia, and western New York.

The next rung on the professional baseball ladder was league membership. But Cum Posey wasn't eager to apply for a league slot. He once stated that in the last half of the 1920s the Grays were courted by both the Negro National League and the Eastern Colored League. Since the leagues were each centered in different regions of the country, with no NNL team east of the Great Lakes area and no ECL club west of Harrisburg, central Pennsylvania represented a potentially profitable area between them.

Posey's counteroffer between the 1926 and 1927 seasons was to keep the Grays independent, but play a total of 20 games at the Pittsburgh Pirates' Forbes Field against Midwestern teams headed east on barnstorming tours and Eastern teams going west on the same mission. Given the popularity of baseball in Pittsburgh, this would undoubtedly have produced profits all around. Most of the money, of course, would have belonged to the Grays, who would have taken a majority percentage of the gate receipts for the home team. As a further proposition, Posey offered a no-raiding packet to both leagues. This agreement had one exception, a big one—the ECL had to return the rights to Oscar Charleston, arguably the greatest player of his era, who had signed a Grays' contract over the winter and then reneged to join Harrisburg.

The leagues turned the deal down, as Posey probably knew they would. It allowed him to boast of the Grays' independence to the home folks in Pittsburgh and tell them that, since the no-raiding clause was dead, "the

Oscar Charleston
Beyond Compare

The great Ben Taylor, who swung a mean bat and played a flawless first base opposite him for many a season, said Oscar Charleston is the "greatest outfielder that ever lived, the greatest of all colors. He can cover more ground than any man I have ever seen. His judging of fly balls borders on the uncanny."

How much was Charleston worth? Ask those fans who saw him hit. "Fans along the Seaboard recall one powerful Ruthian smash of Charleston's that traveled on a line more than 464 feet before it touched the soil. So prodigious was the clout, that Wellington Jones of the Harrisburg Telegraph measured the distance officially and placed the hit at 465 feet."

Alvin Moses called Oscar Charleston the "greatest ballplayer of color produced in this country. Not only is he the finest player of African extraction—but in our judgment he ranks on equality with Cobb, Mathewson, Wagner, and any other American or National league maestro the national pastime has known. Charleston hits with the cunning of a Ty Cobb and the power of a Babe Ruth; runs the bases like a Bob Bescher, Max Carey, or an Eddie Collins; fields his position like only a Tris Speaker could; an arm like Bob Meusel, and the dynamic personality of Johnnie Evars, plus real baseball brains and you have met Oscar Charleston as we have known him and hundreds of thousands of colored and white diamond fans will attest."

Grays are in a position to strengthen any position which becomes weak, and can bolster their pitching staff on a week's notice by getting one of the stars of the league."

In 1929 Posey finally committed the Grays to the newly formed American Negro League, which was to take the place of the late ECL, a victim of the Depression. The new league lasted only a year itself before folding, and surprisingly, Homestead had a mediocre season, finishing only in third place among the six league entries. But it was not surprising that, after the league's demise effectively made most of its players free agents,

Posey snapped up Charleston and William Julius "Judy" Johnson, another future Hall of Famer, from rival Hilldale to make the Grays still stronger.

Being courted by both circuits did not prevent Posey from publicly criticizing both league operations. The 1927 annual joint winter meeting of the NNL and ECL proved to be a fine target for Poesy's barbs. "The magnates will enter the meeting with individual ideas concerning things which might benefit the game and colored baseball; they will forget these ideas while arguing over some minor point and will depart for home having accomplished nothing."

Posey's criticism was not uttered behind closed doors. He had an outlet unique among owners to express his views in the most public of ways—and he used it consistently and with considerable relish. His father was an early stockholder in the company that published the Pittsburgh *Courier*, and had been president of the corporation. His son inherited *Courier* stock and became an employee of the sports department, with a column that ran on and off for many years. This gave him a national outlet for his views. With interests and contacts in many sports, Posey did not restrict his writing to baseball. But he was more than willing to use his position on the sports pages to state what he thought was good and bad about the Negro leagues, and to preach his version of how the sport could be improved.

His unforgiving attitude once led Detroit baseball promoter John Williams to say, "Unfortunately ... you are a gentleman who wants his own way about everything at all times. If you can't have everything as you want it, everything is wrong and everyone unable to do your bidding is a rascal." It seems that if Cumberland Willis Posey, Jr. ever made a mistake in baseball, he kept that fact strictly to himself. He would be a significant presence in black baseball circles across the next two decades.

BASEBALL IN THE SPRING

The 1920s also saw the rise of off-season play. The tradition of spring training in warm climates was present in blackball from even in the sport's earliest beginnings. With the founding of the first league in 1920, that spring rite of baseball became even more important. Teams would head south to where the climate was more conducive to ironing out the kinks, loosening up the arms, and building a team.

When the star outfielder for the 1920s Philadelphia Athletics, George "Mule" Haas, was asked why he thought black players in his day were as good as they were, his answer was simple: "They ought to be good. They play all year." While some white major league players continued to play ball in the off-season in places like California, Florida, and Cuba, their numbers were far less than blackball's stars, and the coverage they received in the white sporting press was miniscule compared to that given in black newspapers to their Negro counterparts. At the end of the Eastern and Midwestern regular league seasons—and for that matter, long before there were Negro Leagues—the best among blackball's heroes scattered across the Western Hemisphere to California, to the Florida hotel circuit, and into the Caribbean for some of the finest baseball available anywhere.

West Coast organized black baseball had existed for a good decade or more before baseball mogul Lonnie Goodwin began to draw on a black population of the Angel City that was about 70,000, many of them from his native Texas, to fill his own park, "modern in every detail, which has a seating capacity of 4500."

Florida, too, had been a popular training ground for black professional baseball. By the 1920s Palm Beach was the center of an annual Florida black winter baseball world that attracted many of the top players of the game.

The 1921 winter season was typical of Florida's Winter League baseball. Chicago's "Big Chief" Rube Foster, aside from a few exceptions, had his American Giants squad intact for the season's opening tussle on January 25. His Giants were to face off against a John Lloyd-led team that represented the best of the colored players of the East. There was in the *Whip*'s account of this situation a note of speculation, indeed doubt, about how well the intact Fosterites would fare against the best of the East. What was a sure thing, according to the scribe, was that if the Western team from his home city lost "there was nothing in the make-up of the Big Chief to indicate a squeal." By the time March rolled around, Foster had little to squeal about.

Pop's Trained Alligator

The fact that John Hennery is bringing an alligator back from Cuba with him as a mascot and bat boy for the Atlantic City Bacharachs is arousing a good bit of interest here in the East. A specially prepared tank is being built for him. And it will be mounted on a flivver chassis.

A standing order has been filed with the various steamship companies for a barrel of Cuban water to be delivered on each trip. This will be used to replenish the water in the tank.

Mr. Lloyd, which is slang for John Henry, cables us that his pet alligator is learning a little bit more day by day. He says that he puts it in a refrigerator for a few minutes every day in order to accustom it to the colder climate of Atlantic City. There is some talk of listing "Money" as a player so he may be sent in as a pinch runner for old man Cummings on those hot days to come when his 'dogs' will be yelping and snapping at the heat. The veteran first baseman says OK if it is for the good of the team.

—Rollo Wilson, Pittsburgh Courier, February 16, 1924

On the fifth of that month his hometown paper reported another victory for the Chicago squad, under the headline "JOHNSON GOOSE EGGS BREAKERS":

> Overseas heroes, Lieut. Johnson, Malarcher and Bobby Williams were the flies that pestered the Royal ointment when the former, hurling for the Poincianas, lived up to his overseas prestige for hand-grenading the enemy, while his aids kept up a barrage lasting one hour and thirty-five minutes in which the enemy was driven back into the dense palm thickets, while Gen. Foster, Capt. DeMoss, Lieut. Johnson and fighters advanced their territorial possession by a count of five games to two. The Breakers are but a few miles removed from the ocean, and fierce and continued fighting will ensue from now on, but it is hoped that the great leader, Lloyd, and his squad will save themselves from the last resort—the Atlantic—in order to avert an overwhelming victory by the Americans.

Victory for Foster's "baseball army" would indeed come shortly thereafter—and shortly after that victory, in terms of bragging rights, its spoils as well. The winning of the Winter League championship by the American Giants was the occasion for hosannas on the home front. "Pitted against a collection of the best ball players in the world, stars picked from the Royal Giants, Lincoln Giants, Hilldale and Bacharachs, the Foster machine still reigns supreme in the baseball field of endeavor" reads the report filed to the *Whip* from Palm Beach on March 15.

Why were there so many black baseball troubadours going south and west every year? The love of the game itself, and the attractiveness of the South and Southern California during cold winter months cannot be discounted. But as the *Kansas City Call* wrote on one occasion, "the coin of the realm was quite welcome to the players in the winter time." Those who chose to play winter blackball were reportedly well paid. Those who didn't, and whose regular season pay was "financially speaking never enough to keep them living a month after the season closes," sometimes had to call on the generosity of club owners to tide them over through the lean months of December, January, and February.

In the middle of the decade A.D. Williams, sports editor of the *Call*, applauded what he hoped was an emerging trend among players of finding gainful off-season employment. He reported Wade Johnson of the Monarchs as the proprietor of a Kansas City barbecue, and Hawkins, the Monarchs' first sacker, operating a profitable taxi service. "There are others too," he wrote, "who are in various kinds of money making venture—but not half enough." Refusing to be discouraged, he saw the gainfully employed half as "a hopeful sign, and we are thankful for progress." But still the winter lure of the South and the West would remain.

BASEBALL IS BLACK AMERICA

Baseball in black, as in white, America of the 1920s amounted to much more than occasional attention to regular season contests and world series battles on the level of the major leagues. By the 1920s, what was now clearly the nation's game had penetrated deeply into the black American consciousness. The great national weeklies fed their readers a steady diet of Negro major league and barnstorming fare across the normal summer season, but also right through the winter from professional leagues in California, Florida, and the Caribbean. Equally as important, baseball was being played on the amateur community level in black population centers across the nation.

Hardly a sports section went by in the *Courier* in Pittsburgh, in New York's *Amsterdam News*, in the *Defender* of Windy City fame, and in the *Call* in Kansas City without some reference to community baseball. The *Chicago Defender*'s sports section was open, as a matter of editorial policy, to all black teams. The paper's policy was to give the results of as many games as it had space for, with teams of national reputation being given more consideration than smaller teams. This openness produced a sports page like that found for June 27, 1919. Alongside notices detailing the doings of top Negro independent teams like the Brooklyn Royal Giants, the Hilldales, and the Chicago American Giants, one finds news of the Southside Junior Giants in Chicago; a strong local race club in Jacksonville, Florida; a black club organized by Nathan Dobbins in Watertown, New York; and the 369th Infantry "Hell Fighters" team reporting a victory from Bay Ridge, New York.

The papers themselves created baseball madness with their own tournaments, teams, and leagues. "THE AFRO BASEBALL LEAGUE GETS START" reads the headline in the Baltimore *Afro American* for May 13, 1921. The newspaper's initiative that started this league had the full approval of Dr. Henry West, Superintendent of Public Schools in Baltimore. School principals throughout the city were asked to form two or more baseball clubs in each school for the Afro League. In November a related headline reads "GOLD FOBS FOR AFRO BASEBALL LEAGUE PLAYERS," noting a generous donation from A. G. Spalding Sporting Goods Company for the Afro-American Public Athletic League schoolboys' champions.

Coverage of black community ball featured the likes of the "Crack Brooklyn Y.M.C.A. Squad" looking out with serious mien at readers of the *Defender* of April 23. "The Carolton Y.M.C.A. baseball club of Brooklyn,

NY," the caption reads, "is out to duplicate its feat of the last two years by wining the Y.M.C.A. championship against college stars who are members of the white Y teams."

Negro major league teams gave direct support—and frequently their name—to youth teams such as the Chicago Young American Giants, the Young Black Sox of Baltimore, and in at least one instance, if scores like 48–2 can be accepted as baseball, the Black Sox Bloomer Girls who showed at Maryland Park in August of 1922 that "they lacked practice while their opponents put up a game equal to a first class male aggregation."

In June 1922 the *Pittsburgh Courier* reports how black industrial workers have caught the baseball bug: "John T. Clark, Secretary of the Pittsburgh Urban League, known as the Judge Landis of the ball teams in Western Pennsylvania among the various industrial plants, is leading with bright expectations into its second season a Negro Industrial Baseball League composed of teams representing Westinghouse Electric and Manufacturing Company; Jones and Loughlin Iron Company; Duquesne Steel Foundry Company and Alpha Club of Carnegie, Pa. The Negro teams representing the three big plants of the Carnegie Steel Company dropped out of the Negro league. They play with the white teams of the company."

Black postal employees would establish a prominent presence on the 1920s baseball scene. As reported in the *Defender* on November 1, 1924, a large crowd was in attendance at a dance to honor the crack Ohio section team of the Chicago Post Office Baseball League "composed of members of our group that have won the city title for three years and now have permanent possession of the Lueder Trophy."

Papers advertised for the creation of amateur twilight leagues as in the *Afro-American's* April 27, 1925, call to "all owners and managers of amateur baseball clubs in the city and suburbs to meet at the Sharp Street Community House on Monday, May 4 to form a twilight league, games to be played in Druid Hill Park."

Independent black teams established a reputation second to none in their baseball circles. "The Columbia Cubs, Harlem's leading amateur baseball team has again come to the front with a win at Central Park against the Caroltons, a fast, hard hitting white team," reports the *Amsterdam News* for July 22, 1925.

Black community baseball could be stickball sponsored by the Y.M.C.A. "The Young Men's Christian Association in an effort to do something for the boys of Harlem gathered the leaders of the various blocks from 130th to 143rd streets and organized them into what is known as the Harlem Stick Ball League" begins a featured story in the *Amsterdam News* for June 2, 1926.

The white press got into the baseball act with black schoolboy teams competing in leagues sponsored by white newspapers. "BLACK DIAMONDS, HARLEM SCHOOLBOY BASEBALL TEAM IN NEW YORK WORLD LEAGUE" reads a lead at the top of the sports page for the *New York Age* for August 21, 1926.

Black baseball in the 1920s was also a church-sponsored activity. The *Chicago Defender* tells its readers that Frank Young, the paper's sports editor; Henry Crawford, physical director of the Wabash Y.M.C.A.; "and last but by no means least, the wives and sweethearts of the aforementioned," were in attendance on October 23, 1926, when Quinn Chapel A.M.E. Church and Sunday school honored its baseball team with a fine banquet for having won the Union Sunday School Baseball League Championship.

Amateur "community" baseball was not confined to blacks in civilian life. Across the state of New York, and presumably elsewhere as well, black National Guard units faced off in games like that reported for July 9, 1927 when "Sergt. George Hill of Company D of the 369th Infantry Regiment pitched for the colored soldiers and struck out 15 batters in an 8–6 victory over the 101 st Signal Battalion at Camp Smith, Peekskill, New York." The game was the first in a series for a cup representing the championship of the New York National Guard.

Nor would "community" military baseball be restricted to the mainland United States. Accompanied by a colorful photograph, the *Amsterdam News* of March 28, 1928, under the headline "U.S. NAVY'S NEMESIS," announced that "down in the Virgin Islands where Uncle Sam sends his Battleships, Armored Cruisers, Torpedo Seaplanes, Lindbergh, Etc., during the winter months the VIRGIN ISLAND ALL STARS meet the sailors and officers on the diamond and always defeat the white players."

Willie Wells
El Diablo

Sportswriters of the time had trouble coming up with enough superlatives to describe the play of shortstop Willie Wells. Wells was the rare shortstop who could combine fielding excellence with a power stroke. A star in both the Negro leagues and Latin America, Mexican fans nicknamed him "El Diablo" (the Devil) because of his relentless style. In fact, Monte Irvin, who once called Wells the best shortstop he had ever seen, said that in Mexico "the players would say, don't hit the ball to shortstop, the Devil's out there."

Black baseball historian Ric Roberts agreed with this assessment, saying, "I watched him play shortstop for 10 years and never saw him make an error." Clark Griffith said, "Willie Wells and Ray Dandridge played the left side as well as anybody." Hall of Famer Larry Doby recalled that "he had good hands, great range, and he could get rid of the ball as quickly as [Phil] Rizzuto did." Another contemporary, Charlie Biot, said, "I think he was the best all-around player at the time I came up. He was one of the best shortstops I've ever seen. He was a fielding gem. I never saw him boot a ball. He was a beautiful hitter. Beautiful fielder and hitter."

Wells was a consistent .300 hitter who would often lead the league in home runs. Buck O'Neil, in the game for more than 70 years, once said, "He could hit to all fields, hit with power, bunt and stretch singles into doubles, and doubles into triples. As great as Ozzie Smith is for the St. Louis Cardinals, old-timers in St. Louis who saw Willie play for the St. Louis Stars still haven't seen his equal." According to Cowan "Bubba" Hyde, Wells "hit 25 to 35 home runs a year and he hit .325 or .330 every year. And he was a smart ball player. He's the best ball player I ever knew."

Though he was never given a chance to play in the major leagues, Wells is given credit for helping the next generation of players, such as Jackie Robinson, Don Newcombe, Joe Black, and Ernie Banks. Black recalled of the all-time shortstop, "Willie told all us young guys: 'Watch yourself. You never know who's looking at you to sign you.'"

For the novelist Thomas Wolfe, who grew up in rural North Carolina, there was nothing that could "evoke spring—the first days of April—better than the sound of a ball smacking into the pocket of the big mitt, the sound of the bat as it hits the horsehide; for me, at any rate, and I am being literal, not rhetorical—almost anything I know about spring is in it—the first leaf, the jonquil, the maple tree, the smell of grass upon your hands and knees, the coming into flow of April...."

Black Americans shared Wolfe's sentiments. From their communities in this time of baseball madness, from early April well into the fall of the year, one often heard "the sound of a ball smacking into...the big mitt, [and] the sound of the bat as it hits the horsehide." Black Americans in the 1920s embraced, along with their fellow whites, a baseball that was "a supererogation to claim as our National Game because such was like solemnly declaring that two plus two equals four." "It is my people's national game as much as it is the national game of whites, because it is above all an AMERICAN game," C. I. Taylor wrote in 1920. "It abides deep in the sports loving nature of all Americans regardless of their creed or color."

END OF AN ERA

When word came north to Chicago in 1902 that a fine pitching prospect was playing for the Waco Texas Yellow Jackets, Jerry Williams, a stockholder of the Chicago Unions, wrote to Andrew Foster inviting him to join that club. Williams told him that they played all white teams, mostly league clubs, and that he would be put to a severe test. Foster answered as follows. "If you play the best clubs in the land, white clubs as you say, it will be a case of Greek meeting Greek. I fear nobody."

If Cum Posey was the future of black professional baseball, Rube Foster was now its past. The decade of the 1920s—America's Golden Age of Sport, it would be called—began with what was seen by black Americans as their own golden moment, the organization of the Negro National League with the indomitable Rube Foster at its center. The decade ended with Rube no longer at the center and the Negro leagues in disarray.

Andrew "Rube" Foster died on December 9, 1930. At his funeral, three thousand people packed St. Mark's church and annex in Chicago, and outside in the snow stood three thousand more unable to gain admission but patiently awaiting their turn to view the remains after the conclusion of the service. News of the death of the baseball giant filled the front pages of all the major black papers, and warranted fine comment on their editorial pages. While the sorrow was sincere, the blow that had hurt baseball the most had occurred four summers earlier when illness took him from the presidency of the Negro National League, and removed from his control the managerial reins of his beloved Chicago American Giants.

Carl Beckwith opened his "THE END OF A GREAT CAREER" piece in the *Kansas City Call* of September 10, 1926, with these words:

> The passing of Rube Foster from the baseball stage means the termination of the career of the best-known Negro baseball player in the entire world. Baseball was his work and his pleasure. On the field, on the corner, anywhere he happened to stop long enough to talk, the subject of his conversation was almost always the same—baseball. He took it to bed with him, and he got up with it in the morning. It was both his life and his living, and his heart was in it.

Without Rube Foster, Beckwith says, there would never have been a Negro National League. While the "Father of Black Baseball" died in the midst of hard times for his game and his nation, the black leaguers and their dreams would have glory days ahead.

Magistrate Ed Henry and Hilldale catcher Joe Lewis in the 1930 season opener.

The Breakdown

Goodbye to Colored baseball! Gracious, the mere thought of such is disgusting. But the rate Negro baseball is going down now, that day isn't far off.

—Leon Hartwick, 1931

On October 13, 1927, the Chicago American Giants of the Negro National League defeated the Atlantic City Bacharach Giants of the Eastern Colored League by a score of 11–4 to capture the fourth and final championship series of the 1920s. In contrast to the well-publicized and profitable major league World Series between the New York Yankees and Pittsburgh Pirates completed five days earlier, the games attracted little attention and flopped at the box office. The overall failure of the series was apparent to Kansas City sportswriter A.D. Williams, who considered the promotion "rotten to say the least... Neither the players or the owners got very much for their time and effort." Sportswriter Rollo Wilson agreed, noting that the losing Bacharachs reportedly earned only $42 per player and suggesting that similar black World Series games "have never paid anybody except the Pennsylvania railroad." Perhaps more damaging, the contests were marred by several controversies, including a threatened walkout by Chicago prior to the series and rumors that Atlantic City had thrown the games.

The disappointing series reflected the startling administrative and financial decline of black baseball by the late 1920s. Devoid of leadership and plagued by numerous problems, black professional baseball faced its severest test in the late 1920s and early 1930s. The financial decline of the industry was hardly surprising, as most "race" businesses encountered similar difficulties during this era. The Great Migration of 1916–1919 had created sizable African-American communities in the urban centers of the East and Midwest, presenting abundant opportunities to develop successful businesses and ideally provide greater employment for the race. Simultaneously, the economic self-determination advocated by the Jamaican Marcus Garvey resonated among many blacks, resulting in the building and expansion of numerous enterprises including banks, insurance companies, hotels, and newspapers. Yet by the late 1920s it became increasingly apparent that black capitalism was an imperfect solution to the economic woes of African Americans. Future NAACP executive secretary Roy Wilkins, for example, rejected the "curious idea...that the starting and maintaining of Negro business will solve the Negro's unemployment problem," arguing that "Negroes...cannot start enough business to employ all the workers in the group—or even to employ the surplus workers who are idle in a time of depression, such as is upon us now." While still insisting that "our only salvation lies in the development of a group economy," the *Pittsburgh Courier* also recognized by 1928 that black entrepreneurs were seriously handicapped by their reliance on a largely impoverished population with limited income.

The gradually deteriorating economic status of urban blacks in the mid- to late 1920s further limited the potential for profitable black businesses. Even the sports pages took note of this reality. As early as 1927, *Chicago Defender* sports editor Fay Young cited the disturbing "lack of employment among our folks," and the onset of the Great Depression dealt a crushing blow to virtually all black enterprises. By 1932, black urban unemployment reached 50 percent, and within three years roughly half of all northern black families were receiving relief. The economic downswing took an inevitable toll on even once enormously successful entrepreneurs such as Chicago banker Jesse Binga and Philadelphia theater magnate John Gibson, both of whom fell on hard times after their businesses collapsed in the early 1930s.

Call the Roofers!

John Beckwith hit some of the most prodigious shots in baseball history. At the early age of 19, he became the first player, black or white, to hit a ball over the roof and completely out of Redland Field, home of the National League Cincinnati Reds. Years later, at Griffith Park, home to the Washington Senators, he hit a home run that cleared the left-field fence and struck an advertising sign 460 feet from home plate—40 feet up the sign. Jake Stephens, a crack batsman himself, said of Beckwith: "Ain't nobody hit a ball as far as that man! Listen, please believe me, no living human could hit as far."

Wielding a 38-inch bat, Beckwith also hit for average. His numbers are astonishing for a slugger: He reportedly hit over .400 during several seasons. Over his career he batted over .300 in the Negro leagues. Is there any doubt why he was known as the "Black Bomber"?

"Superficially," David Levering Lewis writes, "Harlem itself appeared to be in fair health well into 1931." Certainly from a literary point of view it had been in great health for nigh on a decade. With the publication in late 1930 of *Black Manhattan*, America's best known "Black Metropolis" was celebrated in print as it had never been before. "Harlem is still in the process of making," author James Weldon Johnson declared.

But few folks, black or white, there or anywhere in the Depression America of 1931, felt like waving flags. It was hard to be optimistic in the face of the harsh economic reality of those Great Depression years. There were Harlems all across the nation—on the south side of Chicago, on the Hill in Pittsburgh—that were facing the bleakest of times. By the third year of the depression, Lewis tells us, "for the great majority of the population, Harlem, New York was in the process of unmaking."

In so many ways these were not good years for Americans as a whole, and especially not good for those black Americans who heard presidential candidate Franklin D. Roosevelt speak about them in the 1932 campaign as part of the "forgotten Americans one-third of a nation ill housed, ill clothed, ill fed."

From the outside looking in, the problems that black baseball encountered during the depression years pale in comparison to the larger picture of a society whose political, economic, and social institutions many were arguing were in need of radical transformation. But for those within the game the problems were very real and very significant.

In such an environment, the potential to develop and maintain a successful black business such as professional baseball became increasingly slim. By 1931, one observer reported, "many Harlemites do not have the wherewithal—clothes and money—to make their appearance at the ball park, so hard are the times." Virtually all black enterprises regressed, barely remaining solvent until the economic rebound of World War II, and professional baseball was no exception.

Conditions throughout black baseball steadily declined after 1925. In the east, the Eastern Colored League had made an explosive entrance in December 1922, signing several top Western players and driving salaries to an unprecedented high in the early years of its existence. By 1926 the league was forced to retrench, and along with Foster's NNL, imposed a monthly salary cap to hold down wages. Internal squabbles, dwindling attendance, and uncooperative owners further troubled the circuit, whose future appeared questionable after the 1927 season. *Pittsburgh Courier* columnist Rollo Wilson questioned whether "men like the Hilldale Corporation, Colonel Strothers, Alex Pompez and the Bacharach backers [would] continue to throw good money in the ocean" of an ECL in serious decline.

As we have seen, Wilson proved correct. Hilldale, Harrisburg, and the Brooklyn Royal Giants all withdrew from the ECL prior to the 1928 season, and the league itself dissolved by June. The ECL's collapse disappointed a number of observers, including the *Philadelphia Tribune*, which hoped officials would create a new league that would be "a credit to them, their race, and the organizing genius of black men. It can be done, it must be done and we believe they will do it."

A few Eastern officials initially appeared interested in rebuilding the organization, such as Baltimore Black Sox owner George Rossiter, who asserted his belief that "a league is the best thing for all concerned." Yet Ed

Bolden, a major force in the ECL since its inception and previously a strong advocate of league baseball, could no longer see its value. While still "ready to join a real league, which I hope will be in existence some day," Bolden explained that participation in the ECL had ultimately hurt Hilldale, the league's strongest franchise. After losing $18,000 in 1927, the club chose to return to its "old methods" of independent baseball in the metropolitan Philadelphia area, with a greater emphasis on games with strong white semiprofessional teams.

Whether the "old methods" would suffice for Hilldale and other Eastern teams remained questionable. While acknowledging that "the present stand of Hilldale was inevitable," Cum Posey warned, "there is no assurance that independent baseball will be the same for Hilldale as in the past." As Posey and others realized, the heavy reliance on games with white teams at white parks presented its own set of problems. Semiprofessional baseball in many urban centers was now less profitable than it had been a decade earlier, as competing amusements, including the radio and automobile, had cut into attendance. Although Posey claimed that the Grays and Kansas City Monarchs could survive playing only white opponents, the strategy was doubtful for most teams. Fay Young, for example, rejected the notion the American Giants could "withdraw from the league and make more money playing white semipro ball" in Chicago. Although the city had once featured top white teams boasting ex-major leaguers, only a handful of strong clubs remained in Chicago by 1928, and the situation was similar in Philadelphia and other cities.

The declining number of strong white clubs also affected black teams from a competitive standpoint. Black players found it increasingly difficult to hone their skills against mediocre white teams which had little chance for victory. As John Clark, secretary of the soon-to-be famous Pittsburgh Crawfords, later observed, "It isn't fair to the players to have them go out day after day to play teams which have less than one chance in a hundred to win." In an attempt to keep the games competitive and ensure continued bookings at the same site, teams typically used their weakest pitchers or took other steps to keep fans interested in the game's

William "Judy" Johnson

He Could Write His Own Price

"Judy Johnson was the smartest third baseman I ever came across," said Pittsburgh Crawfords teammate Ted Page. "A scientific ball player, did everything with grace and poise. Played a heady game of baseball, none of this just slugging the ball." During his 15-year playing career, Johnson anchored two of the top clubs in Negro leagues history, the Hilldales in the 1920s and the Crawfords in the 1930s.

Another Crawfords teammate, Cool Papa Bell, said, "Oliver Marcelle was supposed to be the greatest third baseman of all time, but he couldn't hit too well. All around, Judy Johnson was better than Marcelle was." Willie Wells added that "[Johnson] had intelligence and finesse."

Johnson honed his skills on barnstorming teams before joining the Hilldales and also played winter ball in Cuba for many years. More of a contact hitter than a slugger, the 155-pounder helped the Hilldales win three Eastern Colored League titles before the league folded, then captained the star-studded Crawfords.

He led by example more than by fire. According to Newt Allen, "He was a great ball player and gentleman. He was a gentleman all through those baseball years when baseball was just as rough as could be. He just went along and played the game. You have respect for a man like that. Never argued with you about anything. Very seldom he argued about a strike or a play on the bases."

Johnson "was like a rock, a steadying influence on the club," said Jimmy Crutchfield. "Had a great brain, could anticipate a play, knew what his opponents were going to do." A renowned sign stealer, he often outsmarted opponents, including savvy players like Leo Durocher in one of many touted appearances against major league teams. Connie Mack saw him play and stated that if Johnson were white, he "could write his own price."

After his playing career ended in 1937, he spent many years as a scout and spring training instructor for several major league organizations. Yet Ted Page felt that Johnson's talents were underutilized. "He should have been in the major leagues 15 or 20 years as a coach. They talk about Negro managers. I always thought that Judy should have made a perfect major league manager. He was a scout, but he would have done the major leagues a lot more good as somebody who could help develop ball players."

"There was sun always shining someplace"— William Julius "Judy" Johnson

outcome. Hilldale's Judy Johnson, for example, later recalled that the team was able to "fool around a lot" against certain white teams. During 1928 Hilldale occasionally used position players as pitchers, shifted other players from their normal positions, and even allowed the starting pitcher to "let up." Yet the strategy seldom fooled fans, whose interest in attending one-sided games noticeably began to wane. As Rollo Wilson observed, "Neighborhood fans are not coming out, when they know that the boys do not have a possible chance to win."

Increasingly frustrated with the widening competitive distance, some white teams and their fans reacted bitterly, creating a hostile climate for black clubs. Alex Pompez, for example, noted in 1928 that his team had not only faced "jeers and insulting names" but "rough stuff" by white players in the metropolitan Philadelphia area. To Pompez, the cause was obvious: "Colored teams are so strong now that it is almost impossible for white semi-pro clubs to beat us...the fans are enraged at the continual spectacle of these clubs being licked." The situation understandably troubled Pompez, who believed "we must have a league and then we can refuse to play any club which cannot guarantee us protection against the vile conduct of fans and players. But now we are handicapped and must accept games wherever and whenever we can get them." Biased umpiring further discouraged patronage, as the veteran player-manager Ben Taylor claimed independent white teams had "set the umpires to regular cheating so as to even the games up. This resulted in disputes and squabbles, and eventually the attendance fell flat."

In terms of dollars, during 1928 Eastern clubs discovered that white semiprofessional baseball, while still an important source of steady revenue, could not by itself resolve the financial difficulties of black teams. Weekend and holiday games with other professional black clubs still offered the best opportunity for generating a substantial payday, yet without a league schedule and policies to follow, such games were now more difficult to arrange. Philadelphia's Hilldale Daisies and Pittsburgh's Homestead Grays haggled for weeks over financial details before finally arranging a home-and-home series in September. Two years later, a highly anticipated series between the Homestead club and New York's Lincoln Giants was delayed for similar reasons. Such uncertainties not only annoyed fans but particularly inconvenienced black teams with parks to fill each week. Short on attractions, Lincoln and Baltimore were occasionally forced to resort to booking white teams on Sunday at their parks during 1928, although such games seldom attracted interest from black fans.

Along with its financial deficiencies, independent baseball, both white and black, exerted only the loosest control over players. Following the breakup of the ECL in early 1928, Baltimore sportswriter Bill Gibson observed that any current arrangement among teams "will not have even the small amount of power that the deceased league had in preventing players from jumping their contracts." Some clubs, however, welcomed the opportunity to pursue top players without restraint. Hilldale, for example, grabbed Oscar Charleston and Daltie Cooper from the disbanded Harrisburg Giants, while Homestead, never a part of the ECL, continued signing stars such as Martin Dihigo of the Cuban Stars and John Beckwith of Harrisburg. Yet without an Eastern league in place, every team faced the constant prospect of losing players not only to regional competitors but to Negro National League teams. An all-out war over talent appeared increasingly likely and as Rollo Wilson warned, "it is going to be a case of dog-eat-dog. The so-called reserve clause in agreements is not going to be respected when the poobahs begin to line up their talent for next season."

THE ONE-YEAR LEAGUE

By the end of 1928, even the harshest of critics recognized that league baseball, regardless of its flaws, provided a measure of stability now sorely lacking among Eastern black teams. As noted journalist Bill Gibson remarked, "The present season has...afforded an excellent opportunity for making a comparison of organized and unorganized baseball—probably we should have said DIS-organized baseball...the absence of legislative, executive and judiciary bodies in eastern baseball has worked the same as the absence of such bodies would with civilized nations." Not surprisingly, several Eastern sportswriters wholeheartedly supported the revival of the ECL. The suggestion was embraced by Ed Bolden and other officials, and a new organization emerged.

In January 1929, Bolden spearheaded the formation of the American Negro League (ANL), featuring five of the original six ECL franchises along with the Homestead Grays, who replaced Nat Strong's Brooklyn Royal Giants. In the sixteen months following a nervous breakdown that appeared likely to end his career, Bolden had reasserted his control of the Hilldale club and now again stood atop the Eastern black baseball world. Reflecting the close ties between the black press and black baseball, Rollo Wilson was named league secretary. The veteran reporter anticipated success for the new organization, citing an "unusual spirit of harmony and consideration among the owners."

Although embroiled in several controversies, including problems with umpires, the ANL operated at a surprisingly high level during 1929, far surpassing the modest standard set by the ECL. Not only were standings and statistics issued on a regular basis, but teams made a genuine attempt to complete the schedule, and five of the six clubs played at least sixty of the eighty games originally planned. While the ANL was arguably the most successful league ever developed in the East, internal disagreements limited the organization to a single season. Cum Posey, for example, quickly became disillusioned with the ANL, complaining of "long trips and rotten umpiring in Philadelphia, Baltimore and New York." The season was also financially disappointing.

With the collapse of the ANL, some Eastern clubs immediately bolstered their position by raiding weaker clubs, including those of the still functioning NNL. The Lincoln Giants signed Turkey Stearnes of Detroit, while Baltimore grabbed Satchel Paige of Birmingham and Mule Suttles of St. Louis. Yet whether a season of independent baseball would ultimately benefit players remained questionable. The always perceptive veteran superstar John Henry Lloyd was doubtful, contending that the ANL's failure would "throw the ball players back about ten years...some of these...players will wish before the season is gone that they had the league to fall back on." Several officials also had serious misgivings, including Black Sox owner George Rossiter, who insisted, "We must have organized baseball in the East at any cost. No one with any sense is going to try to buck against the problems which arise in trying to play independent baseball. The fans want a league, and regardless of the fact that the league last year was not perfect, it was better than no league at all." Bill Gibson agreed: "These same clubs who lost money last year would probably have lost as much if not more, had they played independent baseball, and they will find that out this coming season."

A TIME OF STRUGGLE

Gibson proved correct, as the return to non-league play did little for Eastern baseball, which began an alarming decline during 1930. Several former ANL teams went out of business, including the Atlantic City Bacharachs. After two years of heavy losses, owner Ike Washington gave up on the city, which permanently disappeared as a venue for black baseball. Atlantic City, however, had never drawn particularly well. Fay Young noted, "Every one that goes to the seashore town goes to see the ocean and the boardwalk and not to see a ball game." The Cuban Stars also disbanded, as Alex Pompez, who had already tried to sell his team two years earlier, focused his attention for the next several years on running his illegal numbers operation in New York. Meanwhile, Ed Bolden attempted to dissolve the high-salaried Hilldale club, hoping to forge an alliance with Harry Passon—a former basketball player with the legendary South Philadelphia Hebrew Association, a booking agent, and sporting goods store owner—only to be thwarted by other members of the corporation. While Hilldale survived without Bolden, who remained out of professional baseball until 1933, the team eked out a marginal existence during 1930, averaging only 457 fans per Saturday home date between May 10 and September 20.

Although the Lincoln Giants and Homestead Grays enjoyed relatively successful seasons in 1930, the drop in attendance at most parks was striking. By June, George Rossiter warned that his team would be up for sale if

One of the great independent teams was the New York Mohawk Giants (ca 1931).

the "current business trend continued," and Rollo Wilson questioned whether several Eastern teams could complete their seasons. While the worsening general economic conditions contributed to the lack of patronage, Wilson and other writers cited fans' lack of interest in meaningless non-league baseball. Notably, a hotly contested best-of-ten games series in September between the Lincoln Giants and Homestead Grays played at New York, Pittsburgh, and Philadelphia drew unimpressive crowds. Lincoln Giants' owner James Keenan retired a few months later, spelling the end of his team after 20 years in black baseball.

By early 1931, three major clubs of the Eastern leagues of the 1920s—Atlantic City, Lincoln, and the Cuban Stars—had ceased to exist, leading Cum Posey's to remark that black baseball "has never had a more dreary outlook." The situation discouraged fans such as James Harvey of Baltimore, who lamented, "Negro baseball in this section is dead. The East should be ashamed to let the mid-West know that it is so cheap, having large cities and trying to play sandlot ball." Yet unbeknownst to Harvey, the Midwest was wrestling with similar difficulties.

Unfortunately, conditions improved little in the East during 1931, as the usual problems with attendance, player jumping, and securing attractions continued to plague most teams. As in 1928, a number of observers increasingly believed that a return to league baseball would at least stabilize the industry, yet several proposals, including a mixed league incorporating white semi-pro teams and a round-robin championship series, failed to materialize. With no organization or even tentative plans in place, the future of Eastern baseball appeared bleak. Hoping for a new league in 1932, Washington Pilots' official S.B. Wilkins warned that if fans "are not given the league which they want, it will be good-bye to colored baseball, that's all." Bill Nunn of the *Courier* agreed, gloomily predicting that "unless something is done...Negro baseball is doomed for an early, painful death."

HARD TIMES IN THE HEARTLAND

Although the Midwest enjoyed slightly greater stability than the East between 1928 and 1931, the Negro National League also was suffering. In the absence of league founder Rube Foster, attorney William Hueston presided over the circuit, yet he lacked the authority and experience of his predecessor. The declining economic status of blacks limited the effectiveness of any potential reforms initiated by the new president. Notably, Hueston and Kansas City owner J.L. Wilkinson supported a sensible plan in 1929 to prorate traveling expenses among all league teams, a strategy common in white minor leagues, designed to lessen the financial burden of clubs forced to travel greater distances. Yet the league abandoned the experiment after only a single season, forcing more geographically distant clubs such as Birmingham, Memphis and Kansas City to once again endure a disproportionate share of travel costs.

The failure to maintain the system reflected the general lack of cooperation within the NNL, a chronic problem all along now looming as more crucial in an era of decreasing patronage. Too often owners were less interested in the stability of the league as a whole and more concerned with the short-term success of their teams. The owners of the St. Louis Stars, for example, were reportedly a constant source of conflict, jockeying for better schedules and undercutting whatever authority the league president enjoyed. Team owners refused to contribute enough money for a $2,000 bond required by the Immigration Department to bring Tinti Molina's Cuban Stars, a league member since its formation, to the United States in 1931, leaving the NNL short a franchise. The self-centeredness was apparent as early as 1928 to one Kansas City sportswriter, who noted that several league owners "do not seem to care a rap about anything except the few paltry dollars they are able to wring from the fans who pass their gates. They do not care what happens to the rest of the clubs in the circuit as long as they can go their way and make a few dollars without any undue effort."

Yet, as in the East, the potential for any NNL owner to earn a "few paltry dollars" became increasingly unlikely by the late 1920s. While the league admitted to a "slight recession in patronage" in 1928, the drop became more pronounced in ensuing years. Within a few weeks into the 1929 season, Fay Young claimed that "something is wrong with baseball. Something is radically wrong...the season is hardly started when crowds have suddenly fallen off." The slump affected even normally solid clubs such as the Kansas City Monarchs, who reportedly had a $4,000 deficit by August. By the end of the season, the troubling decline was obvious to managers such as Jim Taylor of the Memphis Red Sox, who assessed the campaign as the "poorest from both playing and attendance since [the] beginning of [the] Negro National League in 1920."

The general deterioration in Western baseball during the late 1920s and early 1930s was most striking in Chicago and Kansas City, the two cornerstones of the NNL. For years Chicago, nurtured by Rube Foster, had been the best Midwestern city for black baseball. Since Foster's incapacitation in 1926, the American Giants had been run by two white businessmen: John Schorling, the lessor of the team's park, and then William Trimble, a florist who purchased the team and the park lease in 1927 from Schorling with the hope of building a dog track at the American Giants' home. Unable to obtain necessary authorization for the track, Trimble found himself saddled with a baseball team and park that he had little interest in maintaining. By 1930 Trimble was eager to sell, even willing to accept a $5,000 down

Catcher Buck Ewing and Edward "Eagle" Durant of the Mohawk Giants (ca 1930).

payment and a portion of the team's receipts during the season. Yet in a reflection of the sagging urban economy, no black businessmen stepped forward to rescue the once proud team, even when the price was lowered to a flat $5000. Although Hueston subsequently announced that the NNL would not operate a franchise in Chicago during 1931, the veteran third baseman Dave Malarcher went ahead and organized a new club, initially known as the Columbia Giants, to play at the American Giants' park. The team, however, was largely a failure, and after a few unsuccessful home dates the park was closed in July, leaving the large local population without regular professional black baseball for the first time in decades. The sad fate of Chicago symbolized the overall fortunes of the once promising league.

Historically one of the best promoted and well-run clubs in black baseball, J.L. Wilkinson's Kansas City Monarchs also encountered problems by the late 1920s. Despite fielding excellent clubs, the team's league attendance in Kansas City began to sag, and non-league games with white semipro teams in Kansas, always an important source of revenue, now became crucial to the club's financial stability. Although the Monarchs' pioneering use of a portable lighting system in 1930 proved to be a brilliant move for the entire industry, Wilkinson was increasingly ambivalent about the NNL and its value to his team, and in early 1931 the Monarchs withdrew from the league entirely. Perhaps more disconcerting to local fans and to black baseball itself, Wilkinson also decided to delay reassembling his team until July, a Depression-driven strategy he would again pursue the following season.

Despite the growing problems of Kansas City, Chicago, and other cities, President Hueston offered a brave public face and continued to insist that there was "nothing the matter with the league." Yet the NNL's financial and organizational problems were inescapable, and the long-term future of the league was increasingly precarious. Fay Young, who had been a close confidant of Foster and long a keen observer of the Midwestern black baseball scene, offered a frank appraisal of the league's administrative difficulties, explaining that the NNL "hasn't any real schedule, doesn't live up to its own rules, pays little attention to the needs and wants of the fans and to add insult to injury, games in the Negro National League take one hour longer to play than in the major leagues." Young concluded, "What Foster built up is going to the rocks." Fittingly, the death of Foster himself in December 1930 coincided with the virtual end of the organization he had founded a decade earlier, although the league would limp through one final campaign before formally disbanding in March 1932.

THE SHORT-LIVED EAST-WEST LEAGUE

As 1932 dawned, black professional baseball in the East and Midwest found itself in virtually identical positions. For the first time since 1919, neither section had a functional league, yet the question remained whether league baseball was an asset or liability in the current economic climate. A number of observers still believed that a league represented the only way to preserve the industry and develop talent. As veteran second baseman and manager Frank Warfield warned, another season of unstructured independent baseball might force players to abandon the game altogether to work "at whatever they can get to do." Despite his past ambivalence toward league ball, Homestead's Cum Posey also supported a movement toward organization, insisting, "This is the year when a baseball league, with baseball men behind it, is needed."

Ultimately, Posey would undertake an ambitious effort in 1932 to unify the East and Midwest into a single organization. In the past the always contentious Posey had been accused of raiding the Negro National League and was involved in scrapes with umpires and players. A single game in Philadelphia on May 17, 1929, demonstrated his pugnacious behavior. He refused to leave after being ejected, charged on the field to protest another call, and was subsequently punched by Hilldale's star outfielder Oscar Charleston. Yet by late 1931 Posey, described by detractors as "not a man who likes to take dictation from others" and "incapable of cooperating," was suggested by Fay Young as "the man to step in and carry on where Foster left off."

Posey, like Foster before him, had much to gain. A new league encompassing Eastern and Midwestern cities would perfectly serve the Grays, whose Pittsburgh location overlapped both sections. Perhaps more important, Posey hoped a league would strengthen his position against an emerging local competitor, the Pittsburgh Crawfords. Named after a local bathhouse and recreation center, the Crawfords, like the Grays, had begun on the sandlots, gradually building a following since the late 1920s while attracting top young local players to their team. By 1930 the Crawfords had begun to pose a threat to the Grays, winning 95 of 114 games (the majority against local semi-pros) and drawing sizable crowds at their home grounds at Ammon Field. The two clubs even met at Forbes Field on August 23, with the veteran Grays topping the newcomers by a surprisingly close 3–2 score.

A new league thus offered the best opportunity for the Grays to bolster their position while isolating the Crawfords from the major black teams. Posey was the driving force behind the January 1932 formation of the aptly titled East-West League (EWL), featuring most of the traditional Eastern cities along with representatives in Detroit and Cleveland. Despite the wide dispersal of franchises, Posey oversaw most aspects of the new league, handling the Grays as usual while indirectly operating Detroit and Cleveland. The clear dominance of Posey in league affairs was apparent to Crawfords' publicist John Clark, who described the Homestead official as "employing all his resources to 'position' certain teams and managers, much as he would checkers on a board." Yet whether the strategic moves of Posey, described by one sportswriter as "the smartest man in baseball," would succeed or backfire remained to be seen.

Despite its evident one-man rule, the league offered at least a few promising new directions, including the hiring of the long-established Elias Bureau to compile statistics as well as the use of salaried traveling umpires. Most surprising, the new circuit planned daily league games, an unprecedented experiment designed to reduce the reliance on white booking agents. Yet the strategy, never again attempted in black baseball, puzzled many observers including Bill Gibson, who warned, "The economic outlook is none too bright, and when one considers that last year it was hard to get many of the fans out on Sunday, it does not seem feasible with conditions now more acute, that more fans will come out for daily games." Coping with one of the worst years of the Depression, black fans failed to come to most parks once the season began in May, and the attempt to play everyday league ball was discontinued after a short period. With few options available, teams eventually turned to Nat Strong and Ed Gottlieb, whose bookings with white semipro teams helped a number of clubs stave off collapse in 1932.

Within a month, it became obvious that league baseball couldn't continue in the current environment, leading to the EWL's quick death by early July. Meanwhile, the short-lived organization failed to achieve any of Posey's objectives. While he initially hoped to crush local numbers man Gus Greenlee (who now owned the rival Crawfords and had built his team

Greenlee Field stadium), the dismal attendance throughout the league soon prompted Posey to reconsider his strategy. By late May a humbled Posey invited the Crawfords to join the league and negotiated an agreement allowing the Grays and other EWL teams to schedule games at Greenlee Field. Although the war between the Grays and Crawfords temporarily subsided, it was clear that Greenlee had eclipsed Posey as the dominant figure in the game. Posey, who had begun the year leading a broad-based eight-team organization, ended the season with his league defunct and team in disarray. Witnessing the decline of the once powerful Grays in 1932, Rollo Wilson suggested that if only one team could survive in Pittsburgh, "I am very much of the opinion that the Grays are closing their books."

Known in Pittsburgh for his "cash and a strong inclination to fight," Greenlee had proven a worthy opponent for Posey, and his position appeared relatively secure for the future. As virtually the only owner able to keep his players on monthly salaries in 1932, Greenlee had continued to strengthen his team, now featuring several stars from the once venerable Grays and recently disbanded Hilldale. Yet the Crawfords were hardly immune to Depression conditions, reportedly losing at least $15,000 during the season. With some clubs collapsing and other teams actually reduced to paying opponents with I.O.U.s, the financial prospects for the industry were bleak and it remained uncertain how Greenlee or any owner could continue to operate.

THE NADIR FOR BLACK BALL

The fragile state of black baseball in the large urban centers of the East and Midwest by the end of 1932 seemingly ended any hopes for a professional league. Assessing the damage, thoughtful observers offered a number of explanations why African Americans had been unable to sustain a strong organization of their own. "Dizzy" Dismukes, a veteran player and manager, believed that the industry had prematurely rushed its development, suggesting that the leagues tried to "accomplish in five or ten years that which it took organizations with millions of dollars of backing to do in fifty years...instead of trying to keep pace with the majors, we should have moulded [sic] our pattern along the lines of the minor leagues." Fay Young, however, suggested that selfishness and not ambitiousness had wrecked the leagues, explaining, "Golden opportunities were passed up a few years ago by short sighted men whose ambitions were more on winning a league championship than...building up baseball and making money."

Regardless of the causes, blackball fell to its lowest point in 1932. Yet most observers hoped that professional ball, a major aspect of African-American life for several decades, would somehow revive in the future. Ed Bolden asserted that baseball "has wonderful possibilities for the bettering of the conditions of a large number of our folks, and for that reason cannot be taken lightly." Ben Taylor expressed a similar view, noting, "It's about the only thing that we have that could be classed as all-colored and if properly handled in a business way, there is money to be made."

A distinct set of problems shaped the dismal course of the major black leagues in the late 1920s and early 1930s. While close observers cited the unwillingness among owners to cooperate, such an explanation identified only the symptoms of a larger issue: inadequate financing. As an economically oppressed community, African Americans had only a small pool of potential entrepreneurs wealthy enough to invest in professional baseball. Not surprisingly, most avoided participation in such a volatile and unpredictable industry, and as Taylor lamented, "Our big business men are afraid to invest in colored baseball. They say they will lose money." The negative experiences of Colonel Strothers with the Harrisburg Giants, George Robinson with the Washington/Wilmington Potomacs, and John Drew with Hilldale in the team's final two years seemingly confirmed that otherwise successful businessmen had little hope of earning a profit in black baseball.

Unable to attract wealthy individuals, the industry often relied on men with limited financial resources who hoped to depend primarily on gate receipts to operate their teams. While acceptable for a few long-established prosperous teams such as Homestead, Chicago, Kansas City and Hilldale, such a strategy was questionable for weaker clubs, as Foster's NNL discovered. According to sportswriter A.D. Williams, the league had not only admitted "dumbbells into the organization" but had also accepted owners unable to meet even the most basic of financial obligations, including a franchise deposit. To keep such weak teams afloat, the league was forced to advance them money, often taken from the deposits of more financially responsible franchises. The East encountered similar problems, particularly in the ANL, where one owner requested to pay his security deposit in installments and another was unable to come up with as little as $50. Meanwhile, an attempt to collect franchise fees in the EWL resulted in bounced checks from some owners.

Even during the financial heyday of the early 1920s, league ball was not without its limitations. Because of the limited income and leisure time of working-class blacks, weekday league baseball was never more than marginally profitable. In 1927, for example, Hilldale's Thursday home games averaged a quarter of what the club typically drew for Saturday and holiday games that season. The situation was similar in the NNL, where Fay Young observed, "Weekday ball doesn't pay in the league. That means if you don't make it on a Sunday you're out of luck." A Kansas City journalist took an even bleaker view, suggesting, "A few lost Sundays—and the chances for making any kind of profit is poor." In such an environment, league scheduling became a logistical nightmare, since teams were reluctant to leave their home parks on their most profitable days: Saturday in Philadelphia, where the blue laws remained in effect, and Sunday in other cities. The reliance on two days of the week, however, disappointed observers hoping that the leagues would replicate the daily schedule of games practiced in white organized baseball.

By 1929 the typical league club began the process of reducing player salaries. With the weak finances and attendance of the era, owners pursued steps to hold down costs. The salary cap imposed by both leagues beginning in 1926 was an initial strategy, followed by subsequent roster reductions to 14 players per team in the NNL. The changes were not popular with players such as Otto Briggs, who suggested that most were underpaid and "the majority of...salaries are based by the owners on what they would make working on the wharf and not on what he draws in the ball park." Bacharach pitcher Hubert Lockhart offered a similar view, not only complaining that the owners were "ungrateful and narrow" but also suggesting that the players would benefit from a union.

The players, however, found themselves with diminishing leverage in salary negotiations by the early 1930s. With a growing number of teams disbanding or unable to pay regular monthly salaries, players were under greater pressure to accept whatever wages were offered by management. As Bill Gibson noted, "The owners have the players practically at their mercy, and they know it." Cum Posey also identified the effect of market forces on salaries, observing at the close of the 1930 season, "The owners had too many players on hand to put up with high salaries and lazy players. There were many good players for every position."

While disheartening, the reduced salaries were less worrisome than the decision by some teams to abandon regular pay altogether during the early years of the Depression. In its place, clubs increasingly gravitated to the "co-op" or "co-plan," a system where 70–75% of the net receipts from each game were allotted to the players and the remainder to management. Under ideal circumstances, players with co-op teams might earn $100 to $125 per month. Yet unfavorable weather and cancelled games often cut into anticipated earnings, as did room and board, a responsibility assumed by the players on co-op teams. Despite grumblings by players, use of the co-op plan became increasingly widespread, and by 1933 virtually every major team had adopted a form of the system.

The lack of guaranteed salaries was only one aspect of an overall lifestyle decline for black players. Schedules, for instance, became increasingly grueling, as owners attempted to recoup losses by arranging more games. As early as 1929, the Homestead Grays occasionally played three games per day on the weekends, and the practice became more common throughout the industry in subsequent years. Yet despite the more exhausting schedule, amenities such as "eating money" on the road and

James "Cool Papa" Bell

Just How Fast Was He?

Cool Papa Bell may well have been the fastest man in the Negro leagues.

How fast was James "Cool Papa" Bell?

Legend has it that he was so fast that when he hit a ball through the pitcher's legs it would hit him in the back as he slid into second for a double.

Another often told tale about Cool turns out to have some fact in it. It's been said that he was "so fast that he could hit the light switch in a hotel room and be in bed before the lights went out. Cool was rooming one night with Satchel Paige when he discovered a slight delay in the light switch. He won a ten spot from his roommate when Cool Papa bet he could reach the sack before the light went out."

And then there are the recollections of those who played with and against him.

"If he bunts and it bounces twice, put it in your pocket," said "Double Duty" Radcliffe.

Bill "Ready" Cash remembers what it was like to play the Homestead Grays when Cool Papa Bell was cavorting around the bases: "All the major leaguers, I don't see anyone in the American or National Leagues playing inside baseball. In our league all we needed was one run. A guy like Max or Leon pitching all you need was one run. You shut the other team down. Play that inside baseball. Lots of times I tell people when we played the Homestead Grays and Cool Papa gets on second base and Jerry Benjamin comes up and lays a bunt down the third base line that's all you need cause Cool gonna dust off at home plate. That ain't no lie."

paid transportation to spring training disappeared or were severely curtailed by 1932. The new policies exerted considerable hardships on most players, recognized by Otto Briggs, who believed, "Some of them would not be able to pay their own railroad fare from [nearby] Chester to Philadelphia." Meanwhile, players no longer enjoyed the train travel common in the early 1920s, as owners began to employ the more cost-efficient but less comfortable buses to transport their teams and equipment.

With conditions at their nadir, the appeal of black professional baseball as a vocation predictably declined. In 1927, four players from the Eastern Colored League and the Negro National League chose to participate in an unsanctioned barnstorming tour of Japan and Hawaii, ultimately missing the first two months of the league season. Despite threats of punishment, the American Negro League was victimized by a similar trip two years later. Independent teams provided a similar safety net for disenchanted players such as George Giles, who left the Kansas City Monarchs to play for the barnstorming Gilkerson Union Giants, and Jake Stephens, who jumped Homestead to join the New England-based Philadelphia Giants in 1929. Others, troubled by the financial uncertainty of a professional baseball career, abandoned the leagues altogether in favor of full-time employment, such as pitcher Rube Currie and several other NNL players who hired on at the Chicago post office.

The experience of pitcher Webster McDonald shows the difficulties the industry faced in retaining its top talent. Between 1928 and 1931, McDonald, a top hurler who enjoyed remarkable success in games against white major leaguers, left his black team each May to pitch for a white semi-pro club in Little Falls, Minnesota. The decision was hardly surprising, as McDonald not only earned more than most Negro league players but also enjoyed a furnished apartment and a lighter schedule in Minnesota. While the absence of the star pitcher disappointed fans, McDonald and other players had little choice but to accept outside offers that black baseball was largely unable to match. The problem would only worsen in the future, culminating in the mass defection of players to other countries in the late 1930s and early 1940s.

ROUGH BEHAVIOR IN ROUGH TIMES

In contrast to the strong authority that white organized baseball enjoyed over its players, black baseball was far less successful in controlling rowdy behavior such as attacks on umpires. During 1929, for instance, assaults on umpires by Buck Ewing of the Homestead Grays at Passon Field in Philadelphia and Chicago manager Jim Brown at Kansas City prompted near riots and police involvement. Despite modest attempts to punish both players and "end player-rule of Organized Negro Baseball," similar incidents followed in subsequent years, much to the chagrin of a veteran like "Candy" Jim Taylor, who believed that unchecked rowdyism "will spell the death to the league by driving its already light patronage away." J.L. Wilkinson also cited the negative effect on attendance, claiming, "This type of ball player is killing the game in the league as well as exhibition cities."

A number of observers complained that the chronic squabbles with umpires resulted in needlessly long games. By 1930 Kansas City fan Larry Gayhardt remarked, "Games are long drawn out, taking from two hours to two hours and forty minutes. I have heard patrons complain of such long games and leave the park in disgust."

Meanwhile, the sometimes less than stellar conduct of players off the field troubled the black bourgeoisie. Kansas City *Call* reporter Roy Wilkins, soon to embark on his national career with the NAACP, wrote about the Kansas City Monarchs' "disregard of passersby at the headquarters on Eighteenth Street....The language of the players... does not have to be so free and easy—and purple." League officials such as Cum Posey also cited players "standing around the street in bedroom slippers, with no collar or tie... drinking in public after 12 o'clock at night or frequenting cabarets after one o'clock." More sympathetic individuals, however, recognized that most players were not "Sunday school boys" but men whose impoverished rural or working-class urban background undoubtedly shaped their behavior.

In reality, the behavior of black players probably differed little from their counterparts in white baseball. But white professional baseball had formal mechanisms in place to maintain a certain level of discipline throughout the industry and squelch the few "malcontents" and "booze-fighters" who created problems. A similar arrangement, however, remained unlikely to develop in black baseball, whose owners resisted cooperation, jealously protected their own interests and remained wary of any strong outside authority. For most officials, a weak administration was an acceptable tradeoff for greater latitude in running their own clubs. Yet this philosophy would obstruct needed reform and cost the industry dearly in the future.

PARKS TO PLAY IN—AND OTHER PROBLEMS

The limited revenue also impacted the choice of a home park, a crucial aspect to the success of any club. Based predominantly in large cities, black teams faced the difficult task of finding suitable grounds that were accessible to fans yet still affordable for owners with limited budgets. Not surprisingly, many of the home parks in use throughout black baseball were substandard.

The situation was particularly discouraging in the East, where two league teams of the 1920s, the Cuban Stars and Brooklyn Royal Giants, had no permanent home grounds of their own. Besides adding uncertainty to an already difficult scheduling process, such clubs were a liability for other reasons as well. Clubs with their own parks bore a cost that teams without did not have to assume. As Otto Briggs explained, "It is unjust to the other clubs that a club without grounds could play at the different parks and carry away thousands of dollars and not have anything to give in return." Eastern teams with parks faced a number of other difficulties. The Catholic Protectory Oval, home of the Lincoln Giants, was small and removed from the Harlem population, while the Atlantic City Bacharachs used a converted dog track as their park beginning in 1928. Meanwhile, despite reasonably strong attendance, Hilldale Park was flawed by its somewhat inconvenient suburban location in Darby.

Perhaps the worst situation in the East was in Baltimore, where local fans were forced to contend with the inadequacies of Maryland Park, leased by the Black Sox but owned by the B&O Railroad. The park was in remarkably poor condition, featuring uncut grass, dirty seats, a leaky roof, and bleachers that had reportedly been condemned. The park's negative effect on attendance was obvious to Baltimore fan James Harvey, who suggested, "If the Black Sox had a good diamond... they would have more people to come to the games." Bill Gibson agreed, noting that Maryland Park's shoddy condition drove away "ladies, who now do not dare go to the Westport ballyard." Yet as a tenant rather than owner, the Black Sox management had little desire to invest the $15,000 to $18,000 necessary to renovate the park, which remained in poor condition and was eventually abandoned in 1935.

The NNL also wrestled with park difficulties in several league cities. In St. Louis, the Stars played at a relatively convenient location, although the park's short left-field fence near a streetcar barn resulted in numerous cheap home runs. The long-term future of the site was also problematic, as the city began to eye the park as a potential municipal playground for blacks as early as 1928. Three years later, after a dismal season at the box office, with reported losses exceeding $14,000, the Stars' management sold the park to the city, spelling the end of the team and permanently destroying league baseball in St. Louis.

Black fans in Detroit also suffered with less than ideal park facilities. Since their formation in 1919, the Detroit Stars had used Mack Park, a site controlled by white entrepreneur John Roesink. Like too many other fields in black baseball, however, the wooden park was in deplorable condition and according to one observer was not only "very shaky" but had been "threatened with condemnation for many years." The worst fears of NNL officials were realized on July 7, 1929, when a fire and subsequent collapse of the grandstand roof injured over 100 fans. A move in 1930 to the newly built Hamtramck Stadium, also controlled by Roesink, hardly solved the team's problems, as the site was less accessible to Detroit's blacks. Moreover, Roesink, by now the team's owner, consistently alienated fans with his references to "shines" and "coons." Not surprisingly, Hamtramck Stadium never developed into a particularly profitable venue for black baseball.

The industry's troubles with parks was illustrated starkly in Chicago, the strongest city in the Midwest during the 1920s. Since 1911 the

American Giants had rented Schorling Park, a former major league facility conveniently located in the heart of Chicago's black belt. Like the Black Sox, however, the team had no incentive to improve the property, which reportedly could be leased for only one year at a time. After Schorling sold the lease in 1927 to William Trimble, whose interest in the American Giants was minimal, the condition of the park rapidly began to deteriorate. By 1931 the stands were in terrible condition, yet, as NNL president William Hueston explained, "under the building code in Chicago, in order to get a stand built now would cost many thousands of dollars, and this, of course, is impractical under the present financial conditions." Moreover, the property was likely to be sold at any time, further discouraging entrepreneurs interested in leasing the facility. Although black businessman Robert Cole gained control of the park in 1932, improvements were few, and the site was abandoned after a 1940 fire.

Surprisingly, three black entrepreneurs did invest a substantial amount in park renovations and improvements during the early 1930s. John Drew, for example, invested a reported $14,000 to refurbish Hilldale Park after purchasing the club in 1931, while Alex Pompez spent an enormous sum remodeling Dyckman Oval in New York four years later. In perhaps the most dramatic example, Gus Greenlee provided half the financing of a new $100,000 park for the Crawfords in 1932. Yet the heavy investment ultimately proved disappointing for each official, as Greenlee Field and Dyckman Oval were torn down by 1939 while Hilldale Park ceased to be a major venue after the collapse of the Hilldale team in 1932. With the risk of construction high, owners generally shied away from future efforts, and most teams would remain park tenants rather than owners.

Despite the organizational woes of black baseball, several positive developments marked the late 1920s and early 1930s. The level of play, for example, remained exceptionally competitive. In 1928 a white baseball "expert" rated the NNL as comparable to an upper-level minor league and suggested that several teams could move into "big league standard" with one or two additions. The grade was particularly impressive since black players appeared likely to perform at an even higher plane under the more favorable conditions enjoyed by whites who, as Rollo Wilson observed, generally had "more experience, more intensive training, better traveling conditions etc. Medical and physical attention are at their call at all times." In a further reflection of the strong talent within the league, two Cubans, Mike Herrera and Oscar Estrada, who spent time with Negro league teams without developing into stars, eventually played major league baseball: Herrera with the Boston Red Sox in 1925–1926 and Estrada with the St. Louis Browns in 1929.

The strong performances in the annual post-season competition with major leaguers perhaps provided the best barometer. During 1927 and 1928 the Grays won 8 of 17 games against a squad of American Leaguers featuring such future Hall of Famers as Harry Heilmann and Jimmie Foxx. In Baltimore, the Black Sox, augmented by several top Eastern players, defeated Lefty Grove in October 1928, followed by a series of victories against major leaguers between 1929 and 1931. Midwestern fans also witnessed solid showings by black clubs, including a reinforced Chicago American Giants team, which took a series from Earle Mack's All-Stars in 1929. Two years later, Willie Foster pitched the Kansas City Monarchs to a 4–3 victory at Muehlebach Stadium over a team featuring brothers Paul and Lloyd Waner of the Pittsburgh Pirates.

The continued success over major league barnstormers revealed that black baseball was still capable of both developing and nurturing talent. Although several greats of the past including John Henry Lloyd, Joe Rogan, Smokey Joe Williams, and Oscar Charleston were past their prime or nearing the end of their careers, a new crop of young stars surfaced, including first baseman Buck Leonard, infielder Ray Dandridge, outfielder Bill Wright, and pitchers Leon Day and Raymond Brown, all of whom made their professional debuts between 1930 and 1934. Satchel Paige and Josh Gibson emerged as recognized superstars during this era, and within a few years would become the two most famous men ever to play in the Negro leagues.

Paige was a standout early in his career. Born in Mobile, Alabama, his play on the local sandlots attracted the attention of the manager of the

Kick, Mule, Kick!

Some of George "Mule" Suttles' greatest feats came during the 1930s when he was instrumental in wining two East-West All-Star classics. A younger contemporary of Suttles, Charlie Biot, recalls a special "Mule" moment:

"The Newark Eagles had a big fella named Mule Suttles that I hardly hear anyone mention. But I never saw a man hit a ball that far with such a beautiful swing. Everyone always talks of Josh, but nobody mentions my buddy Mule Suttles. And he hit some of the furtherst drives I've ever seen in my lifetime. He looked like a big stout fellow. He went about 225 pounds. The only thing small about him was his knee down to his ankle. And he had big feet. But he just stood there and took a couple of waves with the bat. He didn't go through a lot of motion or anything. Then he held it back, and he went through that perfect swing I called it. I saw him one Saturday. I was watching the game from the sidelines. There was a fella named Duffy pitching for the East Orange BBC. In those days they didn't outlaw the spit ball in our leagues. So what he did, he used to bathe the ball in saliva. Put it to his mouth. When he threw a pitch you could see the saliva break off the pitch when the ball started to move. You could see it fly off like a piece of snow. That's how much spit and saliva was on that ball. He threw one to Mule Suttles and you could actually see the saliva fly off of it when it went over the center field fence. I'll never forget it as long as I live.

Chattanooga Black Lookouts, who marveled at the youngster's uncanny ability to hit tin cans with rocks. Paige eventually joined the lower-level Lookouts and debuted in the NNL as a member of the Birmingham Black Barons. The young pitcher, initially often referred to as simply "Satchel" in box scores, soon began to impress onlookers with his "triple windup," pinpoint control, and velocity. A July 1, 1928 game at Kansas City offered a typical performance—Paige threw 15 consecutive strikes at one point, highlighted by a fastball described as "so infernally fast that two were needed to see it."

With no real agreement between the NNL and Eastern clubs after 1927, several teams began pursuing Paige. In 1929, the Homestead Grays announced his signing, yet—in what would soon be a familiar occurrence—the eccentric young hurler failed to report. A year later, Paige jumped Birmingham to join the Baltimore Black Sox, only to return within three months. While Cum Posey complained that "Satchell [sic] acted like a kangaroo throughout the year, bounding from Birmingham to Baltimore and vice versa," Paige remained determined to sell his skills to the highest bidder, regardless of the effect on his teams or their fans. Although justifiable, such a policy invited criticism from sportswriters such as Bill Gibson, who complained after Paige's jump to the Pittsburgh Crawfords in 1931 that the pitcher had "deserted about every team he has ever played with, packing his grip and leaving without notice."

Baseball, however, generally overlooked Paige's frequent transgressions, recognizing that his enviable pitching skills and colorful behavior made him a top box office attraction. Increasingly perceived as a candidate for the major leagues, Paige even began to earn praise from members of the white baseball establishment. After witnessing Paige throw his third consecutive shutout in 1932, former major leaguer Wid Conroy labeled him "the greatest pitcher I've ever seen....He's just about got everything." In a soon to be familiar quote, Conroy noted, "If that guy were only white I'd grab him, make a sale to some major league club, and retire for the rest of my life."

While a less colorful performer than Paige, Josh Gibson would elicit similar comments during his career. Eighteen years old when he joined the Grays in late July 1930, the young slugger soon began attracting rave notices for his hitting. On September 13, Gibson hit one of the longest home runs ever at Forbes Field, followed 12 days later by a mammoth clout at Bigler Field in Philadelphia that cleared the left-field fence and the roofs across the street from the park. Two days later at Yankee Stadium, Gibson blasted another tape-measure home run, this time traveling an estimated 460 feet, reportedly the farthest-hit ball in the park that season. The prodigious homers were the first of many for Gibson, who soon established himself as not only the top hitter in the Negro leagues but perhaps all baseball.

Despite their undeniable skills, Gibson and Paige remained severely underpaid during the Depression. In an era of small crowds and a weak economy, teams were unable to offer high salaries, even to their top performers. Although both players ultimately jumped by 1932 to the financially stable Pittsburgh Crawfords, it is likely that neither man earned more than $500 per month with a league team until 1941. Not surprisingly, black baseball never enjoyed complete control over either player, as both Paige and Gibson willingly accepted lucrative offers to play abroad by the late 1930s. Yet black baseball deserved credit for managing to develop and foster the talents of both players in an era when the league structure was at its most fragmented state.

OUT OF THE DARK

If the rise of Paige and Gibson provided encouragement, the emergence of night baseball in the early 1930s offered another stimulus to an industry in desperate need of attracting fans. Experiments with night baseball had been common for years, including a game involving the black Cuban Giants and a white semi-pro team in the early 1900s, although lighting systems proved inadequate for athletic events until further advances in the late 1920s. After the demonstrated success of college football games under lights during 1929, baseball promoters became increasingly willing to consider the technology.

J.L. Wilkinson began preparing for the Kansas City Monarchs to use a portable lighting system in 1930. Explaining his decision to invest thousands of dollars in the technology, Wilkinson said he had "found that hundreds of people who wanted to see baseball games could not on account of working conditions which did not allow them to get off until after dark....I am well aware...that night baseball will not permit the exact brand of ball to be played ordinarily, but with the rules under which it will be played it will not be far from the regular daytime game."

Not surprisingly, baseball traditionalists remained dubious. The conservative *Sporting News* warned, "The night air is not like the day air; the man who goes to baseball after he has eaten a hearty meal is apt to have indigestion if he is nervous and excited." Despite fears, night baseball was soon a success in the minor leagues during 1930, doubling normal attendance in the Class A Western League, and by early June, 20 cities had installed lights or were planning to do so. Meanwhile, Wilkinson's pathbreaking portable system, utilizing trucks to transport the lights to each venue and a gasoline-powered generator in a bus to provide the electricity, also proved effective, impressing major league officials such as Philadelphia Phillies traveling secretary Jimmy Hagens, who claimed the Monarchs "have it more nearly perfected than any other outfit that I have seen or heard of. From what I saw, I should say that there are wonderful possibilities for semi-pro and minor league ball in this innovation. More people can go to baseball games at night than can go in the daytime and where there are not as many persons to draw on as in the major league cities, night baseball may save the game."

The lights in use at this time, however, were still far from ideal for players and fans. Pitcher Scrip Lee later recalled that he refused to accept a pitching assignment at an early night game, explaining, "I just went out there and threw a ball up and tried to catch it and the ball dropped about a foot in front of me. I couldn't see it." Judy Johnson also cited the inadequacy of the early lights, complaining, "I couldn't see the outfielders out there. If the ball went up above the lights, you'd have to watch out it didn't hit you in the head." Meanwhile, the glare of some lighting systems bothered spectators, prompting one sportswriter to suggest, "With the lights as they are now, a great many fans will find enough objections to be just lukewarm to the innovation."

Despite the technology's flaws, the Monarchs inaugurated night baseball in a number of cities during 1930 and quickly demonstrated its potential value to black teams. A Monday night game in St. Louis in May, for example, drew 4,000 fans, or more than eight times a normal weekday crowd. A month later, a Friday night promotion at Hamtramck Stadium reportedly attracted 7,000 fans, the largest weekday crowd to date for the Detroit Stars. In Pittsburgh, a crowd of over 6,000 turned out to watch a

Now You See It

Smokey Joe Williams was involved in many a pitching duel during his storied career, but few are more famous than the titanic struggle against Kansas City ace Chet Brewer on August 7, 1930. Playing under the primitive light system at the time, the two pitchers battled for 12 long innings. Brewer was known for his cut balls, roughed up with an emery board, and he struck out 19 men. In retaliation, Smokey Joe spat tobacco juice on the ball, making it almost impossible to see. At the ripe old age of 45, he struck out 25 batters that night. The game ended only after the Grays' Oscar Charleston walked and Chaney White followed with a ground ball that bounced wildly off third base. They couldn't see where it went.

July 18 night contest at Forbes Field, including white sportswriter Ralph Davis, who marveled that the field "turned from inky blackness into something approaching mid-afternoon brightness....The scene was a revelation to many doubting Thomases, who went to scoff and left the field, declaring that perhaps after all, the national pastime, if it ever has to be saved, will find night performances its savior."

Unprofitable weekday afternoon and twilight contests were replaced with night games. The impact of lighted white parks was recognized by James Keenan, whose Lincoln Giants participated in the July 2, 1930 debut of night baseball in West New York. The successful promotion not only impressed Keenan, who promised to "play many more games under the lights," but also Dexter Park co-owner Max Rosner, who installed lights three weeks later at his Brooklyn facility, always an important venue for black teams.

The advent of lights ultimately provided black baseball with a desperately needed lifeline during the early 1930s. Not surprisingly, most parks in use by black teams adopted the technology. By late 1932 night lights had been installed at Greenlee Field, Dyckman Oval in New York, Cole's Park in Chicago, Parkside Field in Philadelphia, and Bugle Field in Baltimore. The importance of night baseball for black teams would only increase in the future, recognized by Cum Posey, who accurately assessed night games as the "backbone" of the industry by 1942.

RENTING THE BEST

If night baseball helped stabilize black teams, the gradual movement into major league parks in the early 1930s represented another positive development. Although black clubs had long rented major league facilities (particularly Forbes Field, the Grays' home grounds for several years), rentals of most big-league parks had proved too expensive to be used on more than an occasional basis. Notably, the Cuban Stars of the NNL used Redland Field in Cincinnati for only a single season in 1921, while the ECL's short-lived Washington Potomacs abandoned Griffith Stadium three years later because of cost concerns.

With the Depression in full force, the likelihood of black teams leasing a major league facility for even a single promotion appeared improbable. Yet major league parks continued to intrigue promoters, particularly those readily accessible to urban blacks such as Yankee Stadium, a facility yet to be used by black teams. In 1930, however, the Yankees' management donated the park for a July 5 benefit game for A. Philip Randolph's Brotherhood of Sleeping Car Porters, a major black labor organization struggling to survive during the Depression while it engaged the Pullman Company in one of the period's epic labor management struggles.

Promoted by Brotherhood secretary-treasurer Roy Lancaster, a founding member of the organization, the doubleheader featuring the Lincoln Giants and Baltimore Black Sox drew an estimated 14,000 to 20,000 fans who paid major league prices of $1 to $1.50 for grandstand and box seats. Delighted by the turnout, Lancaster marveled that "the great Yankee Stadium" had been "given to the porters free, to aid them in their fight for a higher standard of living. Truly we have friends in both races."

The Yankees agreed to a second Brotherhood benefit on August 16, 1931, this time involving Hilldale and the Harlem Stars. With barely 2,000 fans in attendance and the Yankees now collecting a third of the gross receipts as a rental fee, the promotion was a disaster for the Brotherhood, ultimately resulting in a loss.

Despite mixed results, the two Brotherhood benefits at Yankee Stadium did succeed in opening the facility permanently to black teams. Following the initial promotion, the Lincoln Giants rented Yankee Stadium for their September 1930 series with the Homestead Grays, leading some observers to anticipate that the team eventually would make the site their home. A year later, Lincoln's successor, the Harlem Stars (later known as the New York Black Yankees) cultivated an even closer relationship with the Yankees, not only renting the Stadium on occasion but also wearing old Yankees uniforms. Not until September 1934, however, did Yankee Stadium finally become profitable for black teams, as two four-team doubleheaders (a soon to be familiar promotion) each drew over 20,000 fans, leading to regular dates in the future. The importance of the Yankee Stadium dates was evident to Cum Posey, who suggested that the 1930 promotions "had a great bearing on colored baseball of the future. No colored teams had ever played to the gross gate receipts as had been taken in at Yankee Stadium."

Chicago's Comiskey Park also became an increasingly important venue in the early 1930s. Seldom used by black teams in the past because it was so close to the American Giants' home, Comiskey began to loom larger with the American Giants' park virtually dormant by late 1931. Within two years Comiskey Park hosted the first East-West game, a soon to be major promotion featuring the top players in black baseball. The annual game at Comiskey Park became the industry's most important date, and by 1939 a record-setting 33,489 fans attended the contest. Black baseball soon became a regular feature at Comiskey, which not only continued to host the East-West game but also became the home of the American Giants in 1941 following a fire at their own park.

Like Comiskey Park and Yankee Stadium, Griffith Stadium in Washington offered enormous potential because of its proximity to a large black community. By the early years of the Depression, the perennially cash-strapped Senators and their president Clark Griffith were eager to lease the park to black teams despite earlier failed attempts with the Washington Braves in 1921 and the ECL's Potomacs in 1923 and 1924. After hosting several successful promotions involving top black clubs in 1931, Griffith Stadium appeared poised to become a major industry venue, prompting the creation of a new team, the Washington Pilots, who planned to use the facility as their home in 1932. The Pilots, however, disappeared within two years, although Clark Griffith, who reportedly looked "with a kindly eye" toward black baseball, continued to rent his park to a number of tenants during the 1930s, including the Elite Giants and Black Senators. By 1937, Griffith's willingness to rent his park drew praise from Cum Posey, who claimed black baseball had "received great cooperation and much valuable advice" from the Senators' official. Posey would finally develop Griffith Stadium into a profitable park after shifting the bulk of Homesteads' home games to Washington beginning in 1940.

In the midst of the Depression, few officials could have predicted that regular promotions at Griffith Stadium, Yankee Stadium, Comiskey Park, and other major league parks would eventually provide the foundation for the renaissance of black baseball. Yet during the war years when black fans supported the game in record numbers, the more spacious facilities easily accommodated the larger crowds and offered the opportunity for unprecedented profits.

Perhaps equally important, the major league milieu contributed to the fight against the color line by generating increased white media attention and forcing uninformed outsiders to reconsider their perception of black teams as little more than semi-pro players. As early as 1933, black entrepreneur and writer Dave Hawkins recognized the importance of placing black teams in a major league setting, promoting a doubleheader at League Park in Cleveland whose "real goal," according to Rollo Wilson, was to sell "Negro baseball to white newspapers and white fans."

The exposure of black players in the East-West games and other promotions at major league parks fulfilled a similar purpose, prompting a number of white journalists and fans to more seriously question the exclusion of such talented athletes from the national game. Impressed by the galaxy of black stars in the 1933 East-West game, Chicago journalist Henry Farrell suggested, "With a plentiful supply of occult calcimine... a bunch of major-league club owners might have their prayers answered." Other observers would gradually reach similar conclusions.

The veteran black journalist St. Claire Bourne reflected on the many games he covered at major league stadiums: "When these guys came along and started playing this kind of ball and people saw them here at Yankee Stadium, people would come out. I always felt that had something to do with the gradual moving of blacks into baseball. Because sooner or later owners were going to get smart enough to realize that the real part of baseball was green, not black or white."

For Negro leaguers who played in these major league stadiums, simple enjoyment outweighed any thoughts they may have had about impacting the integration of baseball. Bill Yancy had the distinction of being the first black player to set foot on the turf at Yankee Stadium. Yancy's excitement was such that he ran out on the field early, pretended to catch fly balls in right field like Babe Ruth, and stood along at home plate pretending to hit home runs into the right field stands like the Babe. Bill Yancy counted playing in Yankee Stadium as one of his biggest thrills.

NEW KINDS OF OWNERS

Despite the high mortality rate of black clubs during this era, entrepreneurs continued to enter the game. Several newcomers who would play a major role in baseball's revival in the 1940s included the Martin brothers, J.B. (a pharmacist) and W.S. (a physician), who purchased control of the sagging Memphis Red Sox of the NNL in 1929. Later joined by a third brother, B.B. (a dentist), the Martins remained fixtures in black baseball for the next three decades. A number of whites also became influential, paralleling the increasing role of whites in other areas of black entertainment. Eddie Gottlieb, a Philadelphia sports promoter known for his involvement in the early years of professional basketball, became a top booking agent in the late 1920s and by the mid-1930s co-owned the newly formed Philadelphia Stars with Ed Bolden. Syd Pollock's nearly 40 years in black baseball also began in the late 1920s as owner of the traveling Havana Red Sox, a Cuban club, although Pollock would gain greater notoriety as the head of the Cincinnati-Indianapolis Clowns in the 1940s. Finally, Harlem Globetrotters owner Abe Saperstein, a powerful yet often heavily criticized booking force in the Midwest in the 1940s, launched his black baseball career in 1932 as owner of a traveling team headed by former American Giant Jim Brown.

Although new white capital was a significant force in helping to sustain the industry in the early 1930s, a greater financial contribution came from blacks, particularly those such as Gus Greenlee, who wasz involved in illegal enterprises. With opportunities in legitimate business minimal, a number of black entrepreneurs instead channeled their energies into operating policy wheels (a popular game in the Midwest) and the numbers lottery, a game in which individuals placed bets, as low as a penny, on any three-digit number, selected in various ways such as the last three digits of the daily transaction totals on the New York Stock Exchange, or racetrack figures. Paying winning players at a ratio of 500 to 600 times the original bet, the numbers game quickly grew in popularity during the mid- to late 1920s, a reflection of the growing hopelessness and weak economic base of urban black communities. As early as 1928, *Courier* columnist George Schuyler cited the "economic forces that drive nine-tenths of a community to gambling," and Depression-fueled unemployment would only intensify the interest in the pastime.

With local law enforcement officials and politicians frequently connected to the game, the numbers lottery offered the potential of enormous profits. By 1930, communities such as Philadelphia, Washington, and New York wagered thousands of dollars daily, enabling entrepreneurs such as Alex Pompez to gross as much as $8,000 per day. In Pittsburgh, where the game operated with little local interference, one observer claimed the numbers generated $100,000 to $200,000 per week, employed over 500 people, and paid an average of $25,000 in weekly salaries.

Illegal enterprises would eventually provide much of the venture capital during the Depression for legitimate black businesses such as baseball. Underworld figures had always been part of the industry, as men such as Tenny Blount (Detroit Stars), Baron Wilkins (New York Bacharachs), Dick Kent (St. Louis Stars), and Alex Pompez invested in league franchises in the early 1920s. Yet the influence of numbers and policy money would grow later in the decade, to the discomfort of some observers. Following the 1927 season, Rollo Wilson noted the "close affiliation...between the gamblers in Atlantic City and the baseball club there. It is reported on more or less reliable authority that whenever the birds of that species sank their rolls on a game it was 'in.' It has been said that at times the payroll was met by the slickers of Arctic Avenue." Bill Gibson warned of the potential problems with such individuals: "Crap shooters, bootleggers and their kind have no business being mixed up with the national pastime. Theirs is a different life."

Yet as illegal lotteries became an inescapable force in black communities in the late 1920s, they became a financial presence in black baseball. Gambling club operator Smitty Lucas, for example, who owned the short-lived Philadelphia Tigers during the final months of the Eastern Colored League in 1928, was implicated for murder three years later. In Atlantic City, Bacharachs' owner Ike Washington was arrested on numbers charges two months prior to the 1929 season, although he was soon released. In the west, William Mosely, dividing his time between his policy wheel, numbers business, and occasional involvement with the Detroit Stars, was murdered in 1935 after reportedly failing to pay off on a $50 hit.

With the risk of owning a team mounting in the Depression, illegal income loomed even larger in the financing of teams. Along with Gus Greenlee in Pittsburgh, several new officials entered the industry in the early 1930s, all with ties to the numbers or gambling, and apparently eager to launder their illegal profits. Robert Cole, the head of the successful Metropolitan Funeral System Association who also dabbled as a "professional" gambler, rescued the Chicago American Giants in 1932, while numbers operator James Semler took control of the New York Black

Yankees, albeit with the considerable financial assistance of Nat Strong. Abe Manley, a leading numbers banker in Camden, New Jersey, also began his involvement in black baseball, initially investing in a sandlot team in 1929 and entering the professional ranks six years later as the owner of the Brooklyn, soon to be Newark, Eagles. Finally, Rufus "Sonnyman" Jackson, a Homestead numbers operator and jukebox entrepreneur, joined the management of the Grays after a nearly broke Cum Posey was forced to seek additional financing for the team in 1934.

Illegal enterprises, despite their volatility and vulnerability to prosecution, thus filled an important role, providing the influx of cash necessary to keep the industry afloat during a difficult period. While the black public embraced the benevolent involvement of underworld figures such as Greenlee, who were perceived as truly interested in the game and the community, the continued preponderance of numbers bankers by the late 1930s ultimately troubled observers such as Baltimore *Afro-American* sportswriter Sam Lacy, who felt the leagues needed to be "more discriminating in...[their] membership requirements." The shady background of several owners would later prove to be a liability to the industry during its attempts to demonstrate its legitimacy to white organized baseball in the early post-integration years.

A NEW ERA

By early 1933, the future of African Americans in baseball was increasingly doubtful. Conditions and salaries for players were at their nadir, and the professional league structure begun by Rube Foster over a decade earlier lay in tatters. Simultaneously, white organized baseball continued to maintain its unwritten exclusion of black athletes. As in other areas of African-American life during the Depression, the question arose whether blacks should now focus their attention on protesting against white discrimination or continuing to build their own institutions.

Yet the early months of 1933 also witnessed the beginnings of a new era in black professional baseball. In January, Gus Greenlee spearheaded the

Mohawk Giant players posed for this 1930s photograph as fans filled up the stands.

formation of the Negro National Association of Baseball Clubs (commonly known as the Negro National League), an organization initially composed of predominantly Midwestern franchises. After Posey's disastrous East-West league of a year earlier, the attempt appeared doomed to failure. As Rollo Wilson observed, "If Gus Greenlee can carry his league through the present campaign this correspondent will be the first to congratulate him on performing a modern labor of Hercules." The new league intentionally set its expectations low, as explained by Crawfords' secretary John Clark: "Members of the league admitted that they could not expect profits...the very best that could be expected was to keep the losses to a minimum, keep the league interest intact, and prepare for 1934."

Black baseball thus stood at the crossroads in 1933. The prosperity experienced just a decade earlier was now a distant memory, and every team faced severe obstacles. Although Greenlee's formation of a new league appeared to be a positive step, the question remained whether league baseball was economically feasible. Notably, Black Yankees official James Semler preferred to remain outside of the league structure and instead maintain his close relationship with booking agent Nat Strong. Explaining his lack of interest, Semler suggested that Strong "can keep the team working and I know the league can not" and insisted that "it will be a long time before a colored league will stand its ground. Finances will stop them dead." Whether the industry would ultimately lean toward Semler's example or the league route advocated by Greenlee remained unclear as 1933 dawned. Recognizing the trials and difficult decisions ahead for the industry, one observer warned, "Baseball has possibilities but must be handled properly or all is lost."

Jimmy Hill, an outstanding lefty for the Newark Eagles, around 1940.

Recovery and Demise

I didn't play baseball because it was a pastime. I played it because I loved it. I played it with what they call "reckless abandon." I ran over hills; I ran into fences; I dove into pigpens. I'll never forget that. Oh, I can smell it now.

—Harold Tinker, Captain of the Pittsburgh Crawfords

1934 COULD HAVE BEEN DUBBED THE YEAR OF THE PITCHER. Historian John Holway characterizes it as arguably Satchel Paige's best season. On the nation's birthday Paige opened Pittsburgh's new Greenlee Field with a 17-strikeout no-hitter for his Crawfords against the Grays. He followed that up with five straight shutouts. A skinny 20-year-old, left-handed version of the great Satchel, Stuart "Slim" Jones waged a season-long rivalry to lead his Philadelphia club to the second-half pennant.

In September a classic showdown was arranged. In game one on September 9 in Yankee Stadium—Monte Irvin called it the greatest game he ever saw—several fielding gems and clutch pitching marked a contest that ended at one apiece as darkness brought a halt to the proceeding after nine innings.

Game two on September 16 before 30,000 fans saw another close-fought battle. Let Holway tell this story:

The teams went into the ninth as the shadows lengthened.

Slim Jones set the Crawford down 1–2–3 in the top of the inning getting Josh Gibson on a hard grounder for the final out.

In the bottom of the ninth darkness was falling fast. Williams raced behind first and threw the speedy Chaney White out. But he made a wild throw on Jud Wilson's slow roller, and Jud charged all the way to third.

After Paige walked Biz Mackey to put the tieing run on first, Judy Johnson called time and trotted to the mound. "Satch," he said, "the boys at the barbershop said they want to shut your big mouth."

"Did they?" Satch said.

It was now so dark that Paige was almost invisible. Webster McDonald, a good hitter, pinch-hit. Satchel mowed him down on three called strikes, Satchel's 17th strikeout of the day.

Pinch-hitter Ameal Brooks was next. He too went down for strikeout #18, and the umps called the game as the fans screamed.

Satchel strode over to the Philadelphia dugout, poked his head inside, and said, "Tell that to the boys in the barbershop."

Final score—Crawfords 3, Stars 1.

FDR, GUS AND CUM

The rejuvenation of black baseball in the 1930s was part of a larger order of change for black Americans as the nation gradually emerged from the depths of the Depression. The job gains blacks had made during World War I and afterward ended by the late 1920s, when the last hired were the first fired. African Americans would continue to feel the economic hard times more acutely than their white fellow citizens.

But even before the coming of the Depression, there were clear signs that the GOP ship they had been sailing on since Reconstruction was ripe for abandoning. In mid-decade Roscoe Dungee captured the growing mood of black leadership, and many among the masses, when he called into question the political mantra uttered by the great Frederick Douglass in the 1870s—the one about the Republican Party being the ship and all else the sea. The radical Dungee told his Oklahoma *Black Dispatch* readers that the Negro had lain down and gone to sleep in the backyard of the Republican Party for 60 years, and it was past time for a wakeup call.

That call came in muted tones in 1928—and then resoundingly in 1932 and 1936. And when it came, blacks answered the ring. In the 1928 national election, two national weeklies, the Baltimore *Afro-American* and the Chicago *Defender*, did the previously unthinkable— something that only a radical like W. E. B. Dubois and his NAACP crowd would have advocated up to then. They urged their readers to jump off the Republican ship to support the Democratic candidate, Al Smith.

If 1928 was a muted call, in 1932 the call was clearly heard. The *Pittsburgh Courier* had reached the position of leading black newspaper, and *Courier* owner and editor Robert Vann was a stalwart who had been in charge of the Colored Division of the Republican Party in the previous two presidential contests. In 1932 he jumped ship. In his famous "The Patriot and the Partisan" speech delivered throughout black communities, he drew the line clearly for all his listeners to see and hear. "Go home and turn Lincoln's picture to the wall. The debt has been paid in full." And so they did on Election Day, when a record percentage of the black vote went into the Democratic column.

Franklin D. Roosevelt's New Deal was ushered in with a flourish of legislation unprecedented in the nation's legislative history. And while the discrimination prevalent through all of American society meant that blacks would fare less well from this legislation than their white counterpart "Forgotten Americans," they would fare better than ever before from a government that had long ignored their plight. Four years later election results announced that the long ride on the Republican elephant was clearly over. It was now time for African Americans to saddle up and mount the Democratic donkey.

During the era of the Depression, black baseball also undertook a search for new direction, with renewed hope for the future. As FDR started the engine again for America, so would Gus Greenlee and Cumberland Posey revive a Negro league that would in time outshine all that had gone before it.

RENAISSANCE AND NEW DEAL BLACKBALL

With Cool Papa Bell flying around the base paths, Josh Gibson drawing accolades as the black Babe Ruth, and Satchel Paige intentionally loading the bases, telling his fielders to sit down, and then striking out the side, Pittsburgh spearheaded the rejuvenation of black baseball during the 1930s. "Coming to Pittsburgh was a big thrill," former Newark Eagle and Hall of Famer Monte Irvin recalled. "You were lucky to win one game, because the Pittsburgh Crawfords and Homestead Grays, you see, they dominated baseball at that time."

In the mid-1930s, Pittsburgh became to black baseball what Harlem had been to black literature and the arts during the 1920s, the catalyst of a renaissance. From the depths of the Depression through World War II, black urban enclaves such as Newark, Philadelphia, and Baltimore witnessed the rebuilding of the Eastern black professional baseball network. Revival would take place in the West as well, with Kansas City leading the way. But the catalyst was found in the Steel City. Pittsburgh became a black baseball crossroads as a result of its central geographic location, the astute leadership of Gus Greenlee and Cumberland Posey, Jr., and the presence of a Georgia-born, Pittsburgh-bred ballplayer named Joshua Gibson.

Together, the Homestead Grays and the Pittsburgh Crawfords captured over a dozen Negro National League championships and contributed to the careers of seven of the first nine Negro leaguers chosen for the Hall of Fame. The incomparable Gibson, perhaps the greatest hitter of all time, starred for most of those championship squads. So did a handful of other talented athletes, including Buck Leonard, Oscar Charleston, and Cool Papa Bell, who wowed opposing players and fans from the city's sandlots to the West Coast and beyond.

Black baseball in Pittsburgh during the 1930s and 1940s was not simply a regional phenomenon. It was part of both a national and international network of athletes firmly embedded in the world that African Americans and Afro Caribbeans had created on their own during segregation. Over a score of African-American communities in major cities fielded professional black teams during these years. To the east, the

The wind up, the strech, the pitch! Baltimore Elite pitchers, late 1930s.

Newark Eagles, New York Black Yankees, Philadelphia Stars, and Baltimore Elite Giants were to their cities what the Grays and Crawfords were to Pittsburgh. To the west, the Chicago American Giants, the Cleveland Buckeyes, the Memphis Red Sox, and the Kansas City Monarchs played comparable roles in theirs. An even greater number of squads played in the Caribbean basin. Cuba boasted of Almendares and Santa Clara, Puerto Rico of Santurce and Ponce, the Dominican Republic of Escogido, Licey, Aguilas, and Las Estrellas of San Pedro de Macoris.

Though black baseball locales differed greatly, they had always shared two defining cultural and social denominators. On the one hand, none could ignore the exclusionary policies of organized baseball at both the minor and major league levels. Nor could they escape the social and political mores that permeated societies that not only tolerated, but promoted racial inequality. On the other hand, these locales drew strength from a shared internal dynamic of community and identity generated within black America. Urban institutions as diverse as national newspapers, black-owned businesses, churches, mutual benefit societies and insurance

Satchel Paige
Methuselah on the Mound

The story of Robert Leroy "Satchel" Paige is better known than that of any other Negro professional ballplayer. It began on the professional level in 1926 in Chattanooga, Tennessee, when he joined a team playing for the Negro Southern League. Baseball took him across the American landscape from Birmingham to Baltimore to Cleveland, Pittsburgh, Kansas City, and down into the Dominican. Later he embarked on a colorful barnstorming tour with his own all-stars, and played again in Cleveland (how old he was, God only knows) to help the big-league Indians win a championship, even pitching three innings with the Kansas City Athletics (reportedly at the age of 59) to become the oldest man to pitch in the majors.

Control was the very essence of his game. At his first professional tryout, he knocked 14 out of 15 cans off a fence from 60 feet. While touring, one of his favorite tricks was to set a ball on a box at home plate and bet he could hit it at least once in three tries. He usually won. It's been said that he could pitch between two batters, facing each other six inches apart, and knock cigars out of their mouths.

In 1934 he was in top form. In the fall he fanned 16 out of 18 barnstorming big leaguers in Cleveland. The next day at Columbia he struck out Mickey Heath, Danny Taylor, and Nick Cullop after deliberately loading the bases. He later won a 13-inning 1–0 battle against "Dizzy" Dean.

In 1941 he reportedly took the mound for 30 straight days

In 1942 he recorded four straight wins over the Grays. Nabbed by a policeman for speeding on the way to the last game, he took the mound with no warm-ups in the third inning with the Monarchs behind 4–3. To give himself time to settle in, he decided to try to pick a runner off first. He would throw one to the plate, and three or four to first base. He blanked the Grays without a hit the rest of the way to a 9–4 victory.

Maxwell Manning, fellow Negro Leaguer, said of him: "There was something strange about Satchel's ball. No matter what angle you looked at it, it was always small. It never looked like the size of a normal ball."

In 1971, finally experiencing the proudest moment of his life, Satchel Paige was elected to the National Baseball Hall of Fame as the first Negro league inductee.

Paige was the first Negro leaguer to be inducted by the Baseball Hall of Fame.

companies; protest organizations; professional societies of black doctors, lawyers and businessmen; and a cultural and entertainment network that spoke to the heart and soul of black America, and on occasion to white America as well, offered respite from American racism. This dual dynamic was at the heart of black professional baseball during these years. Within the boundaries drawn by segregation, a vibrant communal sporting world took shape in black America's urban archipelago and the Caribbean basin.

Black and Latin players were a presence as well in hundreds of white communities during their frequent barnstorming excursions, while word of mouth and the black press carried their exploits even farther. For a variety of reasons, not least the quality of its play, a largely invisible African-American baseball world became more and more visible to the nation as a whole during the Depression and World War II. That visibility would prove to be an important element in the assault on segregated baseball.

Rising from the depths of the Depression and the collapse of the first Negro National League in 1931, the Negro National League was reconstituted in 1933, and the Negro American League shortly thereafter. Their East-West Classic, an annual all-star game in Chicago, attracted new celebrity to black baseball. It often brought more African Americans together at one time than any other event during the year. Black teams, meanwhile, continued to barnstorm the nation, playing two or three games a day before fans who rarely, if ever, saw a white major league game. The crowning of a Negro league champion also resumed, intermittently after 1937 with informal post-season play, and formally in 1942, when the Kansas City Monarchs defeated the Homestead Grays in the first real Negro League Series since the 1927 Chicago American Giants' defeat of the Atlantic City Bacharach Giants. While the series never gained the attention lavished on the East-West Classic, it contributed to black baseball's growing stature as players like Satchel Paige, Josh Gibson, Buck Leonard, Monte Irvin, and Ray Dandridge became national, even international, icons.

THE CRAWFORDS COME TO RULE

When the Negro National League was resurrected, its savior was not the sage Cumberland Posey, Jr., who had dominated the sport in black Pittsburgh during the postwar years, but Gus Greenlee, a relative newcomer to black baseball. Greenlee was an unlikely figure to lead black baseball into its golden age, but hardly an obscure one. In many ways, he was a larger-than-life character.

Almost everyone in black Pittsburgh knew Gus in one way or another. Some patronized his nightclubs, others drank his bootleg liquor, and still more played their pennies and dollars on his numbers. Many came to him for a never-to-be-repaid loan to help pay for groceries, a load of coal, the rent, or tuition to send a child to college. They cheered his stable of boxers, which included John Henry Lewis, the first African-American light heavyweight champion of the world, and recognized Greenlee as the leading patron of black sports in Pittsburgh.

While Greenlee played baseball growing up in Marion, North Carolina, he displayed neither great aptitude nor keen interest in the game. Yet during the 1930s, black Pittsburgh knew Gus as the force behind the Pittsburgh Crawfords, possibly black baseball's finest team ever. Two of Greenlee's brothers became doctors and a third practiced law, but Gus dropped out of college and wound up becoming the "caliph of Little Harlem" instead. "Big Red," as the 200-pound, six-foot three-inch, lightly complected Greenlee was known, commanded attention.

After the outset of prohibition, Greenlee opened a speakeasy, the Paramount Club, on Wylie Avenue in the Hill section, which looms above the city's central business district. The traditional stopping point for newcomers to Pittsburgh, the Hill was absorbing many of the thousands of black migrants from the South.

Though the Hill became the city's principal black neighborhood in the 1920s and 1930s, it was a well-integrated neighborhood of immigrant and second-generation Italians, Jews, Syrians, and Irish. The lower Hill, where Gus Greenlee ran a number of clubs, was the city's tenderloin, complete with "black and tan" cabarets, the rackets, and their integrated clientele. The Crawford Grill became the best known of Greenlee's establishments. The classiest nightspot on the Hill, a mecca for jazz aficionados, and the hub of Greenlee's varied business activities, the Grill attracted a broad mix of people. Athletes, politicians, and entertainers mingled with working men and women. Greenlee could usually be found there most evenings, sitting at the bar, dispensing favors.

He was there one day in 1930 when several members of the Crawfords, a local sandlot team, burst in and asked Gus if he was interested in becoming the owner of their ball club. The Crawfords, who were beginning to challenge the Homestead Grays for local bragging rights, were a popular draw on the Hill, often attracting a few thousand fans to games. Greenlee had no significant connection to local sports, but he had been among the Wylie Avenue businessmen who responded when *Pittsburgh Courier* columnist John Clark solicited contributions for the ball club in 1926. Greenlee demurred when the players asked for his patronage, but they persisted. Finally, he agreed to take the club on and put them on salaries.

"Man, gee whiz! A salary," team co-founder Bill Harris recalled. "That was just a dream to us. We never thought about no salary. We just wanted to play ball."

SANDLOT BALL

The Grays and the Crawfords fit into a larger interracial sandlot scene of self-organized, independent clubs that collectively drew more fans and meant more to many people than the major league Pittsburgh Pirates. The sandlots encompassed a range of sandlot, semi-pro, and company teams that annually took to local diamonds. During sandlot ball's heyday between the two world wars, 200 to 500 teams played in the region each year. Ten to twenty of these teams were composed of black players.

The cost of admission and afternoon starting time of most Pirates games discouraged working-class attendance. African Americans, along with many white immigrant and industrial workers, opted to watch or play sandlot ball instead. There, the cost of admission was whatever they chose to toss into a passing hat. The games were played during the twilight hours after work or on weekends. And the players were often family members, neighbors, or workmates.

Honus Wagner, who grew up in Carnegie, a working-class suburb of Pittsburgh, played for a handful of these sandlot clubs before moving up the ranks of organized baseball. The bow-legged shortstop, who starred for the Pirates for 18 seasons and became one of the Hall of Fame's five original inductees, returned to the sandlots after leaving the majors playing for the Green Cab semi-pros and the Carnegie Elks for another eight seasons, until he was 51.

A center fielder on numerous sandlot teams, Harold Tinker did not dream of playing major league baseball. His fantasy centered on the Homestead Grays. "I had an ambition," Harold explained. "I sat down there in Forbes Field as a kid and I watched them [the Grays] play. I told myself, 'Boy, one day I'm gonna be on a team that will beat these Homestead Grays.' That was my life's desire. And every team that I became a part of, I took that nucleus of players that I knew in my heart would be coming toward that aim."

Spotted running down fly balls on the field near his home when he was 15, Harold was recruited to play for WEMCO, a black team sponsored by the Westinghouse Manufacturing Company. From there he went to the Keystone Juniors, the Pittsburgh Monarchs, and finally Edgar Thomson Steelworks team (ET). Early during the 1928 season, ET played the Crawfords. "We were amazed that we could only beat them two to one or something like that," Tinker explained. "Those kids were really hustlers." Afterward, Bill Harris approached Tinker and his brother Neal and persuaded them and four other ET players to join the Crawfords. With this infusion of older talent, the Crawfords were on their way to becoming the best black sandlot club in the region and a challenger to the Grays.

Shortly thereafter, Tinker, who became the Crawfords' captain and manager, recruited a young ball player who one day would be called the black Babe Ruth. That ballplayer's father, Mark Gibson, had come north in 1921, leaving Buena Vista, Georgia, for a job at a Pittsburgh steel mill. Three years later, his family joined him. His son, Josh, was not quite 13 when he arrived in Pittsburgh. A strong, solidly built young man, Josh left school

Buck Leonard

The Black Lou Gehrig

Smooth at the bat, smooth in the field, Leonard is front row, left.

Buck Leonard started out as a right fielder. The experienced Negro league first sacker, Ben Taylor, was "the owner, manager, everything of his team." Still a great hitter, but getting too old to play in the field, Taylor groomed his young pupil to play his own first base position. He must have taken some pride in the fact that the boy he mentored came as a man to be compared most often to Lou Gehrig. Historian Jim Riley captures Leonard the baseball player well:

"Possessing a smooth swing at the plate, he was equally smooth in the field. In 1941 one media source described four or five sensational stops that were way beyond the reach of 99 percent of major league first basemen. Sure handed, with a strong and accurate arm and acknowledged as a smart player who always made the right play, Buck was a team man all the way. A classy guy, he was the best-liked player in the game.

As adept as he was in the field, he was even more adept at the plate. While teammate Josh Gibson was slugging tape measure home runs, Leonard was hitting screaming line drives both off the walls and over the walls. Trying to sneak a fastball past him was like trying to sneak a sunrise past a rooster."

after the ninth grade and worked at Westinghouse Airbrake, a steel mill, and Gimbel Brothers before finding his calling on the ball field.

Tinker encountered Gibson playing ball on the Northside. "That day I saw him over there, he was playing on a very rough ball field, just rocks and stones. He was playing third base and they were hitting shots down there and he was coming up with them like he was playing on Forbes Field." Tinker thought to himself, "This boy is a marvel." Near the end of the game, Gibson hit a home run. "He hit the ball out of existence," Tinker exclaimed. "They didn't even go after it. It went over a mountain. And I said to myself, 'This is a part of my plan. He needs to be with us.'" After the game, Tinker asked Josh to join the Crawfords. "'Come to Ammon Field next Tuesday and you'll have a job with the Pittsburgh Crawfords.' Those people up there went wild over him and so did we, from the very first day."

The Crawfords played to large, enthusiastic crowds at Ammon Field on Bedford Avenue and traveled into outlying towns where the only other black team to play had been the Grays. Though perceived as the Hill's team, the Crawfords attracted black fans from other parts of the city. White residents of the Hill and a contingent of white fans from Lawrenceville made up between 15 and 30 percent of the crowd at home games, according to former players.

With Gibson behind home plate, the Crawfords continually beat the best white sandlot clubs around. But as the club recruited new players, some of the youths who had formed the team left. Bill Harris and Johnny Moore joined the Homestead Grays while Teenie Harris left to work for his brother Woogie's numbers operation. He returned to Ammon Field, however, to take a photograph of his former teammates as they proudly stood side by side on the sandlot atop the Hill. Harris kept taking photos, earning the sobriquet "One Shot Harris" in a career as the *Pittsburgh Courier's* principal photographer. His shots of Negro leaguers and other black athletes remain among the best ever taken.

The Homestead Grays were the ultimate challenge for the Crawfords. Before they got a game with Posey's team, the Crawfords went through a

Josh Gibson, one of the most popular men in black baseball, greets his fans.

significant change. Seward Posey, Cum Posey's younger brother, approached Josh during a Crawford game in the 1930 season with an offer to play for the Grays. Josh sought Tinker's blessings for the move. Tinker figured that Posey wanted to take the Crawfords' power away before giving them a game. "That was a hard decision," he explained, but he knew what playing for the Grays could mean for Gibson. "If I didn't love Josh, I wouldn't have told him to go."

A different version of how the Grays recruited Josh features the Kansas City Monarchs playing Homestead at Forbes Field on the evening of July 25, 1930. The night game was lit by the portable illumination system the Monarchs used during their travels. But the system did not throw enough light for catcher Buck Ewing and pitcher Smokey Joe Williams to see each other well. A mix-up in signs crossed up Ewing, who split his hand on a fastball. When the Grays' backup catcher hesitated to take Ewing's spot, the Grays called Josh out of the stands to catch.

The Crawfords lost Gibson, but they gained Gus Greenlee later that summer. After Greenlee took on the Crawfords, he put them on a salary and told them they had to devote themselves to baseball full-time to stay with the team. With six children to support, Tinker doubted he could manage on the money Greenlee was offering, especially because it was only paid during the season. Before he made up his mind to quit the team, he had a chance to accomplish his boyhood ambition, beating the Homestead Grays.

The first time the Crawfords played the Grays, they lost by a run, when Grays outfielder Vic Harris, an older brother of Bill and Neal, made a running catch of a line drive with two on and two out in the ninth. The second time, they were beaten 9–0. By the time the Crawfords played the Grays a third time, at Cyclone Park in McKeesport in August 1931, Greenlee had added several out-of-towners to the team.

The Grays led 4–0 early in the third game when former Chicago American Giants shortstop Bobby Williams, whom Greenlee hired to manage the Crawfords, brought in a lanky, sardonic pitcher from the bullpen. "They warmed up this Satchel boy and we didn't know nothing about him," Tinker recalled. "I'll tell you, he was throwing nothing but fastballs. And the Grays hardly hit a hard foul for the rest of the ballgame. We scored five runs and beat 'em five to three. By the grace of God, that's when we beat the Grays." With his ambition realized, Tinker left the Crawfords at the end of the season. "We played for the reputation and the desire to go to the top," Tinker explained. His Crawfords had reached the heights and it was time to move on. "I never did have money as the basis of my interest in basketball and baseball."

The Crawfords replaced Tinker in center field with Jimmy Crutchfield and added left-handed pitcher Sam Streeter and infielders Chester Williams and John Henry Russell to the roster during the 1931 season. Greenlee's revamping of the squad had only begun. The following year, Greenlee continued the team's makeover, signing baseball greats Oscar Charleston, Judy Johnson, Cool Papa Bell, Rev Cannady, Ted Page, Ted "Double Duty" Radcliffe, and Jud Wilson to the team. Greenlee secured several of these players from the Grays, who could not match the salaries he offered. The Crawfords also signed Josh Gibson back from the Grays in 1932, and fielded a team with five players whose careers ended in the Hall of Fame. Most of the original Crawfords were relegated to the bench or the grandstands.

As he remade the Crawfords, Greenlee contended with a dilemma that most black professional teams faced. Few controlled their own playing fields. As a result, they were often beholden to white booking agents or major league owners willing to rent their facilities when their own clubs were on the road.

Greenlee, who sought more autonomy, decided to build a ballpark of his own on Bedford Avenue, a few blocks from the Crawford Grill. To finance construction, Greenlee formed the Bedford Land and Improvement Company. Treasurer Joe Tito and secretary Robert Lane were white. Tito, a longtime friend of Greenlee, had been involved in the numbers with him. Lane was his accountant. The numbers were likely a major source of funds.

The redbrick-walled Greenlee Field cost $100,000 and took 75 tons of steel and 14 railroad cars of cement to construct. *Pittsburgh Courier* editor Robert L. Vann led a standing ovation for Greenlee before offering the ceremonial first pitch at the ballpark's official opening, pitting the Crawfords against the New York Black Yankees.

During its first year, 1932, Greenlee Field attracted 119,000 paying fans to an array of baseball, football, and soccer games, as well as a few boxing cards. In 1933 and again in 1936, two of the few years for which there is documentation, the Crawfords played to over 200,000 paying fans. A drawing for a Ford sedan, benefits co-sponsored with social organizations, and appearances by Olympic star Jesse Owens who raced a horse before games, boosted attendance. Greenlee promoted his teams by showcasing Paige and Gibson, guaranteeing that Satchel would strike out the side and Josh hit a home run. More often than not, they did.

Greenlee's nearby nightclub became a popular after-game destination. "All the people flocked to the games," Newark Eagle Monte Irvin remembered, "and after the games, they would flock to the Crawford Grill #1. And after a while, they were doing so good, they built Crawford Grill #2. They had good entertainment, great food, and there were plenty of girls so that the ballplayers could meet them. This is why we got really excited."

THE RESURRECTION OF NEGRO LEAGUE BASEBALL

The Crawfords were a top-notch squad and Greenlee Field was the foremost black-owned ballpark in the United States. But there was no credible league to legitimize either. In 1932 Greenlee sought a franchise in Cumberland Posey's short-lived East-West League, but Posey was loath to surrender control over black baseball in Pittsburgh. To gain entry in the league, Greenlee would have had to sign a five-year contract allowing Posey to determine the Crawfords' local schedule and the composition of the team. Making clear who was in charge, Posey also stipulated that either he or his brother, Seward, would manage the Crawfords. Greenlee refused to accept these terms. Instead, he decided to reform the Negro National League in time for the 1933 season. He could hardly have picked a worse moment to launch his venture.

The United States was at the lowest point of the Great Depression. Pittsburgh had been especially hard hit as its manufacturing base crumbled. That spring United States Steel was operating at 14 percent of capacity. More than one of every seven white and two of every five black Pittsburghers were on relief. A majority of African-American workers in Pittsburgh were either unemployed or underemployed. Conditions were even bleaker in outlying mill towns.

But the Negro National League became a success, linking ball clubs into black America's preeminent professional league for 16 seasons, from 1933 to 1948. Pittsburgh, with two strong black clubs, was a natural city to serve as its center. It was already well known as a crossroads city on the "chitlin circuit," the informal network of black nightspots linking Eastern and Midwestern cities. Black ball clubs, like black entertainers, passed through the town whenever they traveled from the east to west or vice versa. Headquartered at first over the Crawford Grill, publicized nationwide by the black press, and serving as proof of what African Americans were able to accomplish on their own, the Negro National League propelled black baseball to a new prominence.

The owners in the Negro National League were distinctive on two counts. Except for Effa Manley, the individuals behind these teams were African-American or Latin men. And many of them relied on the numbers game as a key source of revenue, as we have seen. Writing about the numbers barons, Richard Wright observed, "They would have been steel tycoons, Wall Street brokers, auto moguls, had they been white. Instead, they built empires on a betting game that even poor people could play." Given the illegal and decentralized nature of the numbers game, bottom-line figures are impossible to determine. A 1928 story in the Pittsburgh Press asserted that the lottery was then a two-million-dollar-a-year operation in the city.

The creation of the Negro American League in 1937, with fewer owners involved with the numbers, led to two more geographically balanced leagues. The NAL fielded teams in Kansas City, Chicago, Cincinnati, Memphis, Detroit, Birmingham, Indianapolis, and St. Louis its first season. Kansas City, Chicago, and Memphis maintained franchises throughout the 1937–1948 period, with Cleveland (first the Bears, then the Buckeyes) joining this trio in 1939. Birmingham was almost as consistent, missing only the 1939 season.

THE EAST-WEST CLASSIC

Gus Greenlee also played a major role in creating the East-West Negro League All-Star Classic. During the 1933 season Pittsburgh Crawfords' secretary Roy Sparrow and *Pittsburgh Courier* editor William Nunn, Sr. broached the idea of a black all-star game with Cum Posey. Their initial plan was to hold the contest at Yankee Stadium in conjunction with the New York Milk Fund. When that effort failed to materialize, they approached Gus Greenlee. He proposed that they involve Chicago American Giants owner Robert Cole and lease Comiskey Park as the All-Star game's venue.

On September 10, the East-West game was inaugurated before a rain-dampened crowd of 20,000. Fans attending that first black summer classic saw seven future Hall of Famers take the field in a steady drizzle—Cool Papa Bell, Oscar Charleston, Bill Foster, Josh Gibson, Judy Johnson, Willie Wells, and Turkey Stearnes. Earlier that summer major league baseball had held its first all-star game, also at Comiskey. Babe Ruth hit the first white All-Star home run. Fittingly, Mule Suttles hit the first black one. "He hit a drop ball—it may have been a spitter—from Sam Streeter off his shoe tops and drove it between the upper deck and the roof."

Over the next 20 seasons the East-West All-Star Game ranked among black America's favorite sporting events. From 1933 through the 1950s, the mid-summer classic attracted tens of thousands of fans each season. Most of these games were held at Comiskey Park, but New York City, Washington, D. C., and Cleveland also hosted the contest, sometimes in a given season as a second All-Star game. Fans came on special railroad cars along the New York Central, Santa Fe, and Illinois Central lines, congregating in Chicago and making the event more than an athletic showcase.

The East-West game attracted the attention of both the black press as well as white sportswriters and front office personnel, who noted the size of the crowds as much as the talent on the field. The games also served a social role, bringing together African Americans from many cities and regions in what might have been the largest gatherings of blacks from across the country at any time during the 1930s and 1940s. Like a Joe Louis or Henry Armstrong title fight, the games displayed the emerging national identity of African Americans after the Great Migration out of the South. Black sports fans attended by the thousands, and so did black politicians, celebrities, and elite.

Fans voted the players onto the squads, using ballots published by the major black papers. The press reported over a million votes cast in each of the first few years, and though the totals slipped badly in 1935 and 1936, they rebounded by newspaper-published accounts to almost three million in 1938, and soared to over 17 million in 1939.

PATTERSON
EAST WEST

Batter Pat Patterson takes a swing during the 1939 East-West All Star Game.

The Chicago American Giants, Homestead Grays, and Pittsburgh Crawfords dominated the first contest, contributing 20 of 32 players. While eight were future Hall of Famers, some sportswriters questioned the legitimacy of the game, won by the Western squad 11–7. They derided it as little more than a Giants-Crawfords clash, augmented with a few ringers. But the criticism did not deter the game's organizers, who returned to Comiskey the following season and were favored with a classic ballgame, won 1–0 by the East. William Nunn, Sr., one of the game's creators, could hardly restrain himself in his coverage of the contest, which featured future Hall of Famers Willie Foster and Satchel Paige pitching in the final innings. "Today's game was more than a masterpiece! It was more than a classic!" Nunn wrote. "It was really and truly a diamond eye!"

In 1937 Joe Louis became only the second black heavyweight champion when he knocked out James Braddock in a bout held inside Comiskey Park. Two years later he threw the All-Star game opening ceremonial first pitch to Gus Greenlee on the same field. In that same year, a second All-Star game brought over 40,000 fans to Yankee Stadium. The 1941 game attracted a record crowd of 50,000 to Chicago. Monte Irvin, who made his All-Star debut that year, fondly recalled the joy of playing in black baseball's premier showcase. "You didn't go to Chicago to sleep," he noted, not when Count Basie, Ella Fitzgerald, and Billie Holiday were playing the clubs. Players stayed at the Grand Hotel, and found themselves the center of attention. The game featured as fine an array of talent as could be found in baseball. "But more than anything else," Irvin reflected, "our games gave black Americans hope all across the country.... They said, 'If these ball players can succeed under these very difficult conditions, then maybe we can too.'" Irvin and a handful of other Negro League all-stars would reprise their roles in major league baseball's All-Star contests after the end of World War II.

SEASONS IN THE SUN

The resurrected Negro National League charted new waters for the black game, but stability was elusive. Some of the founding teams, such as the

Columbus Blue Birds, Cole's American Giants, and the Baltimore Black Sox, left league play, moved after a season or two, or disbanded. Others, including the Newark Eagles and the Philadelphia Stars, took their place. But while teams came and left, the Crawfords excelled. Between 1932 and 1936 Greenlee's team was the best overall club in black professional baseball. The Crawfords' best years came in 1935 and 1936, when they won back-to-back Negro National League pennants.

In the NNL's inaugural 1933 season, Cole's American Giants came in a game ahead of the Crawfords, but Greenlee awarded his team the pennant anyway. He was, after all, the head of the league, and while the Giants protested, so what? Though both Josh Gibson and Oscar Charleston had strong seasons, Satchel Paige finished with a losing record, going 5–7. Paige rebounded and won 13 games against only three defeats the following year. But in early August 1934, Paige, never known for adhering to contracts, jumped the club to play for the House of David in the *Denver Post* Tournament, an annual championship of the best clubs outside the white majors. After beating the Kansas City Monarchs in the tournament's championship game, Paige returned to Pittsburgh for the rest of the season. The Philadelphia Stars beat Cole's American Giants in the 1934 playoffs to win the NNL pennant. Following the season, Paige celebrated his wedding to Janet Howard with a party at the Crawford Grill.

Satchel Paige did not return to Pittsburgh for the 1935 season. Unable to reach agreement on his salary with Gus Greenlee, Paige jumped to Bismarck, North Dakota, where he formed a battery with Ted "Double Duty" Radcliffe on an otherwise white semi-pro team. His presence, on and off the field, was not missed. Charles Greenlee had worked as the team's traveling secretary before his brother, Gus, helped him attend medical school. Josh Gibson, the younger Greenlee recalled, "was one of the easiest guys to handle…a beautiful man. And Satchel Paige was one of the biggest sons-of-a-bitch that you ever said hello to. He would not do right. He had a brain like a relief recipient. All for me."

Cool Papa Bell, Sammy Bankhead, Oscar Charleston, and Josh Gibson more than made up for his absence between the lines. They powered the

Josh Gibson
The Black Babe Ruth

There's no better judge of an athlete than a competitor. Charlie Biot played against Josh Gibson, the man many refer to as the "black Babe Ruth." Even after 40 years had passed, Biot remembered Gibson as a player "in a class all by himself. He was an uncanny hitter. He never had to do a lot of digging in or moving around at the plate. He just took his back foot and dug it in. And you remember him always rolling up his sleeve. He always rolled up his right sleeve. And then he was set. He took one or two little swings for exercise and held his bat back. He was a perfect hitter. I think he was born with that. Some people say you can develop it, but I think Gibson was more just a natural born hitter. And he swung with such great ease. I never saw him swing, get off balance, fall. I never saw him do the things that I see every day among the major league ball players."

Biot recalls a game against Gibson's Homestead Grays in Richmond, Virginia, that entered the ninth inning with the Pittsburgh club and Biot's Black Yankees tied at two apiece:

"I'll never forget it. The lights were very expensive to run at that time. It looked like we were going past nine innings. The Grays were coming to bat for their last half. Gibson was the lead-off hitter. So the manager ran out, and they got together like they were going to change pitchers, and he said, 'Please, for God's sake, get the game over with. This game is going on too long. We won't have any money left. The electricity bill will beat us. Give Josh a pitch right down the middle and let him end it cause the people would love to see that.' And that's what we did.

"I was pitching and the first ball he pitched was right down the center and went right over my head about 50 feet in the air into the trees 420 feet away. We laughed and kidded about it later that night when we got in the restaurant. We said to Josh, 'We let you hit that one.' And he laughed too. But you did not have to let him hit it."

What about the ones they didn't want to let him hit?

John Holway tells us that Josh Gibson "hit what he called his longest home run in 1932. It was a measured 512 feet against Sug Cornelius in Monessen, PA. 'Why didn't you call for a curve' the players asked catcher Larry Brown after the inning. 'Goddamn!' Larry replied, "If I'd a known he was gonna hit the fastball, I would' a called for the curve.'

Mal Goode tells a story about another of Gibson's great shots: "Ralph

Gibson has been called the "black Babe Ruth."

Kiner hit one just barely over the center-field wall. I sat beside a fellow who said, 'I bet no one's ever hit one that far.' I said, oh yea. I saw a fellow on a team a few years ago, a fellow named Josh Gibson. In August, 1938 I saw him hit a ball 20 feet above that wall which was marked 440 feet which meant it had to be 700 feet into the trees in what they called Schenley Park."

team at the plate while Leroy Matlock, Sam Streeter, and Roosevelt Davis led the pitching staff. Matlock finished that season 19–0, and the Crawfords beat the New York Cubans four games to three in the playoffs. Matlock, who pitched for both the Pittsburgh Crawfords and the Homestead Grays during his career, was selected to the East-West All-Star game in 1935 and 1936. Teammate Ted Page called him "the best left-hander that ever toed the rubber." Streeter, a stocky curveball and spitball pitcher, regarded by many as one of the smartest hurlers in the Negro Leagues.

The New York Cubans joined the league in 1935. Alejandro Pompez, spending a reported $60,000 on the renovation of Dyckman Oval, transformed the grounds into a professional stadium with a seating capacity of 10,000, complete with a covered grandstand, new seats, and floodlights for night games. The renovations were impressive. According to the *New York Age* "There is no comfort that the fans can crave undone by Pompez Exhibition Co., Inc." For the next two years Dyckman Oval served as a gathering place for Harlemites to retreat, a location where they could feel separated from the indignities of racialized treatment in a wider society, a place of their own to celebrate their own.

Although popularly referred to as "Harlem's Own," Dyckman Oval's location just outside Harlem proper could have complicated the team's ability to secure a stable fan base. To validate his team's place in the hearts of Harlem's fans, Pompez fielded a competitive club from the Cubans' inception in 1935 to the team's demise. The impresario's promotional flair led to game-day promotions such as raffling off a new car and bringing to the Oval heavyweight champion Joe Louis and Babe Ruth. And Dyckman hosted more than just baseball games. "Dyckman Oval is rapidly gaining the right to the title of Manhattan's amusement center," Lewis Dial wrote in the *Amsterdam News* of August 24, 1935. "Every branch of sports from races to cricket have been exhibited at Pompez's beautiful miniature stadium." Featured events at the Oval also attempted to connect with Harlem's diverse population as reflected by an August 1935 championship-boxing match featuring Puerto Rican boxer Sixto Escobar.

Led by player-manager Martin Dihigo, the Cubans filled their roster with a stellar cast of African-American, Cuban, Puerto Rican, and Dominican ballplayers. Ten of them were later elected to a baseball Hall of Fame in the United States or the Caribbean basin. The 1935 Cubans bounced back from a slow start to be a winning team. The Cubans headed to victory in the second half of the season and into an exciting playoff against the first-half winner Crawfords. The two clubs were among the strongest ever to face each other in Negro post-season play.

From a pure talent perspective, the 1935 Pittsburgh Crawfords–New York Cubans match-up was arguably the greatest championship series in black baseball. The Crawfords featured a line-up of four future Hall of Famers (Satchel Paige, Josh Gibson, Cool Papa Bell, and Oscar Charleston) among other notable Negro leaguers like Sam Bankhead, Jimmy Crutchfield, and Leroy Matlock. The Cubans squad boasted its own collection of talented players. Directed by player-manager and future Hall of Famer Martin Dihigo, the Cubans line-up included Latin American standouts Ramon Bragana and Lazaro Salazar, and Negro league all-stars Horacio Martínez, Alejandro Oms, and Lefty Tiant.

The 1935 match-up upset the expectations of those who felt the Crawfords would overwhelm the Cubans. Pompez's club jumped ahead in the series by taking the first two games, 6–2 and 4–0, in New York, before Pittsburgh shut the Cubans down in game three, 3–0. With New York ahead two games to one, the series shifted to Pittsburgh. On their home turf at Greenlee Field, the Crawfords claimed game four, 3–2, before the Cubans snapped up a 6–1 win in game five to take a three-games-to-two series advantage. It looked promising for the Cubans, about to clinch the World Series in their inaugural Negro league campaign. Playing under the lights in Philadelphia, the Cubans took a 6–3 lead into the ninth inning of game six, but Oscar Charleston's three-run homer off the Cubans' Martin Dihigo led a determined Crawfords' comeback for a 7–6 victory that tied the series. Game seven took the action back to Dyckman Oval. In a hard-hitting contest featuring three extra-base hits by Chester Williams, home runs by his Pittsburgh teammates Josh Gibson and Oscar Charleston, and round

Hanging by a Thread

Although Jud Wilson was arguably the most prolific hitter in Negro league history, with a lifetime batting average of .354, he also had a bad temper. After the 1935 East-West Game, he was trying to get some sleep when his roommate Jake Stephens came in "all juiced up," records John Holway. When Stephens wouldn't calm down, Wilson grabbed him by one ankle and hung him out the window. Looking down at the sidewalk several stories below, Stephens quickly saw the error of his ways. He was hauled back in, much more sober than he had been just minutes before.

trippers by the Cubans' Clyde Spearman and Paul Dixon, the Cubans took a lead into the eighth inning. In the ninth, however, the Crawfords managed to rally again, this time taking an 8–5 lead. The Cubans mounted a comeback of their own, highlighted by Spearman's two-run homer but fell short, dropping the decisive seventh game 8–7. Greenlee's Crawfords walked away with the Negro League championship.

Satchel Paige was back with the Crawfords in 1936, going 10–3, while his battery mate Gibson led the league in home runs. The Crawfords finished third in the first half of the season, three games behind the Washington Elite Giants, but won the second half. Instead of facing each other in a playoff, the two teams combined ranks, added a few members of the Homestead Grays, and entered the *Denver* Post Tournament, which they swept. They then barnstormed back East, playing against a squad of white major leaguers led by Johnny Mize, 17-year-old Bob Feller, and an aging Rogers Hornsby. The Crawfords continued their post-season by playing in Mexico against a team led by Jimmie Foxx, Heinie Manush, and Hornsby.

Though Paige often took his leave, Gibson was a constant presence on the field for the Crawfords. He led the league in home runs in 1932, 1934, and 1936, and developed into an outstanding defensive catcher. Other Crawford stars included Ted Page, Herbert "Rap" Dixon, and Jimmy

Roy Parlow was a hero to Puerto Rican baseball fans of the late 1930s to early 1940s.

Crutchfield. Page, who delivered at the plate and played the field adroitly, brought a special competitive zeal to the team, while Dixon was one of the league's best all-around players. Crutchfield, a three-time East-West Classic performer, was frequently compared to Pirate Hall of Famer Lloyd Waner, who played in Pittsburgh during Crutchfield's tenure with the Crawfords. Cool Papa Bell regarded his well-rounded and upbeat teammate as the best team player in baseball.

THE LURE OF THE TROPICS

For African Americans, the reasons for heading to Latin America to play ball remained essentially unchanged from the beginning of the 20th century through the end of segregated ball. North American black players could earn good money doing what they loved. What did increase over time was the attractiveness of a Latin American baseball sojourn versus staying in the United States and continuing to face the everyday indignities of Jim Crow. In Latin America black players were welcomed on the basis of their abilitiy to improve the chances of local teams to claim a league pennant.

Future Hall of Famer Ray Dandridge highlighted the economic motivations that led numerous players into the new professional Latino baseball venues of the 1930s and 1940s:

> This is the reason why I left the Eagles to go and play in foreign countries. Because the foreign countries, the places we went to, they paid my expense, my family's expense, gave us an apartment and everything. And if we had stayed with the Eagles, we didn't have nothing. I say for at least ten years for me I left one league and went to another league. I stayed in Mexico for seven years, all my expenses paid, my wife, my kids, my transportation. And my money was clear there. And after I left Mexico I use to go back to Cuba. I was in Cuba, and I took my family there and that was during school time. They put my kids in school and everything else. That was the experience I had, and that was the way I made out my contracts, that was the way I operated with foreign countries.

The players' motivations for jumping to the Caribbean were not just monetary, as Willie Wells so eloquently explained to Wendell Smith from a barber's chair in Mexico City. Wells had left the Newark Eagles for a club in Veracruz in the spring of 1944. "Not only do I get more money playing here," he told Smith, "but I live like a king.... I am not faced with the racial problem.... I didn't quit Newark and join some other team in the United States. I quit and left the country.... I've found freedom and democracy here, something I never found in the United States. Here, in Mexico, I am a man."

The formation of Latin American professional leagues in the 1930s and 1940s created new opportunities for North American talent and enabled the most talented African-American and Latino players to perform year-round. Reflecting baseball's growing popularity in the Spanish-speaking Americas, new professional leagues were formed in Mexico (1937), the

Dominican Republic (1937), Puerto Rico (winter 1938-39), and Venezuela (1946). Hungry for good baseball, the professional leagues recruited African-American talent through the same system of scouting and recommendations that had introduced Latino talent to the Negro leagues. Organizers of Latino professional teams like Abel Linares and Alex Pompez used their time in the States to schedule barnstorming visits by North American teams and also to recruit players they saw perform.

Player recommendations represented the other significant means for Latin American teams to tap into the African-American talent pool. Personal familiarity encouraged cooperation between African Americans and Latinos. Participation in the North American circuit allowed Latino team managers and players to familiarize themselves with African-American players, to develop friendships, and to acquaint the players with the realities of Latino baseball. These Latinos knew all too well the adjustment required in leaving their home country to play ball elsewhere. Winter-league roster spots were at a premium. Teams usually carried only fifteen to eighteen players with the majority reserved for native players. Under these circumstances the practice of players recommending each other for vacant positions on a club's roster became common.

Right-handed pitcher Wilmer Fields is a good example of a player who benefited from the opportunities created by the interdependence of Latino and black baseball. In a career that lasted from 1940 to 1959, Fields performed throughout the Americas. In addition to eight Negro League campaigns and several minor league seasons after integration, Fields also pitched in Mexico, the Dominican Republic, and in Venezuela. The competition in Latin America was intense, as Fields recalled in his autobiography, *My Life in the Negro Leagues*. "Not everyone could make it down there and you better believe if you didn't produce you didn't last long."

League rules allowed each team only to have a small number of *refuerzos* (non-native players) on their rosters. As a result, winter league teams aggressively pursued the best available foreign talent, black or white. Given the shorter season than the Negro leagues, Latino baseball also had a different intensity. It was literally produce or go home. There was little time for a refuerzo to go into a hitting or pitching slump, especially since each team was only allotted three or at most five refuerzos. Reputation from playing in the North created the opportunity; lack of production quickly took it away.

African Americans who had not yet established their reputation in professional baseball often relied on relationships forged during the Negro leagues season to secure a Latin American winter position. On occasion a Latino teammate or manager whom the player had met in the States acted as his agent in locating him a spot on a winter-league team. Joe Black, a hard-throwing right-handed pitcher who worked his way into black baseball's elite with the Baltimore Elite Giants before being signed by the Brooklyn Dodgers, was one of dozens of African-American players whose career and reputation grew through participation in Latino baseball. Toward the end of the 1950 Negro League campaign, Black asked New York Cubans pitching coach Rodolfo "Rudy" Fernández, who was also a manager in the Cuban circuit, to keep him in mind during the winter. Sure enough, when Fernández became aware of a position available on another Cuban team, he recommended the talented pitcher to that team's manager.

The cultural cross-fertilization between the different points within the international baseball circuit clearly had an impact on professional baseball. The exchange significantly elevated the talent level in black baseball in the States and in Latino baseball. North and South baseball circuits came to operate as a development ground. Dozens of the players in the first wave of blacks to perform in the majors, like Orestes Miñoso, Larry Doby, Monte Irvin, and Jackie Robinson, developed their baseball skills against high-quality competition while learning valuable lessons about adjusting to challenging situations, and building relationships in foreign settings and in integrated leagues. Their experiences in this international circuit held them in good stead when it came to making the difficult adjustment required in the majors.

In the spring of 1937, the attraction of the South to North American players, coupled with the chaotic politics of a Caribbean island, brought

Martin Dihigo
Mr. Versatility

Among the standout Negro league stars discovered by Alex Pompez, the immortal Martin Dihigo stands a cut above the rest. The Cuban native excelled at several positions in the field and always represented an offensive threat at bat.

Dihigo began making his mark when he first traveled north with the Cuban Stars in 1923 at the age of 18. A veteran of two Cuban league seasons, the young Dihigo found it difficult to crack into a Cuban Stars starting line-up. By mid-June, however, he secured a spot as a starter at first base, a position he would play when not on the mound throughout the 1923 season.

The versatile Dihigo became the centerpiece of the Cuban Stars. He matured into one of the Eastern Colored League's most potent hitters, ranking consistently among the circuit's leaders in batting average, including a .421 average for 1926, and twice leading the league in home runs (1926 and 1927). The latter year he tied for the crown with 18 home runs in just 181 at-bats.

When the Eastern Colored League collapsed in 1928, Edward Bolden's Hilldale club quickly snatched him up. He stayed with Hilldale through the 1931 season. However, since his talents on the mound and at the plate were highly desired, Dihigo would spend the next two decades playing extensively throughout Latin America, with an occasional return to the U.S. black circuit.

In a career that spanned three decades, his stellar performance and unparalleled versatility took him throughout the Americas and led to his enshrinement in the Hall of Fame of four different countries: the United States, Cuba, Mexico, and Venezuela.

about the Pittsburgh Crawfords' downfall. The Crawfords' fall from grace contributed to the Grays' return to black baseball's elite ranks. The pivotal event in this reversal of fortunes occurred prior to the season, when Gus Greenlee, wearying of salary disputes with Josh Gibson, traded his star to the Grays for catcher Pepper Bassett and $2,500. Although Gibson reported to the Grays for spring training in Hot Springs, Arkansas, he soon headed even farther south, to the island of Hispaniola. Greenlee, who had lost the best hitter in black baseball, soon lost much more. In the spring of 1937, five NNL players jumped their clubs and played in Cuba. Weeks later, the raids resumed, this time from the Dominican Republic.

The Spanish-speaking, baseball-playing Dominican Republic uneasily shared the island of Hispaniola with French- and Creole-speaking Haiti. The Dominican Republic was a baseball backwater in the 1930s, far behind Cuba in its production of talented players, although it sent both shortstop Horacio Martínez and outfielder Tetelo Vargas to the Negro leagues, where both starred. In 1937, the nation was the fiefdom of Rafael Trujillo, a former military officer who had seized power in 1930. Trujillo, a megalomaniac of epic proportions, had the highest mountain peak, towns, and much else renamed for him. Even the capital city, Santo Domingo, was renamed Ciudad Trujillo to honor him. A plaque on the wall of most homes read, "*En este casa, Trujillo es el jefe*" ("In this house, Trujillo is the chief"). In 1936, the Estrellas Orientales from San Pedro de Macoris, aided by a number of Cuban and African-American players, won the Dominican championship. The following season, the two teams in the capital— Licey and Escogido —were combined to form Los Dragones de Ciudad Trujillo, to ensure that the title returned to the city most associated with Trujillo. The club recruited top Cuban and Puerto Rican players, a move its rivals matched, and then turned its gaze northward.

Ciudad Trujillo's emissaries approached Satchel Paige in New Orleans during spring training. They offered him enough money to desert the Crawfords and board a Pan American biplane for the island. Once in the Dominican Republic, Paige realized just how good the other teams were. Cubans Martin Dihigo and Luis Tiant, Sr., Chet Brewer, and Dominican center fielder (and Negro league all-star) Horacio Martínez played for Aguilas from Santiago. Puerto Rican Perucho Cepeda (father of Hall of Famer Orlando Cepeda), Dominicans Pedro Alejando San and Tetelo Vargas, and Cubans Pedro Arango, Ramón Bragaña, and Cocaína García also played for a Dominican team that summer. Paige called Cool Papa

Bell, who recruited a handful of Negro National Leaguers, including Sammy Bankhead and Leroy Matlock, to fly to the island. Most of them were Crawfords. Another was Josh Gibson, recently acquired by the Grays.

Dominicans still talk of the 1937 season. The black American ballplayers were especially popular in and around San Pedro de Macoris, where many of the cane cutters and sugar mill mechanics were descended from cricket-playing immigrants from the Virgin Islands, Nevis, St. Martin, and other small English and French-speaking islands. "That Gibson," recalled cane worker Coleridge Mayers, "he could hit the ball from here to the sky. One Sunday, he was playing and Bragaña strike him out twice and he says to Paige, 'Goddamn! That ball is dropping hard. I can't hit him.' Paige says, 'you'll get him the third time.' When Joshua comes to bat that third time, he has two strikes and a ball, I remember it like it was just now. Paige says, 'Stoop a little more. Stoop a little more.' Whoooo! It was the biggest home run I ever saw in all these Lord's days." Mayers and others recalled the ballplayers carousing in bars and dancehalls, mixing easily with their Dominican fans.

Several of the American ballplayers spoke of armed guards and not-so-subtle warnings that Ciudad Trujillo must win. Chet Brewer, who pitched for Aguilas that summer, went looking for Paige to have a beer one day but couldn't find his friend. A young boy told him that Paige and some of his teammates were "*en la cárcel*" ("in jail"). Trujillo, Brewer explained, "had put them in before they were going to play us so they wouldn't rouse around."

The Negro league imports earned their pesos with their play. Gibson led the league in hitting with a .437 batting average while Paige won eight games and lost two. Bell stole bases and played the field with his customary elan and came in fifth in batting. In the season finale, Ciudad Trujillo rallied from a 2 to 0 deficit to Aguilas in the fifth inning. Chet Brewer, who had beaten them with a one-hitter the week before, started the game. After Martin Dihigo relieved during the fifth inning, Sammy Bankhead hit a grand slam for Ciudad Trujillo. Aguilas closed the margin to 8–6 in the ninth before Paige came in from the bullpen to end the game.

Although the NNL vowed to bar the players who had jumped to the Dominican Republic, the league quickly relented. Stars like Paige, Gibson, and Bell had too much power at the gate to blackball them. Instead, they were fined a week's salary and allowed to return to their clubs. Paige, Bell, and several of the Crawfords chose instead to barnstorm that summer as the Trujillo Stars, winning the *Denver Post* Tournament. Paige never played again for a Pittsburgh team, heading to Kansas City instead. Gibson, however, belatedly joined the Grays, completing their pre-season trade.

Devastated by the Dominican raids, Greenlee's Crawfords never recovered. Already some of the allure of owning a Negro league team had faded for Greenlee. The Crawfords, according to rival team-owner Cum Posey, had never been much of a financial success, losing money on both the 1932 and 1933 seasons. But Greenlee's participation in sports had never been primarily motivated by a desire to make money. By all accounts, he enjoyed the sporting scene and used his numbers revenue to subsidize his involvement in baseball and boxing.

The team stumbled through the 1937 and 1938 seasons on the field, while off it Greenlee's stature diminished. The NNL had retained Eddie Gottlieb, the white owner of the Philadelphia Stars, to represent them with independent clubs east of Altoona, Pennsylvania. With the economy tanking again in 1937, black teams played to the smallest crowds yet in the league's history. Greenlee soldiered on, but was increasingly in the minority within the league against a coalition formed by Gottlieb and the owners of the Newark Eagles, New York Black Yankees, and Homestead Grays. On the field, he had to contend with a new phenomenon, a losing team.

Gus Greenlee's problems were magnified by difficulties making Greenlee Field profitable. With the Depression's resurgence in 1937 and 1938 and the loss of his stars slicing attendance below a break-even point, Greenlee decided to cut his losses. Greenlee Field was torn down, and Bedford Dwellings, the city's first housing project, erected in its place. In February 1939, Greenlee resigned as the league's chairman and accepted its honorary presidency. Two months later, he dissolved the Pittsburgh Crawfords Baseball Club. A number of white businessmen in Toledo pur-

Pure Gold at Third

In the late 1930s the Newark Eagles were held down by what was called the "million-dollar infield." Slugging "Mule" Suttles held down the first base bag, while slick-fielding, no-hit Dick Seay played the keystone position. The incomparable Willie Wells at shortstop was joined on the left side by Ray Dandridge, regarded by many as the greatest third baseman in blackball history. He was bow-legged, and his teammates said, "You could drive a freight train between Ray's legs, but you couldn't get a ground ball through them." He also was a sharp line-drive hitter, amassing a batting average of .350 over 17 years in the Negro leagues. In one of the great losses to major league baseball fans, Dandridge would be signed by the New York Giants but was considered too old to be brought up to the big leagues. That didn't stop his peers from inducting him into the Baseball Hall of Fame in 1987.

chased the team and hired Oscar Charleston as its manager. A year later, the club moved to Indianapolis and then ceased fielding a team.

POSEY WILL REBOUND

In the early 1930s, Gus Greenlee's Crawfords had eclipsed Cum Posey's Homestead Grays, who stayed out of the Negro National League until 1935. Soon after taking over the Crawfords, Greenlee stripped the Grays of many of their key players. At the end of the 1932 season, Courier sportswriter Rollo Wilson wrote that Posey, whom he called "my boy friend from the Monon[gahela] Valley," had just "finished the most disastrous year of his baseball career. He made enemies of men who had once been his best friends; he saw himself become the mighty somnambulist of a vanished dream when his personal league [the East-West League] crashed about his head. He lost his grip on a profitable territory. He saw his club raided by the same ruthless methods which he had employed against other owners in the history years." But, Wilson told his readers, "Posey will rebound."

In 1933, Posey shored up the club's ailing balance sheet by persuading Sonnyman Jackson, a Homestead numbers banker and sportsman, to invest in the Grays. The ball club retained considerable local support and was toasted by community leaders at a reception and dance at Manhattan Hall in 1933. While Greenlee snared several key players, the Grays held onto pitchers Smokey Joe Williams and Ray Brown and were bolstered by the arrival of first baseman Buck Leonard in 1934. When they joined the NNL in 1935, the Grays were a .500 ball club. The following season they had a losing record. But their fortunes revived in 1937.

The catalyst was the reacquisition of Gibson. "We just took off after that," recalled Buck Leonard, the Grays' first baseman from 1934 through 1950. "He put new life into the whole team." With Gibson and Buck Leonard forming the quintessential power-hitting duo of black baseball, the Grays reeled off nine Negro National League pennants in a row.

Josh Gibson, after a winter in Cuba playing with Sammy Bankhead, Ray Brown, and Willie Wells, led the Grays to a pennant-winning season in 1938. Gibson and the Grays played a series in Cuba after the 1938 season and Josh wintered there. Back in Pittsburgh for the 1939 regular season, Gibson and Leonard led the Grays to victory in both halves of the 1939 regular season before losing a post-season playoff to the Baltimore Elite Giants.

"When I had a chance to see the guys play," outfielder Bob Thurman remembered, "I said that's where I want to play, with the best guys, you see, with Josh Gibson and Leonard, um boy. I could see myself batting in front of them or behind them." Thurman was one more powerful bat in an imposing lineup.

Odile Posey Stribling was married to Cumberland Posey's brother, Seward, the club's business manager and traveling secretary during its impressive pennant-winning run. "I do believe in all sincerity that the Pirates couldn't have played us in those days," she explained. "Because we had about five or six fellas that were home run hitters. That Josh Gibson would tear anybody's ball apart. Buck Leonard was the same thing. This

Victor Harris—they were just absolutely good ball players and hard hitters."

The Pirates, Thurman recalled, agreed to an exhibition game with the Grays after World War II. But, he laughed, several Pirates attended a Grays game at Forbes Field prior to the contest. Buck Leonard, Luke Easter, and Thurman proceeded to hit back-to-back-to-back home runs and the exhibition was called off. Clarence Bruce played for the Grays then. "We didn't just play and think we were inferior. We thought we were great ballplayers and I think we walked with that air. When we walked into a town, we held our heads high. We knew we were great players. And the fans knew it. I think the white fans knew it."

The Grays were more than just Gibson and Leonard, who some described as the Ruth and Gehrig of the Negro leagues. The team included Ray Brown, Vic Harris, Sammy Bankhead, Roy Partlow, Luke Easter, Bob Thurman, Cool Papa Bell, Jud Wilson, Wilmer Fields, and other quality ballplayers.

Ray Brown, who had wed one of Cum Posey's five daughters in a ceremony at home plate in 1935, had a great career on the mound and was a major factor in the Grays' success. Brown both pitched and played outfield for the Homestead Grays from 1932 until 1946. He led the NNL in wins in 1939, 1941, and 1942 and is ranked among the all-time pitching leaders in Negro league history. Vic Harris, whose younger brothers Bill and Neal played for the Crawfords, was a mainstay of the Homestead Grays for over 20 seasons. A six-time Negro league all-star and a fine all-around player, Harris left an even larger legacy as a manager, leading the Grays to eight NNL pennants. Sammy Bankhead played most of his 20-year Negro league career for either the Crawfords or the Grays. A versatile athlete who performed in seven East-West All-Star games at three different positions, Bankhead was best known as a shortstop and a team leader. The fleet-footed Bell played for championship teams for the Pittsburgh Crawfords during the 1930s and the Homestead Grays during the 1940s. He was the fourth Negro leaguer selected to the Hall of Fame. Easter, Thurman, and Wilson were best known for their feats at the plate, Fields as a pitcher and an outfielder.

The Homestead Grays are poised to take the field on opening day, May 18, 1940.

While Gibson missed the 1940 and 1941 seasons because he was playing in Mexico, Buck Leonard was a steady presence at first base. The Rocky Mount, North Carolina, native had played semi-pro baseball while working as a shoeshine boy, a mill hand, and finally with the Atlantic Coast Line Railroad. When he lost his job on the railroad in 1933, Leonard turned full-time to baseball. After brief stints with the Baltimore Stars and the Brooklyn Giants, he joined the Grays in 1934. His consistently superior defensive play and ability to hit with power and for a high average earned Buck Leonard selection to the East-West Classic twelve times and jobs in winter ball throughout the Caribbean.

But the fans who saw Leonard and Gibson lead the Grays to victory with mind-numbing regularity recognized their abilities and were not so sure that Leonard and Gibson came up short in comparison with the Yankee's immortals. Washington Senators owner Clark Griffith, who rented his ballpark to the Grays from 1940 through 1948, also realized how good these men were. The Grays played several games a week at Griffith Stadium in Washington, D.C., where they began to draw large crowds.

During World War II, when spending for the war pumped up take-home pay, the Grays and other black clubs thrived.

During the 1943 season, Griffith sent word down to the dugout that he would like to see Leonard and Gibson in his office after a game in his ballpark. Years later, Leonard reconstructed the conversation. Griffith asked them if they would like to play major league baseball. "We said, we like it fine." Griffith then asked, "Do you think you can play major league baseball?" The ball players replied, "We will try." The Senators' owner posed another question: Did they think they could hit major league pitchers? "Well," Leonard answered, "we could hit some of them and some of them we couldn't." At that point Griffith said, "The reason why we haven't got you colored baseball players on the team, the time hasn't come for you fellas to get on the team. The time hasn't come for you to be integrated." So Leonard and the Grays remained in the Negro National League, winning the pennant every year from 1937 through 1945.

MONARCHS OF THE WEST

While the Grays set the standard for baseball excellence in the East, the Kansas City Monarchs dominated Negro league ball in the Midwest. They won 17 Negro American League pennants and two Negro League World Series between 1923 and 1955 and fielded a dazzling array of stars between the lines.

Kansas City's black community not only enjoyed the Monarchs, they felt a sense of ownership of the club. Despite the white complexion of the team's owners, the Monarchs were tied to local black businesses, the music scene, and the very lives of its members. Many of the players, including Frank Duncan and Newt Allen, had been recruited from the city's sandlots. The team added stars from around the country and a few from the Caribbean to become one of Negro league ball's flagship franchises. Black Kansas City embraced them as they built their sporting legacy. African-American Quincy Gilmore, the team's traveling secretary, often served as the Monarchs' public face. Gilmore organized a Monarchs

Booster Club, which held parades on opening day and banquets to honor the team. The booster club also served as a civic organization. Few teams, if any, could claim such solid community ties. The Monarchs held games as benefits for churches, community groups, and national black organizations. Local businesses and organizations, in turn, advertised upcoming ballgames while ministers preached sermons backing the home team.

From the late 1930s through the 1940s, the Monarchs and the Grays set the standard for black baseball. Satchel Paige, who had been the Grays' nemesis when he pitched for the Pittsburgh Crawfords, became the Monarchs' best-known star during this period. In 1938, Gus Greenlee tried to resign Paige, whose contract he still held even though the fireballing hurler had not pitched for the Crawfords for two seasons, but he could not persuade the itinerant pitcher to return to Pittsburgh. Greenlee then sold his contract to the Newark Eagles, but they could not sign Paige either. Instead, Satchel ended up playing ball in Mexico, where he experienced arm troubles that many thought would end his career.

In 1939, Kansas City Monarchs owner J. L. Wilkinson bought Paige's contract from the Eagles and had him pitch for his "B" squad, which toured small towns in the Dakotas and Kansas. That summer Paige's arm came back. He also developed an assortment of off-speed pitches to complement his rejuvenated fastball. In 1940, Kansas City won a third straight pennant with Paige remaining on its "B" team.

In 1941, Paige returned to the Monarchs' regular squad, where he bolstered a roster that already featured Willard Brown, Chet Brewer, and Hilton Smith. Brown, black baseball's premier home-run hitter of the 1940s, was characterized by historian Jim Riley as a "bundle of unlimited and largely unfulfilled potential." Given the record the Kansas City outfielder established, one might have to question the "unfulfilled" tag. But on second thought, given the talent that was present, one might have to agree with Riley's assessment. Riley has it right when he says, "Willard Brown was a slugger who was exceptionally fast in the field, a good base runner, and an excellent gloveman with a great arm. Noted as a big-game player, he was at his best in front of a large crowd."

A dominating pitcher, "with good control and a retentive memory," Chet Brewer "spotted the ball, mixing a wide repertory of pitches that included a live running fastball, a sweeping curve, an overhand drop, a deep sinker, an emery ball, and a good screwball." He was frequently picked for the East–West Classic. Across a 24-year professional career he "toiled on the mounds of black baseball with an assortment of teams thoughout the world, including Canada, Japan, the Philippines, Hawaii, Canada, Mexico, Panama, Puerto Rico, Haiti, Santo Domingo, and in forty-four of the forty-eight continental United States."

Hilton Smith arguably had the best curve ball in black baseball. Known as "Satchel's caddy," for the six innings he would often pitch in relief of Paige's opening three—many would say with no appreciable difference in effectiveness—the tall thin right hander won more than twenty games in each of his dozen seasons with the Monarchs, including a record of twenty-five victories and only two defeats in 1941. He was selected to the Hall of Fame in 2001.

The Monarchs clubs of the 1940s also featured John "Buck" O'Neil at first base. While a fine ballplayer in his own right, and an outstanding manager, coach, and nurturer of the likes of Ernie Banks and Lou Brock, arguably in his senior years he has been even a finer preserver and disseminator of the history of Negro baseball.

THE LURE OF MEXICO

The Grays were without Gibson for the 1940 season. After winter ball in Puerto Rico, Josh went to Venezuela to play during the spring, and then to Mexico for the summer. Mexican League president Jorge Pasquel lured a contingent of Negro League stars, including Chet Brewer, Willie Wells, Ray Dandridge, and Bill Wright, to his nation that season. But the Grays prevailed without Gibson, as Leonard won the batting title and Ray Brown won twenty-four games and lost only four. Kansas City declined an offer from the Grays to play in a post-season World Series.

Mexican baseball gave several Negro leaguers an alternative during the early 1940s. Jorge Pasquel, a politically connected liquor mogul, offered salaries that no Negro league team could match. He also recruited a number of white major leaguers, including Max Lanier, Sal Maglie, and Mickey Owen, to the Mexican summer league. Paid sums they never expected to make, put up in the finest hotels, and adored by the sporting public, many Negro leaguers found their time in Mexico the best seasons of their careers.

Gibson stayed in Mexico in 1941, playing for Vera Cruz alongside Dandridge, Wells, Johnny Taylor, Ray Brown, and Cubans Lazaro Salazar and Ramón Bragaña. Vera Cruz might have been Mexican baseball's best team ever. While many Negro league clubs suffered from the Mexican defections, the Grays won a fifth straight title.

SOUTH OF THE BORDER

As many famous black jazz players opted to live in Europe rather than endure discrimination back home, so did one of the best black hitters of the era decide to move permanently to Mexico. "Wild Bill" Wright had more than established his credentials up north. Over an 11-year career in the Negro leagues the six-foot-four center fielder pounded out a .341 average. Teamed with Sammy T. Hughes, regarded as the best second baseman of the Negro National League, he helped lead the Baltimore and then Washington Elite Giants to consistent upper-tier finishes in the East, even topping perennial power Homestead Grays in the 1939 post-season playoffs. Yet once this seven-time all-star saw that Mexicans adored him, he spent the rest of career, from 1940 to 1951, in the southern climes. He was one of the most popular players in the country, and with a career .335 average and fistfuls of extra-base hits, it's not hard to see why. In Mexico he was treated like the king of the diamond he was.

Back in the states, black blackball continued to impress its viewers—in this case a white one. H. G. Salsinger, sports editor of the *Detroit News*, reported in glowing terms on a doubleheader in early August 1941 between the Elites and the Grays. He found Buck Leonard to be "infinitely faster and more aggressive" than the Tigers' outstanding first baseman, Rudy York. Matt "Lick" Carlisle "made a play that was the best delivered by a second baseman at Briggs Stadium this season." Salsinger's conclusion was telling: "There is one thing that distinguished the Negro National League ball players from their major league brethren, and that is their whole-hearted enthusiasm, their genuine zest. They play baseball with a verve and flair lacking in the big leagues. Thye look like men who are getting a good deal of fun out of it but who desperately want to win. It is a relief to watch two teams as intently bent on winning as these two were yesterday."

WAR YEARS

Josh Gibson returned to the Grays for the 1942 season. Both they and the Monarchs won pennants again that year. This time they met in a Negro League World Series, the first real league series played since 1927. Kansas City swept in "almost" four straight. The Grays did win one game, but their victory was disputed because they had added Newark's Leon Day and Monte Irvin to their roster for that day's contest.

About game two in Pittsburgh, historian John Holway hits a Ruthian—or is it Gibsonian?—home run with this observation:

> On a rainy night Paige was nursing a 2–0 lead with a man on first, no outs, and Gibson the third scheduled batter. What happened next, had it happened in a white World Series, would today be memoralized [alongside] Babe Ruth's "called shot," as a transcendental moment of baseball lore.
>
> "Heh Nancy," Paige called to Buck O'Neil. "I'm gonna put Harris on base, I'm gonna put Easterling on base, I'm gonna pitch to Josh."
>
> "You got to be crazy," O'Neil replied as manager Frank Duncan and owner J. L. Wilkerson charged onto the field waving their arms wildly.

"I'll get Josh out," Satch answered calmly.

At last they shrugged: "It's your funeral."

It took 20 minutes to clear the field.

"The bases was drunk," Paige recalled. To Gibson he said: "I heard all about how good you hit me. Now I fixed it for you. Let's see how good you can hit me now.

"I'm ready," Josh replied testily. "Throw it."

Satchel remembered saying to Josh: "Now I'm gonna throw you a fast ball, but I'm not going to trick you."

Then "I wound up and stuck my foot up in the air. It hid the ball and almost hid me. Then I fired." Sidearm, knee-high. Josh, thinking curve, took it for strike one.

"Now I'm gonna throw you another fast ball, only it's gonna be a little faster than the other one." Strike two.

"One more to go. I knew it. Josh knew it. The crowd knew it. It was so tense you could feel everything jingling. The last one was a three-quarter sidearm curveball. He got back on his heels; he was looking for a fastball." Knee high on the outside corner—strike three. "Josh threw that bat of his 4,000 feet and stomped off the field."

Josh had a phenomenal summer on the field in 1943, but his personal demons tormented him off it. "He was in and out of St. Elizabeth's Sanitarium 'like a drunken monkey,' as Buck Leonard put it. But when he played, he played so well. He hit more doubles, 33, than any man in Negro league history. And he slugged ten balls into the distant bleachers at Washington's Griffith Stadium. The entire American league hit only two there in 77 games."

In the first clash of the 1943 season between Gibson and Paige, Josh hit three home runs and doubled off the center field wall for two more RBI. Next time up Paige walked him intentionally, and he scored a sixth run. That year he led the NNL in hitting, with Dominican Tetelo Vargas and Puerto Rican Pancho Coimbre also having stellar years. Cool Papa Bell

Leon Day was one fiercely competitive pitcher.

returned to the Grays, and Johnny Wright, who would sign with the Brooklyn Dodgers' Montreal farm club in 1946, had a splendid season on the mound. The Grays drew over 150,000 fans to their games at Griffith Stadium and returned to the Negro League World Series.

This time they won, beating the Birmingham Black Barons four games to three. With their backs against the wall, down three games to two, the Barons' John Markham held the Grays to no runs through ten innings. In the bottom of the ninth Hoss Walker, disputing a called third strike, threw the ball at the ump. He was tossed out of the game. Ed Steele replaced him in the lineup. In the bottom of the tenth with two down, Sloppy Lindsay tripled and Steele drove him in with a game-winning single. Two days later the Grays, behind their ace, Johnny Wright, with key hits by Josh Gibson, Howard Easterling, and Vic Harris, won the game by an 8–4 count, and the series four games to three.

During World War II, the Grays widened their geographic base, making both Pittsburgh and Washington, D.C., their home cities. Black teams had tried on five previous occasions to establish themselves in the nation's cap-

Leon Day
Putting Something on Your Mind

Leon Day, pitcher extraordinaire, once said, "When they told me they was gonna pay me to play baseball, I said they must be crazy. I said I'd play for nothing."

Day believed in what he called "putting something on your mind." "You were getting paid to hit the ball and he was getting paid to pitch. And the best easiest thing on his mind was to keep you from hitting the ball. If that meant putting some rosin on it, cut it, lick it, whatever he had to do. And then Leon pitched you close and tight. That's the kind of ball player Leon was."

He didn't hesitate to throw a chin-whiskers pitch to a one-armed ball player. "We were down around Ocean City. We had to go down there one night. They had this Pete Gray. He was a one-armed ball player. He was the lead-off hitter and the first time up we kind of nonchalantly looked around at him and he got a hit off of Leon. He's standing over at first. Leon looked over at him and said I'll tell you what. Wait till you come back up the next time. I guess it was the third or fourth inning he came back again, and Leon threw it right up under his neck, and he didn't hit any more that night."

In the spring of 1995, Day's former teammate Max Manning brought him the news that the pitcher had finally been given his just due with election to Cooperstown. Leon, who was in a hospital in Maryland, accepted news of his induction with a wry smile and a gentle thank you. Within a few days he would pass. His widow, Geraldine, would bring tears to the eyes of the thousands who gathered for the Cooperstown Hall induction ceremony. She delivered an acceptance speech that could only have been more magnificent if Leon himself had been there to deliver it.

ital. But where the Potomacs, Pilots, Elite Giants, Black Senators, and Royal Giants failed, the Homestead Grays were a smashing box-office success. Black Washington had grown during the Depression, when New Deal jobs became available to African Americans, and expanded even more during the war. This larger and more affluent black community welcomed the

Grays, who arrived in town with a reputation as the best black club in the East.

The Grays, now known as the Washington Homestead Grays, filled comparable roles in the capital to the ones they had played in Pittsburgh during that city's transitional migrations. They helped a black community fractured by class come together on a symbolic and social level. Though the Grays drew fewer fans per game in Washington than they had in Pittsburgh their first two seasons, the club began to attract larger crowds and more attention during the 1942 season. The pivotal game occurred on June 18, 1942, when a night game between the Grays and the Kansas City Monarchs drew a crowd estimated at close to 30,000 fans. It was, according to Brad Mitchell Snyder, "the night the Grays took back Griffith Stadium," home to the hapless Washington Senators. Though Clark Griffith gladly rented his ballpark to the Grays and made an estimated $50,000 to $60,000 a season doing so in 1942 and 1943, the Senators complied with the major league color line. They also segregated seating at their games. The game with the Monarchs, which the Grays won 2–1 in the tenth inning, marked both Washington's embrace of Posey's club, and an affirmation of black pride and joy in an otherwise rigidly segregated city. The Grays outdrew the Senators on a per-game basis that season and most likely would have dominated them if the two clubs had met on the ball field.

The Grays played frequently in Washington, D.C., because the city had a large potential fan base and because Pittsburgh's economy was reeling by the second dip of the Depression. Though the team initially threatened to abandon Pittsburgh, it decided instead to commute back and forth, a profitable resolution to its financial difficulties.

With the war in full swing, Satchel Paige proposed that the 1944 East-West contest be a benefit for wounded GIs. When the owners refused, Satch refused to play. The other players then refused to play, voting to strike unless their meager $50 apiece was raised to $200. When the owners agreed to $150, the players relented, and brothers Alex and Ted "Double Duty" Radcliff/Radcliffe (they spelled their last names differently) won the game "for their mother" with hitting heroics that earned each a $700 bonus.

In 1944, the draft and enlistments caught up with the Monarchs, who lost 14 players to the service during the war. Neither Leonard nor Gibson was eligible for military duty, and the Grays won both the pennant and the Negro League World Series, besting Birmingham again, this time four games to one. The Grays, up two games, started their ace, Ray Brown, in game three. At its end Double Duty Radcliffe's single was all that stood between Brown and a no-hitter. Birmingham salvaged some pride with a 6–0 win in game four, with Grays castoff John Huber pitching a 3-hit shutout. Game five in the nation's capital saw the defending champions repeat by a 4–2 margin behind the tosses of Roy Welmaker.

The war wreaked havoc on the rosters of several Negro league teams. The Monarchs' lineup was considerably depleted. The Grays witnessed the departure of 11 players. The Newark Eagles lost a key nucleus of starters, including Monte Irvin, Larry Doby, Leon Day, Max Manning, and half their infield to the armed forces. In all, almost a hundred black players enlisted or were drafted. These losses came at the same time that several clubs suffered defections to the Mexican leagues. The war also caused the Office of Defense Transportation to temporarily order Negro league teams to stop using their buses in order to conserve fuel. That directive especially hurt the Negro American League squads, which had fewer rail options and greater distances in reaching their road games. The Monarchs changed the times of games to make it possible for workers on swing shifts to attend, and did not charge soldiers in uniform. And though play on the field suffered, the war meant more money in the pockets of black fans, and more money coming through the turnstiles for team owners.

Josh Gibson continued his fine play in 1945. Despite a disposition that made him a delightful teammate, the burly slugger often drank in excess. By all accounts, Josh was a favorite among his teammates. Monte Irvin called him "happy-go-lucky" while Harold Tinker said that Josh was a sweet fellow off the field and a wonder to behold on it. Odile Posey Stribling, whose husband Seward Posey helped his brother, Cum, run the Grays, described Gibson as "a big overgrown kid with a smile always on his face." But Gibson's life was not without pain. Josh's woes began soon after he joined the Grays in 1930. His wife, Helen, gave birth to twins but died in childbirth;

the children were raised by her parents. Josh was admitted to St. Francis Hospital in Pittsburgh on occasion to dry out. During the 1945–1946 winter season in Puerto Rico, Gibson was found wandering in a daze one night in the streets of San Juan and temporarily committed to a sanatorium.

Nevertheless, Gibson led the Grays to the pennant for the ninth consecutive time in 1945. In Kansas City, Paige pitched poorly for the second season in a row. The Cleveland Buckeyes, the youngest club in blackball, were the surprise team that year, winning the Negro American League pennant by a comfortable margin over the Birmingham Black Barons. Led by catcher Quincy Trouppe, who had returned from Mexico to take the helm of the club, and in the outfield by speedster and future major league star Sam Jethroe, they got career seasons on the mound from the Jefferson brothers, Willie and George.

The Grays, now a team of aging veterans, proved no match for the youngsters from Cleveland. A four-game sweep, with shutouts in the third and fourth contests, saw the once powerful Pittsburgh machine score a total of three runs in the entire series. Josh Gibson was 34, Sam Bankhead 35, Buck Leonard 38, Cool Papa Bell 40, and Jud Wilson 46. Wilson's long and glorious career was sadly coming to a close in not so glorious circumstances. Suffering from increasing seizures in the later part of his career, teammates that year found him tracing circles in the dirt at third base and exhibiting other odd behavior in this last championship run for the Grays.

POST-WAR HIGHS—BUT MOSTLY LOWS

Homestead's record streak of pennant-winning seasons came to an end in 1946. Jackie Robinson had signed a contract with the Brooklyn Dodgers organization on October 29, 1945, and some saw the handwriting on the wall. Most eyes turned to Robinson and the anticipated reintegration of the game. The Grays, however, were about to suffer two monumental losses. Before the 1946 season began, black baseball lost one of its most far-sighted leaders. As the Grays recovered their dominant position in the Negro leagues, Cum Posey had regained a leadership position in black

An opening day match between the Newark Eagles and the Phillie Stars, May 8, 1946.

baseball. In 1937 he was elected NNL secretary and his partner Sonnyman Jackson was voted to its board of trustees. But on March 28, 1946, Posey died at the age of 53 after losing a battle against cancer. Thousands paid tribute to "the sagacious sportsman who made the Homestead Grays as magic a name in the baseball world as Joe Louis in the fistic firmament." Wendell Smith, in a poem he wrote about Posey, called him the "smartest man in Negro baseball and certainly the most successful." Posey's death foreshadowed the end of professional black baseball.

Black baseball's second loss came after the 1946 season. Despite having a terrible season in Puerto Rico that winter, Josh Gibson rebounded and had another great year at the plate, driving balls out of several ballparks. He blasted another home run out of Forbes Field, the ball soaring above the center field wall at the 457-foot mark. But not even Gibson could lead the Grays to a tenth NNL pennant. The Newark Eagles, with their stars back from the war, opened the season with a no-hit victory by Leon Day against the Philadelphia Stars. Winners of both halves of the split Negro National League season with hefty .739 and .759 percentages, they closed out the Negro League World Series that fall with a seventh-game, 3–2 come-from-behind victory over the Kansas City Monarchs of Satchel Paige and Buck O'Neil. It was a watershed series—arguably the last at the top level of Negro league play. Three future Hall of Famers, Leon Day, Larry Doby and Monte Irvin, suited up for the Eagles, along with Max Manning, who was awarded the Negro National League equivalent of today's Cy Young Award as best pitcher that season. It was Satchel Paige's last appearance in the Negro League limelight that he had lit up on so many occasions.

Before the 1947 season began, Josh Gibson died. He had been fighting physical decline for several seasons, problems exacerbated by his position in the field as a catcher and by weight gain. He likely suffered from hypertension and also from acute bronchitis. The incomparable slugger died, possibly from a stroke, on January 20, 1947, at the age of 35, without ever playing in the majors. "He never got that opportunity," recalled teammate Harold Tinker. "And Campanella couldn't have held Josh's glove, and we went crazy over Campanella. Campanella used to sit on his haunches and

Larry Doby is called safe at home in the 1946 season opener.

throw 'em out but he couldn't throw 'em out like Josh could. And I know Campanella hit home runs but he never hit home runs like Josh. And all he needed was the chance to do it in the majors. He would have been something." Monte Irvin agreed. "Most impressive man I've ever seen as a hitter. He was very strong, broad shouldered, and happy-go-lucky. Confident. Knew he was good but he didn't flaunt it. He just got out and did what he was supposed to do. He could run like a deer. He had a rifle for an arm. And he could really hit." Irvin compared Gibson to the white major leagues' incomparable star. "Josh Gibson was the black Babe Ruth. All the black players will tell you that Josh was our best. He was our best hitter, our best all-around player."

The 1947 season, arguably the last year of high-quality talent for Negro league baseball, saw the triumph of black baseball's perennial bridesmaid, Alex Pompez's New York Cubans. Adding the hitting of Claro Duany and Lorenzo Cabrera to an already potent lineup featuring all-stars Orestes

"Minnie" Miñoso, Silvio Garcia, and Rafael Noble, the Cubans enjoyed their best season ever. But it was the pitching that perhaps changed the team's fate. The ageless wonder Lefty Tiant went undefeated in regular season action with ten wins. Fellow left hander Pat Scantlebury also had his best Negro league campaign in garnering all-star consideration while winning ten games. Paced by the rejuvenated offense and stellar pitching, the team was competitive from opening day. After finishing the first half in second place behind the Eagles, the Cubans surged to claim the National League pennant, qualifying to face off against the American League champs, the Cleveland Buckeyes.

Given the excellent pitching of Tiant, Scantlebury, and David Barnhill across the regular season, a low-scoring series was predictable, but the big three did not pitch up to expectations. Rain prevented completion of the series opener, which was played at the Polo Grounds, the Cubans' home grounds, and ended in a 5–5 tie. Although he was not tagged for the loss, the Buckeyes roughed up Barnhill, who did not make it out of the second inning and left the game trailing 5–0. The Cubans' big bats came through, however, with Lorenzo "Chiquitin" Cabrera's run-scoring double leading a three-run outburst that tied the game in the fifth inning of the rain-shortened, six-inning affair.

The Cubans' pitching again faltered in the series' first completed game, held at Yankee Stadium. The undefeated Tiant was not given much leeway by manager José Maria Fernández, who pulled the pitcher in the first inning after three runs had crossed the plate. The game turned into a seesaw affair, with the Cubans battling back from 3–0 and 7–3 deficits to tie it up. The sloppily played game, which saw Cleveland commit four errors and New York three, came down to the last inning, when the Buckeyes rallied for three runs off a tiring Lino Diñoso, who had entered in the fourth inning and had held Cleveland scoreless for four innings. The 10–7 victory gave Cleveland the initial series advantage.

The sloppy play was perhaps a reflection of the inclement weather affecting the series, but the action in the initial encounters seems to have shaken the Cubans' confidence in their pitching. Turning the ball over to Barney Morris, the Cubans finally got a solid pitching performance.

Morris hurled a five-hit shutout as New York put six runs across in the ninth inning. Inspired by Morris's performance, Dave Barnhill followed up with his own strong performance, shutting down Cleveland's offense except for a four-run outburst in the eighth after the Cubans had amassed an 8–0 lead. New York's catcher Rafael "Ray" Noble led the Cubans' offensive onslaught with a towering grand slam that struck the top of the left-field roof at Philadelphia's Shibe Park.

Pitching woes apparently behind them, the Cubans strode confidently into game four played at Chicago's Comiskey Park. The combination of good hitting and strong pitching did not falter. The Cubans won 9–2, seizing a three-to-one series advantage.

With ace Luis Tiant taking the mound in game five, the Cubans swaggered into Cleveland. Yet Tiant's pitching woes continued. New York found itself down 4–0 in the third inning with their ace on the bench again. Just as in the abbreviated Polo Grounds encounter, Pat Scantlebury came on in long relief and deftly handled the Cleveland batters as the Cubans mounted a comeback. Taking full advantage of the Buckeyes' shoddy defense, New York pushed three runs across in the sixth inning and another in the seventh inning. Entering the eighth down 5–4, game three's hero Ray Noble stepped to the plate with two on. He came through again, slamming a two-run double that put New York ahead, 6–5. It was a pennant-winning hit as Scantlebury made it stick. New York finally had a Negro League champion.

But even while the Cubans were winning their first Negro League World Championship, the heyday of black baseball was drawing to a close. "It didn't hit me until later on," Monte Irvin reflected, "that we were living in a special era. ...We had provided a form of entertainment for a group of people who were downtrodden, who had no hope, who didn't get much encouragement. But then on a Saturday or a Sunday or a Tuesday night, they could come out to the ballpark and see some guy that could play baseball very well and that would give them hope. And say, well, at least somebody is making it."

May Day parade in New York City, 1939. The pressure mounts to integrate baseball.

Crossing the Color Line

Jackie didn't pave the way. We did.
—James "Joe" Green, Kansas City Monarchs

By the late 1930s, with a Second World War looming, much was changing in the world of black professional baseball and in the larger black and white world where baseball was played. But one rule seemed permanent—race prejudice barred blacks from major league baseball and limited opportunities for African Americans in all areas of American life. The separate but equal standard in place in the highest law of the land since *Plessy* v. *Ferguson* was only just beginning to feel the assaults from the NAACP that would lead to the *Brown* v. *Board* decision of 1954. But even with segregation firmly in place, it was clear to some, both black and white, that in baseball and elsewhere the time of separation was coming to an end. Those who believed in equal, not separate, would prevail when baseball's "gentleman's agreement" finally came to an end.

World War II was a watershed for black professional baseball and race relations in the U.S. as a whole. The historian Charles Silberman called the war years a "turning point in American race relations, in which the seeds of the protest movements of the 1950s and 1960s were sown." The movement toward integrated baseball received a major lift from the changing racial climate ushered in by the War. The excellence of professional black baseball itself presented one of the most potent arguments against continued segregation of the national game. Then, the final blow was struck by a talented baseball player and a bold white general manager. In the person of Jackie Robinson, and in the instrument of Branch Rickey, a revolution in baseball was to change the sport forever.

THE FOUNDATION FOR INTEGRATION

Big changes rarely happen in isolation. They are shaped by the groundswell of events that precede them. Just as the 1954 landmark *Brown v. Board of Education* ruling came only after years of challenges in the lower courts, major league baseball's integration in 1947 came after decades of protest over racial segregation in sports.

Equal access for blacks to their nation's playing fields had been a political issue for African Americans since emancipation. Access to recreation and the opportunity to compete, in turn, were part of a larger struggle for rights and equality. The black press kept these questions before its readers, celebrating victories and decrying discrimination on its pages. Occasionally a black journalist's ideas would even find an outlet in a "white" publication. *Pittsburgh Courier* feature writer George Schuyler's 1928 article in the *American Mercury* reflected on the significance of sports and leisure time. "It is...when they set out in pursuit of pleasure and recreation ... that the Ethiops are made to feel most keenly their lowly status. It is when work is finished and, arrayed in Sunday finery, they saunter forth to enjoy the fruits of their toil that they are most frequently wounded." The color line that blocked African Americans from public amusement parks, beaches, and other leisure venues, Schuyler concluded, sorely tested their "patriotism."

Meanwhile, large numbers of African Americans took part in struggles to desegregate swimming pools and ball fields and to win the right to play on teams ranging from local youth leagues and high schools to the major leagues. Sometimes the attacks on racial limits in sports and recreation were frontal assaults. But by the early 20th century, most of black

America's sporting energies were given to a different kind of challenge. The emerging urban population of the great migration era had come to concentrate on building an autonomous sporting life. Certainly from the 1920s onward—and even earlier—networks of race teams and leagues could be found wherever blacks lived in significant numbers.

At the same time that African Americans were building their own sporting world, black voices were also calling for the integration of American sports, especially baseball. These efforts to end baseball's color line took the form of editorials and targeted reporting, lobbying efforts, and actions designed to call attention to the segregated nature of the major leagues.

Black sportswriters raised the issue time and time again. In December 1938, just weeks after *Kristallnacht*, the "night of the broken glass," when Nazis attacked Jews throughout Germany, Wendell Smith pulled no punches, contending that the major leagues played "the same game as Hitler. They discriminate, segregate and hold down a minor race, just as he does. While Hitler cripples the Jews, the great leaders of our national pastime refuse to recognize our black players." At least, he wryly noted, Hitler was straightforward in his anti-Semitism. "He is wrong, of course, but he doesn't think he is. And, he doesn't hide or refuse to answer when asked about it. But you take 'Hitler' Landis, for instance. He, nor any of his aides, have the courage of Adolph. When asked about the inclusion of black 'jews' in baseball, they beat around the bush."

When it came to the question of integration, the black press not only reported the news, they often made it. They surveyed major leaguers' racial attitudes and forced owners to commit themselves on the race question, making the debate over the color line a public one. The majors often took the bait, responding unequivocally to black press queries whether African Americans were indeed eligible to play in their leagues. In February 1933, National League president John Heydler told the *Courier*, "Beyond the fundamental requirement that a Major League player must have unique ability and good character and habits, I do not recall one instance where baseball has allowed either race, creed or color to enter into the question of the selection of its players."

Pittsburgh Courier writers confronted Pittsburgh Pirates owner William Benswanger about the color line in 1933, soon after he replaced his father-in-law, Barney Dreyfuss, at the helm of the club. Dreyfuss, who had died the previous year, considered Cum Posey a friend, and the feeling was mutual. Dreyfuss welcomed black patrons to Forbes Field, the ballpark he had built in 1909, and rented it regularly to the Grays. His son-in-law, William Benswanger, obligingly wrote the paper that he had seen countless Negro league games and was most impressed by the players. "Such men as Charleston, Gibson, Washington, Scales and Cannady and others appear to be of highest caliber and worthy of highest in baseball."

The *Courier* delighted in suggesting from time to time how much the city's hapless major league franchise would benefit from an infusion of black talent. In 1937 sports editor Ches Washington telegraphed Pirate manager Pie Traynor at the winter baseball meetings that he knew how to help the club. "HAVE ANSWER TO YOUR PRAYERS RIGHT HERE IN PITTSBURGH [STOP] JOSH GIBSON CATCHER BUCK LEONARD FIRST BASEMAN AND RAY BROWN PITCHER OF HOMESTEAD GRAYS AND SATCHELL [SIC] PAIGE PITCHER AND COOL PAPA BELL OUTFIELDER OF PITTSBURGH CRAWFORDS ALL AVAILABLE AT REASONABLE FIGURES [STOP] WOULD MAKE PIRATES FORMIDABLE PENNANT CONTENDERS [STOP] WHAT IS YOUR ATTITUDE?" When asked again about black players in 1938, Benswanger not only stated that Negro leaguers were good enough to play in the majors, he said that if the issue came before the major leagues, he would heartily endorse it.

But Benswanger did not volunteer to lead the way, and the *Courier* kept pressuring the Pirates and the other major league teams to integrate. During the 1939 season, the paper interviewed players and coaches from each National League team in order to challenge the argument posed by segregation's defenders that white players would not accept integration.

Many major leaguers had played against blacks on sandlots, during barnstorming tours, or in California. Some had played alongside black and Latin ballplayers in winter ball in the Caribbean basin. The remarks of eight Pirate players and coaches were featured in the final installment of the series. They, like those interviewed for the other articles, unequivocally endorsed the ability of black players. They named names, too, of those Negro leaguers they thought capable of performing in their league. Pirate manager and Hall of Famer Pie Traynor said he would use a black player if given the permission. The go-ahead, however, was not forthcoming.

In 1942, the *Courier* jubilantly reported that Benswanger had agreed to give tryouts to three black players. But when the *Daily Worker*, the Communist Party newspaper, identified the three, Benswanger reneged. He told the *Courier* that the *Daily Worker* had "put words in my mouth" and that he had not made up his mind about the tryout. The *Courier* reported that Benswanger was still willing to give a black player a chance and that he had solicited the paper's suggestion of four players to work out. The paper applauded Benswanger's statement and wrote that he was "the greatest liberal in baseball history."

The tryouts never took place. Benswanger later said that Cum Posey talked him out of holding them on the grounds that integration would destroy the black leagues. "I tried more than once to buy Josh Gibson," Benswanger asserted in 1950, only, he said, to have Posey tell him that if he did, he would set in motion a chain of events that would bring about the end of Negro league baseball. That explanation drew Wendell Smith's wrath. He wrote that Benswanger was "baseball's number one phony."

A handful of white sportswriters aided the black press's efforts to make baseball's segregation a public issue. Jimmy Powers wrote in the *New York Daily News* that he could testify to the ability of at least ten black players to make it in the majors. "I am positive," he wrote in 1939, "that if Josh Gibson were white, he would be a major league star." *Washington Post* sportswriter Shirley Povich saw the disparity of talent between the capital city's American League Senators and the National Negro League's Homestead Grays, who then played regularly in Washington, D.C. "There's a couple of million dollars of baseball talent on the loose ready for the big leagues, yet unsigned by any major leagues," he wrote. Povich described potential 20-game winners, .350 hitters and a catcher—Josh Gibson—he considered superior to major league star Bill Dickey. "Only one thing is keeping them out of the big leagues—the pigmentation of

Monte Irvin
The Last Eagle

Monte Irvin, at right, had a storied Negro league career including six All-Star games.

Monte Irvin's outstanding career in the Negro leagues was followed by a nine-year career in which he helped lead the New York Giants to two National League pennants and a World Series triumph. In 1951 he had an MVP-caliber season when he batted .312 with 24 home runs and a league-leading 121 RBI.

Equally inspired was his play in his beloved Negro leagues. A tremendous power hitter, he hit .403 in 1939 and followed with season averages of .377 and a league-leading .395 in 1941. In 1946, Irvin led the Newark Eagles to the Negro league title, batting a league-high .404.During his career he appeared in six East-West All-Star games. He holds another important distinction, shared only by the great Martin Dihilgo—membership in the halls of fame of four countries—Mexico, Cuba, Puerto Rico and the United States.

Along with Buck O'Neil, Irvin has worked tirelessly to help keep the history of the black leagues alive. Always supportive of the men he played with in the Negro leagues, Irvin has been, in every possible meaning the word could have, a champion all his life.

their skin.... It's a tight little boycott that the majors have set up against colored players."

THE TIMES WON'T ALLOW IT!

In Boston, where the Red Sox and the Braves counted on the city council annually exempting their clubs from a ban on Sunday baseball, Councilman Isadore Muchnick announced that he would oppose the measure unless the clubs agreed to give tryouts to black players. When Red Sox general manager Eddie Collins claimed that in 12 years with the club, no black player had asked for a tryout, Wendell Smith told Muchnick that he could deliver three credible prospects to Boston. He subsequently brought Jackie Robinson, Sam Jethroe, and Marvin Williams to Fenway Park in April 1945. After the Red Sox put the three players off for two days, they ran them through a desultory tryout on the third. Boston made little pretense of taking the tryout seriously and never got back to Smith or the players. The club's indifference and that of the other franchises led black sportswriters to urge their readers to organize boycotts and protest campaigns that placed economic pressure on the big leagues.

Sam Lacy, meanwhile, attempted to work from within. He repeatedly pressed major league baseball executives to meet with representatives of the black press. In 1943, the owners agreed and the *Chicago Defender*, for whom Lacy was then working, reportedly dispatched actor and activist Paul Robeson to address the meeting. Nothing came of the session. But in March 1945, Lacy persuaded major league baseball to study the possibility of integrating the major leagues. Lacy spoke to a meeting of the owners on April 24, 1945 at which they formed a Major League Committee on Baseball Integration composed of Lacy, Branch Rickey of the Dodgers, Larry MacPhail of the Yankees, and black Philadelphia magistrate Joseph H. Rainey. But the committee was never convened.

The major leagues acted as if there had never been a policy blocking African Americans. In 1942, Commissioner Kenesaw Mountain Landis, who had been granted near total authority over the majors in the wake of the 1919 Black Sox scandal, claimed, "There is no rule, formal or informal, or any understanding—unwritten subterranean, or sub-anything—against the hiring of Negro players by the teams of organized ball." But Landis, until his death in 1944, thwarted efforts to bring African Americans into the majors. Reluctant to discuss the color line, Landis broke his silence only after Brooklyn Dodgers manager Leo Durocher claimed in 1942 that the commissioner was the obstacle preventing him from using a black player. Landis responded to Durocher's allegation by stating, "Negroes are not barred from organized baseball...and never have been in the 21 years I have served." But later that season Landis issued an edict ending interracial competition during the winter off-season.

When forced to commit themselves on the race issue, most baseball executives tried to evade the question. In 1939 Ford Frick, National League president, averred that there was no rule explicitly forbidding black players, but that the times were not right. In an interview with Wendell Smith, Frick noted, "Many baseball fans are of the opinion that major league baseball does not want Negro players, but that is not true. We have always been interested in Negro players, but have not used them because we feel that the general public has not been educated to the point where they will accept them on the same standard as they do the white player." Until racial attitudes changed, Frick rationalized, baseball would await a more favorable climate for integration. Cubs owner Philip K. Wrigley, Jr. echoed Frick's remarks three years later when confronted by the Chicago-based Citizens Committee for Negroes in the Big Leagues. "I would like to see Negroes in the big leagues," the chewing-gum magnate assured the committee. "I know it's got to come. But I don't think the time is now.... The public must be prepared to accept Negro players."

These comments reflected the owners' prevailing sentiments. Most had watched black players perform in their own ballparks and realized how good they were. They knew that arguments that black players could not make the grade were specious. But some owners feared losing white fans if they accepted black players, largely because they thought that large black crowds at their games would scare away white patrons.

Josh Gibson and Ted Radcliffe at a play at the plate.

Branch Rickey looked at integration differently. Instead of focusing on the downside, he saw the potential for black ballplayers to turn the Dodgers around and for his team to profit at the gate. Rickey had seen the St. Louis Stars play during his years with the Cardinals when the club had rented out Sportsman's Park for games between all-star teams of Negro and major leaguers. As World War II progressed, Rickey saw the wealth of Negro league and Latin talent and the potential black fan base that had grown apace with the migration of African Americans northward.

A mediocre major league ballplayer and a manager who lost more games than he won, Branch Rickey was a brilliant and innovative baseball executive. Rickey's tenure with the St. Louis Cardinals was distinguished by his creation of the modern farm system, the major leagues' most fecund source of talent in the 1930s and 1940s. It helped the Cards to six National League pennants and four World Series. Devout, loquacious, and ambitious, Rickey was a controversial figure who inspired both respect and criticism. Sportswriters called him the "Mahatma," the "Professor of Baseball," "the Brain," and "El Cheapo." They knew that Rickey was always good for quotable comments, but had little idea just how great a role he was about to play in baseball's history.

In 1942, after a quarter of a century with St. Louis, Branch Rickey parted with the Cardinals. He surfaced not long afterward as the general manager and president of the Brooklyn Dodgers. Rickey also gained an ownership interest in the team. Brooklyn offered a more open racial atmosphere than St. Louis, where ballpark seating was still segregated, and he soon embarked on a program to push his club to the top of the National League. At its core was a plan to tap black baseball talent.

Rickey took over an aging club that had won the pennant in 1941 but had few prospects in its minor league system. By trading off some of his more marketable players, he sought to restock the club's pool of players. Trades and an expanded scouting corps were only the preliminaries. Rickey had a grander scheme. After conferring with George McLaughlin, the president of the bank upon which the club counted to remain solvent, he gained the approval of the Brooklyn Dodgers' board of directors at a January 1943 meeting to undertake a surreptitious search for black and Latin talent.

Rickey received an unanticipated boost to his efforts when Commissioner Landis died in November 1944. His successor was Kentucky Senator Albert "Happy" Chandler. Unlike Landis, Chandler was willing to countenance baseball's integration. *Pittsburgh Courier* journalist Ric Roberts confronted Chandler on Capitol Hill after his selection as commissioner was announced. In response to a question whether he would accept African Americans in the majors, Chandler replied, "If they can fight and die on Okinawa, Guadalcanal, in the South Pacific, they can play baseball in America.... And when I give my word you can count on it."

Branch Rickey always asserted that his motivation for integrating baseball was his abhorrence of segregation. He often cited an encounter with racial prejudice experienced by an African-American member of the Ohio Wesleyan University baseball team he had managed. The player's mortification and sorrow, Rickey related, "haunted me for many years and I vowed that I would always do whatever I could that other Americans did not have to face the bitter humiliation..." There is little reason to question his sincerity regarding race relations. "I could not face my God any longer," Rickey stated, "knowing that his black children were held separate and distinct from his white children in a game that has given me all I own."

But this astute baseball man was also aware of the enormous advantages to be gained by the first team to successfully use black players. He dispatched scouts into the Caribbean and across the United States to evaluate players. Recognizing the obstacles that the first black players would face, Rickey refined his search to English-speaking players. After two years of scouting, Branch Rickey stunned the black baseball world in the spring of 1945, but not by announcing the signing of a black player.

THE "SAVIOR" OF BLACK BASEBALL

In May, Branch Rickey publicly committed himself and the Dodgers organization to support the newly formed United States League, a black circuit that was largely the handiwork of Gus Greenlee. Greenlee had sought to reenter professional baseball for some time. A year after resigning as the president of the Negro National League and the Crawfords, he told Wendell Smith, "I'd like to get back in baseball because I know I can make a go of it in Pittsburgh." He subsequently applied for franchises in both the Negro National and American Leagues but was rejected. Cum Posey likely vetoed his efforts, unwilling to share the Pittsburgh market with another club. Greenlee then resurrected the Crawfords as a semi-pro club and began raiding the Grays and other Negro league clubs for players. He arrived in Chicago before the 1944 East-West All-Star game and was accused by Negro league owners of provoking the players to demand more money. The owners' ire flared again when Greenlee organized the United States League for the 1945 season.

The USL lasted but two seasons, with franchises in Pittsburgh, Brooklyn, Chicago, Boston, Detroit, Cleveland, Philadelphia, and Toledo (although not all at the same time). Greenlee, who served as the league's vice president, headquartered the USL upstairs over the Crawford Grill, his nightclub in Pittsburgh. Attorney John Shackleford was the league's titular president, Greenlee the league's progenitor, and Rickey its unlikely godfather.

What did Branch Rickey seek to accomplish by backing the United States League? At his May 1945 press conference, the "Mahatma" expressed his concerns for the welfare of black baseball. He argued that there did not exist "in a true sense such a thing as organized Negro baseball." The USL, however, would fill that void. Pledging his support for Greenlee, Rickey said that the new circuit could use Ebbets Field or any of the other 22 ballparks that Brooklyn controlled. His public denunciation of the existing Negro leagues as tantamount to rackets made it clear that the USL was designed to supplant them. Newark Eagles owner Effa Manley, skeptical of Rickey's motives, questioned the Dodgers president's newly found interest in black baseball. Even fellow owner Clark Griffith, who had rented his stadium to the Homestead Grays since 1937, challenged Rickey's attempt to "set himself up as the czar of Negro baseball." Fay Young, concluding that Rickey's USL venture was designed to block segregation, wrote that Rickey was "no Abraham Lincoln or Franklin D. Roosevelt, and we won't accept him as dictator of Negro baseball. Hitler and Mussolini are dead! We need no American Dictator."

Rickey's solicitude for black baseball was overstated. His participation in the USL screened efforts to scout and secure the best black players to integrate the majors until the announcement of Jackie Robinson's signing made his intentions public a few months later. Seeking to gain an overwhelming advantage in case other teams went after black players, Rickey soon signed Don Newcombe and Roy Campanella. Furthermore, Rickey's dismissal of the Negro leagues' legitimacy made it easier for him to sign black players without paying compensation to their black teams.

According to Wendell Smith, Gus Greenlee was the key to Rickey's involvement in the league. Greenlee stressed the advantages to be gained by becoming the first major league club to field black players, in terms of talent and additional black spectators. But Rickey, who was thinking along the same lines, did not need much convincing. The USL attracted a fair amount of coverage and left clubs in the "other" Negro leagues less able to hold on to their own players or seek fair compensation for them as major league clubs began to sign them. But the United States League faded as all eyes turned to a black athlete who arguably would become the most visible and best known member of his race.

JACKIE ANSWERS THE CALL

In late October 1945, two months after the end of World War II, the Brooklyn Dodgers announced that they had signed Jack Roosevelt Robinson to a contract and assigned the Kansas City Monarchs infielder to their Montreal Royals farm club. An agreement between Robinson and Branch Rickey had actually been reached in August. The two had then agreed to remain quiet about their understanding as Rickey sought to orchestrate the right moment to go public with the news. But increasing activism made delay difficult. The Communist Party's New York City councilman Ben Davis, who had taken Congressman Adam Clayton Powell, Jr.'s Harlem district seat in 1943, campaigned vociferously for baseball's integration. A state delegation demanded that the three New York teams sign pledges not to discriminate in hiring. Fiorello La Guardia and his Mayor's Committee on Baseball ensured that the issue maintained a high profile. These efforts eventually forced Rickey's hand, and the signing of Robinson was announced on October 23.

At that moment in our nation's history it would have been reasonable to think that any significant change in America's racial landscape would be slow in coming. The Armed Forces were still segregated; the wartime Federal Employment Practices Commission was gone; antilynching legislation had yet to pass Congress; a Civil Rights bill, the first since Reconstruction, was still 12 years distant; and schools in the South remained segregated. But Jackie Robinson and Branch Rickey would change baseball, and American society, in ways few could have expected at the time.

Many observers asked, "Jack who?" But by 1945 Jackie Robinson was far from unknown in America's sporting circles. His incredible range of athletic talents had drawn comparison to Jim Thorpe, perhaps the greatest all-around American athlete of the 20th century. Robinson entered Pasadena Junior College in 1937, where he was known at first as Mack Robinson's younger brother. The older Robinson brother had won a silver medal in the 200 meters at the 1936 Berlin Olympics, finishing behind the incomparable Jesse Owens. But younger sibling Jackie soon established his own identity as a multisport star. In 1939, Robinson enrolled at UCLA, where he became the school's first four-letter athlete. Jackie twice led the Pacific Coast Conference in scoring in basketball, averaged 11 yards per carry in football, and won the NCAA championship in the broad jump. For good measure, Robinson won the Pacific Coast Conference intercollegiate golf championship and played a great game of tennis. One of the most brilliant and versatile athletes ever to attend UCLA, Robinson left school his senior year. Dismissing paltry offers from semi-pro teams to play baseball, football, and basketball, Robinson began working as a coach for the National Youth Administration, a New Deal program. He also barnstormed with the Los Angeles Bulldogs football team until he was drafted into the army in the spring of 1942. Accepted for Officer Candidates School after Joe Louis interceded on his behalf, Robinson served through May 1944.

Negro league baseball beckoned, and Jackie answered its call. He joined the Kansas City Monarchs in 1945. Even though the new Monarch was a rookie with much to learn, he attracted the attention of black sportswriters Sam Lacy and Wendell Smith. In a 1945 preseason article, Lacy wrote that Jackie would be "the ideal man to pace the experiment" to break the color line. Lacy and Smith saw in Robinson many of the psychological and intellectual attributes that soon attracted Branch Rickey's attention. Even so, his signing by the Dodgers organization surprised most people with intimate knowledge of the Negro leagues. He was relatively inexperienced and not considered on a par with at least a dozen other black players.

Black American All Stars, Venezuela, 1945–46.

While the baseball world, and much of the non-baseball world as well, was stunned by Branch Rickey's announcement, African Americans reacted with a mixture of jubilation and disbelief. White reporter Jimmy Powers called Robinson a thousand-to-one shot, while *Atlanta Journal* sports editor Ed Danforth castigated those he saw as carpetbaggers and agitators capitalizing on the race issue. But African Americans saw Robinson's signing as a critical social breakthrough, albeit one freighted with risk. Robinson, Wendell Smith wrote in the *Pittsburgh Courier*, carried "the hopes, aspirations and ambitions of thirteen million black Americans heaped on his broad, sturdy shoulders." The NAACP's *Crisis* called the young World War II veteran the symbol of new possibilities for millions of black people at home and abroad. Roy Wilkins wrote that the end of baseball's color line meant "that in a new and dramatic fashion the fact that the Negro is a citizen with talents and rights is being heralded to the nation." Wilkins, the *Courier*, and other African-American voices antic-

Jackie Robinson at bat for the first time for the Montreal Royals, 1946.

ipated that Robinson's signing would open doors for the race off the playing fields, too. Many lauded Branch Rickey for his courageous decision, and some placed him in the pantheon of African-American heroes not far below Abraham Lincoln.

The adulation was not unanimous. A few doubted Rickey's sincerity. Sportswriter Joe Bostic had campaigned for baseball's integration for years. But decades after Robinson's debut, he told historian Jules Tygiel that when the signing was announced, "I thought it was a trick.... I just wouldn't accept that it would be real." Others questioned if Robinson would be given a legitimate chance of making the Dodgers or whether this relatively raw ballplayer had the requisite talent and disposition to succeed in the major leagues. Some white editorialists objected to the social implications of baseball's integration, but other observers, including New York's first black congressman, Adam Clayton Powell, Jr., hailed the Dodgers' action as "a definite step toward winning the peace" in the fight for racial justice.

CIRCLING THE WAGONS

Jackie Robinson became the most scrutinized African American in the nation as he suited up for the Montreal Royals the next spring. When he debuted on April 18, 1946, before a record crowd in Jersey City, New Jersey, many African Americans in the stands were teetering between euphoria and anxiety. Robinson grounded out in his first at-bat; in his second, he hit a three-run home run. Wendell Smith captured the moment when he wrote, "Our hearts beat just a little faster and the thrill ran through us like champagne bubbles."

The thrill did not extend to the men who owned major league franchises. They focused their attention on how to thwart Rickey's Robinson initiative. A steering committee of major league executives made up of the New York Yankees' Larry MacPhail, Boston Red Sox's Tom Yawkey, St. Louis Cardinals' Sam Breedon, and Chicago Cubs' Phil Wrigley prepared a report during the summer of 1946 that tackled, among other issues, the "Race Question." The internal memorandum was not intended for public distribution, and several owners later denied its very existence. Baseball, the report declared, was under siege from "political and social-minded drum beaters" interested in scoring publicity points. "Every American boy, without regard to his race, or his color or his creed," the committee professed, "should have a fair chance in baseball," but it was incumbent to "look at the facts." The facts, they argued, were that no black player was capable of playing major league ball, and that integration would threaten the financial existence of the Negro leagues, a $2,000,000 a year business employing hundreds of African Americans, and thus cost major league organizations hundreds of thousands of dollars in rental fees. But the most important "fact" the report stressed was the possible doom that could result from increased black patronage. "The situation might be presented, if Negroes participate in major-league games, in which the preponderance of Negro attendance in parks such as the Yankee Stadium, the Polo Grounds and Comiskey Park could conceivably threaten the value of the major league franchises owned by these clubs." The fear of losing white fans was paramount. Integration, the report suggested, could lessen the value of certain franchises.

THE REACTION OF THE ROBBED

African-American baseball owners were shaken by the news. At first they challenged Rickey's right to sign their players, claiming his actions violated their contracts. Tom Baird, the Kansas City Monarchs' owner, contended, "Robinson signed a contract with us last year and I feel he is our property." Baird and his partner J. L. Wilkinson did not object to integrating the majors, but they objected to Rickey's dismissal of the Negro Leagues as he did so. Soon after the announcement, Wilkinson professed, "I want to see Jackie make good.…I would never do anything to mar his chances." But neither Rickey nor Robinson felt that Robinson was legally bound to the Monarchs. Even if Robinson had an ironclad contract, the Monarchs were in a dilemma. As Newark Eagles owner Effa Manley later pointed out, "We were in no position to protest and he knew it.…He had

Lesson Learned

One Sunday at Memorial Stadium, as the guests of Tommy Thomas, my father and I saw an exhibition game between the Orioles and an all-black team called the Baltimore Elite Giants, pronounced Eee-lite. To all the closet Confederates in Memorial Stadium that day, the visiting team was not seen as a group of baseball professionals but as Pullman porters out of their league. And out of their league they were: They were far better than the Orioles.

"Why aren't those Negroes playing in the major leagues?" I said to my father.

"Well, Charlie, they're flashy, all right," he said, "but they're not steady enough to play the whole season."

My father was a decent and intelligent man, but that observation wasn't one to be bronzed. Like the rest of Baltimore, he never dreamed that his own Babe Ruth might not have been as good as the black Josh Gibson, or that the great Red Ruffing might not have been as good as Satchel Paige, whom a Ruffing teammate named DiMaggio called "the greatest pitcher I ever faced" after trying to hit against him in an army camp game.

My father and I both had a lot to learn. In just four years, one of our lessons would be a Montreal second baseman named Jackie Robinson.

—Charles Osgood

us over a barrel....The fans would never have forgiven us, plus it would have been wrong."

In Pittsburgh, Cum Posey and Sonnyman Jackson called Rickey a "thief and robber" when the Dodgers signed the Homestead Grays' top pitcher, John Wright, for their Montreal club for the 1946 season. "We have invested a lot of money in Wright, and Montreal should offer us some kind of financial compensation," Posey asserted. But Rickey paid the Grays no more attention than he had the Monarchs. Negro league owners met in November 1945 and wrote to baseball commissioner Chandler: "We are glad to see our players get the opportunity to play in white baseball....We are simply protesting the way it was done." They asked Chandler to stop major league owners from taking their players without compensation. But the Baltimore Elite Giants received nothing when the Dodgers signed Roy Campanella in 1946, nor did the Newark Eagles for Don Newcombe.

Some owners thought the major leagues might recognize them as minor leagues and establish working agreements covering the movement and purchase of their players. As a result, the leagues adopted major league bylaws and contracts, and their presidents met with Chandler. The commissioner told them to purge themselves of numbers men and develop "a clean bill of health." Little came of these efforts. Yet the Negro league teams tightened up their contracts, and most teams subsequently purchased players from Negro League clubs.

Nor did the black press, agog over Robinson's signing, come to the defense of the Negro League owners. The *Pittsburgh Courier* editorialized on its sports pages that while they supported black baseball and opposed raiding, "We did feel, however, that the signing of Jackie Robinson by the Brooklyn farm club transcended anything else at this particular time." Wendell Smith was less temperate—some might say intemperate. He castigated Negro league owners for only caring about "the perpetuation of the slave trade they had developed" and dismissed their "shaky, littered, infested, segregated baseball domicile" as of little significance.

Smith was right, at least about black baseball's clout. The Negro leagues faded almost as soon as Robinson made his mark on the majors. The black teams began to lose some of both their most established and their most promising players. Their departure hurt at the gate, but even if the black teams had retained their stars, the fans, wanted to see black players in the majors. Eastern teams were especially hard hit. The Newark Eagles had won the 1946 Negro World Series against the Kansas City Monarchs and entered the 1947 campaign with a talented team. But after drawing large crowds while barnstorming through southern and border states, they hit Washington, D.C., Philadelphia, and New York—Jackie Robinson country—and attendance dwindled.

As Wendell Smith so aptly put it, "Jackie's nimble, Jackie's quick, Jackie makes the turnstiles click." African Americans, abandoning the Negro leagues, turned out in record numbers to watch Robinson. The Dodgers drew over 329,000 more fans on the road in 1947 than the previous season, an increase of over 21 percent, as Brooklyn became black America's team. Black attendance at Ebbets Field, the Dodgers' home field, rose 400 percent over the 1946 season. When they went on the road, the Dodgers found black fans turning out en masse. In Pittsburgh, a local businessman organized a contingent of 500 black fans to back Robinson in his Forbes Field debut. "Anyone with the least bit of racial pride should join us and show Mr. Rickey we are grateful," he explained, adding that the Pirates ought to realize "how much money they are missing by not signing black players." When the Dodgers played in other National League cities, they were cheered by sizable clusters of black fans, some who came from far away to support Robinson.

The Newark Eagles, who would lose several top players to the majors, watched their fan base wither from 120,000 paying spectators in 1946 to about 57,000 in 1947 and only 35,000 in 1948. Their bottom line showed losses of $47,000 for these two seasons. Negro National League clubs were the hardest hit. Negro American League teams, farther away from cities where Jackie played, suffered less erosion of their fan base. But as Buck Leonard succinctly put it, "After Jackie, we couldn't draw flies." By the end of the 1948 season, the Homestead Grays, New York Black Yankees, and Newark Eagles had pulled out of the NNL or decided to disband. The three clubs left in the league joined the Negro American League and added the Eagles, who relocated to Houston, to form a ten-team league. The Grays returned to barnstorming, playing their last game in Parkersburg, West Virginia, in September 1950.

The signing of additional Negro league players cemented black America's focus on major league baseball. Rickey soon signed John Wright, a 27-year-old pitcher who had pitched splendidly for the Homestead Grays and the all-black Great Lakes Naval Station team in 1944, and Roy Partlow, another former Homestead Gray then pitching for the Philadelphia Stars. Neither Wright nor Partlow found much success in organized baseball. Nor did Memphis Red Sox pitcher Dan Bankhead, the younger brother of Negro league all-star Sammy Bankhead. A similar fate was in store for outfielder Willard Brown and infielder Hank Thompson,

Larry Doby
The Other Barrier Breaker

Larry Doby (third from left) with teammates from the Newark Eagles, 1947.

Less than three months after Jackie Robinson broke the color barrier in major league baseball's National league, Larry Doby did the same in the American League. In his first full season in the majors he switched from second base to a new position in the outfield, hit for .301 across the regular season, and batted .318 as his Cleveland Indians triumphed over the Boston Braves in the World Series. He had six straight appearances as an all-star. He won the American League home run crowns in 1952 and 1954 with a league-leading 126 RBI in the latter season. Overall, he compiled a lifetime batting average of .283, and he joined baseball's elite with induction into the Hall of Fame in 1997.

His Negro league career was brief—he played only one full season, and parts of two other seasons—but he racked up accomplishments on America's black playing fields. During the full year he played in 1946, he recorded a .341 average, and ended up only one home run behind league leaders Josh Gibson and Johnny Davis. He played in that season's black all-star game, and his play at second base and at bat contributed significantly to the Newark Eagles pennant and Negro League World Series triumphs. Along with Willie Mays, Satchel Paige, and Monte Irvin, Larry Doby holds the distinction of playing in both a Negro League World Series and a Major League World Series.

Jackie Robinson, in spring training, Vero Beach, Florida, March, 1950.

whom the St. Louis Browns purchased from the Kansas City Monarchs in July 1947, and Birmingham Black Barons infielder Piper Davis, on whom they took an option. Brown and Thompson lasted a month. The option on Davis was never exercised.

The entry of additional black players in the white major and minor leagues led to the virtual abandonment of the Negro leagues by the black press. The black newspapers were the means by which most black fans followed the Negro leagues during the season. But while the black papers chronicled Jackie Robinson's every move and noted the at-bats of each black player in the majors in boldface type, they began to ignore the Negro leagues. Coverage became increasingly spotty. When the Homestead Grays won the 1948 Negro League World Series, the last ever played, the *Pittsburgh Courier* noted their triumph in a two-paragraph story buried in a welter of articles focusing on blacks in the majors.

When black journalists did write of black baseball post-Robinson, they often criticized it in the most scathing terms. Sam Lacy described the Negro leagues as a "mongrel puppy licking at the heels of a prospective master." By the following season, the autonomous black baseball world that had nurtured African-American athletes and offered a cultural counterpoint to segregation had shrunk to the Negro American League. Its best years were in the past, its future uncertain.

Richard King, Oscar Charleston and Connie Morgan, in 1954.

Forgotten Legacy

The Negro National League gave colored players a chance to develop skill and prowess and earn a lucrative salary when the majors had their doors barred. It has done commendably well with limited capital and material. It ought to be supported and preserved.

—Georgia M. Scott, Washington, D.C., 1948

For the cause of integration, the 1950s and 1960s were times of hard struggle, but also they were glorious times—the years of the civil rights revolution. These were the "up to the mountain top to at last look down on the Promised Land" times. So much that had been struggled for and fought over for so long was finally being realized. Echoing many of his generation, Negro leaguer Charlie Biot would say: "I knew I had a lot of ability. But it [segregation] didn't make me bitter. Because I just felt as well maybe someday blacks will get a chance. But I used to say to Roy Campanella, it won't be during our time. Those are my very words to him. We'll never see that." But live to see it he did.

The new era, however, was accompanied by the passing of an old era. These were bittersweet days for many African-American institutions, Negro Baseball and the black press among them. Founded during segregation, these race-based institutions had served their people's cause well. Ultimately, their reason for being would be undermined by the integration for which they had fought. "In the early twenties when Claude Barnett and I worked together," Percival Prattis said, "neither of us could have foreseen that come a few years something called integration was going to get the best of us." But it did get the best of them—for redoubtable and talented black journalists like Prattis and Barnett—and for redoubtable and talented black baseball owners like Abe and Effa Manley.

Mal Goode, who had fought against segregation as a crusading journalist, and became the first black correspondent for a television network in 1962, witnessed the trade-offs that the struggle for equality sometimes entailed. He recognized that integration meant an end to the Negro leagues. "We gained something, but we lost something too," Goode reasoned. "But what we gained was the greater. We got our self-respect, and you have to be black to understand what that meant."

Novelist John Edgar Wideman, however, cast integration and the loss of black institutions in a different light. "I think a lot was lost when the Negro leagues went belly up," he said. "I think a lot was lost when the black colleges began to lose students and funds. After all, this is supposed to be a culture, a society, of diversity. And losing institutions that have that long a life and play that crucial a role in the community...it's very worrisome." Wideman argued, "What was contained in those institutions was not simply a black version of what white people were doing, but the game was played differently."

Negro baseball enjoyed a bonanza during World War II and the immediate postwar period, but by 1948 the successful days wer over and forgotten. Attendance at Negro National League games plunged during the 1947 season, when the eyes of African-American fans turned to Brooklyn and the Dodgers' black star, Jackie Robinson, and, to a lesser extent to Cleveland, where Larry Doby was integrating the American League with the Indians.

After the season *The Sporting News* reported that the New York Cubans, Negro National League champions and winners of the Negro World Series, had lost $20,000 for the year, and that it was a "fair guess" that the league's six teams had dropped a total of $100,000. "As a result," the weekly said, "the organization stands in danger of folding."

Sounding an oft-heard complaint, one black sports editor blamed Negro league management. A.S. "Doc" Young of the *Cleveland Call and Post* urged an overhaul of Negro baseball in a column in January 1948. "First, the game must be improved—faster play, more showmanship, less distraction," he wrote. Young said the teams should have farm clubs to develop young talent. "Second," the veteran scribe wrote, "if our leagues are going to take the big league description in name, let's give the fans something big in action. Let's cut out the farce whereby teams play league games all over the country, whereby a team meets one team nearly twice as many times per season as it does another. Let's stop playing the [Negro World] Series all over the world. Set up a real organization, with a commissioner who knows how to lay down the law." Young also proposed that Negro league teams set up building funds so that they could have their own parks and not have to rely on renting stadiums from white owners. Doc Young suggested, too, that Negro league owners should approach organized baseball about better organization and ways to "reap some of the big money that goes for minor league talent."

Black baseball's leaders were already thinking along those lines. In late December 1947 the Negro National and American Leagues petitioned the minor leagues for entrance into organized baseball. The Rev. John H. Johnson, NNL president, said in March 1948 that the two black leagues had asked the National Association of Professional Baseball Leagues to approve their entry into the minors in accord with a recommendation in 1945 by Larry MacPhail, New York Yankees' president, to a committee that was studying Negro baseball's position at the behest of New York City Mayor Fiorello LaGuardia. MacPhail had written:

> If and when the Negro leagues put their house in order—establish themselves on a sound and ethical operations basis—and conform to the standards of Organized Baseball—I favor admitting them to Organized Baseball; and the rights, privileges, and obligations of such membership.

> This would serve to give the Negro leagues greater prestige; help stabilize their operations; and protect the rights of their public and players. I also believe Organized Baseball could help in the establishment of additional leagues where the young Negro player can be developed.

Johnson, who had been a member of LaGuardia's committee, said the Negro leagues had tried to meet MacPhail's conditions by improving scheduling, adopting a new constitution, and instituting uniform players' contracts. Nevertheless, he said, when the black leagues applied for admission to the National Association of the minor leagues at its convention in December, they were turned down. Johnson said he realized that organized baseball had rules about territorial rights, which might be violated because Negro league clubs often used minor league and big league parks, but he pointed out that the majors had condoned the practice for years by renting their stadiums to Negro league teams. Johnson told the *Chicago Defender*, "The Negro Leagues still possess no status, no voice, no rights, no relationship at all to the major or the minor leagues."

After that rebuff, the Negro leagues suffered another blow, this one from Jackie Robinson. While touring Georgia with a vaudeville troupe in early 1948, the Dodger's star told the *Atlanta Daily World* on February l, "Negro baseball needs a housecleaning from top to bottom." He denied that he had violated a contract with the Kansas City Monarchs when he signed with the Dodgers to play with the Montreal Royals in 1946. Thomas Y. Baird, Monarchs owner, subsequently told *The Sporting News*, "Robinson was signed by letter and telegrams," which he said was standard contract procedure in the Negro leagues, but he was unable to produce a formal contract for Robinson, who played for the Monarchs organization for only a few months.

Jackie Robinson expanded on his criticism of the Negro leagues in an article with his byline in the June issue of *Ebony* magazine. He decried low salaries for players, "sloppy umpiring," and "questionable business connections of many of the team owners." Robinson wrote:

> Players have to make the jump between cities in uncomfortable buses and then play in games while half asleep and very tired. Umpiring is unsupervised and quite prejudiced in many cases. The umpires are quite often untrained and favor certain teams.
>
> When players are able to get a night's rest, the hotels are usually of the cheapest kind. The rooms are dingy and dirty, and the rest rooms in such bad condition that the players are unable to use them ....
>
> With the Monarchs I found the rules as far as players were so lax that on many days some of the players would not get to bed at all. They were allowed to drink whenever they pleased.

Negro league owners were not pleased by Robinson's blast. Most vocal among them was Effa Manley, co-owner with her husband, Abe, of the Newark Eagles, who called Robinson "ungrateful and more likely stupid." The opinionated and outspoken Mrs. Manley said: "Frankly, no greater outrage could have been perpetrated. No greater invasion of the good sense of the American people could have been attempted. No greater ingratitude was ever displayed.... How could a child nurtured by its mother turn on her within a year after he leaves her modest home for glamour, success and good fortune? Jackie Robinson is where he is today because of organized Negro baseball."

Effa Manley continued her rebuttal to Robinson in the August 1948 issue of Our World magazine. In an article titled "Negro Baseball Isn't Dead!" Mrs. Manley urged black fans to rescue the leagues by attending games. "Otherwise," she wrote, "400 young men and their families will be dumped among the unemployed." Her biographer, James Overmyer, noted that on a copy of the article she gave to the Baseball Hall of Fame Library, Mrs. Manley had written in longhand beside the title, "But it is pretty sick."

Effa Manly
Queen of the Negro Leagues

Effa Manley was, as journalist Connie Woodward said, a woman who was "ahead of her time. She ran a male-oriented business, a baseball team, like a man. She was a good role model because she was successful at her business and she inspired young women like me to go into a business or be affiliated with a business that was male-oriented. We were living in the days when chauvinism was at its height into the last '30s, and early '40s and '50s. A woman's place was in the home."

Effa Manley was the business side of a husband-wife combination. She and Abe Manley, who saw more to the on-field side of the operation, ran the Eagles franchise for 14 seasons, from 1935 through 1948. They fielded a team in Brooklyn the first year, but then moved to what proved to be fertile ground in Newark, New Jersey. The Eagles, a perennial runner-up to the powerhouse Homestead Grays and finally Negro world champions in their own right in 1946, were an institution in black Newark.

Effa and Abe were constantly maintaining that Negro baseball should be run on a more businesslike basis. She later recalled Abe's assessment, certainly her own, too, that the Negro leagues were run "in a permissive, self-defeating, and entirely unorthodox manner." They advocated an independent commissioner, more reliable scheduling of games, and enforcement of penalties against players who jumped contracts and the owners who happily received the jumpers.

Max Manning, a longtime Eagle, thought that Mrs. Manley consistently upset her fellow owners: "They recognized the woman was sharp, and could see things they couldn't see, and they resented it."

Well-known black sportswriter Wendell Smith shared her desire for more organized Negro leagues, but had little pity for her or the other black owners after major league integration transferred the black fans' allegiance to the new big leaguers. He gave her a fond farewell, even though he too had experienced her "interference." "There are many of us who will miss the "Queen of Newark," he wrote, "because despite the fact that she tried to tell us how and what to write, she was always good copy."

PASSING UP THE NEGRO LEAGUES

That 1948 season brought no good news for Negro league owners. Attendance at games continued to plummet, particularly in cities near major league franchises. Black fans passed up the chance to see Negro league games if they could watch Jackie Robinson and Roy Campanella with the Brooklyn Dodgers in New York, St. Louis, Boston, and other National League cities. Larry Doby and Satchel Paige of the Cleveland Indians were the big attractions for black fans in American League cities.

Kansas City pitcher Hilton Smith said, "All the people started to go Brooklynites. Even if we were playing here in Kansas City, everybody wanted to go over to St. Louis to see Jackie. So our league began to go down, down, down."

Negro league clubs did well to draw 2,000 fans in 1948, even in such major league venues as Yankee Stadium and the Polo Grounds in New York, Shibe Park in Philadelphia, and Comiskey Park in Chicago. Crowds as low as 700 were drawn to big league parks for black league games that season. The attendance drop of 85,000 from 1946 to 1948 for the Newark Eagles, whose home base was only 10 miles from the Dodgers Ebbets Field, was symptomatic of the times.

Before the '48 season started, the Negro National League agreed on a $6,000 monthly cap on a team's salaries in an effort to contain costs. Most teams simply made proportional cuts on individual salaries, much to the dismay of stars that had been earning $900 or more a month during the boom years. Baltimore Elite Giants general manager Vernon Greene took a different tack. He cut his roster from 25 to 20, and was thus able to continue paying top dollar to veteran stars like shortstop Thomas "Pee Wee" Butts, outfielder Henry Kimbro, and first baseman Johnny Washington.

One telling symptom of growing financial troubles was the annual East-West game, usually the highlight of the black leagues' season. The attendance at the 1948 East-West game at Comiskey Park on August 22 was said to be 42,099—not too far off the 48,000 in 1947. But the *Chicago Defender* reported that just a few minutes before the attendance figure was announced, the number was given as 37,099. The *Defender* noted that a few nights earlier, the venerable Satchel Paige had drawn 51,000 to Comiskey Park to see him pitch a five-hitter for the Cleveland Indians and beat the Chicago White Sox, 5–0. Two days after the '48 East-West game, the same all-star teams appeared at Yankee Stadium in New York for what was billed as a "Dream Game." New York's *Amsterdam News* predicted that 40,000 fans would show up for the night game. In the event, fewer than 18,000 turned out to see the East win, 6–1.

At the end of the 1948 season, Effa Manley and her husband, Abe, having lost $25,000, decided to sell the Eagles. Before ending their association with baseball, the Manleys sold their top star, Monte Irvin, to the New York Giants for $5,000, a bargain basement price for a future Hall of Famer. The Eagles wound up in Texas, playing as the Houston Eagles.

The Newark Eagles were not the only casualty of declining attendance. When the season ended, the Homestead Grays, winners of the NNL pennant and the Negro World Series against the Birmingham Black Barons, announced that they were folding. It would be the last official Negro World Series between two league champions. Their co-owner, Rufus Jackson, said the Grays had lost $45,000 in their last two years. The Grays, did, however, continue to operate through 1950, competing in the minor Negro American Association, which was made up of teams in Virginia and North Carolina, and barnstorming in the South.

The New York Black Yankees also folded after using Rochester, New York, as their hometown for the 1948 season. The Negro National League died, too, ending 16 continuous years of operation. The remaining NNL clubs—the Baltimore Elite Giants, New York Cubans, and Philadelphia Stars—joined the Negro American League, which was split into Eastern and Western Divisions, with five teams each, for 1949.

A TALENT DRAIN

Over the winter, in the face of a reality that clearly said otherwise, the ever optimistic Negro American League president, Dr. J.B. Martin, predicted, "Without a doubt, 1949 will be its [Negro baseball's] greatest year."

Owners of most Negro American League clubs, according to the *Defender*, joined Martin in his public optimism. The *Pittsburgh Courier*'s Wendell Smith had a less cheery outlook, calling 1949 a "do or die" year for black baseball when the lights could well go out with a "shocking suddenness."

Attendance at most league games dropped below the dismal figures for 1948, and receipts at the East-West game sank again. The black mid-summer classic at Comiskey Park drew 31,079 fans; only 26,697 bought tickets. The Baltimore Elite Giants won both halves of the NAL's Eastern Division, while the Monarchs took the first half of the Western Division race and the Chicago American Giants the second half. The Monarchs ceded the Western Division championship to the American Giants. Some said it was because they had lost too many stars to white organized baseball; others said it was because they had no place to host playoffs. The Kansas City Blues of the American Association had first dibs on the municipal stadium. It was a telling sign of black baseball's increasing weakness that its young stars went into white organized baseball, and that scheduling problems arose because of the dearth of stadiums that were owned or leased by the clubs. The Baltimore club defeated the American Giants four straight for the league championship.

On the other side of baseball's increasingly porous racial divide, black players appeared for the first time in a major league All-Star game. Jackie Robinson, Roy Campanella, and Don Newcombe, all of the Brooklyn Dodgers, and Larry Doby of the Cleveland Indians made the breakthrough. An overflow crowd of 32,577 jammed the cramped confines of Ebbets Field in Brooklyn to see the first black major league All-Stars.

One bright spot in the financial picture of black teams was player sales to clubs in the major and minor leagues. The *Defender* reported that T. Y. Baird, sole owner of the Kansas City Monarchs after the retirement of J. L. Wilkinson in 1948, had sold six players to teams in organized baseball. The first was Satchel Paige, who joined Larry Doby on the Cleveland Indians in July 1948. The next year Baird sold second baseman Hank Thompson, who had had a cup of coffee with the American League's St. Louis Browns in 1948, to the New York Giants. Monarch pitcher Ford

Smith also went to the Giants. Both he and Thompson were assigned to the Jersey City Giants of the International League.

The New York Yankees bought catcher Earl Taborn and outfielder Bob Thurman and placed them with the Newark Bears of the International League. Baird sold pitcher Booker McDaniels to the Chicago Cubs, who assigned him to Los Angeles in the Pacific Coast League.

Tom Hayes, owner of the Birmingham Black Barons, did well in the player market, too. He sold shortstop Artie Wilson to the Oakland Oaks of the PCL for a reported $10,000. Black Barons pitcher Alonzo Perry went to Oakland for $5,000. Hard-hitting Lorenzo "Piper" Davis, the second baseman and manager, was bought by the Boston Red Sox, who sent him to Scranton of the Eastern League. The Black Barons got $7,500 for him, with the promise of another $7,500 if Davis was still with the club on May 15. On May 1, Davis was leading the team in batting average at .333; in homers with three; and runs batted in, ten, but the Red Sox released him on grounds that they couldn't afford the extra $7,500. It would be another year before Willie Mays of the Black Barons, the Negro leagues' prime young prospect, would be sold to the Giants' organization. The *Defender* reported that the New York Giants paid Alex Pompez, owner of the New York Cubans, $20,000 for three stars—third baseman Ray Dandridge, pitcher Dave Barnhill, and catcher Ray Noble. Dandridge and Barnhill starred for the Giants' farm club in Minneapolis, and Noble spent time in Jersey City and Oakland before going up to the big club in 1951. Pompez would also conduct scouting efforts in the Caribbean, successfully locating new talent Minnie Minoso, Jose Santiago, and Edmundo "Sandy" Amoros—all contributors to the Cubans' 1947 Negro league championship team and future major leaguers. Pompez went on to engineer the opening of the Dominican pipeline to the major leagues, signing Dominican players like Juan Marichal, the Alou brothers, and Manny Mota for the New York Giants.

The major leagues were cherry-picking the most promising young players in the Negro American League—and some who were not so young. Ray Dandridge, for example, told the Minneapolis Millers that he was 29 years old when he joined them. In fact, he was 36. Dandridge batted .364 and was second in the balloting for the American Association's Rookie of the Year award. The next year he was the league's Most Valuable Player. Despite these achievements, Dandridge was never called up to the parent New York Giants roster.

Dandridge was not unique. Other Negro league veterans who hoped for at least a shot at the majors were consigned to the minor leagues—often the low minors—if they were signed at all. Historian Jules Tygiel writes: "Generally underestimating the quality of play in the Negro leagues, baseball officials placed most of the new recruits in classifications far beneath the players' talents. As a result blacks compiled astounding statistics in the early years of integration."

Often the presence of blacks on the field increased attendance considerably. Slugger Luke Easter, Homestead Grays first baseman, is a good example. Easter was signed by the Cleveland Indians and placed on the roster of the San Diego Padres of the Pacific Coast League. His penchant for hitting tape-measure home runs attracted record crowds in Los Angeles and San Francisco. Easter had, however, suffered a painful knee fracture in spring training, and he had to quit on July 1 for recuperation. He had batted .363 in 80 games, with 25 home runs and 92 runs batted in. After Easter's departure, attendance at PCL games dropped abruptly, and team owners said his loss cost them $200,000 in gate receipts.

Late that season the big first baseman was called up to the parent Indians and got into 22 games for them. That was followed by four productive seasons in the majors, with batting averages ranging from .263 to .303 and 93 home runs. Like many other Negro leaguers, Easter shaved several years off his true age to enhance his chances of being signed by a team in organized baseball.

Meanwhile, the Negro National League's teams were losing players to clubs in the Caribbean and Canada, as well as to the minor and major leagues. Philadelphia Stars catcher Bill "Ready" Cash headed south when Mexico City offered him a thousand dollars a month, double his salary with the Stars. Cash was another in a long line of Negro leaguers (and big leaguers) who had been drawn to the Mexican league and elsewhere south of the border even before World War II.

Raymond Brown

Best Player Not in the Hall of Fame?

There are a number of major talents from the Negro leagues who, when this book had gone to press, had still not been inducted into the Hall of Fame. Cannonball Redding, Frank Grant, Homerun Johnson, Sol White, Wild Bill Wright, Jose Mendez, Spotswood Poles, and Louis Santop all come to mind. But maybe the greatest omission is Raymond Brown.

He was not just a fine pitcher in the Negro leagues, his records in Mexican and Cuban play qualify him for consideration as well. The 1936 Cuban season alone gave him immortal status in the annals of that island's baseball history. His 21–4 tied a record for most wins going back to 1903. One of those four losses was to the redoubtable Luis Tiant in an 11-inning contest that ended with a final score of 1–0. Brown completed an astounding 23 out of 26 games he started. His prowess on the mound was matched at the plate with a .311 season average.

None of his achievements in Cuban play would have come as a surprise to his counterparts in the Negro leagues. By 1936 he was the ace of the Homestead Grays' pitching staff. Across his 19-year career he pitched in two East-West All-Star games, was held out of a third by the Grays' ownership, and compiled a 3–2 record in the seven Negro League World Series games he pitched, one of those a one-hit shutout of the Birmingham Black Barons in 1944.

Historian James Riley captures his formidable pitching presence well. "The Homestead Grays' ace had a sinker, slider, and a fine fastball, but his curveball was his best pitch. So confident was Ray in all of his pitches that he would throw a curve with a 3–0 count on the batter. Later in his career he developed an effective knuckleball, and he had good control of all his pitches."

The 1938 squad may have been the Grays' strongest team of their nine straight pennant-winning clubs. The *Pittsburgh Courier* that year listed him among the five Negro League players to be certain major league stars. Brown's four fellow designees, Josh Gibson, Cool Papa Bell, Buck Leonard, and Satchel Paige, have all earned baseball's greatest honor. Of the five, only Raymond Brown remains outside the Hall.

Canada was a new destination for black players. The Provincial League, centered in Quebec, attracted many Negro leaguers in the post-World War II period when the black leagues were faltering in the U.S. So did the ManDak League, with teams in Manitoba, Canada, and North Dakota. Over the eight years the ManDak league lasted, more than a hundred Negro league players appeared on that circuit's teams. Even the ubiquitous Satchel Paige appeared there, pitching three innings in each of the first three games played by the Minot Mallards. As usual, Satch sparkled on the mound, giving up only three hits and no runs in his nine innings while striking out 13. In one game with the Mallards, Paige did not bother to warm up. A teammate recalled, "He was standing beside me during the National Anthem and I asked him why he hadn't warmed up. Satchel turned to me and said, 'I've been warmed up since 1936.'"

In spite of defection northward and southward, the Negro American League managed to get through the 1950 schedule without stumbling, with the Indianapolis Clowns winning the Eastern Division race, and the Kansas City Monarchs the Western Division. Actually, the Clowns placed third behind the New York Cubans and Baltimore Elite Giants in the Eastern's second half but were awarded the championship because they had played more than 30 games in the half, as against only eight for the Cubans and 25 for the Elite Giants. There was no official playoff for the league title between the Monarchs and Clowns, although the two teams went on a barnstorming tour, with games in Kansas City, New Orleans, Houston and Shreveport.

Attendance at games continued to drop off. Television was still a novelty, but it was beginning to cut into the gates of the Negro leagues and of the minor leagues, too. As a possible answer to hard times, teams turned to novelty attractions. The Chicago American Giants attempted to lure more white fans by integrating their club with four white players. Resorting to the tried and true, a year later the American Giants signed Satchel Paige, black baseball's biggest attraction, in hopes of boosting gate receipts. They lost Paige in July when Bill Veeck, who had brought him into the majors with the Cleveland Indians in 1948, signed him for the hapless St. Louis Browns. Thereupon the American Giants added a white

Ralph "Spec" Bebop played for the Clowns 1950-1960.

clown named Ed Hamman, who was noted as a great pepper game player and who was able to do such tricks as throw from third to first behind his back. Novelty sometimes produced its own novelty. Hamman was a victim of Jim Crow in Birmingham when he was ordered off the field and into the stands reserved for whites during an American Giants game with the Black Barons. This white clown later owned the Indianapolis Clowns and created some of their skits. But he and his pepper tricks were unable to save the American Giants, who succumbed to box office anemia in 1952.

Another black baseball legend, the Homestead Grays, gave up the ghost in mid-season of 1951. After the end of the Negro National League in 1948, the Grays had spent a season in the minor Negro American Association, and then a year on the barnstorming trail during which they lost $10,000 before folding in June 1951.

The passing of the Chicago American Giants and the Homestead Grays, two of the bellwethers of Negro baseball, was a clear indication of weakness. Another sign was that East-West game attendance continued to drop. For the 1951 contest a total of 21,312 spectators (14,161 paid) saw the East win, 3–1, at Chicago's Comiskey Park. Miss Carolyn Combs, a 24-year-old senior at Chicago's Roosevelt College, was crowned Queen of the 19th annual East-West game, but her reign seems to have had little effect on the box office. Nor did that of other young women who were crowned in later years.

The Indianapolis Clowns dominated the NAL's Eastern Division in 1951, winning both halves with a combined record of 53–26. The Kansas City Monarchs took both halves of the Western Division, edging out the Chicago American Giants. The Clowns won the playoff for the NAL title.

The Negro American League retrenched to six teams, losing the New Orleans Eagles and Baltimore Elite Giants, in 1952. The divisional system was scrapped, and the Indianapolis Clowns won the first half of the split season, with the Birmingham Black Barons taking the second half. The playoff for the NAL title was a wandering Southern barnstorming tour of 12 games. It was called the Negro World Series, even though the competing teams were in the lone black major league. The Clowns won seven of the 12 games. The star was Clown shortstop Hank Aaron, an 18-year-old

BASEBALL CIRCUS
FUN - LAUGHS - THRILLS
The GLOBETROTTERS of BASEBALL
BASEBALL'S NUMBER ONE SHOW TEAM
SUPER STAR HANK AARON STARTED HIS BASEBALL CAREER WITH THE CLOWNS
44th SEASON
BOBO SMALL
Bobo Small, versatile comedy star of the Indianapolis Clowns. Small, the showboat of comedy will be seen in action when the Clowns play.
ALWAYS A CROWD PLEASER
INDIANAPOLIS CLOWNS
- VS -
Kingston Braves
WED., AUG. 15
Dietz Stadium
8:00 P.M.
STEVE ANDERSEN
Famous One Armed First Baseman who reminds Fans of Former Major League Star One Armed Pete Gray.

Advertising the last of the barnstormers.

who had left the team in June to begin his career in white organized baseball as a Boston Braves farmhand in Eau Claire, Wisconsin, of the Northern League. Aaron won the Northern League's Rookie of the Year award en route to a 23-year major league career during which he set several records, including most home runs (755). The Northern League's season ended early enough that Hank Aaron was able to return to the Indianapolis Clowns for the league playoff series. He batted over .400 and hit five home runs in the 12 games.

The Chicago *Defender* had optimistically predicted a crowd of 25,000 for the 1952 East-West All-Star game, but in the event, the attendance was 18,127, of whom 14,122 paid to see the West win, 7–3.

FIGHTING FOR SURVIVAL

The following season, 1953, was notable for two reasons. In this year, the last of the Negro leagues' potentional superstars went directly to the majors. Ernie Banks, then a 22-year-old short stop for the Kansas City Monarchs, was bought by the Chicago Cubs. Pitcher Bill Dickey was sent to the Cubs' farm at Cedar Rapids, Iowa. The Monarchs were said to have been paid $35,000 for Banks and Dickey.

Secondly, in this same year, the Negro American League introduced a woman player. Marcenia Stone was a talented athlete, a 32-year-old second baseman who had earlier played for the New Orleans Creoles of the Negro Southern League. Ms. Stone, who may have been the highest paid player in the NAL at a reported $12,000 a year, played in 50 games for the Clowns and batted a creditable .243. The following season she was sold to the Kansas City Monarchs, and the Clowns added two other women to their roster—infielder Connie Morgan and pitcher Mamie "Peanut" Johnson.

The Negro American League cut back to four teams for 1953—the Monarchs, Birmingham Black Barons, Indianapolis Clowns, and Memphis Red Sox, who finished in that order. Players from the Black Barons and Clowns made up the East's roster for the East-West game, while the Monarchs and Red Sox represented the West. The West won handily, 5–1, before an officially estimated 10,000 fans at Comiskey Park. Johnny Johnson, sports editor of the *Kansas City Call*, cast doubt on the figure. "Many of the scribes shook their heads in disbelief when it was guessed that 10,000 fans were in the park," he wrote. "A few set their own estimation at 7,000; some of the less generous ones declared the total was 5,000."

Johnson blamed the low attendance on the lack of interest by Chicago's black population. "The Negro citizens of the big city have failed to support this athletic institution as they should," Johnson wrote. "And in their lack of support they are guilty of lack of civic pride." He called for having the East-West game played elsewhere—Birmingham, Memphis, Kansas City, or other cities "where more appreciative persons might have the opportunity to extend a warmer bit of hospitality to the venture." Nothing came of that idea until the last East-West game was played in New York's Yankee Stadium in 1961.

For a season the news got better. The Negro American League, with President J.B. Martin still at the helm, expanded from four to six teams in 1954, adding the Detroit Stars and the Louisville Clippers. The Indianapolis Clowns, managed by veteran Oscar Charleston, won the NAL pennant easily. The West won its third straight East-West game before an estimated crowd of 10,000 at Comiskey Park. Fay Young of the *Defender* was skeptical about the estimate. He said it "must have included the police, the firemen, the ushers and the groundskeepers plus the players on both teams and the four umpires."

The march toward oblivion continued in 1955. The Negro American League cut back to four teams that season. The Detroit Stars replaced the Indianapolis Clowns, who hit the barnstorming trail for good. The other three teams were the Kansas City Monarchs, Birmingham Black Barons and Memphis Red Sox. None of them was thriving. The Detroit Stars were probably better known for a side attraction, a team of black acrobats called the Flying Nesbit, than for their baseball talents.

There was another effort to move the East-West game out of Chicago. According to the *Defender*, the owners voted in February to play the 23rd annual game in Kansas City. However, league president Martin mounted a campaign to keep the midsummer Negro classic in the Windy City. He had the support of the Chicago Negro Chamber of Commerce, and won the battle at a meeting of the owners in June. It proved to be a Pyrrhic victory. According to the *Defender*, 11,257 fans were in Comiskey Park to see the West prevail again, 2–0, in a defensive battle. The crowd was no doubt drawn by the fact that Satchel Paige, now back on the Monarchs roster, was advertised to pitch the first three innings for the West. He did—and gave up no hits, although he did not get credit for the victory.

Even the fabled Kansas City Monarchs club was on shaky legs. The clap of doom for the Kansas City club was transplantation of the big league Philadelphia Athletics to the Monarchs' home city. Monarchs historian Janet Bruce reports that the city's black fans became gripped with interest in the A's two black players, Vic Power and Bob Trice, while the price of playing Negro league baseball in Kansas City mounted considerably.

"The Monarchs, besides losing their fans, also faced increased costs for renting the stadium, now city owned. The city charged 25 percent of the gate receipts and also required (owner Tom) Baird to contract with the A's for ushers, ground crews, ticket agents, and janitors. Altogether, Baird paid out over $3,000 per game, which left him with less than half of the gate receipts to split with the visiting team....After the opening game, the Monarchs returned to Kansas City for only one other game that season."

At the end of that summer, only owners who had sold many players to the majors showed a profit. The league was so disorganized that some sportswriters were not certain that the season had ended and had even less idea about who had won the pennant. Later reports said the Monarchs were 1955 champions.

RETREAT INTO THE SHADOWS

By 1958 the Negro American League was down to four teams. The Detroit franchise was purchased by Reece "Goose" Tatum, a star of the Harlem Globetrotters touring basketball team. Tatum, famed as a showman with the Globetrotters, changed Detroit's name from Stars to Clowns, believing "the new name would help in creating more interest among the fans." He also introduced what he boasted as "the best 'shadow ball' of any team in the country." Shadow ball, with its pre-game whipping of an imaginary baseball around the infield required considerable dexterity and a touch of comedic genius to be carried off successfully. It was also, of course, a throwback to an entertainment stereotype of blacks rooted in the 19th-century tradition of the minstrel in blackface. As a solution for anemic gate receipts, it fell considerably short of the mark.

The renamed Detroit Clowns with the "best shadow ball skit" did do well for at least some games, drawing 10,000 in Birmingham for a contest against the Black Barons. A season highlight was a face-off between Tatum's Detroit Clowns and the Memphis Red Sox, who split a doubleheader in New York's Yankee Stadium on June 1, the first appearance by black teams there in 12 years. *New York Times* sportswriter Louis Effrat observed that six major league scouts were on hand. "The presence of these bird dogs," Effrat noted, "was as important to the Negro American League as were the 9,506 spectators." For him the reasons were obvious. "Without paying fans there would be no Negro American League and without such an organized circuit there would be no real showcase from which might spring the future Jackie Robinsons, Roy Campanellas, Hank Aarons and others of their race who made the big jump to the majors."

The swan song of the Negro American League may have been the 29th annual East–West game, played in Yankee Stadium on Sunday, August 20, 1961. Appropriately, the most valuable player citation went to the ageless Satchel Paige, who had returned to the Kansas City Monarchs in May, and in August pitched the first three innings for the West. Paige, who was (officially, at least) 55 years old, was the winning pitcher as the West triumphed, 7–1. He gave up the East's only hit, a scratch infield single in the first inning by Fred Green of the Raleigh Tigers. The crowd at Yankee Stadium numbered 7,245.

A few days before the East-West game, sportswriter John Drebinger of the *New York Times* mused about the place of the Negro American League in the baseball firmament. In a "Sports of the Times" column, Drebinger wrote that in the 1930s, the New York Giants and Cleveland Indians played exhibition games in southern small towns on their way home after spring training. "It was missionary work of a sort the majors never should have abandoned," he said. "Now four Negro teams are reviving that interest in long-idle minor league ball parks."

Drebinger's column focused on Satchel Paige, whose career he summarized as the biggest attraction in "Baseball's Top Road Show." "What records he would have set had he pitched in the majors in the years of his prime!" Drebinger wrote. "Now, somewhere between 55 and 65, ol' Satch is still baffling them as he rolls up one scoreless inning after another for the Kansas City Monarchs." Two weeks after the East-West game, Paige signed with the Portland Beavers of the Pacific Coast League to finish the season there.

A LONG LEGACY OF TALENT

By 1963 black players were common—and dominant—in the major leagues. The last club had been integrated four years earlier, and now fifteen percent of big leaguers were African American or black Latin Americans. Such baseball men as Bob Feller, Larry MacPhail, and the editors of *The Sporting News* who had predicted that few black players were capable of playing at the major league level had been proved wrong conclusively. Since Jackie Robinson joined the Dodgers in 1947, the National League's Most Valuable Player award had gone to black players eleven times (Robinson himself, Roy Campanella three times, Willie Mays, Don Newcombe, Hank Aaron, Ernie Banks twice, Frank Robinson, and Maury Wills). Jackie Robinson was the league's Rookie of the Year in 1947, and he was followed as the National League's top rookie by Don Newcombe (1949), Sam Jethroe (1950), Willie Mays (1951), Joe Black (1952), Jim Gilliam (1953), Frank Robinson (1956), Orlando Cepeda (1958), Willie McCovey (1959) and Billy Williams (1961). Four of the top five players in the National League in 1963 for batting average, runs batted in, and home runs were African Americans. All five league leaders for stolen bases were black.

The majority of these stars had started in the Negro leagues. Jackie Robinson had been with the Kansas City Monarchs in 1945; Roy

Playing Hardball

At a reunion of Negro League veterans, Willie Mays recalled to John Holway a story from his early years. One day he was hit by a beanball and knocked unconscious. When he came to, he saw his manager, Piper Davis, standing over him. "Are you okay?" Piper asked. Willie nodded weakly. "Can you see first base?" Willie nodded again. "Well then," his manager said, "get up and get on it."

Campanella with the Baltimore Elite Giants from 1937–45; Willie Mays with the Birmingham Black Barons from 1948–50; Don Newcombe with the Newark Eagles from 1944–45; Hank Aaron with the Indianapolis Clowns in 1952; Ernie Banks with the Kansas City Monarchs in 1950 and 1953; Sam Jethroe with the Indianapolis ABCs in 1938 and with the Cincinnati and Cleveland Buckeyes from 1943–48; Joe Black with the Baltimore Elite Giants from 1943–48; and Jim Gilliam with the Nashville Black Vols and Baltimore Elite Giants from 1945–51.

Blacks not only excelled in the big leagues, they changed the way in which baseball was played. Black athletes reintroduced speed and base running into a game that for three decades had been dominated by power hitters. As early as 1949, New York sportswriter Dan Daniel noted that Jethroe, Doby, and Robinson were the fastest men in baseball. "As you will note, all are Negroes," added Daniel. "If that race has contributed nothing else to the game…it has brought the consummate speed of a quality rarely demonstrated since the Ty Cobb heyday."

The injection of speed did not imply the sacrifice of power. The contrasting images of the ponderous, slow-legged home run hitter and the willowy, spray-hitting speed merchant lost their validity. Willie Mays, Hank Aaron, and Frank Robinson, the greatest power hitters of the modern age, were highly proficient base stealers. Mays alone registered more stolen bases in his career than the combined totals of Babe Ruth, Jimmy Foxx, Ted Williams, and Mel Ott, the leading home run hitters before 1960. By the 1960s baseball, in this respect, more closely resembled the well-balanced offensive structure of the Negro leagues than the power-oriented attack of the all-white majors.

THE LAST BARNSTORMERS

By 1963 the Kansas City Monarchs, Birmingham Black Barons, Detroit Stars, a black team called the Cincinnati Tigers, and the Indianapolis Clowns were still barnstorming. So was Satchel Paige's All-Stars, which was loaded with old Monarchs. Paige's pitching buddy Hilton Smith even organized a new black semi-pro club called the Kansas City Braves. But one by one they all slipped into oblivion by the mid-1960s, except for the Clowns.

The Clowns were the longest-running franchise in Negro baseball history. They began as the Miami Clowns in 1929, and ended 59 years later as the touring Indianapolis Clowns. Across their long tenure the team was also called the Ethiopian Clowns and Cincinnati Clowns. During the 1940s and '50s, the Clowns were in the Negro American League and won four championships before dropping out in 1955, but they were best known for their comedy. Catcher Pepper Bassett sometimes played his position in a rocking chair. "Natureboy" Williams would dance with the umpire at his first base position and shoot off a firecracker in his glove as he speared a throw. Spectators with little knowledge of baseball and no appreciation of its intricacies could enjoy the antics of comedians Birmingham Sam, King Tut (real name Richard King), Harlem Globetrotter basketball star Goose Tatum, and midgets named Spec Bebop and Billy Vaughn. Thirty-one-inch tall Dero Austin, who succeeded Vaughn on the Clowns roster, was said to reduce the club's hotel bill by sleeping in a suitcase.

"When I was there," Henry Aaron recalled, "we still did the shadowball routine, taking infield practice without a baseball. But after warm-ups, the players played and left the clowning to Tut and Bebop. They would do routines where Tut would have a toothache and Bebop would yank it out with pliers, or they would pretend like they were fishing and the boat turned over, that kind of thing. They threw buckets of confetti into the crowd—all the same stunts the Globetrotters did. The fans ate it up."

Pitching great Max Manning poses with teammates of his high school team in 1937.

In 1965 the Clowns were sold to Ed Hamman. Satchel Paige continued to pitch both for and against the Indianapolis Clowns during the late 1960s. One week he would go three innings for the Clowns, the next he would be featured by a touring club called the New York Stars. Hamman remembered that he had given the unreliable Satchel "the shortest contract in baseball history—no show, no dough." Paige said, 'Even Bill Veeck didn't do that to me.' I said, 'Bill Veeck wasn't in the bus league either.'" Hamman recalled, "Satchel loved to fish. So he would dress in his uniform in the hotel, and I would take him to the nearest stream. I'd leave and go to the ball game till about the third or fourth inning. Then I would go get him, and he would pitch the last couple of innings and everybody's happy. Now and then Satchel would hand a fish to an umpire."

In 1973 Ed Hamman sold the Clowns, sans Satchel Paige, to George Long, a veteran semi-pro operator in Muscatine, Iowa. The final chapter in the long saga of the Indianapolis Clowns began in 1984, when Dave Clark and Sal Tombasco bought the Clowns from George Long for

$25,000. Clark had been crippled by polio as a child, but he learned to play ball on a leg brace and crutches. Clark and Tombasco were on the Clowns' 15-man player roster. "We also had two clowns called designated entertainers, who were not players," Clark said. "Sal was a ham too. He played in a clown costume and worked with the two clowns." Players were paid $50 a week, plus $5 a day meal money. In their final years the Clowns barnstormed mostly in the East, with an occasional foray into the Midwest. "One day we would be playing in a cow pasture, literally, and the next day we would be in the Metrodome in Minneapolis," Clark recalled. In the club's last years, Clark said, about 70 percent of the players were white.

REMINISCING

By 1970 the veterans of the Negro leagues were pretty much forgotten. Most of them looked back with pride on their time on the ball field and without many recriminations. Many, like Buck O'Neil, saw the Negro leagues for their contribution to a level playing field in the society at large:

> Yet when you look back, what people didn't realize, and still don't, was that we got the ball rolling on integration in our whole society. Remember, this was before *Brown versus the Board of Education* of Topeka. When Branch Rickey signed Jackie, Martin Luther King was a student at Morehouse College. We showed the way it had to be done, by just keeping on and being the best we could. And the victory was finally complete when scouts began signing young black players in Alabama and Mississippi right out of high school. That was great, but it also meant these young blacks didn't need the Negro leagues anymore. That was the last nail in the coffin.
>
> When I look at what happened after Jackie, I get a chill up my spine. But I also get a bittersweet feeling because I remember that a lot of people lost their whole way of life. That was another of those ironies, the hardest one. Not only did a

black business die, other black businesses did, too, the ones that were dependent on black baseball and black entertainment. The Streets Hotel (in Kansas City) had to close because it couldn't compete with the Muelebach Hotel downtown. The Vincennes in Chicago went out because the ballplayers and the entertainers were staying in the Loop now. Instead of the Woodside in Harlem, they were staying in Times Square.

A way of life came to an end along with black baseball. But I guess it couldn't be any other way. The white-only hotels had to die, too, for integration to work, and that ended another way of life."

Jimmie Crutchfield, whose Negro league career stretched from 1930 to 1945, mused about it many years later:

> I have no ill feeling about never having had the opportunity to play in the big leagues. There have been times—you know, they used to call me the black Lloyd Waner. I used to think about that a lot. He was on the other side of town in Pittsburgh making $12,000 a year and I didn't have enough money to go home. I had to borrow bus fare to come home.
>
> It seemed like there was something wrong there. But that was yesterday. There's no use in me having bitterness in my heart this late in life about what's gone by. That's just the way I feel about it. Once in a while I get a kick out of thinking that my name was mentioned as one of the stars of the East-West game and little things like that. I don't know whether I'd feel better if I had a million dollars.
>
> I can say I contributed something.

Max Manning was asked what the game meant to him after a decade in the Negro leagues, a year in the minor leagues, and 28 years as a teacher. He responded:

Ernie Banks jumps for joy after news of his election to the Baseball Hall of Fame.

You can't imagine what memories I had when I left baseball, particularly what happened to African-American ballplayers—where they went and what they did, what they were able to do and the abilities they had—which indicated to me that the Negro leagues were really the Negro major leagues. Look what the early players who entered the major leagues did. They were all big stars!

I have absolutely no regrets, none whatsoever, in terms of what happened to me. I think destiny plays a big part in what happens in people's lives.

I'm just so happy I had the experience.

Statistics

BASEBALL FANS ARE USED TO THE ABUNDANT SUPPLY OF PRECISE AND ACCURATE statistics for most contemporary baseball operations. Unfortunately, data of this caliber is not available for Negro leagues baseball. There exists no official source of statistics for these leagues, there are no compilations of scorecards, and modern researchers have had to dig deep to locate credible figures. There have been several outstanding attempts to rebuild this history, most notably by John Holway, Jim Riley, Phil Dixon, Larry Lester and Dick Clark, but many gaps still exist in the historical record.

There are multiple issues with which researchers must contend when attempting to rebuild Negro leagues statistics. The most important are:

- Which games should be included? Published schedules were not always accurate, and the list of league-sanctioned games was not necessarily stable, so researchers do not have a simple list of games to target. Additionally, there were multiple leagues, independent teams and other exceptions which must be considered.

- How do we locate the game accounts and numbers? For most of this period, the only sources of raw data are the newspaper boxscores. However, these were not consistently reported by any one newspaper, so researchers must work with a wide variety of publications.

- How do we deal with imprecise information? Due to the fact that many different sources must be used, there is an inconsistent presentation of data.

As part of the Hall of Fame sponsored study, Larry Lester and Dick Clark supervised an effort to rebuild the Negro leagues statistics in order to help historians better understand the game. They labored under a strict guideline to include only those numbers for league-sanctioned games where boxscores did exist. Their research team tracked down thousands of entries from over 120 period newspapers, and these have been used to build their data base. The other criterion is that these boxscores must be made available to the archive at the National Baseball Hall of Fame so that others could verify and duplicate their effort. The statistical charts used in this volume are a direct result of their monumental effort.

Because Negro leagues numbers are less precise than major league numbers, it has been extremely difficult to compare the players from these leagues. The numbers may be somewhat imprecise, but when a batter hit .341 when the league average was .262, it is safe to assume that he was a pretty good hitter. Home run totals may not be as high as some assumed, but the home run to at-bat ratio for the best Negro leaguers favorably compares to the best in major league history.

More boxscores will be discovered in coming years, and these will be added to the existing historical records, but Negro leagues data will always contain gaps and inconsistencies. Like other segments of baseball history, the folklore of the game will remain as important as the actual data, but the effort to rebuild this history will continue.

PLAYER STATS

BELL, JAMES THOMAS a.k.a. Cool Papa B: 05.17.1903, Starkville, MS

YEAR	TEAM	G	AB	R	H
1922	St. Louis Stars	12	32	5	11
1923	St. Louis Stars	49	108	24	26
1924	St. Louis Stars	59	223	42	65
1925	St. Louis Stars	70	310	59	99
1926	St. Louis Stars	55	238	59	80
1927	St. Louis Stars	65	273	51	86
1928	St. Louis Stars	82	349	84	115
1929	Chicago American Giants	4	17	3	3
1929	St. Louis Stars	60	244	52	71
1930	St. Louis Stars	40	179	46	62
1931	St. Louis Stars	10	38	6	8
1932	Detroit Wolves	21	86	19	28
1932	Homestead Grays	12	46	12	16
1932	Kansas City Monarchs	14	53	14	21
1933	Pittsburgh Crawfords	40	165	33	48
1934	Pittsburgh Crawfords	52	210	42	64
1935	Pittsburgh Crawfords	40	170	46	53
1936	Pittsburgh Crawfords	22	92	23	29
1937	Pittsburgh Crawfords	5	21	4	7
1937	Trujillo All-Stars	2	7	2	4
1942	Chicago American Giants	20	72	10	23
1943	Homestead Grays	49	204	39	68
1944	Homestead Grays	37	152	27	46
1945	Homestead Grays	18	67	14	24
1946	Homestead Grays	27	88	20	35
	Career Totals:	**865**	**3444**	**736**	**1092**

CAMPANELLA, ROY a.k.a. Campy B: 11.19.1921 Philadelphia, PA

YEAR	TEAM	G	AB	R	H
1937	Washington Elite Giants	2	2	0	0
1938	Baltimore Elite Giants	5	13	3	4
1939	Baltimore Elite Giants	17	55	7	15
1940	Baltimore Elite Giants	27	88	13	25
1941	Baltimore Elite Giants	25	80	16	27
1942	Baltimore Elite Giants	30	110	18	33
1944	Baltimore Elite Giants	21	84	19	37
1944	Philadelphia Stars	1	3	2	1

BATTING

D: 03/07/1991, St. Louis, St. Louis County, MO						B/T, S/L		5'11.5, 150 lbs.	
D	**T**	**HR**	**RBI**	**W**	**SAC**	**SB**	**E**	**AVG.**	**SLUG.**
3	0	1	3	3	0	0	0	.344	.531
5	1	2	17	7	6	1	4	.241	.361
13	2	0	33	17	5	9	4	.291	.368
19	3	7	16	24	3	13	6	.319	.468
14	4	7	16	25	6	4	3	.336	.517
14	2	3	12	23	6	12	3	.315	.414
20	7	5	18	34	6	16	9	.330	.470
0	0	0	1	1	0	0	0	.176	.176
13	5	1	1	27	3	18	1	.291	.398
8	2	4	11	15	0	5	2	.346	.480
2	0	0	0	5	0	9	0	.211	.263
3	0	0	8	6	0	7	1	.326	.360
3	1	0	0	6	0	1	0	.348	.457
4	5	0	3	10	1	3	1	.396	.660
5	3	1	24	16	1	8	2	.291	.376
6	1	1	5	25	1	12	3	.305	.357
3	5	2	10	20	0	7	4	.312	.424
4	2	0	1	7	1	1	0	.315	.402
1	0	2	2	2	0	0	0	.333	.667
0	0	0	0	2	0	0	0	.571	.571
2	1	0	3	8	2	0	1	.319	.375
6	5	0	17	20	2	10	0	.333	.412
6	3	0	19	17	1	4	1	.303	.382
2	0	0	6	12	0	0	1	.358	.388
2	1	0	11	7	1	4	1	.398	.443
158	**53**	**36**	**237**	**339**	**45**	**144**	**47**	**.317**	**.425**

D: 06.26.1993, Woodland Hills, Los Angeles County, CA						B/T, R/R		5' 9, 200 lbs.	
0	0	0	0	0	0	0	0	.000	.000
0	0	0	1	1	0	0	0	.308	.308
1	0	1	6	3	1	0	5	.273	.345
3	1	5	21	4	1	1	3	.284	.511
7	2	4	23	11	2	2	1	.338	.625
3	3	1	28	10	2	1	2	.300	.409
10	1	2	23	3	0	2	2	.440	.655
0	0	0	0	1	0	1	0	.333	.333

CAMPANELLA, ROY CONTINUED

YEAR	TEAM	G	AB	R	H
1945	Baltimore Elite Giants	9	31	8	9
	Career Totals:	**137**	**466**	**86**	**151**

CHARLESTON, OSCAR a.k.a. Charlie B: 10.14.1893 Indianapolis, IN

YEAR	TEAM	G	AB	R	H
1920	Indianapolis ABC's	44	168	21	46
1921	St. Louis Giants	44	163	50	71
1922	Indianapolis ABC's	54	224	49	91
1923	Indianapolis ABC's	84	308	68	112
1924	Harrisburg Giants	54	205	64	84
1925	Harrisburg Giants	68	240	95	107
1926	Harrisburg Giants43	152	37	45	11
1927	Harrisburg Giants32	118	31	43	9
1928	Hilldale Giants	60	212	57	74
1929	Hilldale Giants	50	200	38	63
1929	Hilldale Giants4	13	2	6	2
1930	Hilldale Giants	26	104	19	28
1931	Hilldale Giants	33	134	25	43
1932	Pittsburgh Crawfords	52	188	38	60
1933	Pittsburgh Crawfords	40	158	35	50
1934	Pittsburgh Crawfords	46	168	26	56
1935	Pittsburgh Crawfords	35	132	23	39
1936	Pittsburgh Crawfords	18	51	9	15
1937	Pittsburgh Crawfords	14	46	4	7
1939	Toledo Crawfords	9	33	4	10
1940	Indianapolis Crawfords	3	9	1	4
1941	Philadelphia Stars	1	1	1	0
	Career Totals:	**814**	**3027**	**697**	**1054**

DANDRIDGE, SR., RAYMOND EMMETT a.k.a. Ray B: 08.31.1913, Richmond, VA

YEAR	TEAM	G	AB	R	H
1933	Detroit Stars	12	46	3	9
1933	Nashville Elite Giants	2	2	0	0
1934	Newark Dodgers	32	119	20	48
1935	Newark Dodgers	29	112	11	29
1936	Newark Eagles	16	62	8	16
1937	Homestead Grays	2	8	1	3
1937	Newark Eagles	22	84	15	29
1938	Newark Eagles	27	109	24	42

D	T	HR	RBI	W	SAC	SB	E	AVG.	SLUG.
1	1	1	5	6	0	0	0	.290	.484
25	**8**	**14**	**107**	**39**	**6**	**7**	**13**	**.324**	**.502**

D: 10.5.1954, Philadelphia, Philadelphia County, PA B/T, L/L 6' 0, 190lbs.

D	T	HR	RBI	W	SAC	SB	E	AVG.	SLUG.
4	2	4	12	13	4	9	3	.274	.393
7	8	6	24	21	8	21	4	.436	.687
14	9	12	43	19	3	15	5	.406	.710
25	6	11	94	48	15	26	15	.364	.591
23	5	15	59	29	3	20	0	.410	.790
22	3	20	36	54	13	17	11	.446	.813
1	9	31	33	4	21	2	.296	.559	
4	8	30	21	7	6	4	.364	.712	
7	5	10	32	31	3	10	6	.349	.571
7	4	4	24	24	4	5	6	.315	.450
0	0	0	2	0	0	0	.462	.615	
8	1	4	11	15	2	3	1	.269	.481
7	3	2	3	11	0	2	4	.321	.463
12	3	4	14	26	1	14	12	.319	.479
7	3	5	33	11	1	4	2	.316	.494
6	3	5	25	17	1	2	4	.333	.494
7	1	5	17	16	4	7	5	.295	.477
4	0	3	9	9	1	0	1	.294	.549
1	0	1	3	2	0	0	1	.152	.239
2	0	0	0	3	0	0	1	.303	.364
0	0	0	2	1	0	0	0	.444	.444
0	0	0	0	2	0	0	0	.000	.000
185	**61**	**128**	**502**	**408**	**74**	**182**	**87**	**.348**	**.576**

D: 10.5.1954, Philadelphia, B/T, L/L 6' 0, 190lbs.

D	T	HR	RBI	W	SAC	SB	E	AVG.	SLUG.
0	2	0	6	1	2	0	4	.196	.283
0	0	0	0	2	0	0	3	.000	.000
8	3	0	4	4	0	0	5	.403	.521
7	3	0	3	2	0	5	2	.259	.375
0	0	1	4	5	0	4	4	.258	.306
0	0	0	1	0	0	1	0	.375	.375
2	0	0	2	4	0	1	1	.345	.369
3	0	1	9	4	1	1	3	.385	.440

DANDRIDGE, SR., RAYMOND EMMETT CONTINUED

YEAR	TEAM	G	AB	R	H
1942	Newark Eagles	23	80	10	15
1944	Newark Eagles	21	88	13	33
	Career Totals:	**186**	**710**	**105**	**224**

DAY, LEON

B: 10.30.1916, Alexandria, VA

YEAR	TEAM	G	AB	R	H
1934	Baltimore Black Sox	2	1	0	0
1935	Brooklyn Eagles	12	30	6	5
1936	Newark Eagles	6	11	2	5
1937	Homestead Grays	1	2	0	0
1937	Newark Eagles	8	15	4	6
1938	Newark Eagles	2	2	0	0
1939	Newark Eagles	11	28	2	8
1941	Newark Eagles	35	125	21	40
1942	Homestead Grays	1	4	0	1
1942	Newark Eagles	30	92	11	25
1943	Newark Eagles	20	70	8	15
1943	Philadelphia Stars	2	10	2	5
1946	Newark Eagles	18	35	10	13
	Career Totals:	**148**	**425**	**66**	**123**

DIHIGO YLLANOS, MARTIN MAGDALENO

B: 05.25.1906, Cidra, Matanzas, Cuba

YEAR	TEAM	G	AB	R	H
1923	Cuban Stars East	15	59	9	14
1924	Cuban Stars East	47	180	30	47
1925	Cuban Stars East	40	147	21	47
1926	Cuban Stars East	29	111	29	41
1927	Cuban Stars East	33	134	31	45
1927	Homestead Grays	1	4	1	1
1928	Homestead Grays	18	66	13	21
1929	Hilldale Giants	51	194	48	62
1930	Cuban Stars East	13	54	12	20
1930	Hilldale Giants	1	3	1	2
1931	Hilldale Giants	45	159	36	47
1935	New York Cubans	45	160	30	41
1936	New York Cubans	31	108	26	33
1945	New York Cubans	10	25	5	10
	Career Totals:	**379**	**1404**	**292**	**431**

	D	T	HR	RBI	W	SAC	SB	E	AVG.	SLUG.
	1	1	0	6	11	0	0	5	.188	.225
	8	2	1	18	5	0	3	6	.375	.545
	29	**11**	**3**	**53**	**38**	**3**	**15**	**33**	**.315**	**.400**
D: 03.13.1995, Baltimore, Baltimore City County, MD								B/T, R/R		5' 9, 180 lbs.
	0	0	0	0	0	0	0	0	.000	.000
	2	0	0	0	3	0	0	0	.167	.233
	0	0	0	0	0	0	0	0	.455	.455
	0	0	0	0	0	1	0	0	.000	.000
	1	0	0	1	1	0	1	0	.400	.467
	0	0	0	0	0	0	0	0	.000	.000
	0	2	0	2	1	1	0	0	.286	.429
	8	5	3	29	6	1	1	3	.320	.536
	1	0	0	0	0	0	0	0	.250	.500
	4	1	0	15	8	0	1	3	.272	.337
	2	1	0	6	3	2	2	3	.214	.271
	0	0	0	1	0	0	0	1	.500	.500
	1	0	1	5	7	0	0	0	.371	.486
	19	**9**	**4**	**59**	**29**	**5**	**5**	**10**	**.289**	**.405**
D: 05.20.1971, Cienfuegos, Cuba								B/T, R/R		6' 3.5, 190 lbs.
	2	1	0	10	0	0	0	2	.237	.305
	7	3	2	25	11	1	3	21	.261	.367
	8	1	3	9	17	6	3	15	.320	.449
	9	0	9	20	18	2	6	6	.369	.694
	7	1	9	31	12	0	5	8	.336	.604
	1	0	0	1	0	0	1	0	.250	.500
	1	1	4	10	6	1	0	5	.318	.545
	6	3	11	42	26	4	7	23	.320	.552
	4	1	4	12	2	2	1	4	.370	.704
	0	0	0	1	1	0	0	1	.667	.667
	0	4	7	21	13	1	1	2	.296	.478
	9	1	7	21	17	1	8	10	.256	.456
	6	1	7	19	14	2	5	6	.306	.574
	1	0	1	5	6	1	1	2	.400	.560
	61	**17**	**64**	**227**	**143**	**21**	**41**	**105**	**.307**	**.511**

DOBY, SR., LAWRENCE EUGENE a.k.a. Larry B: 12.13.1923, Camden, SC					
YEAR	**TEAM**	**G**	**AB**	**R**	**H**
1942	Newark Eagles	17	57	12	19
1943	Newark Eagles	19	71	8	17
1944	Newark Eagles	1	5	0	1
1946	Newark Eagles	43	164	39	55
1947	Newark Eagles	8	32	3	9
	Career Totals:	**88**	**329**	**62**	**101**

FOSTER, WILLIE HENDRICK a.k.a. Bill B: 06.12.1904, Calvert, TX					
1923	Chicago American Giants	2	3	1	1
1923	Memphis Red Sox	7	14	2	2
1924	Chicago American Giants	10	13	0	3
1924	Memphis Red Sox	1	3	0	0
1925	Birmingham Black Barons	1	2	0	1
1925	Chicago American Giants	11	23	2	5
1926	Chicago American Giants	33	72	3	13
1927	Chicago American Giants	43	89	13	21
1928	Chicago American Giants	33	91	9	20
1929	Chicago American Giants	27	50	10	12
1930	Chicago American Giants	31	65	5	17
1931	Homestead Grays	10	29	1	0
1931	Kansas City Monarchs	1	3	0	1
1932	Chicago American Giants	20	52	10	13
1933	Chicago American Giants	11	31	5	7
1934	Chicago American Giants	14	39	3	8
1935	Chicago American Giants	8	26	1	6
1936	Pittsburgh Crawfords	5	9	1	1
1937	Chicago American Giants	12	14	1	1
	Career Totals:	**280**	**628**	**67**	**132**

GIBSON, JOSHUA a.k.a. Josh B: 12.21.1911, Buena Vista, GA					
1930	Homestead Grays	21	71	13	24
1931	Homestead Grays	32	124	26	38
1932	Pittsburgh Crawfords	49	191	34	62
1933	Pittsburgh Crawfords	38	138	32	54
1934	Homestead Grays	1	2	0	1
1934	Pittsburgh Crawfords	52	190	39	62
1935	Pittsburgh Crawfords	35	145	37	54

D: 06/18/2003, Montclair, Essex County, NJ — B/T, L/R — 6'1, 180 lbs.

D	T	HR	RBI	W	SAC	SB	E	AVG.	SLUG.
3	2	0	9	5	0	1	2	.333	.456
2	0	3	7	13	2	2	10	.239	.394
0	0	0	0	1	0	0	0	.200	.200
8	6	5	37	25	1	5	7	.335	.549
1	1	1	11	4	1	1	3	.281	.469
14	**9**	**9**	**64**	**48**	**4**	**9**	**22**	**.307**	**.486**

D: 09.16.1978, Lorman, Jefferson County, MS — B/T, S/L — 6'1, 195 lbs.

D	T	HR	RBI	W	SAC	SB	E	AVG.	SLUG.
0	0	0	1	0	0	0	0	.333	.333
0	0	0	1	2	2	1	0	.143	.143
0	0	0	1	0	1	0	0	.231	.231
0	0	0	0	0	0	0	0	.000	.000
0	1	0	0	1	1	0	0	.500	1.500
0	1	0	0	1	3	0	1	.217	.304
2	0	0	1	5	8	0	1	.181	.208
4	1	0	4	6	3	0	6	.236	.303
3	0	0	2	3	5	0	3	.220	.253
2	0	0	2	4	2	1	1	.240	.280
3	0	0	2	3	3	0	1	.262	.308
0	0	0	0	0	2	0	1	.000	.000
0	0	0	1	0	0	1	0	.333	.333
0	3	1	5	2	3	0	1	.250	.423
0	1	1	3	1	0	0	0	.226	.387
0	0	0	0	0	1	0	1	.205	.205
0	0	0	0	1	0	0	0	.231	.231
0	0	0	0	0	2	0	1	.111	.111
1	0	0	1	1	3	0	0	.071	.143
15	**7**	**2**	**24**	**30**	**39**	**3**	**17**	**.210**	**.266**

D: 01.20.1947, Pittsburgh, Allegheny County, PA — B/T, R/R — 6'1.5, 220 lbs.

D	T	HR	RBI	W	SAC	SB	E	AVG.	SLUG.
2	0	5	17	5	0	0	3	.338	.577
8	5	6	23	11	0	0	2	.306	.597
10	5	8	28	21	0	0	4	.325	.555
6	2	8	31	9	1	1	2	.391	.638
0	0	0	0	0	0	0	0	.500	.500
14	3	11	27	19	2	2	6	.326	.605
10	2	8	29	16	0	7	3	.372	.634

GIBSON, JOSHUA CONTINUED

YEAR	TEAM	G	AB	R	H
1936	Pittsburgh Crawfords	26	90	27	39
1937	Homestead Grays	25	97	39	41
1938	Homestead Grays	28	105	31	38
1939	Homestead Grays	21	74	22	27
1940	Homestead Grays	1	2	1	0
1942	Homestead Grays	42	138	36	42
1943	Homestead Grays	55	192	69	91
1944	Homestead Grays	34	123	27	44
1945	Homestead Grays	17	62	12	17
1946	Homestead Grays	33	111	22	32
	Career Totals:	**510**	**1855**	**467**	**666**

IRVIN, MONFORD MERRILL a.k.a. Monte B: 02.25.1919, Halesburg, AL

YEAR	TEAM	G	AB	R	H
1938	Newark Eagles	2	4	0	0
1939	Newark Eagles	21	76	11	22
1940	Newark Eagles	35	131	26	46
1941	Newark Eagles	34	126	28	50
1942	Newark Eagles	4	18	7	11
1945	Newark Eagles	1	5	0	1
1946	Newark Eagles	40	149	34	57
1947	Newark Eagles	13	48	13	16
1948	Newark Eagles	9	30	6	7
	Career Totals:	**159**	**587**	**125**	**210**

JOHNSON, WILLIAM JULIUS a.k.a. Judy B: 10.26.1899, Snow Hill, MD

YEAR	TEAM	G	AB	R	H
1921	Hilldale Giants	29	105	13	28
1922	Hilldale Giants	12	45	5	9
1923	Hilldale Giants	53	191	26	55
1924	Hilldale Giants	80	307	58	106
1925	Hilldale Giants	72	275	59	104
1926	Hilldale Giants	89	344	65	113
1927	Hilldale Giants	59	222	29	55
1928	Hilldale Giants	60	221	21	51
1929	Hilldale Giants	51	210	54	81
1929	Homestead Grays	4	16	1	4
1930	Homestead Grays	27	112	16	33
1931	Hilldale Giants	50	179	23	44

D	T	HR	RBI	W	SAC	SB	E	AVG.	SLUG.
3	2	6	18	13	0	1	7	.433	.711
7	4	13	36	17	0	1	2	.423	.979
4	1	3	9	13	0	1	5	.362	.505
3	2	10	22	20	1	3	2	.365	.865
0	0	0	0	2	0	0	1	.000	.000
6	1	7	38	32	0	2	8	.304	.514
24	5	12	74	39	2	3	10	.474	.839
4	3	9	34	15	0	1	3	.358	.659
2	4	2	15	11	0	0	0	.274	.532
6	2	7	31	12	1	0	7	.288	.568
109	**41**	**115**	**432**	**255**	**7**	**22**	**65**	**.359**	**.648**
D: Living		B/T, R/R							6'1, 195 lbs.
0	0	0	0	0	0	0	1	.000	.000
2	1	2	11	7	0	0	6	.289	.421
9	4	3	36	12	1	2	9	.351	.550
11	1	5	36	10	8	7	2	.397	.619
3	1	1	11	0	0	0	0	.611	1.056
0	0	0	1	0	0	0	1	.200	.200
8	2	6	36	16	0	3	7	.383	.584
1	0	4	10	8	1	1	2	.333	.604
0	0	2	5	4	0	2	1	.233	.433
34	**9**	**23**	**146**	**57**	**10**	**15**	**29**	**.358**	**.564**
D: 06.15.1989, Wilmington, New Castle County, DE							B/T, R/R		5'11, 150 lbs.
2	5	2	3	3	3	2	5	.267	.438
0	1	0	1	2	1	2	3	.200	.244
6	1	2	44	4	1	3	19	.288	.361
27	6	5	55	22	9	10	16	.345	.521
17	11	5	23	23	8	7	16	.378	.575
21	6	1	46	22	14	12	18	.328	.433
5	2	1	15	18	2	2	8	.248	.302
9	4	1	23	7	3	2	9	.231	.321
11	1	5	32	16	5	10	9	.386	.519
0	0	0	0	0	0	0	2	.250	.250
3	3	0	1	6	1	1	3	.295	.375
2	3	1	5	3	1	3	6	.246	.307

YEAR	TEAM	G	AB	R	H
JOHNSON, WILLIAM JULIUS CONTINUED					
1932	Pittsburgh Crawfords	23	93	19	29
1933	Pittsburgh Crawfords	40	151	19	36
1934	Pittsburgh Crawfords	51	192	25	51
1935	Pittsburgh Crawfords	34	130	19	30
1936	Pittsburgh Crawfords	30	112	16	19
	Career Totals:	**784**	**2983**	**476**	**875**
LEONARD, WALTER FENNER a.k.a. Buck 09.08.1907, Rocky Mount, NC					
1934	Homestead Grays	20	79	16	28
1935	Homestead Grays	36	147	26	50
1936	Homestead Grays	17	62	15	15
1937	Homestead Grays	28	105	39	39
1938	Homestead Grays	27	99	21	33
1939	Homestead Grays	22	72	23	30
1940	Homestead Grays	44	152	40	60
1941	Homestead Grays	36	123	40	36
1942	Homestead Grays	26	87	10	18
1943	Homestead Grays	55	200	55	59
1944	Homestead Grays	34	121	30	34
1945	Homestead Grays	16	59	7	17
1946	Homestead Grays	30	102	18	27
1947	Homestead Grays	11	30	7	16
1948	Homestead Grays	10	34	5	9
	Career Totals:	**412**	**1472**	**352**	**471**
LLOYD, JOHN HENRY a.k.a. Pop B: 04.25.1884, Palatka, FL					
1920	Brooklyn Royal Giants	11	44	4	14
1921	Columbus Buckeyes	61	247	42	79
1922	N. Y. Bacharach Giants	26	111	17	31
1923	Hilldale Giants	37	144	30	50
1924	A. C. Bacharach Giants	55	203	36	74
1925	A. C. Bacharach Giants	60	217	42	72
1926	New York Lincoln Giants	46	169	26	61
1927	New York Lincoln Giants	20	77	14	24
1928	New York Lincoln Giants	31	122	28	49
1929	New York Lincoln Giants	35	131	29	49
1930	New York Lincoln Giants	42	156	27	58

	D	T	HR	RBI	W	SAC	SB	E	AVG.	SLUG.
	1	1	1	9	6	0	1	2	.312	.376
	5	0	0	14	6	1	2	4	.238	.272
	11	2	1	13	7	2	4	6	.266	.359
	6	1	2	9	6	0	1	4	.231	.338
	0	1	0	1	7	1	2	8	.170	.188
	126	**48**	**27**	**294**	**159**	**52**	**65**	**138**	**.293**	**.395**
D: 11.27.1997, Rocky Mount, Edgecombe County, NC							B/T, L/L		5'10, 185 lbs.	
	4	0	5	14	3	0	0	5	.354	.595
	10	1	3	10	15	1	3	6	.340	.483
	1	1	2	3	12	2	1	0	.242	.387
	8	1	7	17	20	0	1	3	.371	.667
	0	0	3	8	11	1	0	0	.333	.424
	5	0	5	23	17	9	2	1	.417	.694
	12	3	8	44	32	3	4	3	.395	.671
	4	5	8	29	30	3	6	1	.293	.602
	3	0	0	10	14	0	1	3	.207	.241
	11	7	4	41	38	8	2	10	.295	.480
	8	5	5	27	18	3	1	4	.281	.554
	1	2	0	7	7	0	0	1	.288	.373
	3	1	3	26	24	3	3	7	.265	.402
	0	0	4	8	8	0	1	0	.533	.933
	3	0	3	8	8	0	0	1	.265	.618
	73	**26**	**60**	**275**	**257**	**33**	**25**	**45**	**.320**	**.527**
D: 03.19.1965, Atlantic City, Atlantic County, NJ							B/T, L/R		5'11, 180 lbs.	
	0	0	1	3	2	0	0	1	.318	.386
	17	3	0	14	18	7	15	23	.320	.413
	6	0	1	6	6	3	2	6	.279	.360
	10	1	2	33	3	0	4	9	.347	.472
	11	2	1	43	18	4	7	13	.365	.453
	7	5	3	17	27	9	13	4	.332	.452
	7	3	1	7	24	5	5	9	.361	.456
	7	0	1	3	5	3	0	6	.312	.442
	4	1	5	12	9	3	4	2	.402	.574
	11	3	2	11	14	3	2	3	.374	.550
	5	1	1	11	11	7	6	2	.372	.436

YEAR	TEAM	G	AB	R	H
LLOYD, JOHN HENRY CONTINUED					
1932	N. Y. Bacharach Giants	5	19	4	6
	Career Totals:	**444**	**1692**	**304**	**580**
MAYS, JR., WILLIE HOWARD a.k.a. Buck B: 05.06.1931, Westfield, AL					
1948	Birmingham Black Barons	18	61	9	16
	Career Totals:	**18**	**61**	**9**	**16**
PAIGE, LEROY ROBERT a.k.a. Satchel B: 07.07.1906, Mobile, AL					
1927	Birmingham Black Barons	17	33	2	9
1928	Birmingham Black Barons	32	63	8	19
1929	Birmingham Black Barons	26	76	4	11
1930	Baltimore Black Sox	3	12	1	4
1930	Birmingham Black Barons	12	28	4	10
1931	Cleveland Cubs	5	6	1	1
1931	Pittsburgh Crawfords	1	3	0	2
1932	Pittsburgh Crawfords	17	43	4	9
1933	Pittsburgh Crawfords	10	27	2	2
1934	Pittsburgh Crawfords	20	59	3	9
1935	Kansas City Monarchs	2	3	0	0
1936	Pittsburgh Crawfords	7	24	7	7
1937	Trujillo All-Stars	2	3	0	1
1941	Kansas City Monarchs	9	20	1	4
1942	Kansas City Monarchs	13	29	1	4
1943	Kansas City Monarchs	17	29	3	10
1943	Memphis Red Sox	1	2	0	0
1944	Kansas City Monarchs	10	24	1	4
1945	Kansas City Monarchs	5	11	1	3
1946	Kansas City Monarchs	6	7	1	1
1947	Kansas City Monarchs	1	2	0	0
	Career Totals:	**216**	**504**	**44**	**110**
ROBINSON, JACK ROOSEVELT a.k.a. Cool Papa B: 01.31.1919, Cairo, GA					
1945	Kansas City Monarchs	14	53	11	23
	Career Totals:	**14**	**53**	**11**	**23**

	D	T	HR	RBI	W	SAC	SB	E	AVG.	SLUG.
	0	0	1	2	1	0	0	0	.316	.474
	86	**19**	**19**	**162**	**140**	**45**	**58**	**80**	**.343**	**.450**

D: Living **B/T, R/R** **5'11, 175 lbs.**

	D	T	HR	RBI	W	SAC	SB	E	AVG.	SLUG.
	2	0	0	12	12	0	0	3	.262	.295
	2	**0**	**0**	**12**	**12**	**0**	**0**	**3**	**.262**	**.295**

D: 06.08.1982, Kansas City, Jackson County, MO **B/T, R/R** **6'3.5, 180 lbs.**

	D	T	HR	RBI	W	SAC	SB	E	AVG.	SLUG.
	0	2	0	1	0	1	0	0	.273	.394
	0	3	0	4	0	0	0	3	.302	.397
	1	1	0	2	1	5	0	0	.145	.184
	1	0	0	0	0	0	0	0	.333	.417
	1	0	0	1	1	1	2	0	.357	.393
	0	0	0	0	0	1	0	0	.167	.167
	0	0	0	0	0	0	0	0	.667	.667
	3	0	1	3	0	1	0	0	.209	.349
	0	0	0	1	0	0	1	0	.074	.074
	1	1	0	3	0	2	1	3	.153	.203
	0	0	0	0	0	0	0	0	.000	.000
	1	0	0	0	0	1	0	1	.292	.333
	0	0	0	0	0	0	0	1	.333	.333
	0	0	0	2	1	0	0	1	.200	.200
	0	0	0	0	0	0	0	0	.138	.138
	1	0	0	2	0	1	1	1	.345	.379
	0	0	0	0	0	0	0	0	.000	.000
	0	1	0	2	0	1	0	0	.167	.250
	1	0	0	0	0	0	0	1	.273	.364
	0	0	0	0	0	1	0	0	.143	.143
	0	0	0	0	0	1	0	0	.000	.000
	10	**8**	**1**	**21**	**3**	**16**	**5**	**11**	**.218**	**.276**

D: 10.24.1972, Stamford, Fairfield County, CT **B/T, R/R** **5'11.5, 195 lbs.**

	D	T	HR	RBI	W	SAC	SB	E	AVG.	SLUG.
	7	1	1	15	8	0	1	3	.434	.660
	7	**1**	**1**	**15**	**8**	**0**	**1**	**3**	**.434**	**.660**

ROGAN, CHARLES WILBER(N) a.k.a. Bullet B: 07.28.1893, Oklahoma City, OK					
YEAR	**TEAM**	**G**	**AB**	**R**	**H**
1920	Kansas City Monarchs	37	145	12	43
1921	Kansas City Monarchs	66	199	25	57
1922	Kansas City Monarchs	62	200	40	78
1923	Kansas City Monarchs	68	209	39	76
1924	Kansas City Monarchs	60	195	36	77
1925	Kansas City Monarchs	56	139	20	53
1926	Kansas City Monarchs	57	147	26	45
1927	Kansas City Monarchs	56	116	18	38
1928	Kansas City Monarchs	64	201	40	70
1929	Kansas City Monarchs	71	256	64	92
1930	Kansas City Monarchs	29	107	26	32
1933	Kansas City Monarchs	7	19	5	6
1934	Kansas City Monarchs	7	27	2	2
1935	Kansas City Monarchs	2	6	0	1
1936	Kansas City Monarchs	2	2	1	1
1937	Kansas City Monarchs	16	30	4	8
1938	Kansas City Monarchs	12	24	5	5
	Career Totals:	**672**	**2022**	**363**	**684**
SMITH, HILTON LEE a.k.a. Smitty B: 02.27.1907, Sour Lake, TX					
1932	Monroe Monarchs	2	3	0	0
1937	Kansas City Monarchs	23	49	4	14
1938	Kansas City Monarchs	16	37	4	14
1939	Kansas City Monarchs	16	35	3	6
1940	Kansas City Monarchs	13	21	1	7
1941	Kansas City Monarchs	10	22	4	9
1942	Kansas City Monarchs	13	33	5	10
1943	Kansas City Monarchs	12	24	4	4
1944	Kansas City Monarchs	7	8	0	2
1945	Kansas City Monarchs	7	11	2	4
1946	Kansas City Monarchs	12	21	6	9
1947	Kansas City Monarchs	7	16	2	3
1948	Kansas City Monarchs	2	2	0	1
	Career Totals:	**140**	**282**	**35**	**83**
STEARNES, NORMAN THOMAS a.k.a. Turkey B: 05.08.1901, Nashville, TN					
1920	Knoxville Giants	3	11	0	3

D	T	HR	RBI	W	SAC	SB	E	AVG.	SLUG.
D: 03.04.1967, Kansas City, Jackson County, MO							B/T, R/R	5'7, 170 lbs.	
5	8	0	6	8	3	8	2	.297	.441
9	7	4	13	23	5	19	8	.286	.462
10	6	13	33	30	6	15	1	.390	.695
12	3	7	45	20	4	5	2	.364	.550
11	6	5	51	16	2	8	7	.395	.590
7	8	2	11	15	6	5	0	.381	.590
8	3	1	8	24	7	2	8	.306	.422
3	3	2	9	21	3	1	3	.328	.457
14	5	3	22	18	4	5	6	.348	.512
15	9	7	33	40	7	26	7	.359	.570
6	0	0	5	17	4	5	4	.299	.355
0	0	1	5	3	0	2	0	.316	.474
1	0	0	0	1	0	0	0	.074	.111
0	0	0	0	0	0	0	0	.167	.167
0	0	0	2	1	0	0	2	.500	.500
2	1	0	6	4	2	2	1	.267	.400
1	0	0	2	2	1	1	0	.208	.250
104	**59**	**45**	**251**	**243**	**54**	**104**	**51**	**.338**	**.515**
D: 11.18.1983, Kansas City, Jackson County, MO							B/T, R/R	5'11, 185 lbs.	
0	0	0	0	0	1	0	0	.000	.000
1	0	1	2	2	2	1	4	.286	.367
6	0	0	3	0	0	0	0	.378	.541
0	1	0	1	1	2	0	0	.171	.229
2	1	0	2	0	0	0	1	.333	.524
3	0	0	6	1	1	0	0	.409	.545
3	0	0	9	1	0	0	0	.303	.394
1	0	0	0	0	0	0	0	.167	.208
0	0	0	1	0	0	0	0	.250	.250
1	0	0	4	0	0	0	0	.364	.455
1	0	0	8	1	1	0	1	.429	.476
0	0	1	2	1	0	0	0	.188	.375
1	0	0	0	0	0	0	0	.500	1.000
19	**2**	**2**	**38**	**7**	**7**	**1**	**6**	**.294**	**.397**
D: 09.04.1979, Detroit, Wayne County, MI							B/T, L/L	6'0, 175 lbs.	
1	0	0	0	0	0	0	0	.273	.364

STEARNES, NORMAN THOMAS CONTINUED

YEAR	TEAM	G	AB	R	H
1920	Nashville White Sox	3	12	1	2
1923	Detroit Stars	69	279	70	101
1924	Detroit Stars	55	221	50	77
1925	Detroit Stars	91	354	45	129
1926	Detroit Stars	86	316	25	123
1927	Detroit Stars	83	307	58	108
1928	Detroit Stars	81	318	81	102
1929	Detroit Stars	64	241	60	97
1930	Detroit Stars	34	126	17	40
1930	New York Lincoln Giants	18	72	28	27
1931	Detroit Stars	32	117	25	45
1931	Kansas City Monarchs	12	40	4	2
1932	Chicago American Giants	45	172	43	55
1933	Chicago American Giants	24	109	26	35
1934	Chicago American Giants	46	187	50	64
1935	Chicago American Giants	37	127	35	56
1936	Philadelphia Stars	36	147	30	44
1937	Chicago American Giants	6	26	4	6
1937	Detroit Stars	13	45	9	14
1938	Chicago American Giants	17	69	13	21
1938	Kansas City Monarchs	8	31	4	7
1939	Kansas City Monarchs	29	101	21	30
1940	Kansas City Monarchs	25	86	14	23
	Career Totals:	**917**	**3514**	**713**	**1211**

WELLS, WILLIE JAMES a.k.a. Devil, Chico B: 08.10.1906, Austin, TX

YEAR	TEAM	G	AB	R	H
1924	St. Louis Stars	38	148	24	46
1925	St. Louis Stars	70	270	60	75
1926	St. Louis Stars	53	183	35	60
1927	St. Louis Stars	65	243	54	81
1928	St. Louis Stars	81	324	84	117
1929	Chicago American Giants	4	14	4	8
1929	St. Louis Stars	62	229	63	77
1930	St. Louis Stars	46	181	60	76
1931	St. Louis Stars	12	42	7	14
1932	Detroit Wolves	21	85	13	24
1932	Homestead Grays	10	39	5	10
1932	Kansas City Monarchs	14	52	12	13

	D	T	HR	RBI	W	SAC	SB	E	AVG.	SLUG.
	0	1	0	0	1	0	0	0	.167	.333
	18	14	17	85	17	2	2	5	.362	.710
	7	10	8	60	19	3	1	3	.348	.579
	24	11	19	60	44	2	11	10	.364	.655
	30	8	19	62	37	9	16	8	.389	.715
	23	12	19	66	42	6	12	17	.352	.691
	16	7	24	85	30	7	6	7	.321	.642
	16	4	16	51	36	7	12	6	.402	.701
	9	9	2	15	13	2	6	2	.317	.579
	3	4	6	29	11	0	8	1	.375	.778
	8	1	9	20	14	0	6	4	.385	.701
	0	2	0	2	3	0	1	1	.050	.150
	9	3	5	17	24	2	11	4	.320	.494
	10	2	5	31	7	0	0	3	.321	.587
	5	7	10	29	15	0	10	1	.342	.604
	8	4	6	27	23	1	7	6	.441	.709
	2	1	7	22	13	0	1	2	.299	.469
	1	0	1	4	4	1	0	0	.231	.385
	2	1	1	8	4	0	1	0	.311	.467
	4	1	2	10	5	0	6	1	.304	.478
	0	2	0	1	2	1	2	1	.226	.355
	4	0	3	12	10	4	8	1	.297	.426
	3	1	4	22	14	0	2	2	.267	.465
	203	**105**	**183**	**718**	**388**	**47**	**129**	**85**	**.345**	**.618**
D: 01.22.1989, Austin, Travis County, TX								B/T, R/R	5'8, 170 lbs.	
	12	3	1	28	10	1	0	15	.311	.453
	14	7	6	10	42	9	8	19	.278	.448
	11	3	7	20	36	4	3	9	.328	.536
	14	1	16	44	31	8	5	10	.333	.597
	28	6	22	61	31	7	13	24	.361	.688
	2	1	0	0	1	0	1	2	.571	.857
	9	3	19	58	41	9	15	6	.336	.651
	18	0	10	29	26	3	7	6	.420	.685
	3	1	0	1	9	2	5	2	.333	.452
	5	1	0	6	5	0	2	5	.282	.365
	1	1	2	4	3	0	0	3	.256	.487
	2	3	0	8	9	2	1	1	.250	.404

WELLS, WILLIE JAMES CONTINUED

YEAR	TEAM	G	AB	R	H
1933	Chicago American Giants	21	94	20	28
1934	Chicago American Giants	44	163	25	32
1935	Chicago American Giants	37	146	44	52
1936	Newark Eagles	15	58	14	15
1937	Homestead Grays	2	10	1	0
1937	Newark Eagles	20	77	22	27
1938	Newark Eagles	28	101	19	33
1939	Newark Eagles	22	86	18	17
1941	Birmingham Black Barons	1	1	0	0
1942	Newark Eagles	33	127	34	49
1945	New York Black Yankees	10	36	5	12
1945	Newark Eagles	6	21	4	3
1946	Baltimore Elite Giants	28	104	10	34
1946	New York Black Yankees	7	26	1	5
1947	Indianapolis Clowns	3	11	1	5
1948	Memphis Red Sox	3	8	5	5
	Career Totals:	**756**	**2879**	**644**	**918**

WILLIAMS, JOSEPH a.k.a. Smokey Joe, Cyclone B: 04.06.1886, Seguin, TX

YEAR	TEAM	G	AB	R	H
1920	New York Lincoln Giants	1	4	0	1
1923	New York Lincoln Giants	14	25	4	10
1924	Brooklyn Royal Giants	19	43	1	11
1925	Homestead Grays	1	2	1	0
1925	New York Lincoln Giants	7	12	0	2
1927	Homestead Grays	2	5	0	3
1928	Homestead Grays	3	7	2	2
1929	Homestead Grays	10	29	5	5
1930	Homestead Grays	10	31	6	7
1931	Homestead Grays	9	26	3	6
1932	Detroit Wolves	4	8	2	2
1932	Homestead Grays	7	21	3	6
1932	Pittsburgh Crawfords	1	2	1	0
	Career Totals:	**88**	**215**	**28**	**55**

D	T	HR	RBI	W	SAC	SB	E	AVG.	SLUG.
3	0	0	19	4	0	5	2	.298	.330
7	3	0	2	16	0	9	7	.196	.276
10	3	4	16	21	2	11	4	.356	.548
0	0	2	3	5	2	0	4	.259	.362
0	0	0	1	0	0	0	0	.000	.000
3	1	2	9	6	0	2	3	.351	.494
3	3	2	9	8	3	4	2	.327	.475
1	0	1	3	11	2	2	2	.198	.244
0	0	0	0	0	0	0	0	.000	.000
8	0	3	29	13	1	3	7	.386	.520
5	0	0	7	5	2	1	2	.333	.472
1	0	0	3	2	0	0	0	.143	.190
9	1	1	23	6	0	0	3	.327	.462
0	0	0	2	4	0	1	3	.192	.192
0	1	0	3	1	0	0	1	.455	.636
2	1	0	1	1	0	0	0	.625	1.125
171	**43**	**98**	**399**	**347**	**57**	**98**	**142**	**.319**	**.510**

D: 02.25.1951, New York, New York County, NY B/T, R/R 6'4, 190 lbs.

D	T	HR	RBI	W	SAC	SB	E	AVG.	SLUG.
0	0	0	0	0	0	0	0	.250	.250
1	0	1	10	1	1	0	2	.400	.560
3	0	1	6	3	1	0	2	.256	.395
0	0	0	0	2	0	0	0	.000	.000
0	0	0	0	0	1	0	0	.167	.167
2	0	0	2	0	0	0	0	.600	1.000
0	0	0	0	1	0	0	0	.286	.286
1	0	0	0	2	1	0	1	.172	.207
0	1	0	1	1	0	1	1	.226	.290
0	0	0	1	2	0	0	2	.231	.231
0	0	0	2	1	1	1	0	.250	.250
1	0	0	1	1	0	0	0	.286	.333
0	0	0	0	0	0	0	0	.000	.000
8	**1**	**2**	**23**	**14**	**5**	**2**	**8**	**.256**	**.330**

PLAYER STATS

BELL, JAMES THOMAS a.k.a. Cool Papa B: 05.17.1903, Starkville, MS

YEAR	TEAM	G	GS	CG	IP	HA	RS
1922	St. Louis Stars	12	10	8	92.7	86	52
1923	St. Louis Stars	25	14	9	153.7	180	100
1924	St. Louis Stars	7	4	4	44.0	42	31
1929	St. Louis Stars	1	0	0	1.0	1	0
1944	Homestead Grays	1	0	0	2.0	1	1
	Career Totals:	**46**	**28**	**21**	**293.3**	**310**	**184**

CAMPANELLA, ROY a.k.a. Campy B: 11.19.1921 Philadelphia, PA

YEAR	TEAM	G	GS	CG	IP	HA	RS
1945	Baltimore Elite Giants	1	1	1	9.0	5	6

CHARLESTON, OSCAR a.k.a. Charlie B: 10.14.1893 Indianapolis, IN

YEAR	TEAM	G	GS	CG	IP	HA	RS
1920	Indianapolis ABC's	3	1	0	12.0	17	11
1921	St. Louis Giants	2	0	0	4.7	13	8
1923	Indianapolis ABC's	5	3	1	29.7	31	19
1926	Harrisburg Giants	2	1	1	13.3	11	11
1927	Harrisburg Giants	1	0	0	4.3	13	9
1932	Pittsburgh Crawfords	1	0	0	1.0	0	0
1933	Pittsburgh Crawfords	1	0	0	4.3	2	2
	Career Totals:	**15**	**5**	**2**	**69.3**	**87**	**60**

DAY, LEON B: 10.30.1916, Alexandria, VA

YEAR	TEAM	G	GS	CG	IP	HA	RS
1934	Baltimore Black Sox	1	1	0	1.3	6	7
1935	Brooklyn Eagles	16	12	7	105.7	92	48
1936	Newark Eagles	6	6	3	34.3	31	24
1937	Homestead Grays	1	1	0	4.7	9	7
1937	Newark Eagles	7	4	2	35.3	38	22
1938	Newark Eagles	2	2	0	5.3	11	8
1939	Newark Eagles	12	11	7	85.0	73	46
1941	Newark Eagles	2	2	0	13.3	16	11
1942	Homestead Grays	1	1	1	9.0	5	1
1942	Newark Eagles	10	7	7	68.0	31	17
1943	Newark Eagles	9	6	2	45.0	42	29
1946	Newark Eagles	16	13	10	106.0	85	38
	Career Totals:	**83**	**66**	**39**	**513.0**	**439**	**258**

PITCHING

ER	RPG	ERA	K	BB	WP	HB	SO	SV	WIN	LOSS	PCT
D: 03/07/1991, St. Louis, St. Louis County, MO						B/T, S/L			5'11.5, 150 lbs.		
31	5.05	3.01	49	34	0	3	1	0	6	5	.545
75	5.86	4.39	66	34	4	7	0	0	11	7	.611
13	6.34	2.66	19	16	0	0	0	0	3	1	.750
0	0.00	0.00	0	0	0	0	0	0	0	0	.000
0	4.50	0.00	0	0	0	0	0	0	0	0	.000
119	**5.65**	**3.65**	**134**	**84**	**4**	**10**	**1**	**0**	**20**	**13**	**0.606**
D: 06.26.1993, Woodland Hills, Los Angeles County, CA						B/T, R/R				5' 9, 200 lbs.	
3	6.00	3.00	13	3	0	1	0	0	1	0	1.000
D: 10.5.1954, Philadelphia, Philadelphia County, PA						B/T, L/L				6' 0, 190lbs.	
7	8.25	5.25	6	8	1	0	0	0	0	0	.000
8	15.43	15.43	2	1	0	0	0	0	0	0	.000
15	5.76	4.55	7	13	2	1	0	0	1	2	.333
9	7.43	6.08	6	8	0	2	0	0	0	2	.000
6	18.69	12.46	0	0	0	0	0	0	0	0	.000
0	0.00	0.00	0	0	0	0	0	0	0	0	.000
2	4.15	4.15	1	4	0	0	0	0	0	0	.000
47	**7.79**	**6.10**	**22**	**34**	**3**	**3**	**0**	**0**	**1**	**4**	**0.200**
D: 03.13.1995, Baltimore, Baltimore City County, MD						B/T, R/R			5' 9, 180 lbs.		
5	47.25	33.75	1	1	0	2	0	0	0	0	.000
32	4.09	2.73	39	23	0	1	0	2	7	3	.700
20	6.29	5.24	16	10	1	1	0	0	1	4	.200
4	13.50	7.71	5	1	0	0	0	0	0	0	.000
18	5.60	4.58	19	13	0	0	0	2	4	0	1.000
5	13.50	8.44	0	2	0	0	0	0	0	2	.000
24	4.87	2.54	21	37	0	1	1	0	6	2	.750
6	7.43	4.05	9	7	0	0	0	0	1	1	.500
1	1.00	1.00	14	1	0	0	0	0	1	0	1.000
10	2.25	1.32	59	16	0	0	1	0	6	3	.667
22	5.80	4.40	32	12	0	0	0	0	3	2	.600
23	3.23	1.95	73	31	0	2	2	2	8	2	.800
170	**4.53**	**2.98**	**288**	**154**	**1**	**7**	**4**	**6**	**37**	**19**	**0.661**

YEAR	TEAM	G	GS	CG	IP	HA	RS
DIHIGO YLLANOS, MARTIN MAGDALENO B: 05.25.1906, Cidra, Matanzas, Cuba							
1923	Cuban Stars East	3	2	1	19.7	22	11
1924	Cuban Stars East	9	4	3	49.0	43	17
1925	Cuban Stars East	10	8	7	73.0	69	28
1926	Cuban Stars East	2	1	1	11.7	5	1
1927	Cuban Stars East	1	1	0	2.0	0	0
1928	Homestead Grays	2	2	2	17.0	27	14
1929	Hilldale Giants	6	4	4	36.0	25	15
1931	Hilldale Giants	2	2	2	18.0	19	9
1935	New York Cubans	9	5	4	52.7	44	25
1936	New York Cubans	7	5	4	45.3	40	22
1945	New York Cubans	4	3	2	29.7	24	15
	Career Totals:	**55**	**37**	**30**	**354.0**	**318**	**157**
FOSTER, WILLIE HENDRICK a.k.a. Bill B: 06.12.1904, Calvert, TX							
1923	Chicago American Giants	3	2	0	8.0	6	7
1923	Memphis Red Sox	7	6	5	43.7	26	13
1924	Chicago American Giants	10	7	3	42.3	35	17
1924	Memphis Red Sox	1	1	1	9.0	1	0
1925	Birmingham Black Barons	1	1	1	9.0	1	0
1925	Chicago American Giants	11	8	4	69.0	56	20
1926	Chicago American Giants	34	23	17	226.3	166	63
1927	Chicago American Giants	28	22	20	202.3	172	68
1928	Chicago American Giants	36	26	24	251.0	232	95
1929	Chicago American Giants	28	20	17	176.3	146	66
1930	Chicago American Giants	30	17	15	180.3	162	80
1931	Homestead Grays	10	8	8	80.0	62	30
1931	Kansas City Monarchs	1	1	1	7.0	3	1
1932	Chicago American Giants	23	18	17	165.0	145	57
1933	Chicago American Giants	19	14	10	123.0	73	43
1934	Chicago American Giants	17	11	8	97.0	87	38
1935	Chicago American Giants	13	8	5	84.3	66	51
1936	Pittsburgh Crawfords	5	3	1	21.7	23	19
1937	Chicago American Giants	14	8	2	64.3	57	26
	Career Totals:	**291**	**204**	**159**	**1859.7**	**1519**	**694**
JOHNSON, WILLIAM JULIUS a.k.a. Judy B: 10.26.1899, Snow Hill, MD							
1926	Hilldale Giants	1	0	0	4.3	6	2

D: 05.20.1971, Cienfuegos, Cuba B/T, R/R 6' 3.5, 190 lbs.

	ER	RPG	ERA	K	BB	WP	HB	SO	SV	WIN	LOSS	PCT
	7	5.03	3.20	7	0	0	0	0	0	2	1	.667
	13	3.12	2.39	24	11	0	2	0	1	3	3	.500
	25	3.45	3.08	27	26	2	0	0	1	4	4	.500
	1	0.77	0.77	6	1	0	2	0	0	2	0	1.000
	0	0.00	0.00	0	0	0	0	0	0	0	0	.000
	3	7.41	1.59	14	4	0	0	0	0	1	1	.500
	15	3.75	3.75	11	4	0	0	0	0	4	1	.800
	9	4.50	4.50	11	0	0	0	0	0	1	1	.500
	18	4.27	3.08	35	16	0	0	0	0	4	3	.571
	14	4.37	2.78	25	13	0	0	0	0	4	3	.571
	10	4.55	3.03	16	5	0	0	0	0	1	2	.333
	115	**3.99**	**2.92**	**176**	**80**	**2**	**4**	**0**	**2**	**26**	**19**	**0.578**

D: 09.16.1978, Lorman, Jefferson County, MS B/T, S/L 6'1, 195 lbs.

	ER	RPG	ERA	K	BB	WP	HB	SO	SV	WIN	LOSS	PCT
	5	7.88	5.63	4	4	0	0	0	0	0	0	.000
	9	2.68	1.85	34	10	0	0	1	0	4	2	.667
	9	3.61	1.91	25	17	0	1	2	0	4	1	.800
	0	0.00	0.00	14	3	0	0	1	0	1	0	1.000
	0	0.00	0.00	4	3	0	0	1	0	1	0	1.000
	20	2.61	2.61	45	18	0	1	1	0	5	0	1.000
	51	2.51	2.03	128	80	0	3	7	2	16	6	.727
	51	3.02	2.27	110	65	1	6	4	1	18	6	.750
	77	3.41	2.76	140	72	5	7	3	3	17	11	.607
	57	3.37	2.91	77	44	1	2	5	3	14	7	.667
	64	3.99	3.19	135	55	3	2	1	3	13	9	.591
	20	3.38	2.25	58	19	2	1	1	0	7	2	.778
	1	1.29	1.29	12	4	1	0	0	0	1	0	1.000
	32	3.11	1.75	95	24	1	1	2	2	14	5	.737
	24	3.15	1.76	48	19	0	6	2	2	10	5	.667
	26	3.53	2.41	40	25	1	5	1	0	7	5	.583
	20	5.44	2.13	16	30	0	0	2	0	4	6	.400
	12	7.89	4.98	6	5	0	1	0	1	1	2	.333
	17	3.64	2.38	22	19	1	0	1	0	6	2	.750
	495	**3.36**	**2.40**	**1013**	**516**	**16**	**36**	**35**	**17**	**143**	**69**	**0.675**

D: 06.15.1989, Wilmington, New Castle County, DE B/T, R/R 5'11, 150 lbs.

	ER	RPG	ERA	K	BB	WP	HB	SO	SV	WIN	LOSS	PCT
	1	4.15	2.08	2	2	0	1	0	0	0	0	.000

PAIGE, LEROY ROBERT a.k.a. Satchel B: 07.07.1906, Mobile, AL

YEAR	TEAM	G	GS	CG	IP	HA	RS
1927	Birmingham Black Barons	18	9	5	89.3	69	33
1928	Birmingham Black Barons	26	16	11	134.3	109	44
1929	Birmingham Black Barons	30	19	15	188.3	188	103
1930	Baltimore Black Sox	4	4	3	31.0	35	12
1930	Birmingham Black Barons	14	10	9	96.3	74	35
1931	Cleveland Cubs	6	4	1	32.7	26	12
1931	Pittsburgh Crawfords	1	1	1	8.0	5	3
1932	Pittsburgh Crawfords	22	16	12	132.7	92	47
1933	Pittsburgh Crawfords	13	12	8	95.0	54	39
1934	Pittsburgh Crawfords	22	16	15	154.0	103	37
1935	Kansas City Monarchs	2	2	1	9.0	5	0
1936	Pittsburgh Crawfords	7	5	5	47.7	41	17
1937	Trujillo All-Stars	2	1	1	11.0	16	5
1940	Kansas City Monarchs	2	1	1	11.0	6	1
1941	Kansas City Monarchs	12	11	2	55.0	42	21
1941	New York Black Yankees	1	1	1	9.0	5	3
1942	Kansas City Monarchs	18	15	5	95.0	68	30
1943	Kansas City Monarchs	23	20	3	102.0	90	52
1943	Memphis Red Sox	1	1	0	5.0	0	0
1944	Kansas City Monarchs	14	14	5	82.7	51	18
1945	Kansas City Monarchs	11	9	2	51.7	48	29
1946	Kansas City Monarchs	11	7	2	47.0	40	11
1947	Kansas City Monarchs	3	3	2	19.0	7	2
	Career Totals:	**263**	**197**	**110**	**1506.7**	**1174**	**554**

ROGAN, CHARLES WILBER(N) a.k.a. Bullet B: 07.28.1893, Oklahoma City, OK

YEAR	TEAM	G	GS	CG	IP	HA	RS
1920	Kansas City Monarchs	9	9	8	79.7	67	32
1921	Kansas City Monarchs	22	20	20	181.0	150	68
1922	Kansas City Monarchs	19	14	13	131.3	117	61
1923	Kansas City Monarchs	33	23	19	239.7	209	110
1924	Kansas City Monarchs	27	25	21	204.0	181	94
1925	Kansas City Monarchs	24	18	17	171.3	137	44
1926	Kansas City Monarchs	24	14	13	158.0	145	64
1927	Kansas City Monarchs	27	14	13	144.7	134	49
1928	Kansas City Monarchs	17	10	8	114.3	122	47
1929	Kansas City Monarchs	2	1	0	9.3	10	3
1933	Kansas City Monarchs	1	1	0	1.3	4	3
1935	Kansas City Monarchs	1	0	0	3.0	5	3

D: 06.08.1982, Kansas City, Jackson County, MO **B/T, R/R** **6'3.5, 180 lbs.**

ER	RPG	ERA	K	BB	WP	HB	SO	SV	WIN	LOSS	PCT
21	3.32	2.12	69	26	0	2	2	1	7	1	.875
30	2.95	2.01	112	21	3	2	2	4	12	5	.706
78	4.92	3.73	176	31	6	2	0	2	10	9	.526
8	3.48	2.32	17	6	0	0	1	0	3	1	.750
28	3.27	2.62	69	9	2	1	2	1	7	4	.636
9	3.31	2.48	18	4	0	0	1	0	1	2	.333
2	3.38	2.25	0	1	0	0	0	0	0	1	.000
25	3.19	1.70	92	35	0	3	4	2	10	4	.714
20	3.69	1.89	55	12	0	0	0	0	5	7	.417
24	2.16	1.40	144	26	0	2	5	0	14	2	.875
0	0.00	0.00	11	1	0	0	1	0	0	0	.000
11	3.21	2.08	47	9	0	0	1	0	5	0	1.000
5	4.09	4.09	11	1	0	0	0	0	0	1	.000
0	0.82	0.00	8	0	0	0	0	0	1	0	1.000
10	3.44	1.64	42	6	1	1	0	0	4	0	1.000
0	3.00	0.00	8	0	0	0	0	0	1	0	1.000
19	2.84	1.80	79	11	1	1	1	0	4	5	.444
30	4.59	2.65	74	22	0	1	0	1	6	8	.429
0	0.00	0.00	7	2	0	0	0	0	1	0	1.000
5	1.96	0.54	76	13	1	0	2	0	4	5	.444
6	5.05	1.05	54	14	2	0	1	0	2	4	.333
6	2.11	1.15	45	3	0	0	1	0	5	1	.833
1	0.95	0.47	17	0	1	0	1	0	1	1	.500
338	**3.31**	**2.02**	**1231**	**253**	**17**	**15**	**25**	**11**	**103**	**61**	**0.628**

D: 03.04.1967, Kansas City, Jackson County, MO **B/T, R/R** **5'7, 170 lbs.**

20	3.62	2.26	68	27	2	0	0	0	5	3	.625
45	3.38	2.24	102	57	5	1	3	1	12	8	.600
29	4.18	1.99	80	27	0	1	1	1	8	6	.571
76	4.13	2.85	146	74	9	5	4	3	16	10	.615
61	4.15	2.69	115	66	2	1	1	0	18	6	.750
44	2.31	2.31	102	25	0	0	5	3	17	2	.895
56	3.65	3.19	77	41	1	1	0	1	16	5	.762
37	3.05	2.30	102	29	1	0	3	3	13	7	.650
38	3.70	2.99	54	14	5	2	0	2	10	2	.833
3	2.89	2.89	3	0	0	0	0	0	0	1	.000
2	20.25	13.50	0	0	0	0	0	0	0	0	.000
0	9.00	0.00	1	0	0	0	0	0	1	0	1.000

ROGAN, CHARLES WILBER(N) CONTINUED							
YEAR	**TEAM**	**G**	**GS**	**CG**	**IP**	**HA**	**RS**
1937	Kansas City Monarchs	2	1	0	5.7	5	9
1938	Kansas City Monarchs	1	0	0	1.0	0	0
	Career Totals:	**209**	**150**	**132**	**1444.3**	**1286**	**587**
SMITH, HILTON LEE a.k.a. Smitty B: 02.27.1907, Sour Lake, TX							
1932	Monroe Monarchs	2	2	0	14.3	12	8
1937	Kansas City Monarchs	19	12	6	109.0	84	31
1938	Kansas City Monarchs	17	9	5	87.7	71	24
1939	Kansas City Monarchs	19	10	7	106.0	79	37
1940	Kansas City Monarchs	12	6	4	53.0	51	31
1941	Kansas City Monarchs	15	8	5	78.3	49	20
1942	Kansas City Monarchs	12	6	4	76.3	74	40
1943	Kansas City Monarchs	8	5	3	46.0	34	14
1944	Kansas City Monarchs	8	4	2	37.3	32	18
1945	Kansas City Monarchs	7	6	6	50.7	51	25
1946	Kansas City Monarchs	15	9	6	84.3	64	21
1947	Kansas City Monarchs	7	5	5	49.0	57	26
1948	Kansas City Monarchs	5	1	0	20.3	16	9
	Career Totals:	**146**	**83**	**53**	**812.3**	**674**	**304**
STEARNES, NORMAN THOMAS a.k.a. Turkey B: 05.08.1901, Nashville, TN							
1923	Detroit Stars	1	1	0	7.0	13	14
WELLS, WILLIE JAMES a.k.a. Devil, Chico B: 08.10.1906, Austin, TX							
1945	Newark Eagles	1	0	0	0.7	0	0
WILLIAMS, JOSEPH a.k.a. Smokey Joe, Cyclone B: 04.06.1886, Seguin, TX							
1920	New York Lincoln Giants	2	2	2	17.0	15	9
1921	New York Lincoln Giants	4	2	2	20.0	21	9
1923	New York Lincoln Giants	11	9	6	73.0	84	55
1924	Brooklyn Royal Giants	15	12	8	96.3	107	54
1925	Homestead Grays	1	1	1	9.0	6	3
1925	New York Lincoln Giants	5	2	0	26.7	34	17
1927	Cleveland Hornets	1	1	1	9.0	3	0
1928	Homestead Grays	3	2	1	15.7	16	8

ER	RPG	ERA	K	BB	WP	HB	SO	SV	WIN	LOSS	PCT
5	14.29	7.94	5	1	0	0	0	0	0	0	.000
0	0.00	0.00	0	0	0	0	0	0	0	0	.000
416	**3.66**	**2.59**	**855**	**361**	**25**	**11**	**17**	**14**	**116**	**50**	**0.699**
D: 11.18.1983, Kansas City, Jackson County, MO								B/T, R/R		5'11, 185 lbs.	
8	5.02	5.02	4	0	0	0	0	0	0	0	.000
23	2.56	1.90	74	15	3	3	2	0	11	3	.786
19	2.46	1.95	55	7	2	2	1	0	8	3	.727
22	3.14	1.87	79	14	1	3	2	2	7	4	.636
17	5.26	2.89	43	9	1	2	0	1	4	4	.500
8	2.30	0.92	38	5	0	0	1	2	11	1	.917
23	4.72	2.71	45	18	0	1	0	0	7	3	.700
11	2.74	2.15	15	1	0	1	1	0	3	1	.750
1	4.34	0.24	12	0	0	0	0	0	3	3	.500
5	4.44	0.89	25	5	0	0	0	0	2	4	.333
4	2.24	0.43	53	13	0	0	2	0	8	2	.800
11	4.78	2.02	17	5	0	1	0	0	5	2	.714
0	3.98	0.00	10	4	0	0	0	0	2	1	.667
152	**3.37**	**1.68**	**470**	**96**	**7**	**13**	**9**	**5**	**71**	**31**	**0.696**
D: 09.04.1979, Detroit, Wayne County, MI								B/T, L/L		6'0, 175 lbs.	
12	18.00	15.43	2	4	0	1	0	0	0	1	.000
D: 01.22.1989, Austin, Travis County, TX								B/T, R/R		5'8, 170 lbs.	
0	0.00	0.00	0	0	0	0	0	0	0	0	.000
D: 02.25.1951, New York, New York County, NY								B/T, R/R		6'4, 190 lbs.	
6	4.76	3.18	6	1	0	0	0	0	1	1	.500
7	4.05	3.15	1	0	0	0	0	1	2	0	1.000
32	6.78	3.95	27	1	0	0	0	0	3	6	.333
40	5.04	3.74	55	13	2	1	1	1	3	8	.273
3	3.00	3.00	9	1	0	0	0	0	1	0	1.000
13	5.74	4.39	7	9	0	0	0	0	0	3	.000
0	0.00	0.00	8	0	0	0	1	0	1	0	1.000
7	4.60	4.02	12	2	0	0	0	0	2	1	.667

WILLIAMS, JOSEPH CONTINUED

YEAR	TEAM	G	GS	CG	IP	HA	RS
1929	Homestead Grays	10	8	8	78.3	87	37
1930	Homestead Grays	14	11	8	96.3	69	36
1931	Homestead Grays	7	7	5	53.3	44	22
1932	Detroit Wolves	2	2	1	16.0	16	8
1932	Homestead Grays	9	7	3	55.0	59	25
	Career Totals:	**84**	**66**	**46**	**565.7**	**561**	**283**

ER	RPG	ERA	K	BB	WP	HB	SO	SV	WIN	LOSS	PCT
32	4.25	3.68	38	13	0	0	0	0	3	4	.429
32	3.36	2.99	58	11	0	0	1	0	7	5	.583
16	3.71	2.70	30	8	1	1	0	0	2	3	.400
4	4.50	2.25	5	1	0	1	0	0	2	0	1.000
16	4.09	2.62	10	10	0	0	0	0	3	2	.600
208	**4.50**	**3.31**	**266**	**70**	**3**	**3**	**3**	**2**	**30**	**33**	**0.476**

Index

Acknowledgments

I WOULD LIKE TO THANK THE ENTIRE STAFF AT THE NATIONAL BASEBALL Hall of Fame, most particularly, Dale Petrosky, Ted Spencer, and Jim Gates for their support of *Shades of Glory* and the *Out of the Shadows* research project from which this book is drawn; Kevin Mulroy, Ellen Beal, Rachel Sweeney, Alison Reeves, and Melissa Farris at National Geographic's Books; Elizabeth Barnes of the Union County College History Department for her considerable contribution, Amarjit Kaur and Cris Saladorus, and the College's wonderful "computer doctors. " I owe a special thank you to my family: Sally, Rebecca, Matthew, Elizabeth, Raymond, Shannon, and our grand little ones.

This book draws from the groundbreaking research project, *Out of the Shadows: Black Baseball in America*, which was commissioned by the National Baseball Hall of Fame.

Much gratitude and appreciation goes to my co-authors of the *Out of the Shadows* project for their contribution to this book: to Larry Lester and Dick Clark, who provided the statistical research; Dr. Jules Tygiel, who provided the foreword; James Overmyer, for chapters one and two; Dr. Michael Lomax, for chapters three and four; Dr. Neil Lanctot, for chapter 7; Dr. Robert Ruck for chapters eight and nine; Robert Peterson and Lyle Wilson for chapter 10; Dr. Adrian Burgos for information on Latino baseball; and Dr. Leslie Heaphy for information about the women of black baseball

What we do here, both in its execution and its inspiration, could not be done without the work of those researchers, writers and fellow historians who literally laid the road on which we now walk. At the top of this list are authors Robert Peterson, John Holway, and Jim Riley. Robert Peterson's wonderful book, *Only the Ball Was White*, John Holway;'s *The Complete Book of Baseball's Negro League*, and Jim Riley's several books on the Negro Leagues, including a wonderful biography of Monte Irvin, have been invaluable resources for the writing of this work.

Co-directors for the Out Of *the Shadows* Project, Dick Clark and Larry Lester, deserve a round of applause. They have been fruitful laborers in the field, both in the research they have done, the writings they have produced, and in their dedication to bringing recognition to the men and women whose history they have taken into their own care. Jerry Malloy left a voluminous body of research. He has since passed away, but he is in these pages in substantial ways.

An important bow to Pat Kelly for her wonderful contribution to the photo record that adorns this work.

It seems most appropriate to thank the men who were part of the Negro Leagues, many of whom I have had the pleasure of counting as friends. Thank you for your wit and wisdom. Thank you for all the wonderful times we have had together as you have generously taken us back into who you were, and shared with us who you are and continue to be, gentlemen all.

It is to all of them—to Max, Leon, Benny, "Pint," "Ready," Stanley, Mahlon, Monte, Mr. Mirabal, Buck, and old Doc Sykes and to those on whose shoulders they stood— Top, Pop, Rube, the Cannonball, Smokey Joe, Gentleman Dave, and little Sol, and to the legion of other who march through the pages of this book, that we the editors and authors of Out Of *The Shadows/Shades of Glory* dedicate, with much gratitude, what could only have been, given who it is about, a labor of love.

Illustrations

Page ii: Bettmann/CORBIS; page vi: Bettmann/CORBIS; page xii-xiii: Bettmann/CORBIS; page xxiv: National Baseball Hall of Fame; page 4: Courtesy Lillian Dabney; page 19: Courtesy Lillian Dabney; page 24: Courtesy Dr. Lawrence Hogan/State Museum of New Jersey; page 40: Hancock Historical Museum, Findlay, Ohio; page 42: National Baseball Hall of Fame; page 52: Courtesy Dr. Lawrence Hogan; page 61: Cleveland Gazette, 9/21/1889, Courtesy Dr. Lawrence Hogan, redrawn by Daniel Lapa; page 64: Courtesy Dr. Lawrence Hogan; page 66: Ohio Historical Society; page 74: Kalamazoo; page 81: National Baseball Hall of Fame; page 92: *Chicago Daily News* – Chicago Historical Society; page 94-5: National Baseball Hall of Fame; page 103: Lawrence Hogan collection; page 107: National Baseball Hall of Fame; page 113: *Chicago Daily News* – Chicago Historical Society; page 119: National Baseball Hall of Fame; page 126: Courtesy Frank Keetz; page 132: National Baseball Hall of Fame; page 135: National Baseball Hall of Fame; page 137: National Baseball Hall of Fame; page 140: National Baseball Hall of Fame; page 152: Rutgers University Archives, Alexander Library; page 157: National Baseball Hall of Fame; page 162-3: *Chicago Daily News* - Chicago Historical Society; page 167: Courtesy Dr. Lawrence Hogan; page 194: Ohio Historical Society; page 199: Leland Auctions; page 222: Courtesy Dr. Lawrence Hogan; page 229: National Baseball Hall of Fame; page 234: Courtesy Frank Keetz; page 237: Courtesy Frank Keetz; page 245: National Baseball Hall of Fame; page 264: Courtesy Frank Keetz; page 266: Newark, New Jersey Public Library; page 271: Dick Powell; page 273: National Baseball Hall of Fame; page 278: National Baseball Hall of Fame; page 280: Sport Magazine National Baseball Hall of Fame; page 286-7: National Baseball Hall of Fame; page 291: National Baseball Hall of Fame; page 295: National Baseball Hall of Fame; page 306: Courtesy Dr. Lawrence Hogan; page 313: Courtesy Todd Bolton; page 318-319: Courtesy Dr. Lawrence Hogan; page 321: Photo by Chick Solomon, Courtesy Dr. Lawrence Hogan; page 324: Robert Wagner Archives, New York University; page 330: Craig Davidson; page 333: Bettmann/CORBIS; page 339: National Baseball Hall of Fame; page 340-1: 1946 Negro League Yearbook, page 7, National Baseball Hall of Fame; page 347: Courtesy Dr. Lawrence Hogan; page 348: Bettmann/CORBIS; page 350: National Baseball Hall of Fame; page 364-5: National Baseball Hall of Fame; page 367: Courtesy Dr. Lawrence Hogan; page 375: Courtesy Dr. Lawrence Hogan; page 378: Bettmann/CORBIS.